D1222916

ЭФСИ

Frontispiece and back cover:

This photograph of Lyubov Burda in pre-flight for her half-on, half-off vault was taken by Albrecht Gaebele at the 1973 University Games in Moscow. It was selected by the Montreal Olympic Organizing Committee as the gymnastic poster for the 1976 Olympic Games. Data: 1/500 sec., f/2.8, High Speed Ektachrome exposed as for 650 ASA.

Front cover:

The photograph of Elvira Saadi in an aerial walkover on beam was also taken by Albrecht Gaebele at the 1973 University Games in Moscow. The lens used was the Summicron-R f/2, 90mm on the Leicaflex SL, and exposure 1/500 sec. at full aperture, using High Speed Ektachrome exposed as for 650 ASA.

Women's Gymnastics a history

Volume I
1966 to 1974

by

Minot Simons II

Technical Assistance
Joanne Giannini Pasquale

Photography
Albrecht Gaebele
and other photographers

Women's Gymnastics
A History
Volume I
1966 to 1974

Published by
Welwyn Publishing Company
P.O. Box 222475
Carmel, CA 93922-2475
e-mail: welwyn@aol.com
fax: (408) 624-5294

First Printing 1995

Printed in the United States of America

Design and Production
Valerie Ostenak Taylor

Library of Congress Cataloging-in-Publication Data
Simons II, Minot
Women's Gymnastics, A History, Volume I, 1966 to 1974
Bibliography: p.
Does not include index.
1. Women's Gymnastics.
2. History of, 1966 to 1974
CIP 95-90224
ISBN 0-9646062-0-8

Contents

List of Photographs

Color

Black & White

Photo Credits

Albrecht Gaebele: front and back covers, frontispiece, 51, 56, 62, 63, 80, 82, 83, 84, 86, 110, 144, 151, 159, 163, 172, 176, 178, 200, 202, 205, 210, 214, 222, 225, 226, 227, 229, 230, 238, 242, 243, 244, 246, 248, 249, 250, 251, 288, 291, 293, 300, 303, 306, 316, 317, 318, 321, 324, 324, 331, 334, 337, 342, 342, 344, 345, 346, 359, 395, 396, 397, 400, 401

Don Wilkinson: 50, 68, 71, 73, 74, 75, 81, 91, 142, 146, 153, 155, 161, 165, 166, 169, 170, 179, 209, 216, 217, 218, 224, 232, 235, 236, 241, 246, 362

Rupert Leser: 12, 15, 18, 23, 28, 31, 32, 42, 48, 59
Tony Duffy: 13, 21, 25, 41, 298, 319, 332
Vladimir Safronov: 94, 121, 184, 284, 304, 380
Glenn Sundby, Gymnast: 49, 199, 213, 247, 375
Jean Waldis: 258, 310, 313, 326, 332, 367
Sven Simon: 299, 320, 322, 330, 335
Colin Taylor: 288, 295, 296, 297
Rich Clarkson: 220, 239, 256
Minot Simons II: 259, 265, 376, 378
Novosti Press: 197, 351, 371
Ekaterina Schenev: 107, 109
Swedish Gymnastics Federation: 138, 139
Carl Haberland: 194, 196
Fritz Giessler: 325, 340
City of Landskrona: 136
City of Ljubljana: 140
Klaus Schlage: 180
Lisa Moskowitz: 197
Heinz Kleutmeier: 360
McCoy/Rigby Entertainment: 272
Hansjorg Wieland: 308
Nicholl/Katz: 348

List of Figures: Code of Points

Years refer to the edition of the Code.
Figures are numbered according to their appearance in the text.
Elements are not listed in the order they appear in the Code of Points.

Beam

Floor

Glossary

Terms with French pronunciation:

Arabesque: A position on one leg with the other extended behind. The rear leg is rotated outward and held to a minimum of a 45° angle to the support leg. The arms should make diagonal lines with the palms turned down. The body is leaning forward.

Assemblé: A spring off of one foot onto both feet. The feet meet together at the top of the jump and land simultaneously, "assembled", in demi-plié.

Attitude: A position on one leg with the other raised behind. The back knee is bent and turned out so that the thigh is higher than the foot.

Changement: Changing positions of the feet. Starting in 5th position (feet touching, heel of right foot in front of left toe) spring into the air while changing positions of the feet.

Chassé: A dance step in which a slide on one foot is followed closely and in a gallop-like rhythm by a slide on the other.

Grand jeté: Split leap.

Jeté: A leap from one foot to the other.

Plié: (Demi plié) A slight flexion of the knees, knees turned outward. It is used in preparation for jumps, turns and landings and is done in all 5 positions of the feet.

(Grand plié) Full bending of the knees which are turned out, extending over the toes. The heels come off the floor except in second and fourth positions.

Sissone: A spring off two feet to land on one. A jump from two feet extending the legs to a diagonal split position with the rear leg high and the front leg low. Land in demi-plié, in arabesque.

Tour jeté: Scissors leap forward with stretched legs and half turn (180°).

Terms with English pronunciation:

Aerial: A movement in which the gymnast takes off from one foot to turn completely over in the air and land on the other foot without touching the floor with her hands.

Cast: A term used to describe movements on the uneven bars in which the body is first piked and then extended upward and away from the point of grasp in either a forward or backward direction.

Cat leap: Scissors leap with bent legs. (Hitch kick with knees bent in front of the body.)

Hitch-kick: A jump from one foot to the other while switching legs in front of the body.

Kip: A movement in which the gymnast moves from a hanging position below the apparatus to a support position above the apparatus. In a kip, the body pikes and rapidly extends.

Pass: A sequence of elements in floor exercise or on balance beam that moves along one line of direction.

Pike: A position in which the hips are flexed 90°. The legs and trunk are straight.

Tuck: A position in which the head is forward with the chin close to the chest, the back is rounded and the knees are drawn up to the chest.

Preface

This history is composed of four volumes, the dates of which are as follows:

Volume I	1966 to 1974
Volume II	1975 to 1980
Volume III	1981 to 1988
Volume IV	1989 to 1996.

Originally, the history was conceived as a one-volume work. Consequently, many of the competitions of later volumes have already been written. When it became apparent, however, that the work would be too big for one book, it was decided to break it down into four volumes. Each volume consists of:

- ♦ detailed stories of Olympic and world championship competitions, not-so-detailed stories of European championships and some other important competitions, and brief narratives of the lesser competitions
- ♦ biographies of the medal winners, varying in length from eighteen pages for Olga Korbut to a page or a column for someone who may have won a bronze Olympic or world championship medal or been noted for a single, important accomplishment
- ♦ photographs, both color and black and white. Since women's gymnastics is considered to be one of the beautiful sports and one of the most popular Olympic sports, these photographs are a feature of each book.

Biographies and competitions are grouped together according to the Olympiads, or four-year periods between Olympics, during the years covered in each volume. In this way, the biographies are assembled according to those "waves" of gymnasts who appear, shine, and then disappear as each Olympic period proceeds.

Narratives of the competitions are written to be understood by a general readership. Gymnastic routines are included and gymnastic terms used, but the routines are indented in a different type size so that they may be skipped over if a reader is not interested in reading them. To make it easier for readers who are not familiar with the arcane language of gymnastics, there are figures in the margin taken from the Code of Points which illustrate an element being described. In addition, there is a glossary of some of the more commonly encountered terms.

The figures used are taken from the 1989 Code of Points because they are smaller than those in the 1994 version and fit more easily into the margin of the page. The reader may refer to the List of Figures: Code of Points on page xiv for a complete description of the element in the drawing.

Once a figure has been used—one that illustrates a "walkover," for example—it will not be repeated each time the term is used but the List of Figures may be used where repeat reference is desired.

It is considered important that the writing be understood by non-gymnasts. One group of people who have been kept in mind is the parents of gymnasts. Parents pay the bills, provide transportation, and do volunteer work at their children's club; but often they do not fully understand the sport and may be left in the dark when their children are talking with friends about their activities. Thus, elements and routines are described or illustrated in full and not in some form of telegraphic language.

Because the book is intended for a worldwide readership, the terminology used in the history is the official one, as found in the Code of Points. Thus, the terms "flic-flac" and "stretched" are used instead of "flip-flop" and "layout," terms used primarily in the United States. "Salto" is used instead of "somersault."

For the dedicated gymnast or gymnastics fan, the history provides an in-depth look at who the gymnasts were who made history and what they did in earlier times. Thus, Latynina and Caslavska, for example, become more than just names. We are often not entirely aware of what is going on or what has been going on while we have been living through a certain experience. With this history, readers can more fully appreciate the rich heritage of the period covered by each volume.

In Volume I, there is more about Soviet and East German gymnasts and their performances than about gymnasts from other countries. This predominance will change in future volumes as first Romanian and then American gymnasts become leaders.

One intention of the writer has been that the history should be available indefinitely, that it should not quickly go out-of-print, as so often happens with books offered by the major publishing houses. This history should be available to gymnasts not even born yet, so that the great competitions described should not be forgotten.

Notes

Results are given only for the leading countries or gymnasts. A complete listing of the results of the Olympics or of World or European Championships for both artistic and rhythmic gymnastics is provided in a book called *Liste des résultats.* It is available from F.I.G. at the following address:

Fédération Internationale de Gymnastique
P.O. Box 359
2740 Moutier 1
Switzerland.

It may be purchased by credit card; monetary exchange will be made by the card-issuing company.

More detailed results of lesser competitions may be obtained by application to your favorite gymnastic magazine.

Although the sport described in these volumes is known in America as "artistic gymnastics," in some countries it is known as "sporting gymnastics." In these countries, the term "artistic gymnastics" is reserved for what in the United States is known as "rhythmic gymnastics," which in turn is known officially as "rhythmic sporting gymnastics."

The terms "championship" and "championships" are sometimes confusing. In this history, the term "championship" is used where only one sport, women's gymnastics, is involved, as in most European championships; the term "championships" is used where both men and women's gymnastics are involved, as in world championships.

To differentiate between gymnastics and acrobatics, the following is quoted from Section 12.2, "Contents of the Exercise," from the 1994 "Code of Points."

> "The exercise should be composed from different element groups. The value parts A-, B-, C-, D-, and E- must come from the following element groups:
>
> - *acrobatic elements* with or without flight phase in the forward, sideward or backward movement (round-off counts as a sideward movement.)
> - *gymnastic elements:* Turns, leaps or jumps and hops, step and running combinations, balance elements in a stand, sit and lying position, body waves."

In general, this statement could be construed as indicating that the many different "tricks" performed by gymnasts fall under the category of acrobatics, and the dance skills fall under the category of gymnastic elements.

Typesetting was accomplished using Microsoft Word™ while layout and graphic production was performed using QuarkXPress™. In both instances, the computer used was Macintosh.

All books are case bound. In addition, pages are Smythe-sewn.

If a reader notes a mistake of any kind, the writer would appreciate being informed of it.

Sources

Magazines:

International Gymnast
P.O. Box 2450
Oceanside, CA 92051

USA Gymnastics
Pan American Plaza
201 S. Capitol Ave., Suite 300
Indianapolis, IN 46225

World of Gymnastics
P.O. Box 359
2740 Moutier 1
Switzerland

Le Gymnaste
7, Ter, Cour des Petites Écuries
75010 Paris, France

The Gymnast
Unit 4, Gibbs Reed Farm
Pashley Road, Ticehurst, Wadhurst
East Sussex TN5 7HE, England

Gym Stars
44 Fitzjohn's Avenue
London NW3 5LX
England

Olympisches Turnen Aktuel
Amselweg 5
5908 Neunkirchen
Germany

Videotapes:

Routines described in this volume may be obtained from:

Frank Endo
18011 La Salle Avenue
Gardena, CA 90248

Fred Turoff
5538 Morris Street
Philadelphia, PA 19144

Acknowledgements

To Norbert Bueche, Secretary General of the International Federation of Gymnastics, for permission to use drawings from the F.I.G. Code of Points.

To Albrecht Gaebele, for his willingness to participate in this work.

To Joanne Pasquale for her technical assistance in correcting the routines of the competition narratives and the glossary.

To Dr. Josef Göhler, former editor and publisher of *Olympische Turnkunst,* for the use of some photographs, for supplying some information, and for his unswerving encouragement in this work.

To Glenn Sundby, Director of the International Gymnastics Hall of Fame, for permission to quote stories on the 1966 and 1970 World Championships from *The Modern Gymnast* and *Mademoiselle Gymnast;* and for his encouragement of this work.

To ABC-TV for permission to view their tapes of the 1972 Munich Olympics.

To *Sports Illustrated* for permission to quote from two stories about the 1968 Mexico Olympics.

To *The New York Times* for permission to use excerpts from a story about Vera Caslavska.

To *Sovietsky Sport* for their open policy regarding the use of their material.

To the U.S. Olympic Committee for supplying some information about the 1968 Mexico Olympics.

To Dennis Morimoto of the College of Performing and Visual Arts, University of Northern Colorado, Greeley, Colorado, for providing access to the photographs of the late Don Wilkinson and for permission for their use.

To Tony Duffy, photographer, for the use of certain photographs, particularly three much-needed photographs from the 1966 World Championships, and for 20 years of support and encouragement in my reporting of women's gymnastics in magazines and in this book.

To Rich Clarkson, photographer, for the use of special photographs of Olga Korbut and Ludmilla Turischeva.

To the cities of Dortmund, Landskrona, and Ljubljana for photographs and publicity material.

To Jim Fountaine, Don Peters, and Connie Maloney for allowing my visits to their gyms—the Kips, the Scats, and Verdugo—to watch workouts for many years.

To Luan Peszek of *U.S.A. Gymnastics* and to Dwight Normile of *International Gymnast* for their courtesy and cooperation.

To Frank Edmonds for supplying data on Champions All.

To Murial Grossfeld for some information on the 1966 World Championships.

To Dick Criley for answering certain questions about the 1972 Munich Olympics.

To Patrick Devine, for initial typography specifications.

And, finally, to Valerie Ostenak Taylor, for creating the design of this book and for her untiring efforts in taking my text, the drawings, and the photographs and ending up with the beautiful book you have in your hands.

to

Langdon and Anne Simons

Introduction

Historical Perspective

In 1977, Olga Korbut retired from gymnastics. Yet the sport she so suddenly and explosively popularized in 1972 remains one of the best-loved Olympic sports, not only in the United States, but all over the world.

This durability of women's gymnastics as a vastly popular sport has been gratifying to me, personally, because I had long thought of the days of Olga Korbut and Ludmilla Turischeva as a golden age. These two famous gymnasts caught the fancy of the public at Munich and maintained it for over four years, until the last series of exhibitions they performed following the Montreal Olympics. What will happen, I wondered, when they retire?

Between the Munich and Montreal Olympics, Olga and Ludmilla made six appearances in exhibitions in the United States, as well as exhibitions in many other countries all over the world. Their appearances maintained their own popularity and that of the sport in general. They made one performance together after Montreal in the United States, a visit Olga made famous by her purchase of a wedding dress without having a groom in mind. After that they left the scene and the glamor of gymnastics devolved upon the lovely, personable Nelly Kim and the wonderfully talented but, at the time, distant Nadia Comaneci.

In the United States, the momentum of enthusiasm initiated by Olga and Ludmilla and heightened by the virtuosity of Nadia Comaneci and the charm of Nelli Kim in Montreal carried the sport along until 1980. Then, however, the boycott of the Moscow Olympics and the absence of television coverage that was concomitant with the boycott caused a temporary decline in the popularity of American gymnastics. The boost given by the televising of the Olympics was almost essential to its continued popularity. Major sports like football, basketball and baseball receive constant exposure on television. Until recently, when many more gymnastics events are being televised, such exposure was really limited to the Olympics. When there was no Olympic gymnastics, the sport suffered. Even though there were some wonderful gymnasts in the Soviet Union, East Germany and Romania during the early 1980s, their names were not household words, as were those of Olga and Ludmilla.

After the boycott, enthusiasm for women's gymnastics—in the United States particularly—did not pick up until Mary Lou Retton's electrifying 1984 victory in Los Angeles. Since the 1984 Olympics, women's gymnastics has enjoyed a new popularity.

Because of Mary Lou's early retirement, however, the big development that occurred and which came to a climax at the 1985 World Championships in Montreal was the emergence upon the world scene of two young Soviet gymnasts and a young Romanian gymnast who proved themselves to be the best in the world. Their names were Elena Shushunova, Oksana Omelyanchick and Daniela Silivas. Although Oksana was not able to continue the great success she achieved in Montreal, the other two dominated the sport through the 1988 Olympics. With Elena and Daniela, the future of women's gymnastics was in good hands. They did, in fact, capture the fancy of the public. It was unfortunate that Oksana Omelyanchick, who had that slightly sassy charisma, that special quality that so endeared Olga Korbut to her public, could not, in the end, keep up gymnastically with the other two. Nevertheless, it seemed at the time that another great period of women's gymnastics was at hand. Was it to be as great? In one way, it was much greater.

If great stars are needed to arouse the public's interest in women's gymnastics, another factor maintains the interest not only of the public but also of everyone engaged in the sport. This factor is the astonishing rate at which the sport advances. Gymnasts are constantly striving to learn new elements at higher and higher levels of difficulty and complexity. Some advances are the result of better coaching and of the never-ending creativity and innovative thinking on the part of the better coaches. This development has not proceeded at a steady pace; it seems to come in surges, as, for example, when one famous gymnast breaks new ground.

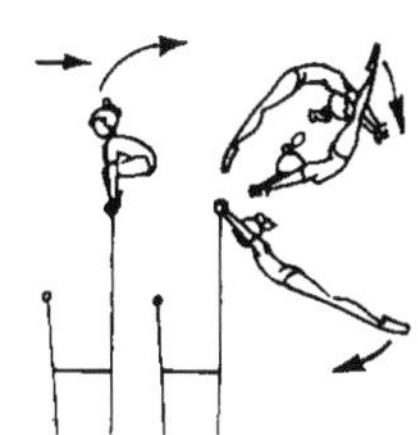
Figure 1

Figure 2

Olga Korbut's example is, of course, the most famous. Although her back flip on the uneven bars was dramatic *(Figure 1)*, it was her back salto on the balance beam *(Figure 2)* that had the more pronounced effect. First, it became controversial; second, it caused people to look at gymnastics in a new light.

After Munich, there was an outcry among many coaches and judges, especially in Europe. These well-meaning people, who had devoted their lives to the sport, felt that Olga's back salto was dangerous, that it would set a trend toward even more dangerous gymnastic elements and that many gymnasts would get hurt. They tried but failed to have such tricks banned by the International Gymnastics Federation, (F.I.G.) Ironically, however, they were right. Olga's salto on the beam, while not extremely dangerous itself, did lead to even more risky gymnastic elements and many gymnasts did get hurt because of them. Yet Olga's tricks did, in fact, cause people to look at gymnastics in a new light. The new approach to the sport was summed up by Olga's coach, Renald Knysh, who said, "Gymnastics is acrobatics on the apparatus."[1]

In the years following Munich, Olga's back salto on the balance beam became commonplace. By 1977 and 1978, many of the beam routines performed by the top gymnasts of all countries included it. In other words, Olga's big advance had been accepted and incorporated. What would be the next such advance?

It actually came about slowly. Olga's gymnastics was like yeast in the dough of gymnastic thinking. It took time before the dough began to rise. Furthermore, the new advances would not be made by the stars of Munich but by a new generation. Foremost among these would be Nelli Kim and Nadia Comaneci. Their Montreal successes were evidence of the ferment going on within the sport.

Far to the south of Moscow, Leningrad, and the republic of Belarus that was Olga's home—parts of the country where the best Soviet gymnasts had traditionally come from—a young coach named Vladimir Baidin had discovered Nelli Kim and was training her not only in the gymnastics of his day but also in the more advanced aspects of the sport that he and certain experts were thinking about. Nelli, whose mother was Tartar and whose father was Korean, lived in Alma Ata, Kasakhstan, a republic in the southern, Asiatic part of what was then the Soviet Union.

Meanwhile, in Romania, a young coach named Bela Karolyi had discovered Nadia Comaneci. Both Karolyi and Baidin had started new gymnastics schools with very young girls. Both had recruited girls from nearby public schools by asking who would like to do gymnastics and by testing them for their aptitude for the sport.

The significance of these two gymnasts over the long term is that together they would elevate the difficulty and complexity of gymnastics to heights undreamed of at Munich and that they would pave the way for still greater difficulty and complexity in subsequent years. Each made her major contribution on a particular apparatus. Vaulting was one of the apparatuses on which Nelli Kim made her special contribution.

Vaults that at Munich were only a handspring with a body twist or a pike of the body after pushing off the horse now suddenly incorporated a back salto off the horse after doing a half twist onto it. Nelli won her gold medal in the Montreal Olympics by doing not only a back salto off the vaulting horse but also a body twist at the same time.

It was on the uneven bars that Nadia made, perhaps, her most dramatic contribution. On this apparatus, she performed for the first time an element that, with variations, has been incorporated into the repertory of all top, modern-day gymnasts. She pushed back off the high bar, did a salto forward with her legs spread in straddle position, and then regrasped the high bar *(Figure 3)*. Olga Korbut gave a hint of things to come at Munich when she did her back flip off the high bar and then recaught it *(Figure 1)*, but that was only half a salto. She started from a standing position and caught the bar with her hands; in floor exercise, that would have been a back handspring. Nadia started with her hands on the bar, let go of the bar, did a complete salto forward and then recaught the same bar. Such an element became known as a "release" move. It has become obligatory for all top gymnasts. In fact, the best of them will incorporate two or even three release moves into their routines. A release move takes both courage and skill—courage, because if the gymnast fails to recatch the high bar, she will fall to the floor; and skill, because regrasping the bar is impossible unless the timing and execution of all aspects of the element are within narrow limits of performance excellence.

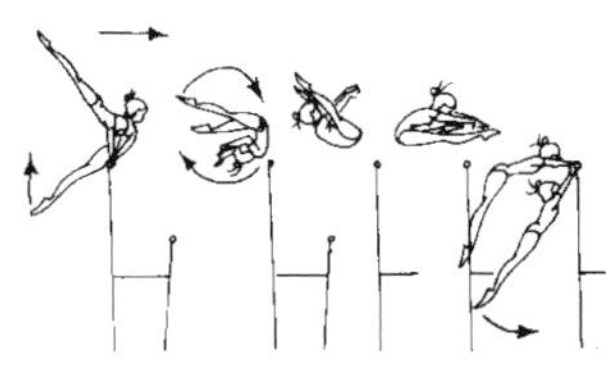

Figure 3

In Montreal, Nadia also completely revolutionized the uneven bars dismount. She greatly expanded the scope of the dismount by first hurling her body off into space using the principle of the slingshot. This she did by going from a handstand, with her hands supporting her body in a vertical position on high bar, to a pike position, with her feet as well as her hands on the bar. Then she let her body drop by force of gravity until, on the way up past the bottom of her arc, she let go and, as she started up, flew off the high bar in the direction she was facing. As she began to fly through the air, she did a half twist with her body so that she was then flying backwards and immediately executed a salto backward tucked to her landing *(Figure 4)*.

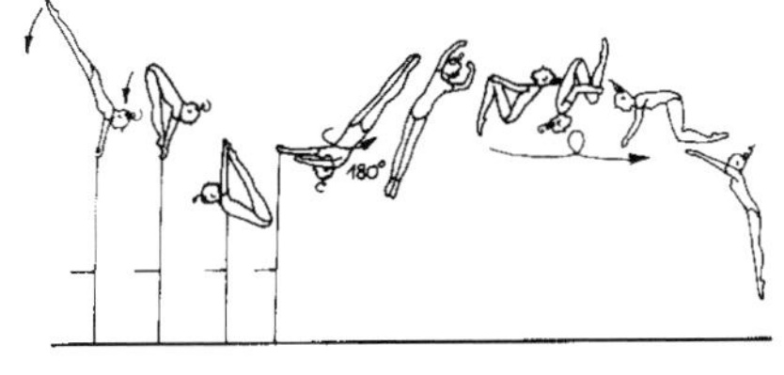

Figure 4

These two elements—her dismount, with its spectacular back salto, and her release move—changed the complexion of the uneven bars. Future top-level gymnasts would eventually use both elements as a matter of course.

On balance beam, Nadia's other specialty, the major advance was the perfection of her work. In the four competitions of the Montreal Olympics, she received three 10s and one 9.9 on balance beam. Actually, in terms of difficulty or originality, there was no notable advance in Montreal over Munich, except that on dismounting she performed a back salto with double twist instead of a single twist. With the double twist, it was a distinctly more difficult dismount than those performed previously but was not in the nature of a major new development. Nadia's contribution to balance beam in Montreal was simply that she did everything so well. Her execution was almost perfect.

In floor exercise, in Montreal, on the other hand, there was a major innovation. There Nelli Kim performed the first double salto backward in Olympic competition. She did it in tucked position *(Figure 5)*. She was the only gymnast to do it. As with her back salto in vault and Nadia's release move and dismount on the uneven bars, Nelli Kim's double salto backward set an entirely new trend in floor exercise. Interestingly, it did not come into widespread use until, as mentioned previously with regard to Olga's back salto on balance beam, a new generation of gymnasts came into being. The double salto backward is an element that needs to be learned early in one's gymnastic career. Gymnasts of the Montreal era were already too old to learn such a new trick. Many tried, but even at the 1978 World Championships in Strasbourg, there were few who did it successfully. One reason was that not only were these gymnasts too old, they were also too big and heavy. A trend toward smallness and lightness in gymnasts had been set in motion by the major advances of the Montreal Olympics.

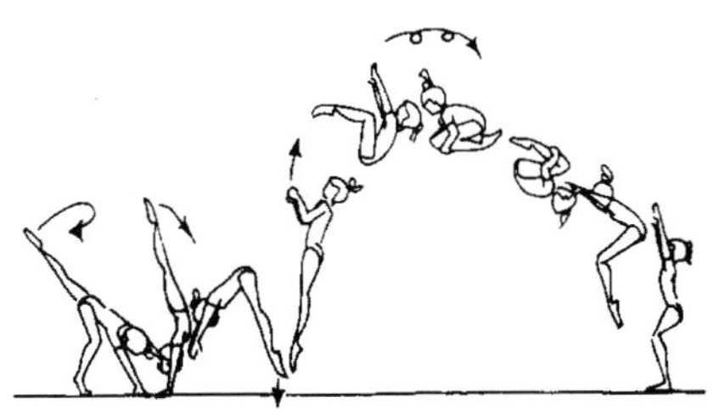

Figure 5

Photographs of the 1976 and 1980 Soviet Olympic teams demonstrate this trend conclusively. The youngest and smallest gymnast on the team in Montreal was Maria Filatova, who celebrated her fifteenth birthday during the Olympics. In group pictures, she stood at one end of the line; at the other end stood Elvira Saadi and Ludmilla Turischeva, in comparison to whom

Maria Filatova looked tiny. She was, in fact, 4 feet 6.5 inches tall, a full 9 inches shorter than Saadi and 6.5 inches shorter than Turischeva. In the group picture of the Soviet team for the 1980 Olympics, Maria is as tall as three other gymnasts; the tallest girl, Nelli Kim, was 6 inches shorter than Saadi in Montreal. This trend would continue and become even more pronounced in future teams, not only of the Soviet Union but of all countries. Smallness and lightness among the world's top gymnasts were characteristics that walked hand-in-hand with the ever-advancing developments within the sport itself.

For several years after Montreal, there was some derision in the press about the smallness of gymnasts and about their young age. Within the sport, we had to put up with this criticism because, at the time, the major effort was to keep up with the progress the leaders were making in pushing out the boundaries of difficulty and complexity in gymnastic elements and combinations; only small, light gymnasts were able to keep up. Much more was being demanded of gymnasts in this matter of difficulty and complexity if they were to achieve good scores.

The requirements concerning difficulty and complexity are spelled out in an official "Code of Points," an illustrated guide for judges, gymnasts and coaches of all countries, published by the international federation, which tells them exactly what they must do. This "Code of Points" comes in a 3-ring binder so that it can be easily updated. After each Olympics, the code is reviewed thoroughly. The large number of 10s awarded at the Los Angeles Olympics, for instance, resulted in major changes which demanded even higher levels of difficulty and virtuosity if perfect scores were to be won.

The word *virtuosity* is important in gymnastics. It is derived from Webster's dictionary definition of the word, as "great skill in the practice of the fine arts, especially in music; as, a pianist noted for his virtuosity." We use the term in gymnastics to describe excellence in the execution of difficult elements or combinations of elements. Nadia Comaneci displayed virtuosity on the balance beam in Montreal, for example. Part of the excitement in gymnastics today is that the level of virtuosity is the highest it has ever been and continues to go higher and higher. A comparison of the scores in the 1972 Munich Olympics, the 1976 Montreal Olympics, and the 1988 Seoul Olympics, for example, bears this out.

All-around gold medalist in Munich, Ludmilla Turischeva, received 9.4 on beam both in the all-around competition and in the women's apparatus finals. Her low scores resulted from "bobbles" (unsteadiness). She had received 9.05 for beam compulsories and 9.75 on beam during optionals of team competition. These preliminary scores gave her a 9.40 average going into the all-around and into apparatus finals during both of which she received that same score. Thus, she was averaging 9.40 on beam throughout the Munich Olympics.

In 1976, Nadia Comaneci received 9.90 for compulsory beam and 10.00 for optional beam, two scores which gave her a 9.95 average for team competition. Then she scored 10.00 on beam in the all-around and 10.00 in apparatus finals on beam. All in all, she averaged 9.9833 on beam in all-around and apparatus finals, almost 0.6 higher than Ludmilla's score.

In 1988 at the Seoul Olympics, all-around gold medalist Elena Shushunova received a 9.925 average on beam both for compulsories and optionals in team competition, then 9.925 again in the all-around finals and a 9.950 in apparatus finals. Thus, she averaged 9.93125 throughout the competition—more than 0.5 higher than Turischeva in Munich. Nadia and Shushunova not only had greater difficulty in their routines but showed virtually no unsteadiness whatever.

In Munich, the entire Soviet team averaged 9.41 on beam in team competition; in Seoul, the Soviets averaged 9.875. This is clearly an enormous leap forward in the excellence with which exercises are performed.

The trend toward young, small, and light gymnasts and the great strides made in raising standards of difficulty, complexity, and virtuosity did for a long time result in a loss of artistry, at least in floor exercise. People remembered the dance and gracefulness of fairly tall young women of 18 or 19 years of age at the Munich and Mexico Olympics. All of a sudden they were watching strenuous acrobatics performed by small 14- and 15-year-olds for whom choreography had been created that was less mature than it had been. In fact, some of it appeared childish. It was difficult for people to believe that tiny gymnasts could also be artistic. Fortunately, even though gymnasts continue to be small, there has been a return to artistry. This reawakenng of artistry has come about in some surprising ways.

For example, artistry has finally come to that most brutal, that most inelegant apparatus, the vault. It used to be that gymnasts ran at the horse—almost charged at it—with ever-increasing speed and "punched" off the beat board forward toward the horse. They then pushed off the horse into their salto forward or salto backward after their twist *(Figure 6)*. Mary Lou's vault at the 1984 Los Angeles Olympics was the supreme example of this brute force approach. In the 1985 Montreal World Championships, all the Soviet gymnasts, without exception, made a change that altered the complexion of this apparatus forever: in

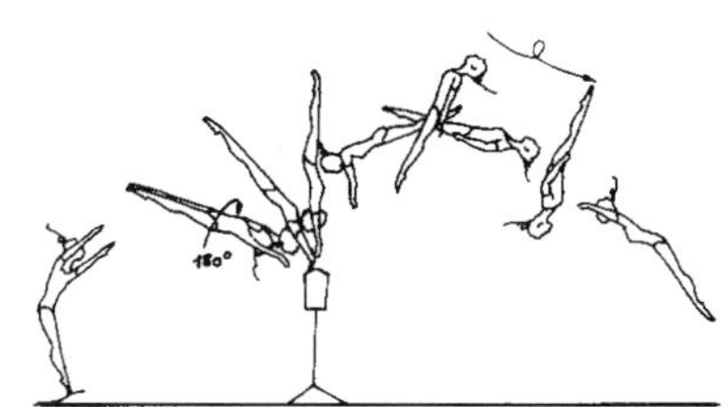

Figure 6

Figure 7

the last part of their run, they performed a round-off that changed the direction of their motion from forward to backward. They then punched off the beat board **backward** with their feet and so got far more force into the punch than is possible going forward *(Figure 7)*. (Most tumbling in floor exercise is accomplished in this way, as are dismounts and saltos on the beam.) Since the force is generated by their backward punch off the beat board following their round-off, the run-in need not be made at great speed. On the contrary, it is done rather precisely so that the gymnast can be sure of arriving at the right spot along the run to perform her round-off. It all adds up to a more artistic and beautiful aspect of gymnastics. This vault is known as the "Yurchenko" after the Soviet gymnast who first performed it. It and vaults derived from it have become the basis of most vaults by leading gymnasts since its introduction in Montreal.

Artistry on the uneven bars has come not only with virtuosity of execution but also with the refinement of release moves that are breathtakingly beautiful to watch. There is, of course, no chance on bars for the posing and dance that characterize exercises on beam or for the opportunity which floor exercise offers the gymnast to display her personality. Routines on the uneven bars do, however, provide an opportunity for the gymnast to display flair and style. She can perform elements that are spectacular as well as beautiful. Principally, these elements have come about as a further development of the release move Nadia introduced in the Montreal Olympics. This expansion of the release move concept developed as the leading coaches of the sport began to incorporate into women's uneven bars one of the important elements of men's high bar: the "giant" circle. The "giant" is the circle about the bar which the gymnast makes with her body in the "stretched" or straight-body position.

Although innovative coaches of women's gymnastics had long been giving their attention to giants, it had been considered impossible to perform them on the uneven bars because the low bar got in the way. This was particularly so for the taller gymnasts who were competing in the 1960s and 1970s. As gymnasts became smaller, however, it became evident to these coaches that if the bars could be separated a few inches more, these shorter gymnasts could perform the giant circle. With the approval of the international federation during the latter years of the 1970s, the equipment manufacturers began to supply longer spacers. These are the horizontal parts of the uneven bars apparatus that control how far apart the low bar is from the high bar. The new spacers allowed the bars to be separated further. Gymnasts still had to pike their bodies or to straddle their legs as they came down or went up between the bars, but they could now circle the high bar the rest of the way with their bodies extended and gain the momentum needed for more complicated release moves.

When women gymnasts began to perform the same giant circles on the uneven bars as the men did on their high bar, they began to be able to do many of the same tricks as the men. The centrifugal force generated by successive giant circles made it possible for gymnasts to perform release moves of much greater amplitude than that performed by Nadia in Montreal. There she performed a quick, tight salto forward with her legs straddled and she got into her salto from what we call a "cast." That is to say, after a kip from low bar to high bar, she used the backward momentum generated by this kip and augmented it by pushing herself further away from the high bar in a horizontal direction backward. This gave her the necessary separation from the bar so that she had space in which to execute her salto forward and to regrasp the bar. It was a very quick salto *(Figure 3)*.

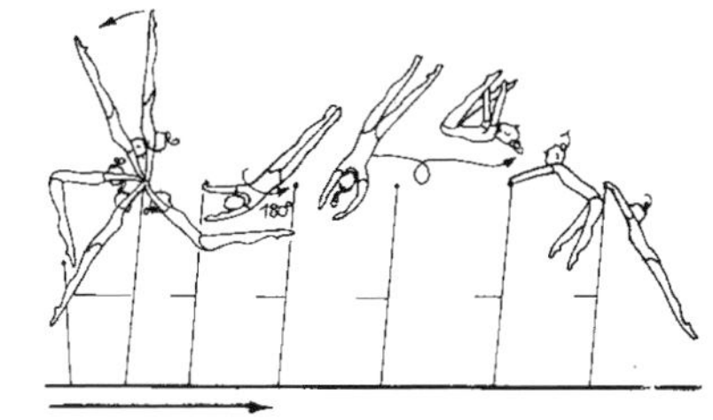

Figure 8

Since then, however, gymnasts have been going into their release moves out of giant circles. For example, if a gymnast swings down facing the direction of her motion, she can release as she begins her upswing, do a half twist, and then a salto forward to recatch the bar as she begins to come back down again *(Figures 8 and 9)*. (Maria Filatova of the Soviet Union, one of the first to do this, performed such a combination in the 1979 World Championships in Fort Worth.) If she swings down facing away from her direction of motion, she can release and do a salto forward without a twist to recatch the high bar *(Figure 10)*. These release moves out of giant swings are much more extended than that performed by Nadia. We say they have more "amplitude."

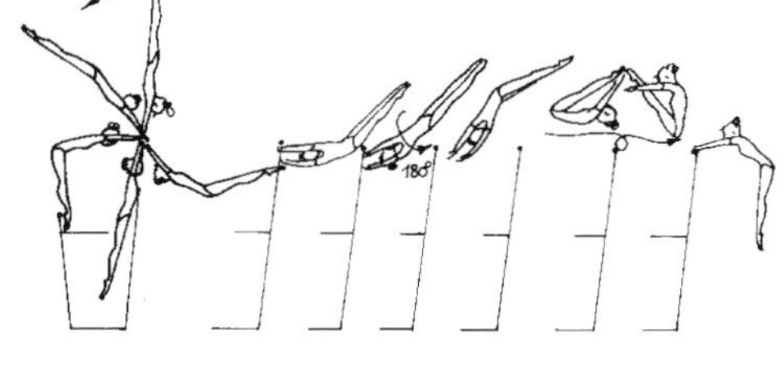

Figure 9

In recent years, the more advanced gymnasts have performed two successive release moves off the high bar before dropping to the low bar. Advanced gymnasts have often combined release moves with other elements that lesser gymnasts consider difficult by themselves. One example is a release move on the high bar followed immediately by a salto backward between the bars as the gymnast drops to the low bar.

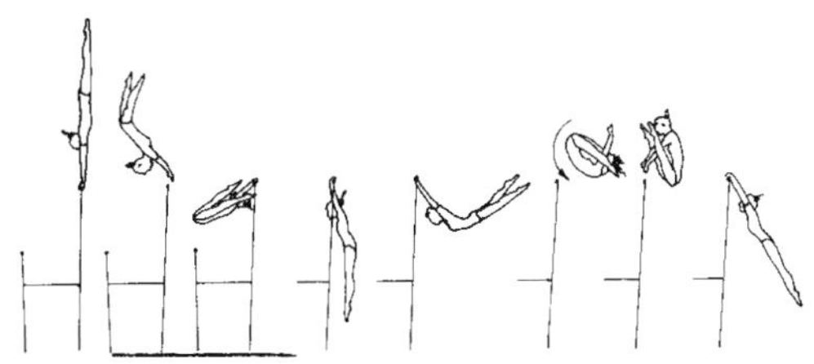

Figure 10

Finally, the gymnast can display artistry on the uneven bars by the originality and flair of her dismount. These have progressed from Nadia's back salto after a half twist in the 1976

Olympics to double saltos backward and even double saltos backward with full twist. Exciting flyaways with double saltos backward make thrilling and impressive ways for a gymnast to finish her uneven bars routine.

Balance beam has retained the artistry it had under Olga Korbut and Ludmilla Turischeva. Combinations of handsprings and saltos on the beam are far more complex than those performed in Munich and there have been some new strength moves. Top-level gymnasts now dismount with a double salto backward. By and large, however, balance beam remains an apparatus from which artistry was never lost.

In floor exercise, the little girl routines with their childish choreography are no longer evident in major competitions. Choreography today is tasteful and original, even though it may be created to fit the personality of the gymnast, who may be very young.

The tastefulness of floor exercise choreography is evident in the routines of almost all countries. The childishness evident in former years has given way to something far more attractive, as was demonstrated in Barcelona by gold medalist in floor exercise, Lavinia Milosovici.

Summing up, women's gymnastics today is the most exciting it has ever been because of the astonishing developments in the tricks the gymnasts perform, because of the superior skill or higher virtuosity with which they perform them, and because everything on each apparatus is done with grace and artistry. We can look forward with lively anticipation to major competitions in the sport for many years to come.

Reference

[1]Michael Suponev, *Olga Korbut. A Biographical Portrait* (New York: Doubleday, 1975), 33–34.

A New Wave

Part One

1966 to 1968

Natalya Kuchinskaya performing a three-quarter turn in clear straddle support on the beam.

World Championships

1966

Dortmund, Germany

Westfallenhalle

September 20th to 25th

This history begins with the 1966 World Championships in Dortmund, Germany, because it was a milestone—a watershed—in the development of women's gymnastics. Ever since the Soviet Union had reentered international competition with the 1952 Olympics in Helsinksi, Finland, the Soviet ladies had dominated women's gymnastics and would continue to do so. In 1966, however, there was a big change in the make-up of the Soviet team. Until 1966, it had been composed of adult ladies and had been led since the 1956 Olympics in Melbourne by Larissa Latynina. This great gymnast still holds the record for the most medals won in Olympic and World Championship competition: between 1956 and 1964, Latynina won twelve

Larissa Latynina

The Westfallenhalle

gold, eight silver, and four bronze medals. She was first all-around in the 1956 Olympics in Melbourne, the 1958 World Championships in Moscow, the 1960 Olympics in Rome, and the 1962 World Championships in Prague. She was second all-around to Vera Caslavska in the 1964 Olympics in Tokyo. In addition, she won seven gold, six silver, and one bronze medal in the European Championships: first all-around in the 1957 European Championships in Bucharest and the 1961 European Championships in Leipzig and second all-around to Vera Caslavska in the 1965 European Championships in Sofia. She also won gold medals in finals on the apparatus, most notably in the 1957 European Championships in Bucharest, where she won them all: a total of five gold medals. She won a total of 38 medals in these top-level competitions, spanning a ten-year career during which she captained the Soviet national team. Her career in world class competition had actually begun in 1954 at the Rome World Championships, where as Larissa Dirii, the 19-year-old novice of the team, she had placed 14th. During the latter part of her long career, Latynina was supported by Polina Astakhova, who placed third all-around in both the 1960 and 1964 Olympics.

This protracted dominance by Latynina had, of course, to come to an end sometime. By 1966, she was 31 years old, was married, and had given birth to daughter Tanya. The beginning of the end came in the 1964 Olympics when Latynina, then 29 years old, lost to Czechoslovakia's Vera Caslavska, who was then 22. The Soviet team as a whole, however, did not make its changeover to a more youthful team until the 1966 World Championships in Dortmund, where Latynina and Astakhova ended the competition in fourth and fifth positions on the team. Ahead of them were the young ladies of a new wave, a wholly new generation of gymnasts, all of whom were under twenty years old.

A preview of things to come took place during the 1964 Soviet National Championships. The new all-around champion was a fifteen-year-old from Vitebsk, Belarus, named Larissa Petrick. She was a student of Vikenti Dmitriev, who would later produce bronze-medalist all-around in the 1972 Olympics, Tamara Lazakovich. Petrick's victory caused a big stir within Soviet

Larissa Petrick in clear straddle support on high bar.

women's gymnastics: she was the youngest national champion the Soviet Union had ever had. It began to be clear that the Soviet team would, in the future, be made up of more youthful gymnasts.

Two years later, not only was Larissa Petrick on the Soviet World Championships team but also two other young gymnasts who, with Petrick, would later distinguish themselves at the 1968 Olympics in Mexico. They were Natalya Kuchinskaya, who had won the USSR World Championships selection trials, and Zinaida Druzhinina. (Druzhinina subsequently married Mikhail Voronin and changed her name to Zinaida Voronina. Voronin was the Soviet gymnast who won the Men's Championships at Dortmund.) Kuchinskaya became the star not only of the Dortmund World Championships but also of the 1968 Mexico Olympics, even though she did not win the all-around in either competition. In Mexico, because of her charm and popularity, she became known as "the bride of Mexico."

All three of these new Soviet gymnasts were young and beautiful, and Kuchinskaya was particularly so. All-around winner both in Dortmund and Mexico, Vera Caslavska later said that it was at Dortmund where she definitely decided when to terminate her career.

"The first time I really thought about leaving (competitive gymnastics)," she said, "was when Kuchinskaya appeared on the world championships podium—so young, so beautiful. It seemed to me I could not compete with her. But then I felt a certain impulse: I wanted to beat just such a multifaceted rival." Thus, Caslavska continued competing until Mexico but left the world of top-level competition immediately thereafter.

"It is important for an athlete to leave at the right time," she said, "to set a date and to set that date when one is 'in flight'—that is, to break off one's sporting song on the highest note."[1]

Coincident with the arrival of Kuchinskaya, Petrick, and Druzhinina on the Soviet team was the appearance of nineteen-year-old Erika Zuchold on the team of the German Democratic Republic. Another young gymnast who had both the talent and the appearance of a star, Zuchold was destined to play a leading role on the East German team for the next six years.

Thus, Dortmund was the beginning of a new era, of a period of big change, and was the event that set the stage for the gymnastics we know today. At that time, eleven-year-old Olga Korbut was training seriously with Renald Knysh in Grodno. In just three years, she would be known throughout the Soviet Union; in three more years, she would be known throughout the world.

In addition, two other important developments occurred in Dortmund. One was the achievement of the team from the United States. The American women gymnasts had competed only once in the world championships: in 1962 in Prague, where they placed eighth. In three Olympic competitions—1956, 1960, and 1964—they had placed ninth. Now in Dortmund, they placed sixth. This was a definite step up and was a position they maintained two years later at the 1968 Olympics in Mexico. The gymnastics community was on notice that the United States team would be a factor to be reckoned with in future major competitions.

The other significant event was a milestone in the development of routines on the uneven bars. It was the routine of the American gymnast, Doris Brause. She placed 27th all around and did not make finals in the uneven bars, but her optional routine was considered—at least by one impartial judge—to be the best of all bars routines displayed in Dortmund. The failure of the judges to reward her properly caused an uproar among the spectators, which stopped the competition for an hour and three minutes.

The secret of her success and the cause of the uproar was Brause's technique of never stopping her routine on bars even for an instant. There was no pause to get ready for another move (or element, as they are called). There were no stops between parts of her routine. Hers was one continuous movement from beginning to end, as routines are nowadays. Thus, it was similar to men's high bar routines. In Dortmund, gymnasts from the leading countries were allowed to make pauses or stops in their routines and they made them, as we shall see. Generally, there was only one such pause per routine, but it was enough to arrest the momentum and interrupt the harmony. Consequently, it was a sensation when one gymnast performed her routine swinging from bar to bar and from element to element without any stop. A description of Brause's routine comes later. It is time now to describe the atmosphere of the event and to narrate the competition itself.

One eye witness to the championships, Mr. Herb Vogel, coach of one of the American gymnasts, had this to say in a story he wrote for the December 1966 issue of *The Modern Gymnast* magazine. It is reprinted here by kind permission of the International Gymnastics Hall of Fame.

> 10,000 spectators . . . flooded the Westfallenhalle to see the XVI World Championships of Gymnastics. And what a world championship did they see!
>
> The World Gymnastic Championship is more than a competition between the leading amateur gymnasts of the world. It is a battle of politics and international prestige where only one place is actually being contested . . . who is "number one." Second best is, as the name implies, just second best!
>
> The moment you step into the arena you can feel the tension and you know that it is going to be a reenactment of the historical report of the "Christians versus the Lions." Even the most casual observer, let alone the highly-tuned contestant, cannot help feeling . . . that the "Lions" are there: trim and hungry, ready to make short work of the opposition, eager to get to the dessert of bronze, silver and gold medallions.
>
> The crowd is there, too, in this case . . . Friends, Germans, and country-men . . . eager with anticipation. They are a gymnastically informed lot. Yet, true to the spirit of the arena of old, they are quick to criticize and abandon the faltering champion or herald the prospect of the crowning of a new queen. In this "arena" tradition, they sit, ready to "thumbs up" or "thumbs down" the performance of these modern age gladiators, as they compete in the greatest skill test of all, against woman's greatest adversary, woman's mastery of herself. The test, World Class gymnastic competition.[2]

In Dortmund, as in all Olympic and World Championship competitions prior to Munich, there were only three competitions: compulsory and optional team competitions, and the individual event finals. There was no separate all-around competition until Munich. Therefore, the individual all-around winner was that gymnast who achieved the highest combined score from compulsory and optional team competition. Then as now, the real excitement did not begin until the latter part of optional team competition, when the top teams were on the floor.

The story of Dortmund is written primarily from the point of view of those actors in the drama who would play a significant role in Mexico in 1968 and in subsequent major competitions. Those gymnasts who placed highly but then left the gymnastics scene will be listed in the results section only. After compulsories, the standings and scores of the leading countries follow.

1. URS	191.358
2. TCH	190.995
3. JPN	190.894
4. GDR	187.494
5. HUN	186.527
6. FRA	183.193
7. BUL	182.694
8. USA	182.360

Note: Romania did not compete in the 1966 World Championships.

Note: TCH stands for Czechoslovakia; GDR, for German Democratic Republic (East Germany).

The standings and scores of the leading, significant individuals were as follows:

1. Caslavska	39.032
2. Kuchinskaya	38.865
3. Ikeda	38.599
4. Zuchold	38.265
5. Petrick	37.966
6. Druzhinina	37.831

Note: Keiko Ikeda of Japan is included in this group although Dortmund was her last world class competition. She deserves recognition because she placed sixth in the 1960 Olympics in Rome, sixth in the 1962 World Championships in Prague, and sixth again in the 1964 Olympics in Tokyo. Regrettably, she is the last woman gymnast from Japan to achieve such success in gymnastics at this level, even though the Japanese men continued to perform with distinction.

Natalya Kuchinskaya and Zinaida Druzhinina

Optional Exercises: September 23rd

First Rotation

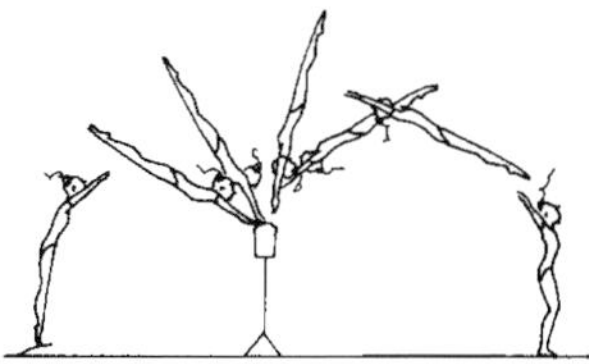
Figure 11

The Soviet gymnasts, being the leaders after compulsories, began their competition on vault. They exhibited a variety of vaults. Zinaida Druzhinina and Polina Astakhova performed simple handspring vaults, a straight-forward flight onto the horse followed by a handspring off *(Figure 11)*. Olga Kharlova and Larissa Petrick performed the Yamashita vault. This is a direct flight onto the horse followed by a piking of the body in the handspring off *(Figure 12)*. Larissa Latynina and Natalya Kuchinskaya performed a vault that consisted of a handspring onto the horse with a half turn followed by a half turn off the horse in after flight *(Figure 13)*. The Soviet vaulting scores were: 9.666 for Kuchinskaya and 9.50 for Latynina for their half-on half-off vaults; 9.50 for Kharlova and Petrick for their Yamashitas; 9.533 and 9.333 for Druzhinina and Astakhova for their handspring vaults. (Incidentally, Olga Kharlova, who has not previously been mentioned, competed in the 1968 Olympics, and the 1970 World Championships under the name of Karasyova, after her marriage. Like Kuchinskaya, Petrick and Druzhinina, she was one of the young Soviets making their debuts on the international stage.) The ladies of the second-place Czech team began their competition on the uneven bars. Vera Caslavska, being the leader of the team, was the last to perform. She scored 9.833, a score matched later by Kuchinskaya and Ikeda but nevertheless the highest score on the uneven bars in both compulsory the optional competition. Although her routine differed markedly from today's uneven bar routines and contained none of today's very complex elements, it was an exciting routine. The only pause came near the end of the routine, which was as follows:

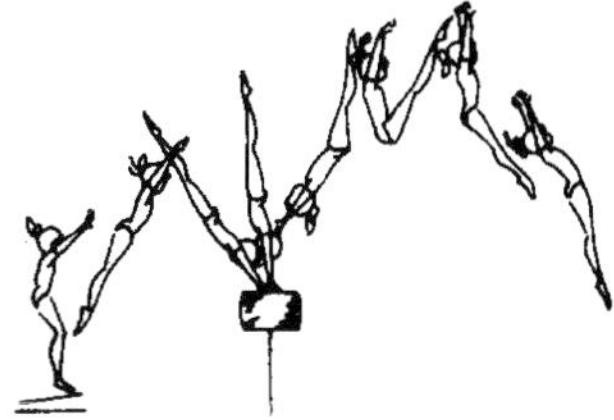
Figure 12

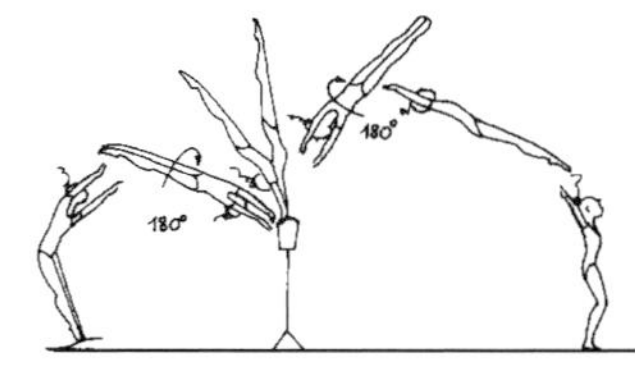

Figure 13

> Starting from the low bar side, Caslavska ran hard at the low bar, jumped off the beat board and wrapped herself forward around the low bar in free hip circles two full times *(Figure 14)*. As she came up on her second hip circle, she piked her body and placed her toes on top of the low bar between her arms. She swung back down in underswing below the low bar, released on the upswing and flew with a half turn to catch high bar facing low bar. She dropped to low bar, kipped on low bar to catch high bar and kipped on high bar through clear support position on the side away from the low bar and did an immediate full turn as she swung down to beat low bar. On her return swing, she executed a second full turn in back of the high bar.

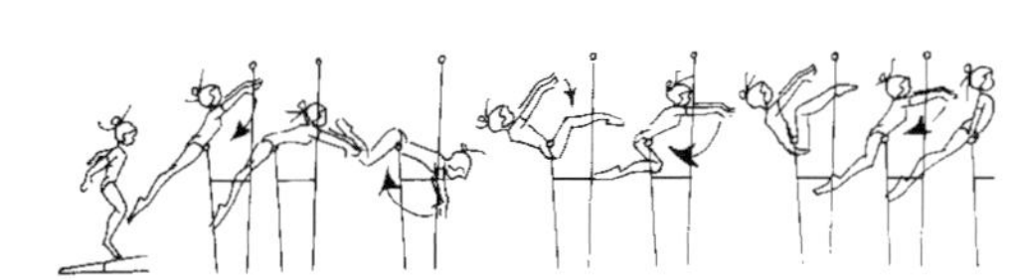
Figure 14

Figure 15

> She swung down to beat low bar a second time and kipped up on high bar to place her toes on top of high bar outside her hands. She swung back under high bar and on up between the bars above the height of the low bar, stretched her body over the low bar, made a half turn and allowed her body to drop down onto low bar. She wrapped backwards around low bar and then paused in front support position, that is, her hips on the low bar, her legs stretched behind her and her hands on the low bar. She then brought her right leg over the low bar in a half turn and grasped high bar so that she was now in rear-lying hang, with her hands on the high bar and her seat resting on the low bar. From there, she kipped on high bar to clear support position back of the high bar, began a hip circle backwards with her hips against the bar and released on the way up in hecht dismount to fly forward over the low bar and land (*Figure 15* shows a hecht off low bar).

The Czech team as a whole did better on bars than the Soviets did on vault. The Czechs averaged 9.633, almost a tenth better than the Soviets' 9.54. At the end of first rotation, the Czech team did, in fact, move ahead of the Soviets into first place. Meanwhile, the third-place Japanese were on beam. They did not do so well on beam as the East Germans did in floor exercise, their event in first rotation, but because of their strong lead after compulsories, they retained their third-place position. The team average was 9.266. The leading gymnast, Keiko Ikeda, scored 9.466 for this routine:

> Ikeda mounted diagonally from her left side near the far end of the beam by jumping off the beat board and landing on her right foot to immediate squat. She stood, made a quarter turn to her left to face across the beam and stand on her left leg with her right leg held diagonally up to the side with her right hand. She then made another quarter turn to her left to line up with the beam. She posed and danced to the other end. She made a cat leap and a half turn and returned with a split leap and dance steps. After a half turn to her right, she leaned forward and lowered herself into lunge position, her left knee bent and in front of her, her right leg extended behind her. From lunge position, she leaned into a forward roll and finished in vee-sit position just beyond the middle of the beam. She stood, made a high kick with her right leg, stepped forward to the end, went into squat position and made a quarter turn to her left. In squat position, she made another quarter turn to her left to face along the beam and entered a cartwheel with a half turn to her left, which she completed in a forward scale. She danced to the far end, turned a quarter turn left to face across the beam, turned back to the end, leaned forward into lunge position again and made a three-quarter turn to her right to face across the beam.

Vera Caslavska performing a full turn back of high bar as she swung down to beat low bar.

> She paused in lunge position after her three-quarter turn, then slid her left leg along the beam so that she was in side splits but facing along the beam. She leaned forward over her right leg while gesturing with her arms. Then she brought her left leg up onto the beam beside her right and lay back in supine position on the beam. She put her hands behind her head on the beam, elevated her legs over her until her right leg was on the beam behind her. She momentarily assumed a standing split position, her left leg vertically upward (although not quite), her hands on the beam, her arms straight and her head and body in line with her left leg. She lowered her body and brought her arms and legs together in squat position. She stood, took a step back, made a half turn to her left and stepped from the middle of the beam to the other end. She made a half turn to her right, stepped forward to the middle of the beam, squatted down, made a full turn to her right during which she rose to stand, elevated her right leg diagonally upward to the side and held it with her right hand. She lowered her right leg, danced forward to the end and made a half turn to her right. She advanced to the middle of the beam where she entered a handstand with her legs split front and back and her back leg bent. She brought her legs together in handstand and then made a forward roll into a pose in which she rests on her right foot in squat position, her left foot ahead of her on the beam with her left knee slightly bent and her right arm diagonally forward and her left arm diagonally up behind her. She stood, made a half turn to her right and returned to the other end with dance steps. She made two consecutive half turns and dismounted off the end with a front aerial walkover.

In floor exercise, the East German team averaged 9.59. Their leader, Erika Zuchold, scored 9.666. At the end of first rotation, the standings and scores of the leading teams and individuals were as follows:

	Initial Score	**First Rotation**	**Subtotal**
1. TCH *(bars)*	190.995	48.166	239.161
2. URS *(vault)*	191.358	47.699	239.057
3. JPN *(beam)*	190.894	46.299	237.193
4. GDR *(floor)*	187.494	47.931	235.425
1. Caslavska *(bars)*	39.032	9.833	48.865
2. Kuchinskaya *(vault)*	38.865	9.666	48.531
3. Ikeda *(beam)*	38.599	9.466	48.065
4. Zuchold *(floor)*	38.265	9.666	47.931
5. Petrick *(vault)*	37.966	9.500	47.466
6. Druzhinina *(vault)*	37.831	9.533	47.364

Second Rotation

The second rotation brought the fourth-place German Democratic Republic to vault, where Erika Zuchold scored 9.666 for her Yamashita. The East Germans averaged 9.54, the same as the Soviet team on vault. The now second-place Soviet team moved on to bars, where they improved considerably in their team average. It was 9.64, a full tenth higher than their 9.54 on vault. Zinaida Druzhinina was first up on bars for the Soviets, among those we are discussing. She scored 9.50 and was followed by Larissa Petrick, who also scored 9.50. Last up on the Soviet team was their star, lovely Natalya Kuchinskaya, who performed this routine:

Facing low bar under high bar, with her hands on low bar, she performed a glide kip to shoot her legs through between herself and the bar. Then she swung backwards around low bar, with her body piked, up through rear support position, that is, with her seat momentarily on the bar and her legs stretched in front, facing away from high bar. She continued backwards half way round, then reversed her swing so that she came back up to rear support position on low bar. There she reached up and grasped high bar. She then performed glide kip on high bar to make a vertical full turn behind the bar to hang on high bar. She dropped to low bar, kipped on low bar to catch high bar and then kipped on high bar again to stoop-through position, her legs piked through her arms as she hung on high bar on the side away from low bar. Again she swung down backwards around high bar and on up past rear support position, where she stretched her body out of pike. She piked again as she went over the top, swung back down and dropped

Natalya Kuchinskaya performing a vertical full turn behind high bar before dropping to low bar.

to low bar, where for the third time she kipped and caught high bar. There she paused with her hands holding high bar and her legs extended over low bar. She rolled half way to her right on her hips so that she now faced high bar, put her feet on the low bar, bent her knees to squat on low bar and jumped off to straddle support position on high bar, that is, she supported herself with her hands on the high bar, her body upright just above the bar and her legs horizontally in front of her but straddled forty-five degrees. There she swung back down around high bar, having put her toes on the bar as she swung back, released her toes on the way up, stretched her body and performed a half turn horizontally out from the high bar. She then swung down, wrapped around low bar and, as she came up, forcefully extended her body from pike to stretch position so that she bounced off the bar and allowed her momentum to carry her forward to land (Hecht dismount) *(Figure 15).*

Kuchinskaya performed a fast-paced routine, with a pause near the end, as in Caslavska's routine, to prepare for her final series of elements. She scored 9.833 and moved a bit closer to Caslavska, who would score 9.80 in second rotation. Furthermore, the strong Soviet team score of 48.199 would be a hard one for the Czechs on beam to match. As expected, the Czechs did not do quite so well on beam as they had done on bars. The team averaged 9.59. Caslavska, however, scored 9.80 for the following routine, one which would be similar to the one she would later perform in Mexico.

Figure 16

Figure 17

Figure 18

Caslavska ran toward one end of the beam, jumped off the beat board, landed on her left foot and immediately assumed an attractive pose in squat on her left foot with her right leg stretched in front, her right arm diagonally down in front and her left arm diagonally up in back. She stood, danced toward the other end, and finished in a split leap *(Figure 16)*. After some body waves at the end of the beam, she did a back walkover, *(Figure 17)* paused and leaned back into handstand, paused, continued to swing down to cross straddle sit *(Figure 18*) and then performed a backroll to stand at the end of the beam. She returned with a big step forward into a forward scale, then after dance steps and a high kick at the end of the beam, she performed a lunge half turn. She came back with dance steps and poses and made a squat half turn to her right. She stepped forward, made a very high kick with her right leg and then slid her right leg forward until she was in split position on the beam, facing along the beam. She posed in split position, brought her left leg around next to her right and assumed a vee-sit position with her legs tightly piked and her arms wrapped around them. She came out of this tight vee-sit by flaring her arms and then allowing her legs to swing down and back up into a position where she was supported by her right knee and shin on the beam, her left leg stretched diagonally up behind her and her body horizontally forward with both hands on the beam. In this attitude, she made a quick full turn, supported by her right knee and shin. She stood by bringing her left leg forward onto the beam and straightening it. After a pose, she dropped down onto her right knee again, with her left leg out in front, let her left leg swing down behind her and performed a forward roll, supported by her hands, to stand at the end of the beam, where she made a half turn to her right. She moved to the other end of the beam with dance steps, made a half turn and prepared for her dismount: she performed a forward walkover, stepped forward, performed a cartwheel to her left and punched off in salto backward stretched to land. (*Figure 19* shows salto backward tucked and with a half twist.)

Vera Caslavska in splits on the beam.

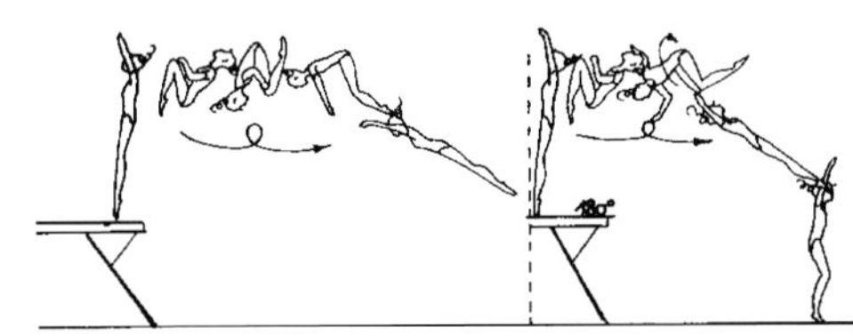

Figure 19

For the third-place Japanese team now in floor exercise, Ikeda scored 9.666 for her routine and helped the Japanese team remain in third place. At the end of second rotation, the team and individual standings and scores of the leading teams and individuals were as follows:

	Initial Score	**Second Rotation**	**Subtotal**
1. URS *(bars)*	239.057	48.109	287.256
2. TCH *(beam)*	239.161	47.933	287.094
3. JPN *(floor)*	237.193	47.899	285.092
4. GDR *(vault)*	235.423	47.697	283.122
1. Caslavska *(beam)*	48.865	9.800	58.665
2. Kuchinskaya *(bars)*	48.531	9.833	58.364
3. Ikeda *(floor)*	48.065	9.666	57.731
4. Zuchold *(vault)*	47.931	9.666	57.597
5. Petrick *(bars)*	47.466	9.500	57.066
6. Druzhinina *(bars)*	47.364	9.500	56.864

Third Rotation

In third rotation, the tight contest between the Czechs and the Soviets moved to beam for the Soviets and to floor exercise for the Czechs. The Japanese moved to vault and the East Germans to bars.

The Japanese achieved only a modest average on vault, 9.46. Ikeda scored 9.433 for her Yamashita, Taki Shibuya scored 9.50 for her Yamashita and, remarkably, Hiroko Ikenaga scored 9.50 both in optionals and finals for her simple handspring vault. For Ikenaga, reaching finals for a less complicated vault was the result of both good technique and a strong 9.60 score in compulsories.

On bars, the East Germans averaged only 9.58 on what is normally their strongest event. Their rising star, Erika Zuchold, scored 9.733. Unfortunately, she scored only 9.50 in compulsories and did not make finals. Her routine was unique to her in that it contained an unusually large number of elements in which she piked her legs through between herself and the bar and then swung backward around the bar. She also stopped her swing and reversed it in what is known as a counterswing. It was a technique she would continue to use both in Mexico and Ljubljana. (She changed her routine entirely, however, for Munich.) Her routine also contained another unusual element, as we shall see.

> Standing away from low bar on the low bar side, Zuchold jumped forward to grasp low bar, made a long glide and, on swinging back, shot her legs through between herself and the bar, so that she was hanging on low bar in pike position. She made a full and a half back seat circle around low bar and, on the way up on her second circle, paused while sitting on the low bar, then reached forward and grasped high bar. She immediately shot her legs up between her arms so that her legs were between herself and the high bar and she was hanging on high bar. She swung backwards until she was under high bar, then reversed direction and swung forward and up between the bars to sit on the bar, facing outwards. From sitting on high bar, she stretched her body into rear support position and circled backward around the bar. When under the bar, she reversed direction in a counterswing. As her body reached the inverted position between the bars, in rear clear support, she let go of high bar and flew to handstand on low bar, facing away from high bar (Zuchold-Schleudern) *(Figure 20)*. She entered a hip circle on low bar in the direction away from high bar and circled the bar until she reached front support position on top of the bar. Then she cast her body from the bar so that she could tuck her body to place her feet on the bar. She stood, reached for highbar and jumped up to toe-on position on high

Figure 20

bar, her feet outside her hands. From there, she swung back down under the bar and, on her way up, stretched her body away from the high bar and performed a half turn horizontally. She swung back down toward low bar, wrapped around it and flew back to catch high bar in eagle grip. She kipped her legs over the low bar, changed her grip to normal overgrip and, on completing her kip, swung back and shot her legs between herself and the bar, but this time on the side away from low bar. She swung back down and up between the bars, with her body in pike position, over the high bar and down the far side under high bar until she was part way up between the bars again. There, like a pendulum, she swung back in the direction her head was pointing. When she was under the high bar at the bottom of her swing, while her body was piked upside down and she was looking up, she kicked out of her pike, released the bar and stretched her body *(Figure 21)*. As she did so, her body rotated, as in a partial back somersault, and her head came up so that she was looking at the bar. As she concluded this unusual sequence, she regrasped the bar and swung forward to wrap around low bar. She came off the bar in hecht dismount and flew forward with a three-quarter turn to land.

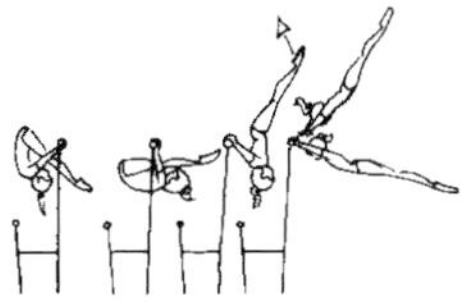

Figure 21

The East Germans moved six-tenths closer to the Japanese after third rotation but still could not overcome the 3.4 points separation between the two teams after compulsories.The two top competitors on beam for the Soviets—as they would be in Mexico—were Larissa Petrick and Natalya Kuchinskaya. Their routines had much in common.

Petrick ran toward one end of the beam, jumped off the beat board to place her hands on the beam. She pressed up to handstand with her legs straddled on the way up and then split front and back in handstand. She proceeded on over in walkover to stand. She danced to the other end with dance steps, a small split leap and skip steps. She made a half turn to her right, stepped forward and performed a one-arm cartwheel on her right hand *(Figure 22)*, paused and performed a one-arm back walkover on her left hand to the end of the beam. She did some body waves and poses, stepped toward the middle of the beam, made a half turn to her left, extended her left leg back and dropped down into lunge position. She executed a lunge full turn and then stretched into side splits along the beam She posed in splits, put her hands on the beam, raised herself with her legs in straddle position and made a three-quarter turn on her hands to the left to sit on the beam with her legs now hanging down, straddling the beam. She raised her legs to vee-sit position, let them drop onto the beam with her left leg bent and her right leg extended straight out in front of her. She

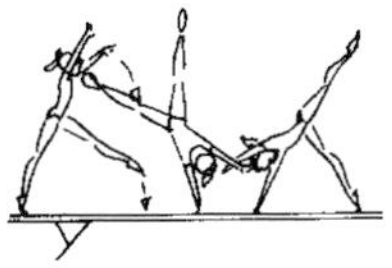

Figure 22

Figure 23

immediately executed a valdez to stand near the end of the beam *(Figure 23),* facing forward. She stood, posing with her right leg forward, her right knee bent, her body leaning forward in line with her left leg, which was diagonally back. She posed for two seconds while gesturing with her arms. She then leaned her body forward until it was horizontal, her weight on her right leg, now straight, then elevated her left leg vertically upward and held it with her left hand. She maintained this vertical split pose for two seconds. She ran toward the other end, performed a split leap and made a half turn to her right at the end. She came back with a big step, followed by a high kick with her right leg and performed a forward walkover *(Figure 24).* At the end, she made a deep body wave, performed some dance steps, made a half turn, stepped forward and dismounted to her left side with a gainer salto stretched while placing her right hand on the beam for support *(Figure 25).*

Natalya Kuchinskaya performing a split leap on the beam.

Kuchinskaya mounted by running to one end of the beam, jumping off the beat board with her hands on the beam and pressing up to handstand, straddling her legs on the way up. She proceeded in walkover to stand. She danced and made a split leap to the other end, made a half turn to her right to face along the beam and posed with her right leg bent in front of her, her back first bent forward and then arched back, her arms doing graceful waves. She took a big step forward, made a high kick with her right leg, lowered herself into lunge position with her right leg forward and made a three-quarter turn to her right. She extended her legs sideways into splits, placed her hands on the beam directly in front of her and pressed on up into handstand. Then she brought her legs back down outside her arms into clear straddle support position and made a three-quarter turn on her hands to the left to face along the beam. She dropped her legs momentarily on each side of the beam, extending rearward in cross straddle sit, brought them back up to vee-sit, legs together, lowered her left foot onto the beam with her knee bent and lowered her right leg onto the beam extended straight ahead. She bent her right knee to put her foot onto the beam and pushed off in valdez to stand and pose at the end of the beam. She danced forward to the end, performed a little tuck jump, which she finished in squat position. She jumped, stretched her legs and returned to squat, still facing out from the beam. She stood, paused, performed a back walkover, paused and leaned back into a stag handstand, which she held for a second. She split her legs, continued her backward movement to place her right foot on the beam and then to stand and pose at the end of the beam. She made a high kick with her right leg, danced forward to the end and made a half turn to her left. She came forward with dance steps to just beyond the middle of the beam, paused and dismounted to her left side with a gainer salto stretched while placing her right hand on the beam for support *(Figure 25)*.

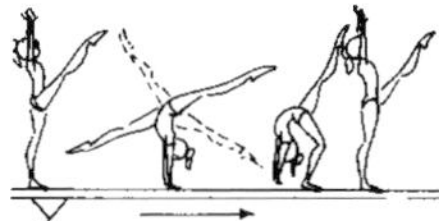

Figure 24

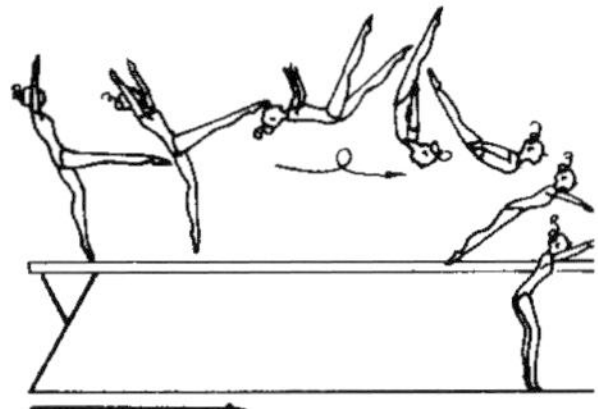

Figure 25

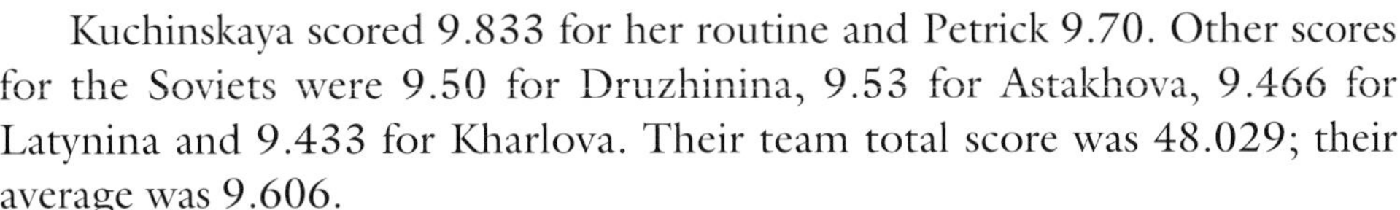

Kuchinskaya scored 9.833 for her routine and Petrick 9.70. Other scores for the Soviets were 9.50 for Druzhinina, 9.53 for Astakhova, 9.466 for Latynina and 9.433 for Kharlova. Their team total score was 48.029; their average was 9.606.

Meanwhile, the Czechs in floor exercise were getting a number of high scores. The five scores that would count were 9.50 for Jindra Kostelova, 9.633 for Bohumila Rimnacova and Jaroslava Sedlackova, 9.80 for Jana Kubickova, and 9.90 for Vera Caslavska. The Czech team total was 48.532 in floor exercise and this put them back into first place. Their average was 9.706. Caslavska's floor exercise was as follows:

She started in the middle of the floor and performed many turns, body waves and poses as she worked her way into a corner for her first tumbling run: she ran, performed a round-off, two flic-flacs (*Figure 26* shows one flic-flac), and a salto backward stretched *(Figure 27)*, at the conclusion of which she dropped right down into splits. Standing, she moved into the middle of the floor and over to the adjacent corner to her right with many turns and leaps before going directly into her second pass: a cartwheel into a side salto and then an immediate cartwheel, which she ended, as in her first pass, by dropping down into splits. She did not pause in her splits this time, however, but rolled forward with a half turn on her back, stood facing the corner and made another half turn to face toward the middle of the floor. She danced, turned and posed while she moved to the adjacent corner on her left for her last pass: a round-off, two flic-flacs followed by a half turn into a forward handspring stepout. She made a very brief pause and then performed a back handspring. Upon landing this last back handspring (also

Figure 26

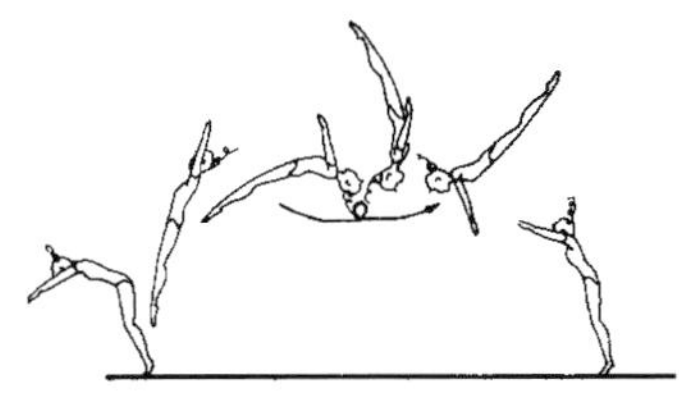

Figure 27

known as a flic-flac), she intentionally fell forward into a tight tuck on the floor with her head almost touching the mat. She stretched her body to stand on her toes, made a number of turns and leaps toward the middle of the floor, where she did a round-off into a salto backward stretched. She ran forward into the middle of the floor again, paused and arched her back so steeply that she could put her hands on the floor just outside her feet. She then allowed her body to roll forward through prone position to her final pose: her knees and shins on the floor, her back arched steeply back with her head and arms hanging behind, her arms stretched.

At the conclusion of third rotation, the standings and scores of the leading teams and individuals were as follows:

	Initial Score	**Third Rotation**	**Subtotal**
1. TCH *(floor)*	287.094	48.532	335.626
2. URS *(beam)*	287.256	48.032	335.288
3. JPN *(vault)*	285.092	47.299	332.391
4. GDR *(bars)*	283.122	47.898	331.020
1. Caslavska *(floor)*	58.665	9.900	68.565
2. Kuchinskaya *(beam)*	58.364	9.833	68.197
3. Zuchold *(bars)*	57.597	9.733	67.330
4. Ikeda *(vault)*	57.731	9.433	67.164
5. Petrick *(beam)*	57.066	9.700	66.766
6. Druzhinina *(beam)*	56.864	9.500	66.364

Fourth Rotation

The Soviets were now faced with the challenge of regaining their lost first-place position in their only remaining chance, floor exercise. To do so, they reshuffled their line-up and made Zinaida Druzhinina the lead-off gymnast, even though she had the capability of winning a gold medal in floor exercise finals. The strategy was that, if Druzhinina got a high score, the scores of the gymnasts following her would be pushed up. As it turned out, the Soviets did get a higher score in floor exercise than in vault, bars or beam and they got a higher score than the Czechs did in vault. They did not, however, score high enough to take the lead away from the Czechs, and Druzhinina, though she scored 9.80, lost her chance for the gold medal in finals. One 9.90 and one 10.00 were awarded her by the judges; if she had been last up, she might have scored 9.90 instead of 9.80. Her routine was as follows:

Figure 28

Druzhinina started in the middle of the floor and, with dance steps and an aerial cartwheel *(Figure 28)*, moved into a corner for her first pass: a

Vera Caslavska in floor exercise.

round-off, flic-flac into a salto backward stretched with full twist. She danced out of the corner along the side of the mat to her right as she finished her back salto with a hop and many very quick small dance steps backwards. She did a series of turns and a split jump, more turns and another split jump as she moved into the adjacent corner for her second pass: she ran and performed a forward aerial walkover, stepped out, ran and performed a second forward aerial walkover. She posed in the corner, made several steps back along the side to the right of her second pass diagonal, turned to her left toward the center and did a forward walkover. After some turns and dance steps, she did a back handspring (flic-flac) and dropped down into splits on the floor. She then stood, posed and with dance steps moved into a corner for her final pass: a round-off, flic-flac, into a salto backward stretched. She danced forward into her final pose, standing erect with her feet spread apart front and back, her right arm held vertically upward, her left arm extended straight in front of her and her head looking to her left.

Druzhinina's sacrifice did not really help the other team members, except perhaps Kuchinskaya, who scored 9.90. Petrick scored only 9.60. Her routine and that of Kuchinskaya may be compared with those they performed later in Mexico. They were as follows:

Figure 29

Zinaida Druzhinina in floor exercise.

Petrick started near the middle of the floor and proceeded along a diagonal to a corner with a high scissors leap and a forward aerial walkover. She stepped into the corner, posed, made a half turn and began her first pass: a round-off, flic-flac, salto backward stretched with full twist *(Figure 29)*. Leaving her corner, she moved to her right and made a circle counterclockwise around the floor with dance steps and skip steps until she came near the adjacent corner to the left of the one she had just left. She made a jump full turn around her left leg with her right leg held up and then some slow, graceful turns and poses. She moved into the corner with two back walkovers. She began her second pass, which consisted of three consecutive forward aerial walkovers *(Figure 30)*. She then danced to her left and performed a high jump full turn with her left leg straight and her right knee bent. Upon completing her turn, she dropped down into splits and posed facing along her right leg, which was stretched out in front of her. She made a three-quarter turn to her right on her seat, stood, made a full turn on her right foot with her left leg extended behind her and immediately leaned forward into a forward walkover. She paused and posed while standing after her walkover, then leaned forward and performed a second forward walkover. She then made two deep body waves, first turning to her left and then to her right. From looking and turning to her right, she swung left into a butterfly turn and followed this consecutively with two more butterfly turns *(Figure 31)*. She then performed a quick full turn on her left foot with her right knee tightly bent and then performed a fast, spinning, double turn to her left with both knees deeply bent, which she finished rolling out onto the floor on her back. She continued her roll into kneeling position, her knees on the floor but her body upright. She gestured gracefully with her arms and made a half turn to her right as she stood up. She stepped forward into a forward scale and made another step into the corner from which she had just begun her second pass. She turned, posed and began her third pass: a round-off, flic-flac into a salto backward stretched. She stepped forward and ended her routine, standing with her knees slightly bent, looking down to her right and holding her right arm diagonally down to her side and her left arm bent over her head.

Kuchinskaya's exercise was much more fast-paced than Petrick's. It was not more graceful nor more artistic, but her movements were much more quickly done. Like Petrick, Kuchinskaya started well away from a corner, but she began her exercise half way along one of the sides of the floor. From standing, she turned to her right to face the corner, kicked her left leg up behind her and moved into the corner with turns and dance steps. In the corner, she turned to face along the diagonal, moved her left leg quickly from side to side behind her and and her arms from side to side in front of her. Then she began her first pass: a round-off, flic-flac into salto backward stretched with full twist. She moved away from the corner toward her right with a few quick hops on her right foot along the side of the floor and made a running circuit around the floor clockwise. She performed a forward aerial walkover and three consecutive split leaps, ending her circuit at the corner to the right of where she ended her first pass. In the corner, she made a double turn while flexing her arms above her. Then, after a pose, she began her second pass, which consisted of a round-off, flic-flac into a half turn followed by a salto forward (arabian) *(Figure 32)* so that she ended facing the corner. She turned to her left and proceeded along the adjacent side with a forward aerial walkover. She made a half turn to her right and dropped down into splits, facing along her right leg which was stretched out in front of her. She posed in splits, stood, while making a quarter turn to her right, posed again, arched her back steeply, then made another quarter turn to her right before dropping down onto her left knee on the floor. She leaned over her right bent knee and drooped her arms down to the floor. Then she leaned back, turned to her left and rolled out into sitting position from which she entered a back walkover to stand. She circled to her left past the middle of the floor, near to the adjacent side, posed and made long steps and sweeping arm gestures first to one side, then the other, crossing her legs and arms in front of her. She made a three-quarter turn to her left and leaned back into back walkover. She stopped her walkover as her first foot reached the floor and pushed back into split-leg handstand. She then bent her arms so that her elbows were on the floor and her chin was also on the floor. She held this chinstand for a second, rotated her legs above her a half turn so that they exchanged position, then rolled out to her right into splits on the floor. She continued turning to her right a full turn as she stood up. Now facing a corner, she danced into it, turned and began her third pass: a round-off, flic-flac into a salto backward stretched. She stepped forward into a graceful final pose: her weight on her straight right leg, her left leg extended diagonally back, her elbows close together in front of her with her right forearm and hand pointing up, her left forearm and hand slightly up, her head tilted back.

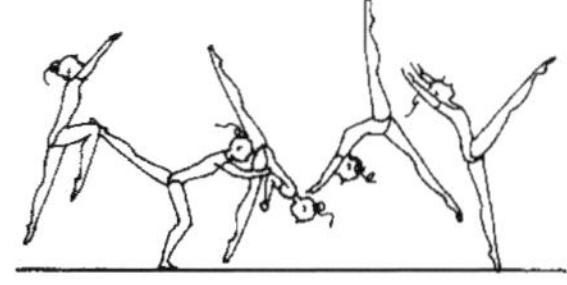

Figure 30

Figure 31

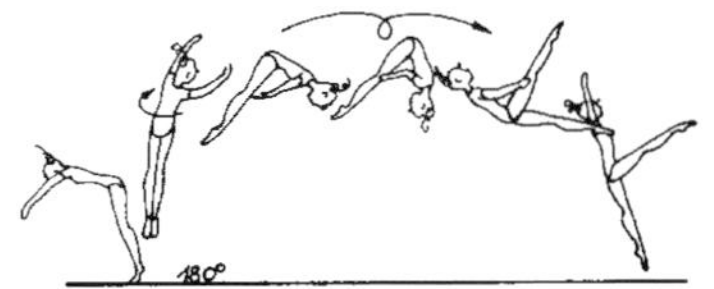

Figure 32

Although floor exercise, with its characteristic of affording the gymnast a chance to show off her personality and to display some original choreography, often yields higher scores than the more cut-and-dried vaulting event, the Czechs on vault nevertheless met the Soviet challenge commendably. None of the Czechs scored less than 9.533 and their average was only 0.002 of a point less than 9.60. Caslavska was highest with 9.733 for her two Yamashita vaults.

Thus, the battle between the Czechs and the Soviets ended in favor of the Czechs. Caslavska held off Kuchinskaya's challenge. Her optional total of

39.266 was a bare 0.034 ahead of her rival's 39.232, but with her lead from compulsories, she ended comfortably in front with a margin of 0.2. Although Caslavska would win the all-around medal again in Mexico, the Czech team would not. In fact, Dortmund was the high-water mark for the Czechs. They would slowly sink in both team and individual standings during the 1970s and 1980s. The Soviets' chief rivals would become first the East Germans and then the Romanians.

Meanwhile, the Japan-East Germany contest ended easily in favor of the Japanese. As with the Czechs, Dortmund was the high-water mark for the Japanese women. The East Germans would win third place in Mexico and the Japanese would go from fourth in Mexico and Ljubljana to seventh in Munich.

On bars, the Japanese scored very well. Their 48.532 team score matched the Czechs on floor in third rotation as highest for any event and was an average of over 9.70 per gymnast. Keiko Ikeda scored 9.833 for the following routine:

Figure 33

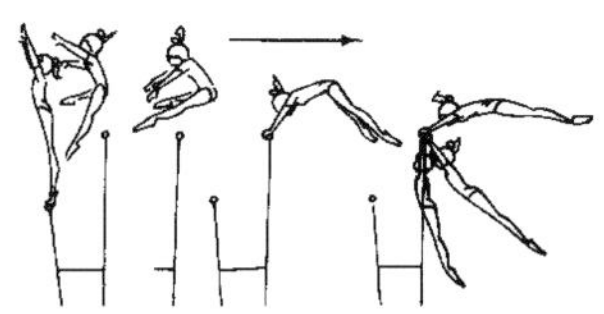

Figure 34

> She ran at the low bar from the low bar side, jumped off the beat board, grabbed low bar and made a half turn to her left above the low bar with her legs in straddle position *(Figure 33)*. She swung down backwards under the low bar, as in a straddle circle, until half way up, at which point, she stopped, brought her legs from straddle to pike under the bar, swung back and made a forward hip circle and then a half hip circle until she could stoop and put her feet on the bar. Amazingly, she then stood up straight on the low bar and posed for a second, holding the high bar with her right hand and stretching her left arm out in front of her. She then flexed her knees and jumped back off the low bar, over the high bar with her legs straddled, grabbed high bar with both hands and swung down to beat the low bar *(Figure 34)*. She swung back and used her momentum and arm strength to hold her body upright and vertical against the high bar, at which point she did a back hip circle around high bar and entered a second back hip circle. As she came up between the bars with her body vertical but inverted, she stretched her body, made a half turn and allowed her body to swing down onto the low bar. She wrapped around the low bar backwards, then kipped and performed a hip circle around low bar in the opposite direction from her wrap, namely, forward toward the high bar. At the conclusion of this hip circle, she paused, reached out to grab high bar with her right hand, lifted her right leg over the low bar and made a half turn to her left so that she was facing away from the high bar with both legs together, her seat on low bar and her hands holding high bar. From this "rear lying hang" position, she kipped directly into forward hip circle around high bar.

As she finished it, holding herself in clear support on top of the bar, she released high bar for a fraction of a second, brought her piked legs which had been slightly straddled, over the bar and together between her hands. She then swung backwards around high bar with her body in piked position one and a half times. Half way around on her second circle, she stopped, swung back and up. Near the top of her circle, she released her hands, allowed her legs to straddle to the side, recaught the bar (a "cut-catch") and swung down with her body stretched to wrap around low bar. As she released from the bar and flew back, she caught high bar in eagle grip *(Figure 35)*, swung forward to place her legs over low bar, changed her grip from eagle grip to under grip and kipped up to clear support position on high bar. She swung down and up in back hip circle around high bar. As she came up, she thrust with her hips off high bar in hecht dismount and allowed her momentum to carry her forward to land.

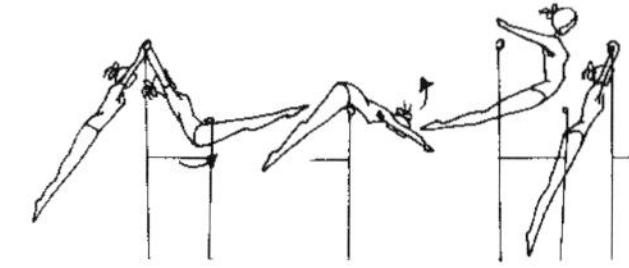

Figure 35

It was obviously an extremely active routine. Although she had two definite stops—one in which she posed standing on the low bar and one during which she made a half turn to bring her seat onto the low bar—she compressed a large number of elements into this one routine. Ikeda's final score in the championships was more than 0.8 higher than the number two Japanese gymnast. She had made a significant contribution to the Japanese team effort.

The fourth-place East Germans finished their competition on beam. Erika Zuchold's 9.266 marred an otherwise excellent competition and kept her from winning bronze medal all around. She would, however, lead her team to bronze medal in the 1968 Mexico Olympics and would win the gold medal on beam four years later in the 1970 World Championships in Ljubljana.

As with Ikeda of Japan, the leaders of the other three leading countries were far ahead of their number two gymnasts. Zuchold was 0.666 points ahead of Angelika Stiegler, Kuchinskaya was 1.7 points ahead of Petrick, and Caslavska was 1.833 points ahead of Jaroslava Sedlackova.

The final standings and scores of the leading teams and individuals were as follows:

	Initial Score	**Fourth Rotation**	**Final**
1. TCH *(vault)*	335.626	47.999	383.625
2. URS *(floor)*	335.288	48.299	383.587
3. JPN *(bars)*	332.391	48.532	380.923
4. GDR *(beam)*	331.020	46.798	377.818
5. HUN			373.889
6. USA			367.620

(table continued on next page)

	Initial Score	Fourth Rotation	Final
1. Caslavska *(vault)*	68.565	9.733	78.298
2. Kuchinskaya *(floor)*	68.197	9.900	78.097
3. Ikeda *(bars)*	67.164	9.833	76.997
4. Zuchold *(beam)*	67.330	9.266	76.596
5. Petrick *(floor)*	66.766	9.600	76.366
6. Druzhinina *(floor)*	66.364	9.800	76.164

It is appropriate now to consider the optional uneven bars routine of Doris Brause. She performed this routine in the group of teams just preceding those we have been discussing. Since the United States had placed eighth in compulsories, it competed optionals in the second senior group, which included Hungary, France, and Bulgaria. In optionals, the United States moved up from eighth to sixth place.

Brause had long been an innovator on bars. Possibly because she did not have a set of uneven bars in her gym for a long time, she did her training on the men's high bar. Therefore she got used to performing as the men do: swinging from element to element without stopping. This aspect of her routine had such an explosive impact on the crowd that they were outraged when she received a score of 9.766 instead of 9.9.

At a time when gymnastics was all but unknown among the American media and almost completely ignored, a German newspaper, the *Sports Telegram*, had this to say, as recorded by Mr. Herb Vogel, from whose article were recorded some impressions at the beginning of this narrative:[2]

ZUSCHAUER-SKANDAL IN DER
WESTFALLENHALLE
Das War Betrug

> The literal translation is "Spectator-Scandal in Westfallenhalle! It is a fraud!"
>
> This front page, 2-inch, bold-type headline points up the description of the one hour and three minutes of irate spectator whistles, cat-calls and rhythmic stamping of feet. It was the longest, and perhaps now, the proudest hour in the gymnastic career of Doris Fuchs Brause, the "uncrowned queen" of the uneven bars.
>
> "Uncrowned" champion, but the true champion she is. The German "Sports Telegram" described the optional routine as a "brilliant, mistake-free and fantastic endeavour." To the German audience, the jury score of 9.766 was simply not high enough to suit them. Their shouts, "Das War Betrug! . . . it was a fraud! . . . " still echo clearly. This report is not an exaggeration by an American writer, for in support, German judge Irma

Walter is credited with this published news quote, "This (Brause's) routine was the best of the competition. It (the routine) contained five of the highest difficulty parts and all were exacted without a flaw. That is why I must award a score of 9.9; a 9.8 would not have been high enough."

From this writer's coaching point of view, Doris' routine presented an illusion of horizontal bar (men's event) execution, in that it was free-swinging and total. Her changes and transitions from bar to bar created the illusion that a low bar did not exist. While we coaches, and our stateside judges, allow our girls unnecesssary stops and stands for preparation . . . merely because the Europeans do, . . . Doris Brause "swings" bars. No pause to get set is ever made . . . . The future trend is, as it has been all along, "Swing is the thing" . . . with each movement carried to its ultimate . . . .

Doris Brause's routine was as follows:

Facing high bar, standing away from the apparatus, Brause ran, jumped off the beat board to catch high bar, swung forward to beat low bar, swung back in uprise to clear support position off high bar. She did a clear hip circle backward on high bar and swung back under high bar to catch low bar. She did a glide kip on low bar and a front hip circle on low bar. Then, from front support on low bar, facing away from high bar, she cast back and performed a front somersault (salto forward) between the bars, with legs straddled to catch high bar, an element known both as a "Brause" and a "Radochla" *(Figure 36)*. After her "Brause," she hung momentarily on high bar, facing low bar, then dropped to low bar. She performed a glide kip, did a half turn under the bar in her glide to face back toward high bar and performed another glide kip from which she performed a front hip circle on low bar. She came out of her front hip circle in handstand on low bar, with her face looking away from high bar, and then arched back to sit on high bar. (This was possible in those days because the bars were so close together.) Sitting on high bar, facing away from low bar, she did a partial seat circle forward with her body piked, at the bottom of which she was able to place her feet onto the low bar, lean her shoulders under the high bar and stoop forward to place her hands on low bar outside her feet. She made a sole circle backward and released on the upswing from under the low bar to catch high bar facing away from low bar but with a cross grip. Her cross grip caused her shoulders to rotate a half turn so that she hung from high bar looking towards low bar. She immediately dropped to low bar, did a front hip circle to a very quick squat on low bar. She then jumped off low bar with a half turn to land on her stomach on high bar, facing out, the low bar behind. She did a front hip circle to handstand on high bar, made a half turn on high bar to face away from low bar and swung down to wrap around low bar and fly forward in hecht dismount to land.

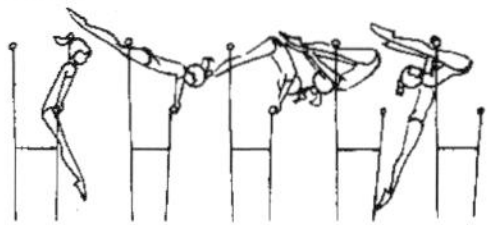

Figure 36

Uneven bars routines would not change dramatically until the late 1970s and early 1980s when giant swings, release elements, and flyaway dismounts would displace the low-bar wrap-arounds, seat circles, and hecht dismounts common during the Dortmund era. (These new elements were made possible by the technical equipment change that greatly increased the separation between the bars.) Brause's routine, while not immediately rewarded, did ultimately have an impact. Its execution and smooth flow might well have been factors that led to the coming, memorable performances on uneven bars by Karin Janz of East Germany in Mexico, Ljubljana and Munich.

Finals on the Apparatus: September 25th

In finals on the apparatus, the only routine not so far recorded is that of Taniko Mitsukuri of Japan, who won the bronze medal on the uneven bars for the following routine. It had two unique elements: her release at the top of her wrap around low bar and, later, her vault over the high bar.

> Mitsukuri mounted with a run to jump over the low bar in tuck position to catch high bar. She swung out with a half turn and swung back to wrap around low bar, release at the top of her circle with her body stretched and her arms out to the side in a quick flair, recatch low bar and kip to catch high bar. On high bar, she kipped but not to handstand. She kipped until she could shoot her feet vertically through her arms behind the bar, swung down backwards in pike position under the bar until she could put her feet on the low bar, grasped the low bar with her hands—her feet still on the bar—and initiated a sole circle backwards around low bar. On the upswing on the far side of the low bar, she released her feet from the bar and made a half turn. She kipped on low bar and made a forward hip circle around low bar until again she could put her feet on the bar. From a squat position on low bar, she reached for the high bar in undergrip, jumped upwards from low bar to high bar, tucked her feet through her arms over the bar and then swung down forwards around high bar. As she came up between the bars, she vaulted over high bar with a half turn and swung down to wrap around low bar. As she came off low bar, she flew with a half turn to catch high bar, dropped to low bar, kipped to high bar, then kipped on high bar—with an assist of a push off low bar with her feet—to clear support position off high bar. She performed a clear hip circle backwards around high bar, swung down to wrap around low bar, released and allowed her momentum to carry her forward in hecht dismount to land. Mitsukuri received a 9.80 in finals.

Most notable in apparatus finals was Kuchinskaya's achievement in winning three gold medals. It is possible she might not have won her gold medal in floor exercise had Druzhinina not been assigned the lead-off role during optional team competition. Druzhinina's high score of 9.933 indicates how she, too, could have scored 9.90 in optionals as Kuchinskaya did. Under her new name of Zinaida Voronina, Druzhinina would, however, win medals both in Mexico in 1968 and Ljubljana in 1970.

In any case, Natalya Kuchinskaya ended up as queen of the championships and was thunderously cheered by the 10,000 knowledgeable spectators in Dortmund's Westfallenhalle.

Final scores in apparatus finals were as follows:

	Compulsories	Optionals	Average	Finals	Total
Vault					
1. Caslavska	9.766	9.733	9.750	9.833	19.583
2. Zuchold	9.666	9.666	9.666	9.733	19.399
3. Kuchinskaya	9.633	9.666	9.650	9.666	19.316
4. Starke, GDR	9.533	9.566	9.550	9.666	19.216
5. Krajcireva, TCH	9.533	9.600	9.566	9.633	19.199
6. Ikenaga, JPN	9.600	9.500	9.550	9.600	19.150
Bars					
1. Kuchinskaya	9.800	9.833	9.816	9.800	19.616
2. Ikeda	9.766	9.833	9.800	9.766	19.566
3. Mitsukuri	9.733	9.700	9.716	9.800	19.516
4. Caslavska	9.800	9.833	9.816	9.666	19.482
5. Astakhova	9.733	9.700	9.716	9.700	19.416
6. Shibuya, JPN	9.666	9.800	9.733	9.600	19.333
Beam					
1. Kuchinskaya	9.666	9.833	9.750	9.900	19.650
2. Caslavska	9.666	9.800	9.733	9.600	19.333
3. Petrick	9.600	9.700	9.650	9.600	19.250
4. Ikeda	9.600	9.466	9.533	9.700	19.233
Ducza, HUN	9.600	9.600	9.600	9.633	19.233
6. Sedlackova, TCH	9.566	9.600	9.583	9.600	19.183
Floor Exercise					
1. Kuchinskaya	9.766	9.900	9.833	9.900	19.733
2. Caslavska	9.800	9.900	9.850	9.833	19.683
3. Druzhinina	9.666	9.800	9.733	9.933	19.666
4. Petrick	9.700	9.600	9.650	9.766	19.416
5. Kubickova, TCH	9.533	9.800	9.633	9.700	19.363
6. Furuyama, JPN	9.700	9.600	9.650	9.666	19.316

Beam Finalists: 1st–Kuchinskaya (URS); 2nd–Caslavska (TCH); 3rd–Petrick (URS).

Upon the conclusion of the 1966 World Championships in Dortmund, the upcoming Olympics in Mexico became the objective on which the gymnastics world's attention would now be focused. There we will meet not only more young Soviet gymnasts but also promising young stars from East Germany and the United States.

Kuchinskaya and Caslavska—the outstanding names of Dortmund—would, with Zuchold, Petrick, and Druzhinina, as well as newcomer Karin Janz of East Germany, be the outstanding names of Mexico. Ironically, Kuchinskaya and Caslavska would leave the scene after Mexico, as Latynina and Astakhova did after Dortmund. As gymnastics became more complicated and physically demanding, careers would become shorter. Four to six years at the top would be the norm.

References

[1]O. Polonskaya, "Faith, Hope, Love," *Sovietsky Sport*, May 1987.

[2]Herb Vogel, "Carbon Copy," *The Modern Gymnast*, Dec. 1966. (Now known as *International Gymnast.)*

Descriptions of the routines of most gymnasts were taken from a video tape made from films taken by Frank Endo; some were taken from a video tape made from films taken by Bill Coco and supplied by Frank Turoff.

The description of Doris Brause's routine on the uneven bars was taken from the ABC Sports video, "Gymnastics' Greatest Stars."

Although she was 25 in Amsterdam, Vera Caslavska leapt just as high as today's gymnasts—and on a bare beam.

European Championship

1967

Amsterdam, Netherlands

and other Important Events

May to October

Important events in women's gymnastics continued without let-up in 1967. Among the most important were the European Championship in May in Amsterdam, the Pan American Games in Winnipeg in July, the Spartakiade in Moscow in July, and the third pre-Olympic competition in Mexico in October.

While European Championships seem to have lost some of their former prestige, perhaps as a result of the annual World Championships that were instituted in 1992 by F.I.G. (International Gymnastics Federation), in former times they were rated very highly. This was natural because all the best women gymnasts were in Europe. The 1967 European Championship was eagerly awaited because of the rivalry between Caslavska and Kuchinskaya.

The first European Championship was held in May 1957 in Bucharest, Romania, where Latynina won gold medals in the all-around and all four apparatus finals.

The second European Championship, held in May 1959, in Cracow, Poland, was Caslavska's first. Here she won the floor exercise gold medal and placed second in vault.

In the third European Championship, held in June 1961 in Leipzig, East Germany, Latynina won the gold medal all-around, Astakhova placed second, and Caslavska tied Ingrid Föst of East Germany for the bronze medal all-around. Caslavska's only medal in apparatus finals was bronze in floor exercise.

Because of some disagreement, none of the top countries competed in the fourth championship in Paris in April 1963.

The fifth European Championship in Sofia, Bulgaria, in May 1965, was Caslavska's first big triumph. She won the all-around and all four apparatus finals, as Latynina had done in 1957. Her principal rivals were Latynina (second, all-around) and Birgit Radochla of East Germany (third, all-around), whose name is associated with that of Doris Brause as first to perform the salto forward between bars. In this last major competition in which she won medals, Latynina placed third in vault and second on bars and beam and in floor exercise. Radochla tied Latynina for second place in floor exercise and tied Petrick for third on beam.

Caslavska repeated her 1965 triumph in 1967 in Amsterdam. Once again she won the all-around and all four apparatus finals. Webster's *New World Dictionary* defines "hat trick" as any of various unusual feats, especially the act by a single player in sports such as ice hockey or soccer of scoring three goals in one game. The term originated in cricket from the practice of rewarding a noteworthy feat with a new hat. Certainly Caslavska's feat of winning five medals in consecutive European Championships qualifies as a hat trick.

The confrontation between Caslavska and Kuchinskaya had been anticipated since the Dortmund World Championships eight months before. It did not pan out as expected, however, because Kuchinskaya had a major break in vault and only placed ninth all-around. She did, however, place second on beam and in floor exercise. Zinaida Druzhinina (Voronina) continued her upward climb. After placing tenth all-around in Dortmund, she placed second all-around in Amsterdam and third on beam and in floor exercise. Karin Janz did well in her first major international competition and Erika Zuchold continued her excellence in vault. Results of major 1967 competitions follow.

European Championship

Amsterdam: May 27th–28th

All-around

1. Caslavska, TCH	38.965
2. Druzhinina, URS	38.533
3. Krajcirova, TCH	38.199
4. Janz, GDR	38.065
5. Zuchold, GDR	37.898
6. Oroszi, HUN	37.565

Vault

1. Caslavska, TCH 19.733
2. Zuchold, GDR 19.533
3. Janz, GDR 19.333

Bars

1. Caslavska, TCH 19.199
2. Janz, GDR 19.166
3. Krajcirova, TCH 19.066

Beam

1. Caslavska, TCH 19.833
2. Kuchinskaya, URS 19.666
3. Druzhinina, URS 19.499

Floor Exercise

1. Caslavska, TCH 19.866
2. Kuchinskaya, URS 19.733
3. Druzhinina, URS 19.666

Pan American Games

Winnipeg, Canada: July

Across the ocean, in the Pan American Games, the United States easily dominated the team event and Linda Metheny became the individual champion. Besides the all-around, Linda won vault, beam, and floor exercise and took second place on bars. Results were as follows:

1. USA 362.377
2. Canada 336.775
3. Cuba 334.526
4. Mexico 289.130
5. Brazil 112.231

1. Linda Metheny 74.03
2. Joyce Tanac 72.99
3. Marie Walther 71.61
   D. Schaenzer 71.61
5. Debbie Bailey 71.34
6. Kathy Gleason 70.28
7. MacDonnell, CAN 70.28

IVth Spartakiade

Moscow: July 24th–30th

Meanwhile, in Moscow, an event of much greater significance for the future was taking place. The reason for its significance is explained in this comment by Dr. Josef Göhler, editor of *Olympische Turnkunst* magazine in the issue for December 1967: "There were nowhere in the world as many gymnasts coming up to international standard as in Russia. On the occasion of the IVth Spartakiade, some 50 girls were able to exceed the 72-point limit, although evaluation was severe. Phenomenal: a 14-year-old girl placed third!" Results were as follows:

1. Natalya Kuchinskaya	76.500
2. Larissa Petrick	75.700
3. Lyubov Burda *(14 years old)*	74.575
4. Polina Astakhova	74.150
5. Ludmilla Turischeva *(15 years old)*	72.375

Pre-Olympic Tournament

Mexico: October 15th–19th

This was, in fact, the third and final pre-Olympic tournament in Mexico. It was attended by Arthur Gander, then President of the International Gymnastics Federation, in his responsibility to see that the preparations were being made properly. Evidence of the interest Mexicans were taking in this most popular of Olympic sports was in the number of spectators: 15,000 saw the women's compulsories; 12,000 saw the men's compulsories; and the four other meets had a total attendance of more than 40,000. Vera Caslavska was not one of the competitors. Results were as follows:

All-around

1. Kuchinskaya	77.10
2. Krajcirova, TCH	76.65
3. Petrick	75.80
4. Noack, GDR *(15 years old)*	75.30
5. Voronina	75.25
Kubickova, TCH	75.25
7. Janz, GDR *(15 years old)*	75.00

Vault

1. Kuchinskaya	19.350
2. Krajcirova	19.316
3. Janz	19.283

Bars

1. Janz	19.433
2. Rimnacova, TCH	19.250
3. Kuchinskaya	19.233

Beam

1. Kuchinskaya	19.485
2. Krajcirova	19.150
3. Noack, Marianne	19.133

Floor Exercise

1. Kuchinskaya	19.508
2. Krajcirova	19.408
3. Petrick	19.300

Caslavska's victory in the European Championships and Kuchinskaya's in Mexico added to the anticipation of next year's Olympics. Caslavska's score in optional exercises in Amsterdam was 38.965; Kuchinskaya's score in optionals in the Mexico pre-Olympics was 38.70. Would this difference have any significance?

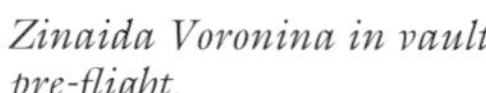

Zinaida Voronina in vault pre-flight.

Olympics 1968 Mexico City, Mexico

Auditorio Municipal

October 21st to 26th

The Olympics are, of course, far more than just gymnastics. Although some people in the gymnastics community erroneously refer to gymnastic's world championships as "world games," the Olympics are, in fact, *the* world games—"games" referring to all sports. And while the 1966 World Championships of Gymnastics in Dortmund, a city located in Germany's dull, gray, industrial heartland of the Ruhr, were significant for this one sport, the 1968 Olympics, set in bright, sunny, colorful Mexico, were significant for all sports. In contrast to the 1964 Olympics in Tokyo, which have been called the "happy games," because everything went so well and everyone went home happy, the 1968 Olympics in Mexico will be remembered as the games that almost, at the last minute, did not happen because of the rioting and demonstrations at the 90,000-student National University.

A look back at the happy Olympics. Vault finalists Vera Caslavska (1st); Birgit Radochla and Larissa Latynina (tie–2nd).

The extent of the rioting and demonstrations was, perhaps, unforeseen by the government. In preparation for the Games, Mexico had gone to great expense and effort not only to build or renovate venues but also to pretty itself up. The city had cleaned, swept, and painted itself; it had planted acres of flowers and had placed bright new statuary along the boulevards leading to the venues. Olympic theme posters—a white dove of peace on a blue background—were all around town. Pretty señoritas were on hand to greet visitors. Mexico, the first city in Latin America to host the Olympics, had created a beautiful setting for the Games. The Mexico Olympics were also the first in which a woman had carried the torch into the stadium and lighted the flame. Mexicans in general had been looking forward to this moment ever since they knew they would host these Olympics. Yet the possibilities for trouble were inherent in the times.

The year 1968 was a time of student unrest in both the United States and Mexico. In the United States, the unrest was primarily, or at least initially, against American involvement in the Viet Nam war; in Mexico, the students, for their own reasons, did not like the government of President Gustavo Diaz Ordaz and were trying to bring it down. In Mexico, a poor country, the gov-

Auditorio Municipal, exterior

ernment had already spent $150 million preparing for the games, a paltry sum when compared to the billions the South Korean government spent on their own games. Nevertheless, $150 million was a large sum for Mexico and the students could not see any good accruing to the country from the spending of this money. The Mexican students had resolved to stage demonstrations and to time them for maximum publicity when the media and visitors from all over the world would be there.

It was the time also of the generation gap, when young people believed that older generations did not understand them. Demographically, there was an upsurge in the proportion of people between 18 and 28 years of age, that is, people born during the war and the postwar years of 1940 to 1950. Never in the history of the United States had the proportion of young people to older people been so large. With their energy and restlessness, these young people were activated initially by what they considered an unjust war, entered into without the consent of the people. Later, their cause became the whole question of civil rights. The antiwar protests and civil disturbances in the United States were widespread, led to the early retirement of President Johnson, and found sympathetic adherents in young people in many countries. In Mexico, a land long dominated by a single political party and where political corruption was a way of life, young activists saw the Olympics as an opportunity for change.

The story of the final confrontation between students and the army was best told by correspondent Bob Ottum of *Sports Illustrated*. Portions of the following article are reprinted courtesy of *Sports Illustrated* from the October 14, 1968 issue. Copyright © 1968, Time Inc. "Grim Countdown to the Games" by Bob Ottum. All rights reserved.[1]

> The students and the army had been feuding for weeks before the Olympians started arriving and by the time the Games were pulling together, the crisis had worsened to the point of explosion. There had been rioting, gunplay and a general smashing-up of things on the university city

campus. President Diaz had appealed for all sides to calm down while the strangers were in town—citing such things as image, the fact that visitors could be hurt, Mexico's big investment in tourism and, finally, motherhood. "Please keep your boys and girls off the street."

But inside the medical center on campus, surrounded by smashed windows, barricades of classroom chairs and splashed paint slogans saying, "No volveremos," which means, "We will not turn back," members of the student strike committee took a different view.

"We like the Olympic Games," one of the leaders said, "but we feel our cause is more important. These should not be related, because Mexico has spent a lot of money on the Games. But that is the way it is. The generation gap that everyone speaks of has grown to world-wide proportions now. It is everywhere. Your way of life, with your mechanism and your Olympics, does not suit us."

That was Wednesday. (The Opening Ceremony of the Games would be on Saturday, October 12.) The students would rally that evening, he said, on the Plaza de las Tres Culturas (in Tiatelolco, a suburb a few miles outside of Mexico City). From there, they would march on a nearby school still occupied by police and liberate it. They came by the thousands. The Plaza sits in the center of Tiatelolco, a condominium housing project. Several of the marchers had made special signs for the occasion—brightly colored posters, many of them showing the Olympic ringed emblem in the foreground—with drawings of police bayonetting students in the background. There were grim invitations for the world to come to these bloody Olympics and other invitations to stay away.

After a while, the belligerent scene became almost festive; it might have been a pep rally at the University of Kansas, seeking free love. A strike leader, speaking from a balcony, had called off the proposed march. Too many soldiers waiting with guns, he said. And then, while students and spectators milled around, came the scene that was to leave its mark on the 1968 Olympics.

It was dark. A green flare suddenly arched high overhead to light the scene and the plaza exploded with gunfire and students running in panic. Soldiers had them surrounded and for three hours and more the place rang with gunfire.

By Thursday, the size of the tragedy was determined: more than 25 had been killed, hundreds more were wounded, jails were full. By the end of the week, the toll had gone up to 34 dead and would go higher. Police closed off the housing area. Foreigners were urged to stay away and, in effect, to take their Olympic business elsewhere. And across town, in the luxurious Camino Real Hotel, the IOC went into emergency session.

> Next day, Mexico City's "The News" headlined THE SHOW WILL GO ON and printed Brundage's statement. And, for all its tension, the show began, slowly, to go on. In the hotel's Presidential suite, Brundage (IOC President Avery Brundage) paced back and forth like a well-tailored old blue bear and admitted that news accounts of the disorders were alarming. "But," he said, "I was at the ballet last night and we heard nothing of the riots. You wouldn't know it in a city this size. After all, you think of the precautions taken to protect the President of the United States and yet he is murdered. We live in that kind of world."
>
> And on the inside with the athletes, it was a different sort of world. There were the games to get ready for and no time to spare. In the Village, all was calm. At the venues spotted around town, such as the Auditorio Nacional near Chapultepec Park, where the gymnasts will perform, soldiers strolled around in groups of three, each carrying a rifle and bayonet and looking fixedly at all strangers until he was sure of their intent. "We sort of noticed when we went to play a warm-up game," said U.S. water poloist Dean Willeford, "that there were soldiers all around us. But you just learn to live with it."
>
> Hectic days lay ahead. On several of the pop-art statues around town, night raiders were scrawling *Vittoria o Muerte* spoiling the beauty of the scene—and as a final grim touch—someone was getting to those white doves. All across town, small blobs of red paint were being dotted in the center of the dove images, creating the effect of a bird shot through the heart, blood dripping down.
>
> There was talk of more demonstrations coming up—that bands of students would strike at various Olympic sites. It was clear that when the big show moves into the stadium on opening day, there will be almost as large a crowd of soldiers outside the place—guarding it.
>
> On Saturday morning, the IOC and 124 National committees put out a statement. It called upon all of Mexico to declare a spiritual truce and unite for the Games. The only thing anyone could do was wait and see. The stage was set, still all prettied up, and Mexico was making a run for it.

This incident, important as it was, was not the only occurrence for which Mexico will be remembered. During the track and field portion of the Games, the two black sprinters who had taken first and third places in the 100-meter sprint, Tommie Smith and John Carlos, raised their straight, right arms high above their heads, held them there with black-gloved clenched fists and looked down during the playing of the U.S. national anthem. The effects of this action were described by John Underwood in the October 28 issue of *Sports Illustrated*. Portions of the following article are reprinted courtesy of

Sports Illustrated from the October 28, 1968 issue. Copyright © 1968, Time Inc. "A High Time for Sprinters—and Kenyans," by John Underwood. All rights reserved.[2]

> They were booed. At a press conference afterward, Carlos flayed into white America in a familiar soliloquy, demanding as he did that reports quote him accurately or not at all. There followed—after midnight the next day—the suspension of the two runners by the U.S. Olympic Committee, with a 48-hour notice to pack their bags and move out. The USOC at first wanted to keep the sentence light, no more than a censure, but the International Olympic Committee demanded more, although this was later denied in some quarters. In one version of the still untold story, the IOC dangled the possibility of expelling the whole U.S. team, swimmers, fencers, weight lifters and all. It said it could not let such abuses of the Olympic rules against political activity go unpunished, because if it did the Games would degenerate into sociopolitical symposiums.
>
> The uproar lasted a day, with newsmen and photographers chasing after the two runners and conducting whose-side-are-you-on opinion polls whenever a new head popped out of a building. British journalists seemed especially eager to take a crack at being sympathetic, but since Carlos and Smith had prepared themselves well for martyrdom, there was no doubt they came out the heavies. Carlos had spurned the support of the all-white Harvard crew—"Who needs 'em?" Not even all the black girls on the track team were quick to back Carlos, who had found it easy to antagonize people. He had stepped on a lot of toes, including those in the chow line, at the end of which he cared not to stand. The last and loudest word from Carlos was that he was going to sue the U.S. Olympic Committee.
>
> The Carlos-Smith affair took much of the play away from the Games themselves and away from some marvelous performances . . . .

Athletes were at first concerned about the altitude—Mexico City is at 7,349 feet above sea level—but soon found they could live with it. Some benefited from it. For example, in the long jump, 28 feet had until then been considered a barrier, like the 4-minute mile, that could not be surmounted. In Mexico, Bob Beamon jumped 29 feet, 2.5 inches through the high, thin air and set an Olympic record that even Carl Lewis could not break. In Los Angeles in 1984, he jumped 28 feet, 0.5 inch.; in Seoul in 1988, he jumped 28 feet, 7.2 inches and in Barcelona, he jumped 28 feet, 5.5 inches.

In gymnastics, held in Mexico City's Auditorio Nacional, the altitude did not have a noticeable effect upon the gymnasts' performance. They were able to perform routines at the same level of difficulty as in Dortmund. During the gymnastics competition, however, there was in the back of everyone's mind, when considering the women's competition, the brutal invasion of Czechoslovakia by the Red Army just two months before, under the orders of the Soviet Union's General Secretary, Leonid Brezhnev. Twelve years earlier, the 1956 Olympics in Melbourne were held shortly after the Soviet Union's invasion of Hungary and the Hungary vs. USSR water polo match had been a bloody affair. This time, although there would be no physical retaliation among the ladies of women's gymnastics, the psychological hurt might put Vera Caslavska at a disadvantage. If there had been any effect, Vera did not show it until the very end, floor exercise, the last event of finals of the apparatus. In *The Complete Book of the Olympics* [3] David Wallechensky writes:

> In the floor exercises she shared first place with Larissa Petrick of the Soviet Union, which meant that the two women stood together on the top platform at the medal ceremony and listened first to Czechoslovakia's national anthem and then to the USSR's. Political observers noted that Caslavska bowed her head and turned away during the playing of the Soviet anthem.

An excellent narrative of the women's gymnastics competition was written by Rex Bellamy of *The Times* of London, who contributed this piece (transcribed in part) for the official U.S.O.C. Team Book:[4]

> It was a gloriously exciting and highly accomplished competition in which craft and art were magically blended. In Mexico, as in Tokyo, gymnastics was one of the great attractions of the Games. Since the Mexicans themselves are not experts (their teams both finished 14th), this was superficially surprising. But only superficially. Mexicans like throwing themselves about. Even the children's playgrounds dotted about the city are mostly equipped with parallel bars and the circuses around the world are mostly equipped with Mexican tumblers and acrobats. But the dedicated discipline demanded by the Olympic routines does not suit their nature.
>
> Besides their enthusiasm for the sport itself, the Mexicans had other incentives. They have a flair for—and appreciation of—the beautiful and the artistic, which attracted them to the Auditorio Municipal. Also Czechoslovakia's finest Olympic athlete in any sport was the blonde and attractive pocket dynamo, Miss Caslavska, who had the engaging good taste to select the "Mexican Hat Dance" for her floor exercise. Small wonder that the crowds were queuing for tickets long before the competition began.
>
> Inevitably, this vast and enthusiastic Mexican crowd did not so much watch the gymnastics as take part in it. When Miss Caslavska was given only 9.6 for her optional exercises on the beam, there was a roar of protest—and its volume steadily increased. Berthe Villancher, president of the women's technical committee, hustled over to the judge-referee concerned. After five

Auditorio Municipal, interior: the gymnastics venue

minutes of bedlam, the mark was changed to 9.8 . . . . The crowd then permitted the gymnasts to carry on the show.

A case of overmarking occurred in the floor exercises. This time Natalya Kuchinskaya of Russia was the lucky gymnast. Miss Caslavska's luck was irrelevant to the final placings, but Miss Kuchinskaya's flattering mark clinched her a bronze medal in the free exercise. This was tough on Larissa Petrick (Russia) and Erika Zuchold (East Germany).

Though slightly exaggerated by the final statistics, the gap between Miss Caslavska and the rest was indisputable. Her closest rival was expected to be the 19-year-old Miss Kuchinskaya, but an early fall from the uneven parallel bars ruined the Russian's chances. Miss Caslavska knew how it felt; in Tokyo, she had trouble with the same piece of apparatus. In Mexico, her mastery was such that it was an astonishing 9.9 on the uneven bars that made her title secure. She stepped down to an echoing ovation and a series of hugs from her teammates. Perhaps the greatest single example of Miss Caslavska's greatness was her floor work in the apparatus finals. She was already overall champion. She had already tucked away one medal after another.

But on the floor in the free exercise, those slim and lovely Russians were marvelous. Their work was a dazzling marriage of gymnastics and ballet, with every movement beautifully coordinated. Miss Caslavska had to follow them—and it quickly became apparent that, merely to share the

> gold medal, she had to do the best floor work of her life. The pressure on her was immense. When she stepped up to face the challenge, you could have heard a pin drop. Then, suddenly, there was that jolly little "Mexican Hat Dance" and she swung gaily through a routine as close to perfection as you could get. It was Miss Caslavska's last challenge—and she rose to it like the peerless competitor she is. On the final count, she made Olympic history, with four gold medals (including the all-around award) to add to the three she won in Tokyo. She was beaten only on the beam—by Miss Kuchinskaya, who is her likeliest successor.
>
> But the 26-year-old Champion was the only Czechoslovak to win an individual medal. The Russians showed us the depth of their resources. Zinaida Voronina, at 20 the "old lady" of the Russian team, collected a gold, a silver and two bronze medals (her husband did even better with seven medals). Miss Kuchinskaya won four medals, Miss Petrick three. These four—and Miss Zuchold and 16-year-old Karin Janz, the East Germans—were the stars of the show. But make a note of the fact that the gymnastics "Establishment" came under fire from America. Linda Metheny, 21, was only 0.025 of a point away from a bronze medal on beam. Cathy Rigby, only 15 and a diminutive 4 feet 10 inches (she looked like an animated blonde doll) finished 16th overall, 1.8 points behind bronze. The American women finished sixth, the men seventh.

Thus we see that the principal actors in the Mexico drama were the same as in Dortmund, with a few additions: the Americans, with Linda Metheny, who placed fourth in finals on beam, and Cathy Rigby, who placed sixteenth all-around but who would win a silver medal on beam in the 1970 World Championships in Ljubljana and become famous in Munich; Lyubov Burda of the Soviet Union, who placed twenty-fifth but who would place fifth in 1970 and sixth in Munich; and, more importantly, 16-year-old Ludmilla Turishcheva. Young Ludmilla placed only twenty-fourth in this her first international competition at this level, mainly because of a major break in beam optionals. Almost immediately, however, her star would begin to ascend: to third place in the 1969 European Championships, to World Champion in 1970, and to Olympic Champion in 1972. Only slightly less important was the arrival of Karin Janz, 16-year-old from East Germany, who placed sixth in Mexico. Her star, too, would quickly ascend to gold medal all-around in the 1969 Europeans and silver medal all-around in Munich.

In Mexico, there was no alternating of the lead between Czechoslovakia and the Soviet Union to add tension to the team competition, as there had been in Dortmund. As a team, the Soviets led all the way, while Caslavska led individually. Kuchinskaya, however, made a game fight for the all-around title, particularly since she had suffered a fall during compulsory bars and had been given a confidence-shattering score of 8.45 for that apparatus. In spite of this setback, she worked her way up to bronze medal with a total score in optionals (39.00) second only to that of Caslavska herself (39.40).

The Japanese had no top-ranking gymnast, their best being Kazue Hanyu, who placed thirteenth. The Japanese team took fourth place, however, because of their strength in depth: five Japanese team members placed between 13 and 22. Interestingly, the USSR and East Germany each had two gymnasts with all-around standings lower than 22.

After compulsories, the standings and scores of the leading teams and individuals were as follows:

1. URS	191.15
2. TCH	190.20
3. GDR	189.40
4. JPN	187.10
5. USA	185.70
6. HUN	184.75

1. Caslavska	38.85
2. Voronina	38.35
Petrick	38.35
4. Janz	38.25
5. Zuchold	38.20
6. Kuchinskaya	37.75

Optional Exercises: October 23rd

First Rotation

Right away in first rotation, Kuchinskaya showed her determination: she scored 9.85 for her vault, which consisted of a half turn onto the horse in preflight and a half turn off the horse in afterflight. Petrick also scored 9.85 for her half-on, half-off; these were the two highest scores in vault. Voronina scored 9.75 for her Yamashita (a handspring onto the horse with piking of the body in afterflight). The Soviets did very well on vault as a team: they averaged 9.72.

The Czechs were on bars during first rotation. As a team, they did not do well: they averaged 9.46. Caslavska, however, scored a brilliant 9.90 for the following routine, one which readers will find quite similar to her routine in Dortmund.

> Facing low bar on the low bar side, Caslavska ran at the beat board, jumped off it and wrapped once around low bar in a free hip circle forward,

pike position. (In Dortmund, she had performed two free hip circles forward around low bar in tuck position in her mount.) On completing her circle, she cast, piked her body again, placed her feet on the bar between her hands, swung back down under low bar, released and flew to catch high bar with a half turn. She dropped forward to low bar, kipped on low bar and performed another forward hip circle. As she came up, she released low bar and in her upward flight performed a front somersault between the bars with her legs straddled and caught high bar—she had learned the Brause

Vera Caslavska executing her Brause.

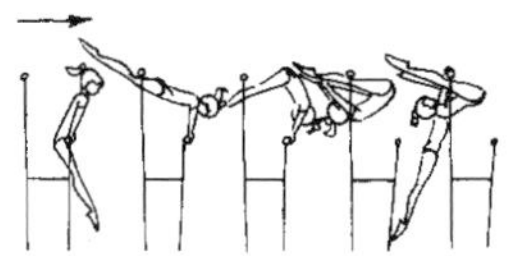

Figure 36

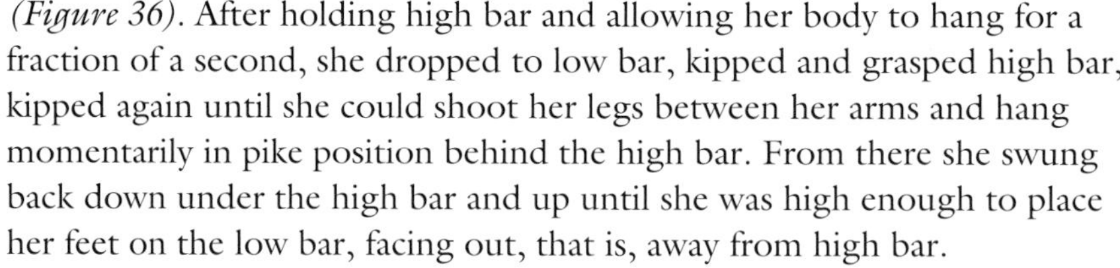

(Figure 36). After holding high bar and allowing her body to hang for a fraction of a second, she dropped to low bar, kipped and grasped high bar, kipped again until she could shoot her legs between her arms and hang momentarily in pike position behind the high bar. From there she swung back down under the high bar and up until she was high enough to place her feet on the low bar, facing out, that is, away from high bar.

She stood for a second in pose on the low bar, balancing herself by holding high bar with her left hand while she held her right arm out in front of her. From her pose on low bar, she jumped backwards over high bar with her legs straddled, grasped the bar and swung down to beat low bar. She swung back, released high bar and made a full turn behind the bar, her body vertical. After recatching high bar, she dropped forward to catch low bar, kipped to catch high bar and kipped up to clear support position back of high bar. She then made a backward hip circle around high bar. As she came up, she pushed off the high bar with her hips and flew forward, straddled her legs over low bar and landed, in hecht dismount.

In spite of Caslavska's efforts, the Czechs' position in second place became precarious after they ended first rotation only 0.05 ahead of the East Germans, who had done well on beam, averaging 9.61. Karin Janz and Erika Zuchold, leaders of the team, scored 9.60 and 9.55 respectively. Zuchold's beam routine was as follows:

Figure 37

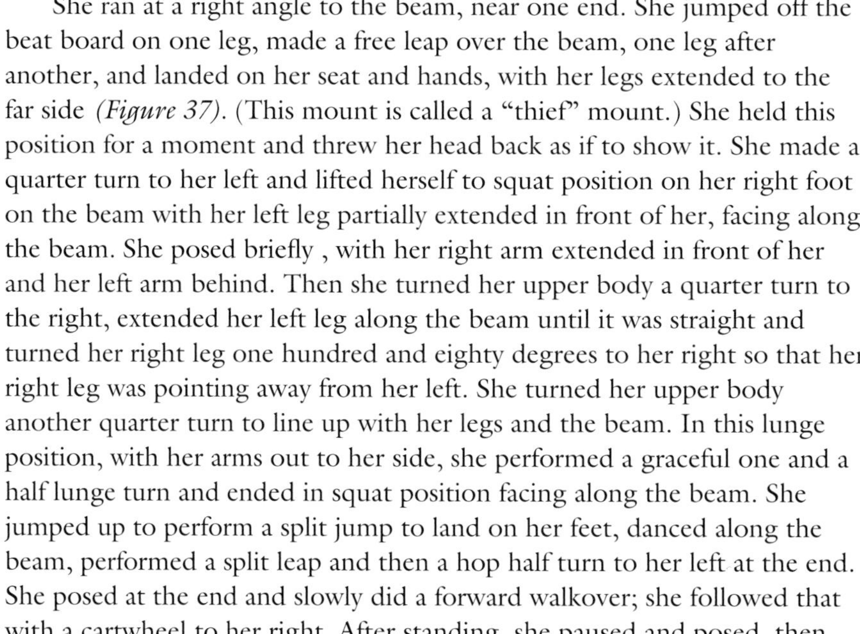

She ran at a right angle to the beam, near one end. She jumped off the beat board on one leg, made a free leap over the beam, one leg after another, and landed on her seat and hands, with her legs extended to the far side *(Figure 37)*. (This mount is called a "thief" mount.) She held this position for a moment and threw her head back as if to show it. She made a quarter turn to her left and lifted herself to squat position on her right foot on the beam with her left leg partially extended in front of her, facing along the beam. She posed briefly , with her right arm extended in front of her and her left arm behind. Then she turned her upper body a quarter turn to the right, extended her left leg along the beam until it was straight and turned her right leg one hundred and eighty degrees to her right so that her right leg was pointing away from her left. She turned her upper body another quarter turn to line up with her legs and the beam. In this lunge position, with her arms out to her side, she performed a graceful one and a half lunge turn and ended in squat position facing along the beam. She jumped up to perform a split jump to land on her feet, danced along the beam, performed a split leap and then a hop half turn to her left at the end. She posed at the end and slowly did a forward walkover; she followed that with a cartwheel to her right. After standing, she paused and posed, then

Figure 38

> performed a back walkover to the end of the beam and posed in attitude *(Figure 38)*. She made a jump half turn and then a half turn on her feet. She posed again in attitude, stepped forward and made a double turn on her right foot with her right knee bent, her left leg straight behind her and her arms out to her side. She stepped forward and made a half turn to her right at the end of the beam. She stepped forward into stag handstand, split her legs and continued on over to stand. She skip-stepped to the end, while also making a high back kick with her left leg and flaring her arms out to the side. She made a half turn to her left on her left foot with her right leg kicked high in front of her during the turn. She proceeded down the beam with dance steps and two leaps, her left leg being extended behind her. At the end, she dropped to squat position, raised herself, made a half turn to her left and posed while standing and making a sweeping gesture with her left arm. She made a full and a half turn, so that she faced the near end of the beam and proceeded to execute a back walkover, followed immediately by a half turn to her left and then a full turn to her right with her left leg held high. She stepped to the end and made a half turn to her right. She made a body wave, a few expressive arm movements and prepared for her dismount: she stepped forward, performed a walkover forward and continued on into an aerial cartwheel off to land.

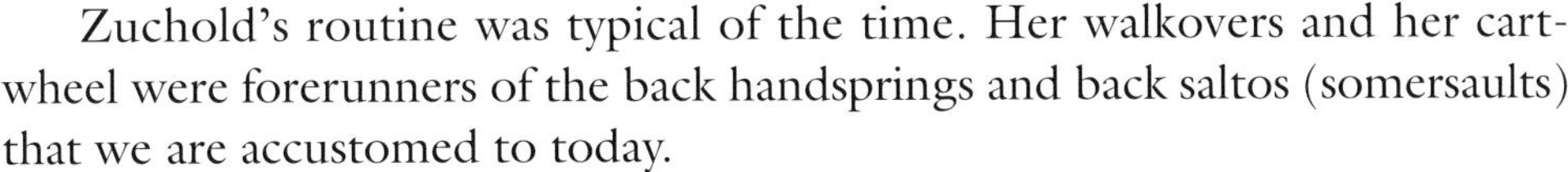

Zuchold's routine was typical of the time. Her walkovers and her cartwheel were forerunners of the back handsprings and back saltos (somersaults) that we are accustomed to today.

The Japanese did creditably on floor, with an average per team member of 9.51.

At the end of first rotation, the standings and scores of the leading teams and individuals were as follows:

	Initial Score	**First Rotation**	**Subtotal**
1. URS	191.15	48.60	239.75
2. TCH	190.20	47.30	237.50
3. GDR	189.40	48.05	237.45
4. JPN	187.10	47.55	234.65
1. Caslavska *(bars)*	38.85	9.90	48.75
2. Petrick *(vault)*	38.35	9.85	48.20
3. Voronina *(vault)*	38.35	9.75	48.10
4. Janz *(beam)*	38.25	9.60	47.85
5. Zuchold *(beam)*	38.20	9.55	47.75
6. Kuchinskaya *(vault)*	37.75	9.85	47.60

Kuchinskaya was still in sixth place, but she was making progress.

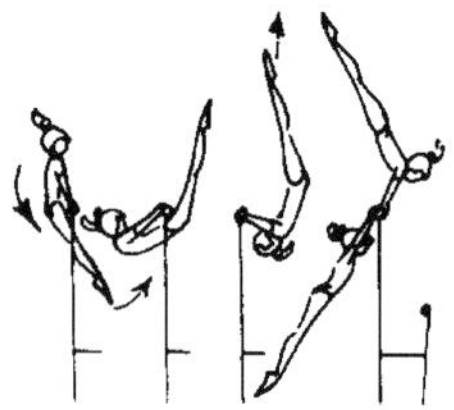

Figure 39

Second Rotation

In second rotation, the top-ranked Soviet team moved to bars and scored only 47.45, for an average of 9.49 per gymnast. In contrast, the Czechs on beam scored 48.00, for an average of 9.60. Interestingly, the Soviets increased their lead over the Czechs from compulsories by 2.25 points during first rotation. The Czechs, however, scored higher than the Soviets during second, third, and fourth rotations and closed the gap to only 0.65 points at the end. Zinaida Voronina was the highest scoring Soviet on bars. Her routine was as follows:

Zinaida Voronina performing half turn after handstand on high bar as she began to swing down to wrap around low bar.

> Standing away from low bar on the low bar side, she ran and jumped off the beat board over the low bar with a half twist to catch high bar. She dropped to low bar, kipped to catch high bar and kipped on high bar, bringing her legs from straddle to together over the low bar, her seat resting on the bar. She paused and changed her grip from under grip to eagle (over) grip. Then, with her feet on low bar, she pushed herself back under high bar and came forward again to stand on low bar, holding high bar with her right hand and extending her left arm horizontally forward, a pose which she held for a second. She dropped both hands to her side, flexed her knees and jumped off low bar to fly back over high bar with her legs straddled. She caught high bar and swung down under high bar to beat low bar with her hips. She swung back and did an uprise to front support position on high bar on the side away from low bar. Her hips were against the high bar and her body was vertical, supported by straight arms. She did a clear hip circle backwards around high bar with her body straight *(Figure 39)*, swung down under high bar and wrapped backwards around low bar. She flew

back with half twist to catch high bar with crossed grip. She made a half turn back to face low bar, dropped to low bar, kipped on low bar to catch high bar and swung forward, once again bringing her legs from straddle to together over the low bar. She paused, put her right hand on the low bar and, still holding high bar with her left hand, lifted herself off the low bar. Now suspended between the bars, she made a 180° turn with her knees fully bent and placed her feet on the low bar. She stood on the low bar, facing high bar, and threw herself forward to place her hips on the high bar and began a forward free hip circle around high bar. Halfway through, she put her hands on the bar and continued on up to handstand, straddling her legs on the way up and bringing them together in handstand. She made a half turn as she swung down from high bar on the side away from low bar (photo opposite). She swung under the high bar and wrapped backwards around low bar. As she came up on top of low bar, she released and flew forward in hecht dismount with full twist to land.

Figure 40

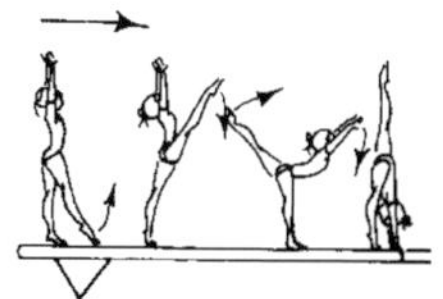

Figure 41

As with Zuchold's routine on beam, Voronina's routine on bars was typical of bars routines at that time. She scored 9.70. On beam, Caslavska received another high score, a 9.80. Her routine, which contained many elements similar to those in her Dortmund routine, as did her routine on bars, was as follows:

She ran and jumped off the beat board at one end to land and assume the same pose she had in Dortmund, except that this time she landed on her right foot and remained in squat position on her right foot with her left foot extended ahead, her right arm extended forward and down and her left arm extended back and up. In Dortmund, these arm and leg positions had been reversed. She held this pose only briefly, then stood, kicked her left leg up behind her and proceeded down the beam with two split leaps. At the end, she made a deep body wave and came back directly with a back walkover, a back straddle down and a roll backward through handstand to stand *(Figure 40)*. She danced forward to the end she had just left, made a half turn to her right and made a running step and a hop into a forward walkover. She finished her walkover and went right into a standing split forward, her right foot on the beam, her left foot extended vertically upward and her head down between her arms, both hands on the beam *(Figure 41)*. From her standing split (also known as a "needle scale"), she raised her upper body to the horizontal, lowered her left leg slightly and held her arms out to her side in a forward scale. Standing again, she made a squat half turn to her right, took a big step with her left leg and then slid her right leg forward so that she assumed a split position on the beam, facing to her left. She posed in splits, turned her body to the right to face along the beam,

Vera Caslavska in standing split forward with hand support in front of support leg.

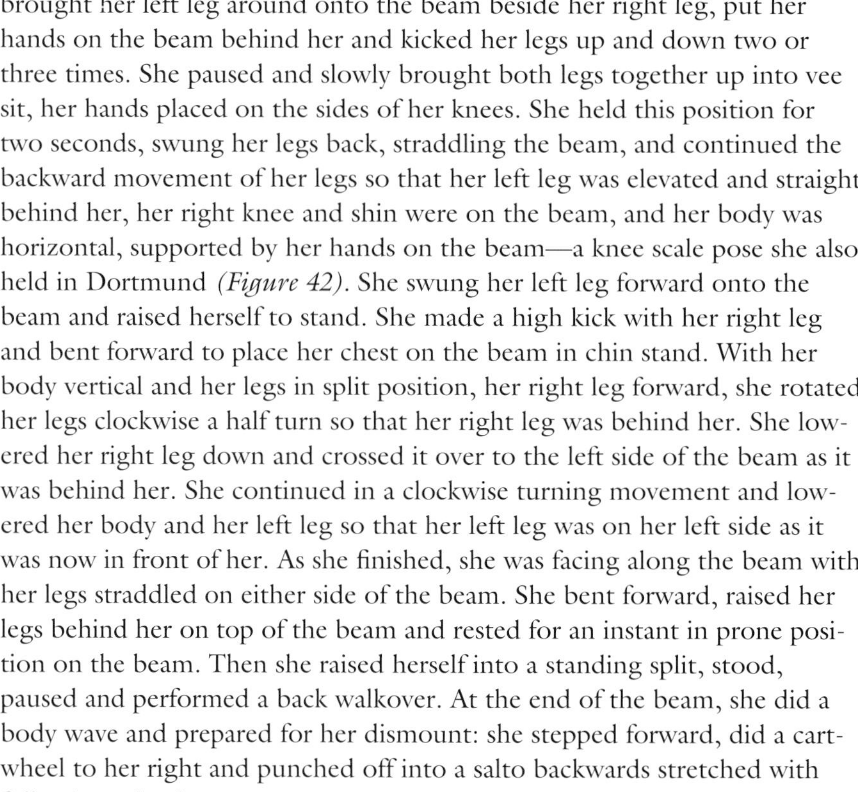

brought her left leg around onto the beam beside her right leg, put her hands on the beam behind her and kicked her legs up and down two or three times. She paused and slowly brought both legs together up into vee sit, her hands placed on the sides of her knees. She held this position for two seconds, swung her legs back, straddling the beam, and continued the backward movement of her legs so that her left leg was elevated and straight behind her, her right knee and shin were on the beam, and her body was horizontal, supported by her hands on the beam—a knee scale pose she also held in Dortmund *(Figure 42)*. She swung her left leg forward onto the beam and raised herself to stand. She made a high kick with her right leg and bent forward to place her chest on the beam in chin stand. With her body vertical and her legs in split position, her right leg forward, she rotated her legs clockwise a half turn so that her right leg was behind her. She lowered her right leg down and crossed it over to the left side of the beam as it was behind her. She continued in a clockwise turning movement and lowered her body and her left leg so that her left leg was on her left side as it was now in front of her. As she finished, she was facing along the beam with her legs straddled on either side of the beam. She bent forward, raised her legs behind her on top of the beam and rested for an instant in prone position on the beam. Then she raised herself into a standing split, stood, paused and performed a back walkover. At the end of the beam, she did a body wave and prepared for her dismount: she stepped forward, did a cartwheel to her right and punched off into a salto backwards stretched with full twist to land.

Figure 42

In floor exercise, the East Germans averaged a modest 9.54 per gymnast. Nevertheless, their total score maintained their third-place position. Erika Zuchold scored a brilliant 9.85 for the following routine:

Standing in from a corner on a diagonal, Zuchold ran into the corner, posed, made a half turn and began her first pass: a round-off, two flic-flacs and a salto backward stretched. She stepped forward, did a cat leap with half turn to face back into the corner and then did a 360° illusion turn *(Figure 43)*. She turned toward the center of the floor, stepped forward and performed a scissors leap *(Figure 44)* and then a double turn during which she squatted down and ended in sitting position. She then began a back walkover, stopped half way and went into a forward walkover with a half turn. She turned toward a corner on a cross diagonal, danced toward it and performed a double turn. She posed, stepped into the corner, made a half turn and began her second pass: a round-off, two flic-flacs and a salto backward stretched, from which she stepped back and posed. She stepped forward out of her corner, did a round-off flic-flac and rolled out into prone

Figure 43

Figure 44

position face down on the floor. She made a half turn in prone position onto her back and sat up with her legs split to the side. She rolled to her right, stood and posed. Then in a long arc proceeding clockwise around the floor, she performed a cat leap followed by two cartwheels with flight phase *(Figure 45)* to her right, a pause while she posed and performed a full turn, and then three butterfly turns, which she ended sitting on the floor. She made a full turn on her seat on the floor and finished her routine with her legs straddled, her arms extended forward and her head tilted slightly upward.

Figure 45

Karin Janz scored 9.50 for the following routine in floor exercise, one which readers may want to compare with her routines in Ljubljana and Munich:

Karin started in a corner and went right into her first pass: she ran, performed a front handspring into a salto forward tucked *(Figure 46)* and continued into a round-off, flic-flac and salto backward stretched step-out. She danced out of her corner toward the center of the floor, performed a quick one and three-quarter turn on her toes and leaned back immediately into a back walkover. Half way through her walkover, she paused in needle scale, her left leg pointing vertically upward and both hands on the floor. She stood by completing her walkover, made a half turn to her left, danced past the center of the floor, leaned forward onto her right knee and pushed off into another walkover, this time forward. She danced with slow steps toward the corner on her left, made a left turn to line up with the adjacent side on her right and lowered herself into splits on the floor. She faced along her right leg extended in front of her, paused for two seconds while gesturing with her arms, brought her left leg around in front of her, extended, put her left hand on the floor behind her, bent her right knee and pushed off in valdez to stand. She turned left toward the nearby corner, stepped into it, posed and turned to her right to line up with the diagonal and began her second pass: a round-off into two flic-flacs and a salto backward stretched with full twist. Upon landing, she turned and danced out of her corner parallel to the adjacent side to the left of the direction of her second pass. Half way along the side, she made a jump full turn to her left with her knees bent. Upon landing, she leaned back into a back walkover. Now near the corner across from the diagonal of her second pass, she made many turns and poses before proceeding toward the center of the floor. She performed a split leap *(Figure 47)* and a free (aerial) walkover forward. Without stopping, from a position now half way between the center of the floor and the nearby corner, she turned to her right, did a full turn to her right and then, in an arc clockwise part way around the floor, she performed a

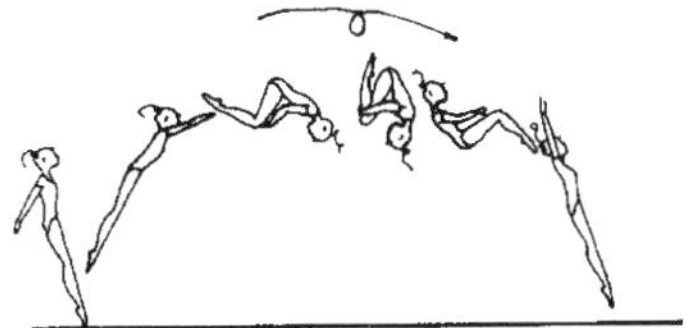

Figure 46

Figure 47

> cartwheel to her right followed by three butterfly turns to her right. She was now well in from the corner from which she had begun her second pass. Nevertheless, she paused, lined herself up with the diagonal and began her final pass, using only about two thirds of the diagonal. It was round-off, flic-flac, salto backward stretched. She landed her salto lightly, feet together, then dropped down into splits, facing back along the diagonal. She did not stay in splits but immediately stood up and made a full turn to her left to stand and pose facing along the diagonal. She then made a deep body wave and a half turn to her left to face into the corner and assume her final pose: she stood on her right leg, with her left foot in front and her left knee bent. She put her left hand on her hip, extended her right arm in front of her and threw her head back.

In vault, the Japanese average 9.42.

At the end of second rotation, the standings and scores of the leading teams and individuals were as follows:

	Initial Score	Second Rotation	Subtotal
1. URS	239.75	47.45	287.20
2. TCH	237.50	48.00	285.50
3. GDR	237.45	47.70	285.15
4. JPN	234.65	47.10	281.75
1. Caslavska *(beam)*	48.75	9.80	58.55
2. Voronina *(bars)*	48.10	9.70	57.80
3. Petrick *(bars)*	48.20	9.50	57.70
4. Zuchold *(floor)*	47.75	9.85	57.60
5. Janz *(floor)*	47.85	9.50	57.35
6. Kuchinskaya *(bars)*	47.60	9.65	57.25

Third Rotation

In third rotation, the Czechs moved to floor and the Soviets to beam. Now we were to see two of the most memorable routines of the whole competition: Caslavska on floor to her "Mexican Hat Dance" music, for which she received 9.85, and Kuchinskaya on beam. Kuchinskaya scored 9.80 in these optional exercises of team competition, but she would later score 9.85 in finals and win the individual event gold medal. Her routine was as follows:

> Kuchinskaya ran and jumped off the beat board at one end to place her hands on the beam and press up to handstand, her legs going from straddle to together in handstand. She continued on over in walkover to stand, took two steps, made a split leap to the end and then a half turn to her right. She

made an extended pose, first leaning forward over her bent right knee and then arching her back steeply back while performing graceful arm movements. She then stepped forward, made a high kick with her right leg and lowered herself into lunge position with her right leg forward. She made a full turn to her right in lunge position, extended her right leg and slid her left foot along the beam to assume splits position. After posing for a moment in splits, she put her hands on the beam and pressed up to handstand, facing across the beam, her legs going from straddle to together at the top. She held her handstand for two seconds and then brought her legs down outside her arms in straddle position horizontally. Holding her legs in this clear straddle support position and supporting herself on her hands, she made a three-quarter turn left to line up with the beam. She sat on the beam, allowed her legs to drop down on either side of the beam, swung them backwards and flung her arms out to the side. She held this pose for a second, then swung her legs forward into pike position in vee sit, with her hands on the beam behind her. She lowered her feet onto the beam and then did a valdez to stand at the end of the beam from which she had started this series of elements. She proceeded down the beam with a step hop, a step assemblé, a deep squat to a stretch jump, another deep squat and another small stretch jump. She made a half turn to her left with her right leg held high and returned along the beam with dance steps and a split leap. At the end, she made a half turn to her left, posed and then executed two forward walkovers. At the far end, she made a half turn to her left, did a chassé and leaned back into a stag handstand, which she held for two full seconds. She straightened her right leg and continued on backwards to stand. She made a full turn, danced to the end and made a squat half turn to her right. Without pausing, she performed a cartwheel to her left and immediately pushed off into a salto backward stretched to land beside the beam, with her right hand on the beam for support.

Natalya Kuchinskaya in clear straddle support. Over her right shoulder, Mitsuo Tsukahara can be seen, intently watching.

The other Soviet gymnasts scored only modestly on beam. Even with Kuchinskaya's 9.80, they averaged just 9.54. Larissa Petrick's beam routine, for which she received 9.50, contained many of the elements of the routine

Larissa Petrick in standing split while holding elevated leg with one hand.

she performed in Dortmund. Readers may wish to compare these two routines with the one she would perform in Ljubljana. Her routine in Mexico was as follows:

> Facing one end, she ran, jumped off the beat board, placed her hands on the end of the beam and pressed up to split-leg handstand. She continued on over in walkover to stand. She danced forward with split leap and more dance steps to the end, where she made a half turn to her right and came back with a one-arm cartwheel to her left on her right hand. Now about two feet from the end, she leaned slowly back and performed a one-arm back walkover on her right hand. She danced forward, performed a cat leap with half turn. She lowered herself into lunge position, her bent right knee forward and her left leg extended behind her, and performed a full turn in lunge position. She extended her right leg and slid her left leg back until she was in splits, her body facing along the beam. Placing her right hand on the beam for support, she then stood, made a half turn to her right and entered a standing split forward on her right foot, her left leg being held vertically upward by her left arm and her right arm extended first diagonally downward in front of her and then slowly raised until it was vertically upward. She made a graceful gesture with her right hand. After coming down from her vertical split, she made a quarter turn to her right, posed facing across the beam, made another quarter turn to her right and danced along the beam with a split leap to the end. She made a half turn, a deep body wave and then a forward

walkover. She danced with skip steps to the end, made a half turn to her right and performed another forward walkover. Upon landing it, she leaned forward into another standing split forward on her right leg. Both hands were on the beam and her head was down between her arms, looking backwards. Her left leg was vertically upward. She lifted her head, brought her left leg down onto the beam, danced to the end and made a half turn to her left. She posed and made graceful arm gestures while preparing for her dismount. She stepped forward and executed a gainer salto backward stretched to the left of the beam to land, with her right hand on it for support.

It will be interesting now to look at the beam routine of 15-year-old Ludmilla Turischeva in this, her first of three Olympics. Readers wishing to compare the following routine with her routines in 1970, 1972, 1974, and 1976 will be struck by their similarity.

Standing on the floor, facing one end of the beam, Ludmilla placed her hands on the beam and hopped up to clear straddle support, that is, her hands and straight arms held her body a few inches above the beam and her straight legs were held horizontally 45° on either side of the beam. She pressed up to handstand, bringing her legs together in handstand, split her legs, with her right leg ahead of her, lowered her right leg forward onto the beam and continued in walkover to stand. She stepped forward and performed a diving cartwheel to her left to stand at the end of the beam, facing back along the beam. She made a half turn to her left to face the end of the beam, kicked her left leg up in front of her, lowered it to the beam and bent her left knee steeply so that she was now in lunge position, with her right leg extended along the beam behind her. With her arms out to the side, she made a three-quarter lunge turn to her left to face across the beam. She placed her hands on the beam and raised her hips so that her feet were clear of the beam. She lowered her hips down so that she was in clear straddle support position and made a quarter turn to her left to face the end of the beam. In doing so, however, she lost her balance to the left and her left foot touched the floor. She repositioned herself, sitting on the beam with her legs hanging on either side, raised herself to place her feet on the beam, stepped to the end and made a half turn to her left to face along the beam. She proceeded down the beam with a low split leap and dance steps. At the end, she made a half turn to the left with her knees bent and ended in squat position facing back along the beam. Then she performed her two consecutive rolls forward without hand support *(Figure 48)* to end in prone position, face down at the end of the beam—a combination that would be her trademark thoughout her career. From prone position, she raised her body, turned it to her left and brought her right leg around onto the beam so that

Figure 48

> she was in splits facing across the beam. She leaned her body forward, extended her seat backward to retain balance and gestured gracefully with her arms. She then placed her hands on the beam, lifted herself up into clear straddle support and made a quarter turn to her right to face the end of the beam. She sat on the beam, threw her arms out to her side and allowed her legs to swing down and slightly back on either side of the beam. She brought her legs up together in front of her and leaned back into vee-sit with her hands behind her on the beam. She lowered her legs down to the beam, with her left knee bent, kept her left hand on the beam behind her and pushed off in valdez to stand, landing on her right foot. She leaned back into a back walkover with her legs split. As she passed through handstand, she switched the position of her legs, so that instead of landing on her right foot again, she landed on her left. She paused, kicked her right leg up and danced down the beam with a couple of little tuck jumps *(Figure 49)*. At the end, she posed with her left knee slightly bent and her right leg extended diagonally forward, her arms held up in front of her with her elbows bent. She leaned back into back walkover, which she finished in a crouch. Then she stood and performed a back handsping. She paused and made a half turn to her left. She did a round-off to the end of the beam, paused and dismounted with a salto backward, full twist.

Figure 49

It is noteworthy that Ludmilla performed a diving cartwheel and a back handspring on the beam and dismounted with a salto backward stretched, full twist. Neither Kuchinskaya, Petrick, nor Caslavska performed these elements.

While the Soviets were on beam, the Czechs were on floor. Her teammates made a big effort to drive up Caslavska's score—she would be the last to perform—and averaged 9.73. Their team score knocked almost a full point off the Soviets' lead. Caslavska's routine was as follows:

> She started her exercise near one side, a few steps from a corner, facing along the side. When the music started, she took a step forward with her left foot, posed, made a double turn to her right, paused, made a half turn to her right to face the corner and danced into the corner. She made a jump half turn to her right to begin her first pass: she ran, did a round-off and immediately a salto backward stretched. Upon landing, she made a hop and dropped down to splits on the floor. She stood, posed, came back along the diagonal with some dancing tap steps, danced forward with a chassé toward the middle of the floor, made a turning, dancing sequence to her right and a leap full and a half turn to her right to face the corner on her right across from the diagonal of her first pass. She danced toward the corner and performed a split leap. In the corner, she did a half turn to her right, while continuing to dance, and immediately began her second pass: a round-off

into a salto backward stretched. She made a half turn toward the corner and an immediate forward walkover, which she landed in splits. Without pausing, she brought her legs together behind her and lowered her upper body to prone position on the floor. She dropped her head down onto the floor. She got up slowly, while rotating her body in a full and a half turn to the left so that she was facing back along the diagonal and posed. She took some slow, straight-leg steps forward to the middle of the floor, where she did some body waves, graceful arm movements, turns and poses. She then turned toward the corner from which she had begun her first pass and proceeded into it with dance steps, turning leaps and poses. She seemed lighter on her feet than the other floor exercise leaders. She began her third pass, this time parallel to the adjacent side to her left: a cartwheel to her left followed immediately by a side salto to her left *(Figure 50)* and another cartwheel to her left. She was now near the middle of the opposite side facing back toward the center of the floor. She moved in a slight arc to her right with a full turn, a split leap, another full turn and a quarter turn to her right to end facing the side in a lunge pose. She turned to her left, performed a butterfly turn to her left, an illusion full turn to her left to splits on the floor, her legs being parallel to the side but her face directed toward the center of the floor. She rolled to her right on her back a half turn so that she faced the side but her legs were still split parallel to the side. She continued with a full and a quarter turn to her right as she rose to face the adjacent side. Standing, she posed, made long dance steps in an arc to her right going clockwise half way around the floor. She finished this arc with a round-off into a salto backward stretched and continued on back through handstand to lie in prone position facing down on the floor. Without pausing, she bent her knees and pushed off with her hands to assume a crouch position, her head nearly touching the floor. Finally, she raised her upper body to kneeling

Vera Caslavska

Figure 50

position on the floor with her body vertical. She flung her right arm straight up and her left arm down and back and looked up toward the ceiling in her final pose.

Vera Caslavska's exercise was a paragon of the floor exercises of the old style—tumbling that is considered elementary today but grace and artistry in her dancing. She scored 9.80.

Both the East Germans and the Japanese scored relatively poorly in third rotation. The East Germans averaged 9.39 on vault and the Japanese 9.31 on bars. Erika Zuchold scored 9.50 for her Yamashita vault.

At the end of third rotation, the standings and scores of the leading teams and individuals were as follows:

	Initial Score	**Third Rotation**	**Subtotal**
1. URS	287.20	47.70	334.90
2.TCH	285.50	48.65	334.15
3. GDR	285.15	46.95	332.10
4. JPN	281.75	46.55	328.30
1. Caslavska *(floor)*	58.55	9.85	68.40
2. Voronina *(beam)*	57.80	9.40	67.20
Petrick *(beam)*	57.70	9.50	67.20
4. Zuchold *(vault)*	57.60	9.50	67.10
5. Kuchinskaya *(beam)*	57.25	9.80	67.05
6. Janz *(vault)*	57.35	9.50	66.85

Fourth Rotation

Figure 51

Figure 52

Fourth rotation brought the Soviets to floor exercise, an event always keenly watched by spectators because of the beauty of Russian choreography. It also brought the East Germans to bars, an event in which they always do well.

Floor exercise was the event that finally brought Kuchinskaya back up into medal contention. Her 9.70 was the highest Soviet score. She could not overcome Voronina's lead, but she slipped past Petrick and Zuchold to earn the bronze medal. As related earlier by Rex Bellamy of The Times, her score was, perhaps, higher than it deserved to be. This generous score was especially hard on Larissa Petrick, who had a lead of 0.15 over Kuchinskaya after third rotation and who was tied with Voronina for second place. The differential of 0.20 between herself and Kuchinskaya in floor exercise scoring, however, wiped out that lead and dropped her to fourth place. She made up for this loss when in floor exercise finals she tied Caslavska for the gold medal.

Five floor exercise routines of the leading Soviets were as follows:

Natalya Kuchinskaya

Natalya Kuchinskaya started her floor exercise in a corner. After a brief pause following the beginning of the music during which she gestured with her arms, she went right into her first pass: a round-off, three flic-flacs and a salto backward stretched. She made a quarter turn to her right during the last part of her salto, landed on her left foot and stepped out with her right foot in another quarter turn to end standing in the corner and facing into it. She turned to her right, extended her right foot and made deep lunge body waves first toward her right knee and then back to her left. Then, moving parallel to the side of the floor, she made a long series of body waves with expressive arm movements, slow graceful steps, turns on one leg with one leg raised, a forward scale and deep poses. She ended this progression with an aerial forward walkover toward the nearby corner, followed by a pose in a deep lunge position *(Figure 51)*, facing the corner, a few feet back. She straightened up, stepped into the corner, made a small cat leap half turn to her left and began her second pass: a round-off, flic-flac into salto backward stretched with full twist. She stepped forward, back along the diagonal, with the same sort of expressive movements and gestures as after her first pass but at a faster pace. She executed a stag leap *(Figure 52)*, an assemblé and a ring leap *(Figure 53)*. After her ring leap, she fell back to lie on her back on the floor. She raised her body into bridge position—her back arched between hands and feet on the floor—and then pushed off with her feet through handstand down to knee-scale position, resting with her right knee and shin on the floor, her left leg extended behind her and her body supported by her arms. From this knee-scale position, she dropped into a chin stand with her legs split above her. She rotated her split legs a half turn to the left, then rolled to her right to sit with her legs straddled. She turned to her right, gradually standing as she turned, making expressive arm movements, and ending her

Figure 53

Natalya Kuchinskaya

uprise on her right foot, with both arms extended straight above her erect body, and her left leg extended back. She made a full turn to her right, lowered herself onto her left knee and lay back into a pose in which she was reclining. She moved toward the corner from which she had begun her first pass and which was across from the diagonal of her second with a step hop and a standing split backwards, her left foot on the floor, her right leg and left arm straight up and her right arm straight down behind her touching the floor, her back steeply arched. She came forward into the corner, made a full and a half turn to her left, posed and prepared for her final pass: a round-off, flic-flac into a salto backward stretched step-out. She stepped forward and ended her exercise in a pose reclining on her left side and left elbow on the floor, her left leg tucked under her, her right leg extended and her right arm thrown across her chest

As mentioned earlier, Kuchinskaya received a score of 9.70.

Larissa Petrick started her exercise in one corner, facing along one side of the floor. She ran in three big steps along the side, performed a split leap, dropped down on her hands and knees, pushed forward into a forward walkover, stepped forward and performed a hurdle into an aerial forward walkover into the adjacent corner. She turned to her right to line up with the diagonal and began her first pass: a round-off, flic-flac into a salto backward stretched with full twist. She paused and posed, then turned to her right to align herself with the side of the floor to the right of her first diagonal, her backside facing the direction of this side. She took three large steps backwards parallel to this side and posed, with her upper body leaning forward horizontally, her left knee bent and her right leg straight ahead of her as if in a deep bow. Standing upright again, she made a half turn to her right and some slow, graceful dance steps forward parallel to the same side

Natalya Kuchinskaya, just before entering into her final pose.

of the floor, a full and a quarter turn to her right into a forward walkover toward the center of the floor, a full turn to her left in back attitude position (on her right foot with her left leg extended behind and her arms extended overhead) into a second forward walkover from which she leaned forward through lunge position down to put her right knee on the floor and continue down to roll a half turn on her seat and a half turn on her knees to her right. She ended these turns in a pose with her feet on the floor and her body arched back, supported by her extended right arm on the floor and her left arm extended vertically upwards. From this pose, in which her back was toward the floor, she turned quickly so that she faced the floor and assumed a more elegant pose: her body was supported by her arms straight to the floor, her right leg was extended diagonally behind to the floor and her left leg was elevated vertically above her. She brought her legs down to the floor on her knees, elevated her body to vertical and posed in the kneeling position, facing to her right with her arms extended to her right. She stood, took a few steps forward, turned to her left and ran back toward the center into a jump full turn. She paused, made a half turn to her left and immediately performed a back walkover. She paused and posed, made a slow half turn to her left, danced forward and performed a forward aerial walkover into a corner across from the diagonal of her first pass. She turned and began her second pass: she ran and performed a cartwheel and two dive cartwheels to her left. She danced out of the corner and ran with windmill motions of her arms and a stag leap in a circle three quarters of the way counterclockwise around the mat to the corner where she had ended her first pass. From this corner, without stopping, she entered her third pass: a round-off, flic-flac into a salto backward stretched from which she stepped back and posed with her back arched backwards, her right leg forward bent sharply at the knee and her arms and head thrown back. She then fell forward into a pose nearly prone on the floor. She raised herself to a final pose: her right knee was bent ninety degrees with her foot on the floor ahead of her, her left leg extended behind her, her body and head thrown back and her arms wrapped around her chest.

Petrick scored 9.50 for this routine, which, as recorded was in fact her optional routine in team competition. In finals on the apparatus, she left out her split leap with change of legs early in her routine but scored 9.90.

Zinaida Voronina scored 9.65 for her routine, a score high enough to enable her to retain her silver medal all around. Her routine was as follows:

> She started her floor exercise near the center of the floor, facing along a diagonal. After an initial pose, she turned back along the diagonal toward the corner, ran toward it and performed a half turn in split leap with change of legs and then a deep body wave before beginning her first pass: a round-off, flic-flac into a salto backward stretched, followed by another flic-flac and another salto backward stretched, from which she stepped back. She posed, stepped forward out of her corner along the same diagonal with long, slow steps, stopped while standing straight and leaned back through chin stand to roll out in prone position on the floor, roll to her right on the floor while slowly raising herself first on her hands and then onto her feet to end up posing in lunge position. She moved her body forward from lunge into knee scale position, resting on her right knee and shin with her left leg elevated behind her and her hands on the floor for support. In this position, she made a full turn to her right and then executed a forward walkover to stand, pose in attitude and do a full and a half turn to pose again in attitude. Meanwhile, she had been moving along one side toward an adjacent corner, which she reached by doing some steps backwards out of her pose and then a back handspring. After some dance steps in the corner, she started her second tumbling run: a round-off, flic-flac into salto backward stretched with full twist. She then proceeded left with some dance steps and an aerial forward walkover and turned to her right with an aerial cartwheel. Now near the far side, to her left from where she had finished her second pass, she lowered herself into splits, performed a full turn to her right on her seat, stood and made a long passage with dance steps, skip steps and turns into the corner where she had finished her first pass. From it, she began her third pass: a round-off, flic-flac into a salto backward stretched. She stepped forward into her final pose: her knees half bent, her body erect with head raised and her arms extended in front of her in a supplicating attitude.

I am pleased to be able to record the floor exercise of Ludmilla Turischeva. Readers may wish to compare her exercise in Mexico with those recorded on later pages for Ljubljana, Munich, Varna and Montreal.

> In Mexico, Ludmilla began her floor exercise standing on a diagonal, about three steps in from the corner. She stood with her right leg forward, her left leg back, her right knee bent, her right arm at her side, and her left

arm extended vertically upward. She was facing across the diagonal. She made a full turn to her right, a side step to her left toward the corner and a three-quarter turn to her left to face along the diagonal to begin her first pass: a round-off, flic-flac, salto backward stretched with full twist followed immediately by a flic-flac. She jumped up upon landing and came down again with her feet spread apart, her head thrown back and her arms thrown diagonally upward to the side. She made some playful poses, leaning to one side with bent knee, then turning and leaning to the other side. Then she danced out parallel to the side to the left of her first pass, made a full turn into two waltz steps and an aerial cartwheel into the adjacent corner facing along the diagonal. She paused for a second and began her second pass: a round-off, flic-flac into a salto backward stretched followed immediately by a flic-flac. She turned to her right and moved along the side to the right of her second pass, making a sideward step, crossing her left leg over in front of her right for another step, made a side step to her right and dropped down into splits, facing the side. She turned her body to face the corner while leaving her legs in splits, posed and made a full and a quarter turn to her left on her seat to face the center of the floor. She began to stand, but instead pushed off into forward walkover. She then danced toward the center, did a split leap with change of legs *(Figure 54)* and dropped down into a crouch position. She made a half turn to her right as she stood up and immediately entered a forward walkover with change of legs. She paused in handstand, lowered herself down to chin stand, her elbows on the floor, and came down onto her left knee on the floor. She made a three-quarter turn to her right on her knee and made a free forward roll parallel to and close to the opposite side. She jumped up to stand near the side and posed, making slow steps from side to side, while gesturing with her arms and turning toward the opposite direction along the side. She danced toward the nearby corner, made a split leap and a second leap. Then she ran in a long arc counter-clockwise half way around the floor to the opposite corner. In doing so, she performed an aerial forward walkover and two full turns. She approached the corner and moved into it, while performing some graceful arm gestures. She turned to face along the diagonal and begin her final pass: a round-off, flic-flac into salto backward stretched with full twist. She stepped forward into her final pose, standing on her left leg, her right foot forward and right knee bent, her right hand on her hip, her left arm extended vertically upward and her head thrown back.

Figure 54

Ludmilla's teammate, Lyubov Burda, was her teammate also in Ljubljana and Munich. Her routines there have been recorded in later pages. In Mexico, Burda's routine was as follows:

Figure 55

She started one step out of a corner, close to an adjacent side, facing in toward the floor. She posed, while turning left and right and gesturing with her arms. She turned to her left, stepped into the corner, turned to her left again and leaned forward quickly into a scale. She stood again, paused and posed, then began her first pass: a round-off, flic-flac into an arabian salto (half twist followed by salto forward stretched) and stepped forward into the corner. She turned to her left and proceeded along the adjacent side to her left with long, slow steps, her arms extended out to her sides. Half way along the side, she made a full and a half turn to her right and leaned back into a back walkover on her left arm (*Figure 55* shows forward and backward walkover). As she passed through handstand, she put her right hand onto the floor, made a half turn to her left and ended in forward walkover. She made a full turn to her left on her left foot with her right foot raised and continued with another slow dancing turn to her left to end in a deep curtsy. Now near the corner across from the diagonal of her first pass, she turned toward it and slowly danced into it. She made several turns and poses and executed another quick forward scale facing into the corner. She turned back to face along the diagonal and begin her second pass: a round-off, flic-flac, salto backward stretched with full twist. She paused for just a second and leaned back into a back walkover. She stopped in handstand, made a quarter turn to her left, rolled out onto her back and continued her roll until her feet were on the floor. As she rolled first on her shoulders, then on her back and her seat, she let her body come up off the floor until, when her feet touched the floor, she was momentarily standing and leaning diagonally backwards. She pushed off into back handspring which she ended in splits on the floor. She paused and posed only for a second in splits, then began to stand, making a full turn to her left as she was getting up. After she was standing, she arched her back steeply and touched her left hand to the floor. Then she turned to her right to touch her right hand to the floor, lean to her right to bring her knees down onto the floor and continue her turn to the right as she stood. Still in the corner at which she had completed her second pass, she ran out of it back along the diagonal and performed two split leaps. At the center of the floor, she paused, kicked her left leg up in front of her and performed an aerial forward walkover. Now moving at a faster pace, she made sweeping half turns first to her left, then to her right and then a quarter turn to her left to run a few steps parallel to the adjacent side. She made a jump full turn and ended in splits on the floor, her left leg in front. She brought her right leg around in front, her right knee bent, put her right hand behind her and pushed back in valdez to stand. She had now turned so that she was facing the corner at which she had finished her second pass. She kicked her

Figure 56

right leg up behind her, extended her arms out to her side and stood on her right leg in momentary scale *(Figure 56)*. She leaned forward and performed a free forward roll, keeping her arms out to her side. She rolled out to stand, ran forward toward the corner, performed a tour jeté and stepped into the corner with other turns and poses to begin her third pass: a round-off, flic-flac, half turn handspring forward into an aerial forward walkover. She performed many turns and poses as she came a few steps out of her corner into her final pose: she stood on her straight left leg, her right leg diagonally behind her, toes on the floor, her left arm at her side and her right arm extended vertically upward.

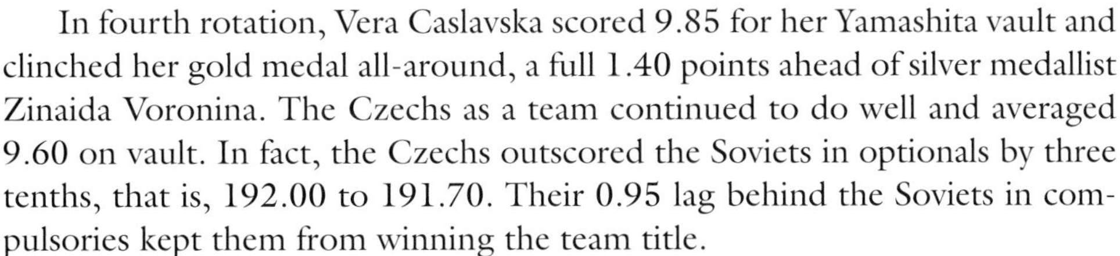

In fourth rotation, Vera Caslavska scored 9.85 for her Yamashita vault and clinched her gold medal all-around, a full 1.40 points ahead of silver medallist Zinaida Voronina. The Czechs as a team continued to do well and averaged 9.60 on vault. In fact, the Czechs outscored the Soviets in optionals by three tenths, that is, 192.00 to 191.70. Their 0.95 lag behind the Soviets in compulsories kept them from winning the team title.

The East Germans on bars showed surprising weakness in depth. Erika Zuchold scored 9.60 and Karin Janz, who would win the gold medal for uneven bars both in Ljubljana and Munich, scored 9.70. As a team, however, they averaged only 9.40, so there were some low scores. Zuchold's routine was similar to the one she had performed in Dortmund. Janz's routine also contained the backward seat circles popular in East German gymnastics but was cleaner: there were no interruptions while on low bar to get ready for the next element. She had taken a cue from Doris Brause's routine in Dortmund!

The routines of Zuchold and Janz were as follows:

Zuchold made a running straddle jump over low bar to catch high bar. She kipped on high bar until she could shoot her legs through between herself and the bar to assume a pike position, hanging on high bar between the bars. She swung backwards and on up to rear support position on high bar, facing away from low bar. From there, with her body stretched, she swung forward and around high bar until on her way up between the bars, she let go of high bar and flew to low bar to catch it in handstand, facing away from high bar (Zuchold-Schleudern) *(Figure 20)*. She allowed her legs to swing down away from high bar and then performed a clear hip circle backwards around low bar and continued circling backwards. As she came up between the bars toward high bar from under low bar, she paused while her legs were together and straight and piked over the low bar and while she was facing down. Then she started to go back under low bar in the

Erika Zuchold in pike hang from high bar.

direction away from high bar. As she did so, she passed her right leg under the low bar, her left leg remaining over the bar. During this forward hip circle, one leg was over the low bar and the other under, but as she came up over the low bar, the relative positions of the legs were reversed. As she came up over the low bar, she released low bar with her hands, reached to grasp high bar and made a half turn to the left, her seat resting on low bar. She was able to make this turn without pausing because in splitting her legs as she did, she was in effect making the turn as she performed her hip circle. She did not have to pause and lift her hips off the bar to make the turn as other gymnasts had had to. She finished this maneuver facing low bar with her legs in straddle position above the low bar. She quickly let her legs drop down between the bars, swung back under high bar and then swung forward again as she dropped to low bar. She kipped and caught high bar, kipped and shot her legs between her arms behind high bar, so that her body was in tight pike position again, this time hanging outside the bars. She swung back down and up over high bar, paused in clear, rear support, continued on around to begin another backward circle in this piked position. As she passed through the bottom of this second circle, she stopped and reversed her swing, kicked out of her pike and stretched her body, making a quick release and recatch of the bar as she did so. She then swung down to wrap around low bar, fly back to catch high bar in eagle grip, that is, her hands over the bar. She began a kip over low bar with her hands still in eagle grip. As her legs rested momentarily on low bar in her kip, she quickly changed her grip to normal and kipped on high bar to clear support position back of the bar. She swung back in clear hip circle until she was up, over the bar, then released and let her momentum carry her forward in hecht dismount with full twist to land.

Karin Janz mounted by running at the low bar and jumping off the beat board in tuck jump over the low bar. She grasped high bar, stretched

Erika Zuchold in clear, rear support on high bar.

her body, swung forward, then flew back over the low bar with her legs in straddle position and caught low bar. She kipped on low bar, shot her legs over the low bar between her arms and reached for the high bar. She kipped on high bar until, nearly on top of the bar, she placed her toes on the bar outside her hands. She swung back and under high bar. On her upswing, she stretched her body and made a half turn, her body being in a position diagonally upward and away from high bar as she began her half turn. Then she swung back under high bar, wrapped around low bar and flew to catch high bar in eagle grip. She hung momentarily from high bar, then dropped forward to catch low bar and begin her kip. She kipped on low bar to catch high bar. She kipped on high bar until her hands were at waist level behind the bar, stopped her kip and made a half turn so that her seat was against the bar. Then she began to circle upwards over and around high bar on her seat and piked her body. After she had passed under the bar, she released her hands from the bar, stretched her body, made a half turn to her left, with her body vertical, regrasped the bar and swung forward to drop and catch low bar. She kipped on low bar until she could shoot her legs between her arms and the bar, while hanging from low bar between the bars. Then she made a second seat circle backwards but stopped it after she had swung under the bar, reversed her swing and circled back up, shooting her legs up and over the low bar. Then she reached up to grasp high bar. She kipped on high bar up to clear support position, that is, until her body was horizontal and held away from the bar by her straight arms. She made a clear hip circle backwards until her body was in the same horizontal position, then swung down, wrapped around low bar, released and performed full twist to land in her hecht dismount (see photo page 82).

Karin Janz in hecht dismount with full twist off low bar.

The Japanese team's 9.43 average on beam nailed down their fourth-place position. Their 375.45 final score was more than 5.5 points ahead of the fifth-place Hungarian team's 369.80, but they were 3.65 points behind the East Germans. Thus, the top three teams were really in a class by themselves. The sixth-pace United States team was close to the Hungarians at 369.75.

The final standings and scores of the leading teams and individuals were as follows:

	Initial Score	Fourth Rotation	Total
1. URS	334.90	47.95	382.85
2. TCH	334.15	48.05	382.20
3. GDR	332.10	47.00	379.10
4. JPN	328.30	47.15	375.45
5. HUN			369.80
6. USA			369.75

	Initial Score	Fourth Rotation	Total
1. Caslavska *(vault)*	68.40	9.85	78.25
2. Voronina *(floor)*	67.20	9.65	76.85
3. Kuchinskaya *(floor)*	67.05	9.70	76.75
4. Petrick *(floor)*	67.20	9.50	76.70
Zuchold *(bars)*	67.10	9.60	76.70
6. Janz *(bars)*	66.85	9.70	76.55
7. Bohumila Rimnacova, TCH			76.00
8. Olga Karasyova			76.00
9. Mariana Karajcirova, TCH			75.85
Miroslava Sklenickova, TCH			75.85
11. Hana Liskova, TCH			75.65
12. Maritta Bauerschmidt, GDR			75.45
13. Kazue Hanyu, JPN			75.30
14. Agnes Banfai, HUN			75.10
15. Jana Kubickova, TCH			75.05
16. Cathy Rigby, USA			74.95

Team winners: URS, 1st; TCH, 2nd; GDR, 3rd

All-around winners: Caslavska, 1st; Voronina, 2nd; Kuchinskaya, 3rd

Finals on the Apparatus: October 25th

Describing them, one eyewitness wrote[5], "The finals, although a very slow meet, proved to be a tough competition. All six girls in every event hit their routines . . . . It is the first finals where I've seen so many routines hit. I can only remember one miss on the bars by one of the Czech girls."

Vault

In vault, Caslavska, Zuchold, and Voronina performed their Yamashita vaults, Caslavska scoring 9.90 and the other two 9.80. This was Caslavska's second gold medal. Zuchold's final score, with the preliminary counted in, was higher than Voronina's, so she got the silver medal. Kuchinskaya placed fifth. The standings and scores were as follows, the preliminary score being the average of compulsory and optional scores from team competition:

	Preliminary Score	Finals Score	Total
1. Vera Caslavska	9.875	9.900	19.775
2. Erika Zuchold	9.825	9.800	19.625
3. Zinaida Voronina	9.700	9.800	19.500
4. Mariana Krajcirova, TCH	9.725	9.750	19.475
5. Natalya Kuchinskaya	9.725	9.650	19.375
6. Miroslava Sklenickova, TCH	9.675	9.650	19.325

Uneven bars

Caslavska won her third gold medal on bars, again with a 9.90 in finals. Karin Janz got well-deserved recognition and gymnastics enthusiasts all over the world got a preview of things to come when Janz received her silver medal. Voronina was on the victory stand for the second time, again for a bronze medal. Their routines have previously been described.

The standings and scores of the finalists in bars competition were as follows:

	Preliminary Score	Finals Score	Total
1. Caslavska	9.750	9.900	19.650
2. Janz	9.650	9.850	19.500
3. Voronina	9.625	9.800	19.425
4. Rimnacova	9.650	9.700	19.350
5. Zuchold	9.525	9.800	19.325
6. Sklenickova	9.550	8.650	18.200

Beam

On beam, Natalya Kuchinskaya finally came into her own. She had won three gold medals in Dortmund, and now had the chance to win one gold medal in Mexico. Her mood at the time was described in an article she wrote eight years later.[6] At that time, she was a judge of floor exercise in the Soviet selection trials for the Montreal Olympics, 1976.

> When the team competition is over, when the finals of the all-around are finished, then begins, in my opinion, the most difficult test—the championships of the individual apparatus.
>
> Then you do not feel the support of your friends, as you do in team competition. You and you alone contend. You, in silence, go out to the apparatus all by yourself, and nobody can help you. Everything—victory, triumph, defeat—is in your hands. Your very own.
>
> In Mexico, there was still no supplementary day for the finals in the all-around. They determined the absolute champion during the team competition. It made no difference, however, for we who had reached the finals in the apparatus felt great fatigue and the effort of the tournament began to tell on us.
>
> What a heavy life gymnasts have nowadays! What strength, what endurance is required in Olympic battles! Victories go only to those sportsmen who are truly well-rounded and well-grounded, that is to say, who have no weak spots. In fact, any gymnast who aspires to be all-around

"Oh, woe is me, to have seen what I have seen, see what I see!" ***Hamlet,*** *Act III, Sc. 1, Line 166.*

"I missed my vault!" Natalya Kuchinskaya.

champion must have routines capable of delivering knock-out blows. On one's own apparatus, it should be possible to earn, shall we say, a bonus, to create an advantage, even a small one, over the other competitors. For me, such an apparatus was beam. Going into the finals, I had received the highest preliminary score. This did not guarantee a gold medal, however. You see, as I have already said, on this last day, nervousness combined with fatigue increased double. We knew that we, our Olympic team, very much need the highest score because Vera Caslavska had become the absolute champion. That responsibility troubled me.

"I must win, I must win," I thought; and even as I prepared for the vault, I repeated in my mind the exercise on the beam. Of course, this was a mistake. In the vault, I did not do well. My mood was spoiled. After this, is it possible to win on the beam?

I went out into the wings of the hall. I had to pull my thoughts together, to calm down. "On me are their hopes, from me they expect victory—but can I do it?" In such a way was I tormented. And suddenly, soberness, calmness descended on me. "On the beam, I have not failed for a long time. Why should I not be able to perform the routine now? I can, I can . . . ."

My turn. My favorite apparatus. I began the exercise and felt that ease and inspiration were with me. I wanted to laugh and fly like a butterfly along the narrow beam. Everyone was watching. After all, the leading Soviet was on the beam in head to head competition with Caslavska. I did win the gold and the crowd seemed to be as happy about it was I was.

Kuchinskaya's 9.85 was tied by Caslavska. Similarly, the two had tied with 9.80 during optional team competition. The score in compulsories, way back on the first day, decided the outcome. Then, Kuchinskaya had scored 9.80 and Caslavska, 9.65. So, Kuchinskaya won the gold medal and Caslavska, the silver.

The standings and scores of the finalists in beam competition were as follows:

	Preliminary Score	Finals Score	Total
1. Kuchinskaya	9.800	9.850	19.650
2. Caslavska	9.725	9.850	19.575
3. Petrick	9.500	9.750	19.250
4. Linda Metheny, USA	9.575	9.650	19.225
Janz	9.525	9.700	19.225
6. Zuchold	9.500	9.650	19.150

One competitor on beam in finals who has just once previously been mentioned was American gymnast Linda Metheny. Though she placed only 28th all around, she came into beam finals with a compulsory-optional average of 9.575, which put her in third place going in, behind Kuchinskaya and Caslavska. She received 9.650 in finals and finished in fourth place because Larissa Petrick, who had come into finals tied for fifth place with Erika Zuchold, scored 9.75 in finals and scooted ahead of her to win the bronze medal. Nevertheless, Metheny's fourth-place finish in finals was the highest achievement to date by any American woman gymnast. Her routine was as follows:

> After mounting at the far end of the beam, Linda proceeded down the beam and performed an assemblé, a half squat turn to her left, a half squat turn back to her right and a double stag jump. At the near end of the beam, she did a half turn to her left, posed, danced forward to the middle of the beam, executed a full turn and leaned forward with a quarter turn to her left to begin a handstand facing across the beam. She slowly pressed her legs up to handstand with her legs straddled, then brought them together to hold momentarily in handstand. She then brought her legs back down between her arms and up into pike position, while supporting herself with her hands on the beam. She held this pike position for a moment, facing across the beam, then lowered her legs, leaving her left leg on the side of the beam she was facing and bringing her right leg through her arms to the side of the beam behind her. Then, still facing across the beam, she brought her left leg up on top of the beam, bent at the knee and tucked under her, and brought her right leg up just above the beam but stretched along it to her right. She balanced herself with her left hand on the beam, her left arm straight, and held her right arm out straight diagonally above her right leg. She held this attractive, side-reclining pose for a second, then made a quarter turn to her left into a momentary lunge position and raised herself to stand. She made a half turn to her left and walked along the beam to the far end. Near the end, she kicked her left leg up and leaned forward into lunge position, her left leg bent in front of her and her right leg straight behind.

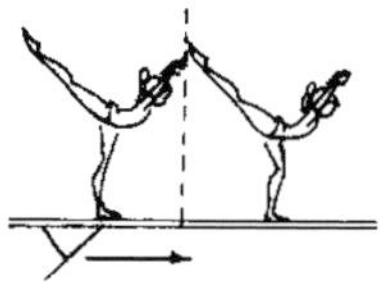
Figure 57

From lunge position, she simply straightened her left leg, kept her right leg straight horizontally behind her, held her arms out to the side and she was balanced in a forward scale *(Figure 57)*. She lowered her right leg down to the beam, made a half turn to her left, posed and came along the beam with skip steps and a split leap. She stopped in pose at the near end with knees slightly bent. She straightened her legs as she made a half turn to her left, stepped forward and leaned forward with a quarter turn to her left into handstand across the beam. She held this handstand for a second, made another quarter turn to her left, this time on her hands, while at the same time lowering her feet down onto the beam ahead of her, in the direction she had been going, and posed, with her left leg partially bent and her right leg extended behind her. She straightened her legs and initiated a back walkover but stopped in a standing split, her left foot on the beam, her right leg extended vertically upward and her hands on the beam. After holding her standing split, she completed her walkover by dropping down onto her left knee and shin, with her right leg straight behind her in knee scale. She then swung her right leg forward, straightened her left leg and stood. From the far end, she proceeded down the beam to the middle, made a half turn to the left and paused with her knees partially bent, posed while gesturing gracefully with her arms and made another half turn to her left. She continued to the near end and made a high kick with her right leg in a full turn to her left. She took two steps back and did a back walkover down to splits. Now near the middle of the beam, she posed in splits swung her right leg forward onto the beam, bent at the knee so that her right foot was on the beam, with her left leg extended in front of her. She then performed a valdez to a dismount to the side of the beam to her left.

Floor Exercise

Floor exercise finals gave spectators a chance to have a last look at those gymnasts who had been in the lead throughout the competition: Caslavska, Petrick, Kuchinskaya, and Voronina. All received high scores. As previously related, Petrick tied Caslavska for the gold medal. The routines of those leaders have all been described.

Vera Caslavska again brought pleasure to the audience with her "Mexican Hat Dance." Petrick's routine also pleased them. There is an interesting story to Petrick's routine, which she related in an article,[7] nineteen years later:

> I always went out onto the podium with a light heart; never did I necessarily strive to win a championships. Was I lacking in ambition? It seemed to me that it was more important to win the hearts of the audience than the

"gold." I dare say the constant pursuit of medals does not give a young gymnast the opportunity to reveal herself . . . .

In my time, floor exercise was considered the main event—win here and you will be queen. Why are floor exercises so good? In them, you show both acrobatics and choreography; then it is possible to display your character. I loved this event more than any other event. I wanted to do something in floor exercise so that people would accept me, would separate me from those who had gone before. Around the sports arenas, people used to ask, "Does anybody have an extra ticket?" So I wanted to justify the expectations of the people, that they had not come for nothing. Therefore, in floor exercise, I always tried to present a small spectacle.

I dreamed of preparing a routine to the music of *Carmen*. The passionate, strong characters had always attracted me. It was a dream, but at the beginning I learned a routine to the music of Strelnikov from his operetta, *The Bondmaid*. In some way here I had to show her temperament. There were in my routine three of the very simplest steps. In showing these three steps, I had time to run around half the floor. How I was able to pull it off, I don't know, but the audience liked it. Because of that, I was very happy, but I never forgot about *Carmen*.

After the Soviet national championships, I was included in the national team and I began training for the Olympics in Mexico. For them it was necessary to make up an entirely new program, but here it was spring 1968 and I still had not prepared a new floor exercise. Then I boarded a train and went off to Leningrad to visit the accompanist of our team, Evsey Gdalyevich Vevrick, and his wife, Aida Alexandrovna Saleznova. I came to them and said, "I want to do *Carmen*." But then Vevrick advised me not to do an étude to the music of Bizet yet. They prepared a routine to the aria of "Tatyana" from *Eugene Onegin*. Then Evsey Gdalyevich proposed to do some kind of pop song for exhibition performances. They selected music from the film, *The Last Camp*. It was an old gypsy love song. In two days, they created still another routine.

Returning to Vitebsk, I performed "Tatyana." Everyone was generally satisfied. But then they sent us to an exhibition performance in Switzerland, where I performed "The Little Gypsy" for the first time. The audience applauded; I was delighted. I returned home and head coach Larissa Latynina said to me that I should perform the routine I had performed on the tour. I will do "The little gypsy." The unfortunate "Tatyana" was forgotten. For the Olympics, they approved my "gypsy romance."

Mexico . . . I will never forget it! The finals! I went out onto the podium and a miracle happened! I forgot everything that had gone on before; I did not think about what will come after. If it is possible to say

> that I soared on the floor, then that's what it was. I ran out onto the last diagonal, literally I ran—I did not stop before the final acrobatic connection but with momentum I completed it. I did the final element and stood stock still. I came to myself in the storm of applause. I do not know what happened to me, but something happened. Not once have I experienced such a sensation. Of course, I fixed it into my consciousness and then tried to tune myself to it but it never happened again. It was a moment of true happiness—not a matter of the Olympic gold medal but of the highest meaning of sport—to express yourself right to the end.

In finals of floor exercise, there remains only to record the routine of one gymnast who did not make floor exercise finals but whose all-around standing represented another achievement for the United States and who would become well known for what she accomplished in Ljubljana and Munich. I refer to Cathy Rigby. Her floor exercise was warmly received during team competition and was as follows:

> Cathy started her floor exercise a few steps away from a corner and along one of the sides, facing the center. She took a few steps toward the center, turned and assumed a playful pose, standing with her arms out to the side, her upper body tilted slightly forward and her seat projected backwards. Then she moved toward the corner to her left with a cat leap half turn, a half turn back and another playful pose, as if preparing for a tumbling run. This time she stood with her left knee partially bent her right leg straight with her left foot on the floor in front of her, her right arm bent with her hand pointing toward her chin and a teasing expression on her face. Instead of starting a tumbling run along a diagonal, she turned to her right and proceeded to the adjacent corner with a cartwheel and two back handsprings stepout. After a tuck jump and a few dance steps in the corner, she did turn and begin her first pass: a round-off, flic-flac into a salto backward stretched with full twist. After landing and posing in the corner, she danced out slowly and gracefully, performed a half turn to her right in attitude, did another half turn to her right and proceeded back along the diagonal of her first pass with dance steps, deep body waves and expressive arm movements. She continued with a jump full turn into a pose with her right knee and shin on the floor, her left knee bent and her left foot on the floor in front of her and her upper body erect. She posed, while looking left with her arms extended down on either side of her. She then danced forward, continuing back along the diagonal of her first pass, and performed a forward aerial walkover into split position on the floor near the corner from which she had started her first pass. She leaned forward over her knees and

then arched her body steeply back while gesturing with her arms. She then rolled partially to her right, made a full turn on her seat and leaned to her right to lie on her side on the floor, her body extended. She sat up and posed in sitting position, near a corner facing one of the sides. She then performed a valdez, parallel to the adjacent side of the floor, to stand. She continued backwards in a slow back walkover after which she stood and posed for a second. Then she ran forward in an arc clockwise toward the corner at which she ended her first pass and made a second short tumbling pass of a cartwheel into a side salto. Speeding up the pace of her movements, she did not stop after this second tumbling pass, but came out of the corner toward the center with some running steps, a half turn to her left into a back handspring and then another half turn and a split leap with a quarter turn to her left. She changed direction with half turn to her left again, walked along the adjacent side and bent over to perform a forward roll to stand. She performed some body waves and poses, a jump half turn down to a pose on one knee, and then stepped backwards into a corner to prepare for her final pass: a round-off into two flic-flacs and a salto backward stretched. She ended her exercise in a pose sitting on the floor, her legs on the floor in front of her, her right hand on the floor behind her and her left hand outstretched in front.

Cathy Rigby

The standings and scores of the finalists in floor exercise competition were as follows:

	Preliminary Score	Finals Score	Total
1. Petrick	9.775	9.900	19.675
Caslavska	9.775	9.900	19.675
3. Kuchinskaya	9.800	9.850	19.650
4. Voronina	9.700	9.850	19.550
5. Olga Karasyova, URS	9.575	9.750	19.325
6. Rimnacova	9.575	9.750	19.325

As with Petrick, looking back on her floor exercise routine, the final words on Mexico were spoken by Vera Caslavska and Natalya Kuchinskaya in interviews nineteen years later. These two great gymnasts were tied together in a bittersweet relationship. As we said in the Dortmund story, so it was in Mexico. Caslavska said, "In Dortmund, everybody loved her. And, oh, how it was in Mexico! Do you remember? The name 'Natasha' was on everybody's tongue. 'The Bride of Mexico.' Yet I had so many times defeated her. Everyone wants a new champion. It is natural."[8]

Ironically, when asked if she had an ideal, someone whose example she wants her students to follows, Kuchinskaya, now a coach, replied, "I think girls don't need an idol. Let them keep to themselves. For me, however, my ideal was Vera Caslavska from Czechoslovakia. I could never win over her, although I wanted to badly. She was a surprisingly strong, strong-willed, serious gymnast. At that time, I looked upon gymnastics as a hobby. I think that attitude hindered me. Any job you do you should do wholeheartedly."[9]

For both gymnasts, Mexico was their last competition. Hard times were ahead for Caslavska in her newly-subjugated country. Kuchinskaya also had a difficult time adjusting to life after leaving Olympic-level sport. Both eventually found fulfillment, Kuchinskaya coaching young gymnasts at the Central Children's Sport School in Kiev and Caslavska as a coach at the Sparta Club in Prague. Finally, after 1989, Caslavska became an advisor to President Vaclav Havel. (See biography.)

References

[1]Bob Ottum, "Grim Countdown to the Games," *Sports Illustrated*, 14 Oct. 1968: 36. Reprinted by permission of Time, Inc.

[2]John Underwood, "A High Time for Sprinters—and Kenyans," *Sports Illustrated*, 28 Oct. 1968: 18. Reprinted by permission of Time, Inc.

[3]David Wallechinsky, *The Complete Book of the Olympics* (New York: Penguin Books, © 1984, 1988).

[4]Rex Bellamy in the *U.S. Olympic Committee Team Book*, 1968.

[5]Dale Flansaas, "1968 Olympic Report," *Mademoiselle Gymnast,* Nov./Dec. 1968: 10. (Now *International Gymnast)*

[6]Natalya Kuchinskaya, "My Apparatus," *Sovietsky Sport*, 25 May 1976.

[7]Larissa Petrick, "I Always Searched for Inspiration," *Sovietsky Sport,* 10 July 1987.

[8]O. Polonskaya, "Faith, Hope, Love," *Sovietsky Sport*, May 1987.

[9]Natalya Kalugina, "Natalya Kuchinskaya: Gymnastics is My Life," *Sovietsky Sport*, 2 Sept. 1987.

Descriptions of routines were taken from a video made from films taken by Frank Endo and from a video made from films taken by Bill Coco and supplied by Fred Turoff.

The 1972 team at Leselidze. Left to right: Korbut, Lazakovich, Burda, Saadi, Koshel, Turischeva, Sikharulidze.

Larissa Semyenovna Latynina

1934 Born in Kherson, Ukraine.

1953 Member Soviet National Team, age 19, as Larissa Dirii. Her coach throughout her career was Alexander Mishakov, who was also coach of World and Olympic Champion Boris Shaklin.

1954 World Championships, Rome, June–July: 14th, all-around.

1956 Olympics, Melbourne, November, as Larissa Latynina: 1st, all-around; 1st, vault; 1st (tie) floor; 2nd, bars; 4th (tie) beam.

1957 First European Championship, Bucharest, May: 1st, all-around; 1st, vault, bars, beam, floor.

1958 World Championships, Moscow, July: 1st, all-around; 2nd, vault; 1st, bars, beam, floor.

1960 Olympics, Rome, August: 1st, all-around; 1st, floor; 2nd, bars, beam; 3rd, vault.

1961 European Championship, Leipzig, June: 1st, all-around; 1st, floor; 2nd, bars,beam; 4th, vault.

1962 World Championships, Prague, July: 1st, all-around; 1st, floor; 2nd, vault, beam.

1964 Olympics, Tokyo, October: 2nd, all-around; 1st, floor, 2nd, vault; 3rd, bars, beam.

1965 European Championship, Sofia, May: 2nd, all-around; 2nd, bars, beam; 2nd (tie) floor; 3rd, vault.

1966 World Championships, Dortmund, September: 11th, all-around; did not place in finals.

1967 Head coach, Soviet women's team, to 1977.

1977 Head coach, Moscow women's team, to 1987.

1980 Director, gymnastics organization, Moscow Olympics.

1989 Awarded Olympic Order in silver by International Olympic Committee.

1990 Deputy director, charitable fund to assist former athletes financially.

1991 Retired.

In our day, Larissa Latynina should be remembered as the creator of the great 1972 Munich Olympic team, the person who presided over the transformation of the team from its 1966 defeat to its victories from 1968 to 1976. Her own gymnastic achievements should not be underestimated, but they are subject to the qualification that they could never be repeated. In her day, the Soviet Union had such a head start and had developed such an extensive training organization that no other country was in the same class. Teams that challenged the Soviet Union came from the old East Bloc, the former communist countries in the Soviet political sphere of influence. These were Hungary in the 1950s, Czechoslovakia in the 1960s, East Germany in the 1970s, and Romania since the 1970s. It was not until the 1980s that the United States, the strongest western country, could begin seriously to challenge this preeminent gymnastic power.

Latynina told the story of the transition from 1966 to 1972 in her little book *Kak zovut ettu devochky?, (What Is This Little Girl's Name?),* written in 1974 and published by Pravda. This biographical sketch is initially a précis of that book with excerpts; other articles bring her life up to date.

> The 1966 team defeat in Dortmund by Czechoslovakia was a shock to the Soviets. It was their first defeat in four world championships. (Latynina had participated in the first one, 1954.) They had also, however, won the previous four Olympics, beginning in 1952. The 1966 defeat was the first in eight major championships. These had given birth to the myth that the Soviet women's gymnastics team was invulnerable. Dortmund made them realize the cruel law of sport: that there is no such thing as an invulnerable team.
>
> Upon reflection, Latynina conceded that the Czech victory was justified: the Soviet team was weaker than its predecessors. Yet the defeat raised a poignant, agonizing question in her mind: would this defeat be the first in a series of dry years? She and Polina Astakhova, her long-time friend, had competed knowing they had no chance for a medal but knowing also that without them the team would be weaker. At the age of 32, it had been difficult to compete. Afterward, the two of them talked at length about their years on the Soviet team, Latynina since 1953 and Astakhova since 1955. They made no promises, no decisions, no clear plans; but several months later, Latynina became head coach of the Soviet women's team.
>
> She was not stepping into a vacuum, however. Exciting things were developing. Already, 15-year-old Larissa Petrick had won the 1965 Soviet national championships. Then in 1966, Natalya Kuchinskaya had won it and would win again in 1967 and 1968. In addition, there had appeared talented coaches who were devoted to working with their young girls: Yuri Shtukman found Lyubov Burda; Vikenti Dmitriev first had Larissa Petrick, then Tamara Lazakovich; under Renald Knysh, Olga Korbut was being noticed; Vladislav Rastorotsky had discovered Ludmilla Turischeva. Although Latynina and Astakhova would leave the team, Kuchinskaya, Voronina and Karasyova, in addition to Petrick, would carry over from Dortmund. Into the two vacancies, she placed Burda and Turischeva for the Mexico Olympics.

At that time, Kuchinskaya was the star. "We fell in love with Natasha! It was impossible not to love her. A lively spirit was evident in each of her performances. For a long time, I could not get used to the contrast: on the podium, a mature master; but down below, a little girl."

Natasha became the leader of the team and she became a strong leader. In Mexico, Natasha fell from bars in compulsories, but recovered and placed third all-around. She won the gold medal on beam.

"Such an acclaim began to grow around the name of Natasha even before Mexico that I wondered: what was the reason for it? Was it for her successful performances in the Mexico pre–Olympics in 1967? Perhaps her smile and her charm had a special effect upon Mexicans. To this day, I don't know. One thing I will say: the role of 'the bride of Mexico,' which was fastened to her, seemed very difficult for her in the face of her responsibilities toward the competition. Clearly the leader, she drew people toward her. We worried about the competition.

"A strong team brings out a strong leader and she gives a special coloring to the whole team. In Mexico, we competed with just such a team and we won."

Mexico was the first victory since the defeat at Dortmund, but it was the last competition for Natasha. She fell ill. Furthermore, she lost interest, as she was having trouble with her coaches. She made an effort to come back and went to Leningrad for the 1969 National Championships. As she watched the opening of the competition, she said, "I am not afraid of not being first. But then what? Who needs it?" So she did not compete. Latynina summed up Natasha's story: "As leader she came to the team; as leader she left."

Who would take Natasha's place as leader? Ludmilla Turischeva's coach, Vladislav Rastorotsky, had great expectations for her. He was, as Latynina said, a "maximalist," that is, a person who favors direct or revolutionary action to achieve a goal. In 1967, Ludmilla had won the USSR Cup in a competition without the strongest competitors. At that he said: "Next year we'll beat Caslavska!" It did not happen. In the 1969 European Championships, she took third place. Karin Janz won it; Karasyova was second. Was Rastorotsky ready to give up? No. His answer, instead, was to add difficulty to her routines. In the 1969 Soviet National Championships, she lost first place all-around on the last apparatus. In any case, Turischeva had moved from last place (with Burda) on the team in Mexico to a place up among the leaders.

Before the 1970 World Championships in Ljubljana, Latynina gathered her team together in Leselidze, a resort on the Black Sea. The East Germans had also come and were staying in the same hotel.

Olga Korbut had a clear objective: to place seventh in trials and become first reserve; but she placed eighth and so became second reserve. Rusiko Sikharulidze became first reserve.

Facing Latynina and the other coaches was the important question: how to place the team members? The coaches knew that the order was of vital importance to the eventual winner: the last person on the team was always treated more kindly by the judges. Besides standings in the trials, other factors were experience and age: the oldest, Karasyova was 23; the youngest, Lazakovich, was 16.

The debutante Tamara Lazakovich would lead off. She had placed fourth in trials, but the coaches felt they could not rely on her. Following her would be Larissa Petrick. After Petrick, Karasyova was in third place. Even though Karasyova had placed second to Karin Janz in Landskrona and had won a gold medal in floor exercise, she had had major breaks both in the national championships and the USSR Cup. She was, therefore, not placed in one of the last positions. Nevertheless, with two former champions, there was an abundance of talent in the lead-off three. "Even so," wondered Latynina, "would the championship be easy?"

The leaders—Zinaida Voronina, Lyubov Burda and Ludmilla Turischeva—knew they had been given an advantage and would have to justify themselves. Voronina had just given birth to her son, Dima, but was working out unconstrainedly. She was soon in top form. Lyubov Burda and Ludmilla Turischeva: so soon at the top? How would they bear their responsibilities as leaders? In fact, before the competition, there were no recognized leaders: all were of about equal strength. There could be several leaders and that could be a risk.

On the first day, Lazakovich fell twice from beam in compulsories. It might have been a staggering blow for the team, but they rallied and ended up only a tenth behind the east Germans.

During the night that followed, imperturbable Vikenti Dmitriev, coach of Lazakovich, tried to calm his friend, the fiery, emotional Rastorotsky, Turischeva's coach. Lazakovich had no chance for a medal. Would Turischeva be able to overcome Janz?

"You know, Vikenti," he said, "I had three talented girls in my group. About one, I said: 'she will be a national champion.' About another, 'she will have a place on the team.' About the third, 'she might also get somewhere.' The third was Ludmilla Turischeva."

Nagging him in the back of his mind was the tradition that whoever won the European Championships would win next year's world championships or Olympics. Win a gold medal in the odd year; win another in the even year. This tradition favored Janz.

As it turned out, the Soviets regained their confidence. "When did I believe for sure we would win?" Latynina wrote. "It was when I saw the faces of our coaches before the second day's competition began. They looked at the podium of the Tivoli Hall confidently and firmly, like masters of the situation."

"Nothing happened," we told the girls. "We're only one tenth behind. Anyone can make that up." And so they did.

As for the all-around, it was a tense competition. Karin Janz was leading but fell on the last apparatus on her beam dismount. Ludmilla Turischeva became world champion.

"Finally, after Ljubljana," Latynina wrote, "we had an experienced, hardened team. Why then in 1971 did we begin to lose those who had experience in Dortmund, Mexico, and Ljubljana?

"It was because Larissa Petrick left. It seemed just yesterday that we met her in Kiev where she became national champion. Yesterday? Six years ago! Because of this, the positions of Olga Karasyova and Zinaida Voronina appeared less strong."

Petrick thought, "Youth is coming; my day is over," and she quit. Voronina and Karasyova competed in the 1972 National Championships and the USSR Cup Olympic selection trials for a place on the Munich team, but they lost. Latynina had hoped for them very much.

"Larissa Semyenovna," said one of the coaches, "you want Olga and Zina to win more than they do."

"Of course, that's an exaggeration," Latynina wrote. "They themselves wanted to win, but they could not. For the senior coach, who is not directly coaching any gymnast, all members of the team and candidates must be equal. That's the way it is. I did not want to believe, however, that I was saying good-bye to Zina and Olga.

"In any case, a team went to the 20th Olympics in which only two gymnasts had competed in the previous Olympics and only three in the 1970 World Championships. Even so, I believe that it was just the team which after Dortmund would not yield to anybody."

To the Ljubljana veterans, Turischeva, Burda and Lazakovich were added Olga Korbut, Elvira Saadi, and Tatyana Koshel. Olga had won the trials, which had been held in Minsk; the other two placed in the top six. The story of Munich is narrated in detail in this book. The following reflections in Latynina's mind and flashbacks in her memory are taken as excerpts from her book.[1]

Olga Korbut won gold medals on beam and floor exercise. "Who in the Olympic Village could predict that she would become what she became?" asked the German magazine *Stern* after the competition. I shall try to answer.

I remember the winter of 1970, the snow-covered airport in Grodno (Olga's home town). Red in the face from the cold or agitation, Olga met me with a bouquet of flowers. Then I had a conversation at her home.

"Look how thin she is," said her mother. "Here's her older sister who also does gymnastics and she still looks like a girl. But Olga! And you still say she can't have butter on her bread."

Fortunately, with us was our doctor, Mikhail Kuznetzov. I quickly nominated him to handle the problem.

While sitting there, I happened to look at Olga's gymnastics diary. It was opened to a page on which were written these words: "1972, Munich, Olympic Games—1st place."

One could imagine how Olga could be inclined to these words, sticking her tongue out in defiance. I looked up from the notebook and caught the eyes of Renald Ivanovich Knysh, Olga's coach. I understood: my doubts expressed in the form of a questioning smile offended him. Yes, why should I have doubted?

"In my opinion, it's well thought out," I said.

"To do it will be difficult, Larissa Semyenovna," admitted Knysh. "Have you seen her hairdo? Her hair sticks out, flares up, no matter how she tries. It's the same with her character."

In 1969, Olga, who had just turned fifteen, was admitted to the national championships in Rostov. There she performed two unique elements, but she fell from bars. From the high bar in squat position, she pushed off into a back handspring to hang on high bar. On beam, she performed a salto backward tucked.

I liked her element on bars better. There and on beam there was more than enough risk, but there was more amplitude on bars. They say that sport hardens character. True! I am strongly persuaded, however, that one must have a foundation for the hardening. If a gymnast is afraid, for example, in big-time gymnastics, there is nothing to be done—until she decides courageously to take a risk. Then once, twice, three times and she moves ahead.

Risk and courage do not have equal significance, especially for the young. That is why it is sometimes more important to see how a girl does not do a risky element, how she loses, how she falls. Yes, at that moment you see more than in a minute of winning. At the ball of success, everybody dances well; but when a gymnast falls, her hopes fade and many points are lost. Then I see how she picks herself up, what she does, whether she risks again tomorrow.

We all lose our grip on the bar; we all fall. I had that experience in Rome at the world championships in 1954; Astakhova had it at the Olympics in Rome in 1960; Burda and Turischeva fell in Mexico. After her fall in Rostov, Olga picked herself right up. That means character. That means Renald Ivanovich found what he was looking for. A coach searches for it. After his student, Lena Volchetskaya, had finished performing, Olga Korbut did not appear for several years.

I continue my conversation with Renald Ivanovich in Grodno in 1970.

"It is difficult to do, but are you going to do it?"

"You see, I would not think of any other way. I know why I am doing it. It's difficult but possible."

Before Ljubljana, Olga had free exercises that were not bad. One could say that for that time they were good. Before Munich we would change them. Aida Alexandrovna Seleznova and Yevsey Gdalovich Vevrick (the accompanist) prepared "Flight of the Bumble Bee" for Olga. Was it suitable? An excellent composition! And the performance was good. A little girl. Dynamic music associated with a beautiful story.

"I don't like it, Larissa Semyenovna."

There was not much time before the Olympics. I looked at Olga with indignation but asked quietly, "Why don't you like it, Olga?" But you don't deceive Olga with feigned quietness.

"It's a very good floor exercise, but something is lacking in it," and she spread her hands apart.

"What is lacking that you can't explain with just a gesture?"

"Larissa Semyenovna, I need something that will show breadth of spirit. But here is a bumble bee!" And she lifted her head high so as to look me courageously right in the eye.

"You have, of course, so advised Renald Ivanovich?"

"He is looking," said Olga, and lowered her head.

"OK," I concluded indefinitely.

Later, Knysh agreed. "We will look," he said. "Perhaps we can show a fragment of something."

So here we are, looking at fragments from a new combination using music from "Kalinka." Something in it is hackneyed and something in it is new.

"No, Renald Ivanovich. Kalinka won't do."

"Neither will 'Flight of the Bumble Bee,'" said Korbut.

There are five days to the trial competition. Five days! Time is inexorable. I walk about my room in the hotel. Time . . . .

Probably Knysh is not sleeping but thinking. On the telephone, our choreographer, Galina Savarina, says: "Why did I get involved in this gymnastics? And this girl. She handed us this problem, but she's probably placed her little, clenched fist under her pillow and is smiling in her sleep. She'll get up in the morning after us . . . ."

Galya Savarina was thinking about how to place old acrobatic combinations in a new composition. A new floor exercise is not a repetition of the old. Did they promise her a gold medal in Munich? No, but they promised a big success. Most importantly, this was an independent step by Olga Korbut toward creativity.

Any prediction in sport is an extremely thankless task. To me the moment of Olga's downfall on bars and then her performance on beam on the third day of Munich revealed much. Such defeats, which lead to victory, happen. They force a gymnast to find within herself strengths she did not know she had. And she feels so free, so relaxed, so bold that she could do anything. That is what happened in Munich with the 17-year-old girl, although she was only 154 cms tall (5 ft. 1 in.) had her hair in pigtails and ran barefoot. That is how were born the two victories of Olga on the first of September.

Since childhood, they had called her the sparrow. But even a nightingale until it begins to sing is just an unremarkable gray bird. In what was the secret of Olga's becoming the favorite of the spectators in the twentieth Olympic Games? The secret of any popularity is something that remains a mystery. Who can guess? As always, the youth of a winner and her bravery are factors in the unexpected victory. And there is something else. Contemporary sport is complicated. For the Olympics, you have to train for many years. Besides coaches, doctors help athletes as well as physiologists, psychologists, biochemists. There's much research. All this is very serious. And people following sport know about this complicated and necessary preparation. But if they see only youth, joy, happiness, they forget about what went before.

Olga Korbut's artistry was so natural that it was not noticed as such. The ballet sorceress, Anna Pavlova, once said: "In its highest form, art consists in the ability to conceal the technique of art." In this, evidently, is the secret of Olga Korbut.

And now we are in the Munich Sporthalle, flooded with bright light, resounding with the modulations of little Bavarian bells. During the last minutes I want to be distracted. I try to look at the girls through the eyes of a spectator. White leotards, red handbags. Good! Whatever people may say, elegance and taste enter into the style of gymnastics. That's not the most important thing, however. The most important thing is the mastery and it does not allow us to take a detached view of the gymnastics podium. The last seconds fly from the dial, like magnesium from the palms of the gymnasts. Polina Astakhova leads the team out to the first apparatus. We look at the rectangle on which the bars are secured and to which Elvira Saadi goes up. The countdown begins—minutes, seconds, tenths, hundredths . . . .

In Minsk in the selection trials, all the apparatus was from the same firm as in Munich. It was so arranged. And there were enough spectators. But a model is a model, although they did not exactly coincide. The podium in Munich seemed lower than is standard. The lighting was four times more than normal: eleven and a half thousand happy spectators would see everything well, as would millions of television viewers. These were not striking differences; the big difference was the judges. Here the judges were not the same as they were in Minsk.

We had the leadership, but how much worry! On the next apparatus—beam—I am able to reconstruct the picture only from stories and from the record. Yes, as in Yugoslavia, I could not stand it and closed my eyes. Shameful weakness? I accept reproach. When I opened my eyes I saw already the sixth on the team, Lyuda Turischeva, making her landing after salto with full twist. The landing, mildly speaking, was not very well done, but she would not lose much.

After the compulsory program, we led the girls from the GDR by almost two points. To a certain extent the result was what chess players call "building a reserve." Really, in 1972 our compulsory program was noticeably close to our optional. We received from the international federation only the set elements, from which we built the combinations. It turned out that our interpretation won.

Here are two conversations from many between the first and second days of the competition.

Jumping up and down, Elvira Saadi ran up to me. "Oh, Larissa Semyenovna, really did we not do well? Tell me, truly, was it good? And we'll do the optionals! You'll see how we'll get it together! We'll do very well!"

She said "we," but I understood she was talking about herself. Her coach, Vladimir Philipovich Aksyonov, had prepared a beautiful gymnast for the national team. This happened 15 years after her fellow Uzbekistaner, Galina Shamrai, made the team.

Now it can be said that we had many arguments about the place of Saadi on the team, even after she had won two gold medals in the national championships.

"Her physical preparation is not enough. Doubtful condition. Now she's flying, but will she in Munich?"

So it goes in gymnastics . . . Elvira, delicate, flexible and actually without athletic training, showed real fighting character. That was why she's here. I nodded my head at her, twittering from happiness: she did not let down the team! Only, don't think you are already Olympic champion!

And here are the sad eyes of Lyuda Turischeva. After the first day, she was two tenths behind Tamara Lazakovich and one tenth behind Karin Janz. Under the new format, the absolute champion is determined after the three-day competition. Nobody is now ahead, but I understand why Lyuda is uncomfortable when she began this conversation and asked if I was not worried.

"Lyuda!" I answered "Before you are still two days. Do not be concerned over such a small trifle! Just think, all you did was miss your landing from beam. You can do it all in optionals! You can!"

As always, Lyuda listened seriously and thoughtfully and nodded.

Again the Sporthalle. After optionals, the team competition was decided. The team is immeasurably more than six good gymnasts. That's the way it is. No matter how you change its composition, no matter who is on the right or left flank, traditions will be preserved. Gather all your strength for the team, even when it is intolerably difficult for you. Such are the traditions of our team.

For Tamara Lazakovich, her personal mark on the second day was very important. Even so, her duty was first for the team. One could only slightly discern the steel-like self-control and obstinate character in the blond, slim, pretty girl. Even her little smile belied it. Those who were close enough to see her bright eyes, however, could read in them, "I will not falter. I will not give an inch."

In the optional competition, we did not have the right to perform more than four identical vaults out of twenty (each gymnast vaulted twice). Four well-learned "bend-unbend" (Yamashita) vaults were assigned, one each to Elvira Saadi and Lyuda Turischeva and two to Olga Korbut. For Tamara, a more complicated vault was assigned—a handspring on, full turn off.

Vikenti Dmitriev spoke quietly, as always, but I saw that he was anxious.

"We must hedge a bit. One vault will be "bend-unbend" (Yamashita).

Was he right? Probably. You know, Dmitriev was asking something not only from his student but from the leader of the championship. But it will be the fifth vault of one type and from the team result they'll take away three tenths of a point. Of course, now, after the victory, one may say: what's three tenths to us? Look by how much we won! But then, before the treacherous apparatus we were not so bold. To risk the team medal? I look at Vikenti and he sighs. He is not only the coach of Tamara Lazakovich; he is coach of the Soviet team.

"Let's just see how she vaults," he said.

We go to the warm-up room and watch how Tamara is doing her handspring on, full turn off vault.

Of, course, the Yamashita is more reliable. Tamara knows this, so do I and so does Dmitriev; but if she does it well, she'll get a better score for this more difficult vault. In the competition, this vault twice let Tamara down. Her only mistakes in four days of competition. In this way were lost hundredths of a point without which she could not attain to the silver medal in the all-around. Conscientiously lost! For the sake of the team! To this day, I feel guilty towards Tamara.

The traditions of the team. They are such that you will shine more brightly if you have stumbled on the day before. Not to yield but to attack. The girls from the GDR team performed on beam before us. They had decided not to risk and left something out of their optional programs. The difficulty was not sufficient. It seemed this was the only retreat from this strong, well organized team, and it did not lead to success: three gymnasts made serious mistakes. Well, from this nobody is insured. Our decision was this: on the last apparatus, beam, where balance is difficult, we would demonstrate everything that we had prepared, not to give up a single thing. As it happened, things got going better and better, and when Lyuda Turischeva landed, it seemed that our team in this last exercise scored even more than in our crowning floor exercise. For the first time in my memory, three gymnasts on one team received the same score of 9.75 (Turischeva, Korbut, and Lazakovich).

These traditions of the team are the reason, I believe, why we won the team championship.

In the all-around, Olga Korbut, as we know, made mistakes on bars and lost two whole points. She cried after she left the podium but wiped away her tears, shook her head and strode off to the next apparatus. When she completed her exercise on beam, her last apparatus, I remembered the phrase, "Nothing in life can knock you out of the saddle."

Of Ludmilla Turischeva's ultimate victory in the all-around, I reflected that there are puzzling swings in sport in which stand coach and student: on the one end, an adult person; on the other, a little girl. Not so long ago, Rastorotsky asked, "Kak zovut ettu dyebochku?", "What's the name of this little girl?" And nobody knew then that this name would be repeated in gymnasiums, would be keyed on teletypewriters and written out on illuminated scoreboards. Of course, on that day of first acquaintance the coach could not think of such a metamorphosis, but he dreamed of it, as he did with his other students.

How difficult it is to realize one's dreams. In 1966 in Tashkent, I accidentally heard almost a monologue from Shtukman, almost because it was in answer to a question.

"Everything is clear to me. But how to communicate it? How?"

It was Shtukman who taught Lyubov Burda the "Burda Twirl" (a one and a half horizontal turn on bars). Nobody knows how much time it took Shtukman to create this twirl and how much time it took him to create the floor exercise to the music of Bach. Coach and student worked on it for three years.

Burda performed well in Munich, but her fifth place all-around did not please Shtukman. That means he will continue his search. You see, the strength of a coach lies in that with each new student he strives to walk

> along a new path. With Shtukman, after Tamara Lyukina and Irina Pervushina, there was Lyubov Burda; for Dmitriev, after Larissa Petrick, he brought up Tamara Lazakovich; and with Knysh, after Elena Volchetskaya and Tamara Alekseyeva, he discovered Olga Korbut. And Knysh maintains: "I needed all my former experience only to disprove it in Korbut."

This is the end of excerpts from Latynina's book.

In the years that followed Munich, Lazakovich, Burda, and Koshel were replaced in the 1974 World Championships in Varna by Nina Dronova, Rusiko Sikharulidze, and Nelli Kim. For the 1976 Olympics in Montreal, Dronova and Sikharulidze were replaced by Maria Filatova and Svetlana Grozdova. Throughout the long four-year period 1972 to 1976, Latynina held the Soviet team together with a nucleus of Turischeva, Korbut, and Saadi. The brightest spot in the history of that period for Latynina, however, was the emergence of Nelli Kim. Yet even that was not enough to withstand the effect upon her of Nadia Comaneci's performance in the Montreal Olympics.

The Soviets won the team competition but lost the all-around. The managers of Soviet gymnastics thought Nadia's victory presaged a basic change in women's gymnastics. "You with your choreography have become out of date."[2] The future, they said, lies with such acrobatically-gifted stars as Maria Filatova. "I was convinced that the gymnastics of super tricks is no more than a tribute to fashion, a temporary appearance and that it is necessary to preserve with care our own traditions of elegant choreography and artistry. The arguments went on more and more bitterly, and I felt that what they wanted was for me to leave. They seemed to want this very much. So I left."[3]

"My departure from the post of senior coach of the USSR women's team in 1977 was very painful for me. The officials of the sports committee of that time imputed to me the blame for the natural gifts, the outstanding talent of the famous gymnast, Nadia Comaneci. We lost to her then (in the 1976 Olympics) although our team was stronger. Only Nelli Kim could stand up to her. I was not able to explain to the bureaucrats that the beautiful outward appearance and physical abilities of the Romanian gymnast were gifts from God against which we could not compete. But mine was like a voice crying in the wilderness: nobody wanted to understand me; they only wanted to blame me. I was not able to endure the undeserved shame and wrote my letter of resignation. It was very hard for me to leave the women's team which I had nurtured."[4]

"Now after so many years—years which were happy, for I was not lost, I was not forgotten—I am proud in that I was proved right. Gymnastics has recovered its beauty."[3]

"The elegance of Svetlana Boguinskaya, the artistic nature of Elena Shevchenko, the lyricism of Svetlana Baitova, the soft lines of Natalya Kalinina . . . are pleasing returns from the gymnastics of supertricks . . . to the gymnastics of inspiration."[3]

Of the three, she esteemed Boguinskaya most highly. "When (in 1987) I first saw Svetlana Boguinskaya, I immediately said she should be on the team getting ready for the world championships in Rotterdam. And, you know, when the question was decided who should be on the team—Boguinskaya from Minsk or Shevchenko from my own Moscow team—people could not understand why I supported the candidacy of Svetlana. But it was because of her beauty, her artistry."[5]

Later she said: "I am happy that women's gymnastics is leaning more and more toward femininity and beauty. You know, it was not so long ago that everything was subordinated to stunts and difficulty. Such an approach was justified when gymnastics had become stale and needed to be moved in a new direction. Now difficulty has become normal and judges more and more give preference to gymnasts who are older and beautiful."[6]

Latynina today.

The bitterness of her departure in 1977 from the post of senior coach of the Soviet women's team gave way to happiness and satisfaction as gymnasts from her Moscow clubs began to shine. (After accepting her resignation as national coach, the gymnastics authorities had given her the consolation of appointment to the post of senior coach for Moscow gymnastics.) Such gymnasts were 1981 world champion Olga Bicherova, 1983 beam world champion Olga Mostepanova and 1988 team member Elena Shevchenko.

A further reward came in 1989 when she was awarded the Olympic Order by the International Olympic Committee. "When they (the Soviet

Gymnastics Federation) gave me the telex of congratulations from President Samaranch, I was overjoyed. I consider this award given not only for my sporting past but for my 10 years as national coach, for having given 36 years of my life to big-time sport."[6]

In September 1993, correspondent Lilya Kovalyova was able to interview Latynina.

> For almost a year I have not been working and I am happy about it. For the previous two years I was deputy director of a charitable fund, 'Physical Culture and Health.' (This was a special commission to help former sportsmen who were in financial difficulty. Latynina saw it as a real opportunity to help people.)
>
> **Where are you living now?**
>
> I live in a one-room apartment. It is big enough, however, and is cozy. It is on the old Moscow street, Vakrushina. I was able to convert my three-room apartment and give two rooms to my daughter and grandson. I like my home today very much . . . . We have a lot suitable for a dacha outside of Moscow, but gardening and looking after the land is not my cup of tea. I love simply to ramble in the picturesque countryside.
>
> **Would you mind telling us about your married life?**
>
> Not at all. It is what stimulates my life today. I am happy in my marriage. I was lucky: I met a wonderful man, with whom I have been able to live not one but several lives. My husband, Yuri Feldman, is an electrical engineer by profession, but he is now general director of the Dynamo Association. In his day, Yuri was national champion of velo-sport (cycle racing). He also sang in the 'Seekers' ensemble. He is still able to work with his hands. In a word, he can do many things.
>
> **Has your career had an influence on your family?**
>
> It is difficult to answer that question. For many years I had to do not only women's work but also men's. Now I have reliable support and I can relax. My home is good for me. Therefore, when my husband proposed that I should leave the charitable fund and occupy myself with the home, I agreed with pleasure. I do not regret anything. It is only now that I feel what it means to be a woman: it is wonderful.
>
> **Tell us about your children.**
>
> I have a daughter Tanya. Since she was 17 she danced in the 'Beryoska' ensemble. She worked with them for 15 years. Then four years ago, her husband said 'Enough'. And she, like me, obeyed. Now she spends her time bringing up my only grandson, 12-year-old Konstantin. In addition, Tanya is studying foreign languages. Our Kostick (Konstantin) is also studying for-

eign languages and takes a great interest in Karate. I am well pleased with my children.

Do you take part in any sport now and what is it?

Yes. For several years Yuri and I with great pleasure have been playing tennis, even though it was only a short time ago that I first picked up the racket. This year we vacationed on the Black Sea. Out of 12 days, we devoted 11 to tennis. From this game I receive a great amount of positive emotion."[4]

References

[1]Larissa Latynina, *Kak zovut ettu devochky?* (Moscow: Pravda, 1974) No. 35 in a series of booklets located in the Ogonyok library.

[2]I. Marinov, "Was Nadia Comaneci Really My Fault?" *Sovietsky Sport,* 10 Oct.1992.

[3]Vladimir Golubev, "The Inimitable Larissa Latynina," *Olympic Panorama,* Mar. 1989, published by *Sovietsky Sport.*

[4]Lilya Kovalyova, "With Latynina Everything is OK," Sept. 1993. Article written for this book.

[5]Natalya Kalugina, "Athletes Have a Difficult Character," *Sovietsky Sport,* 5 Jan. 1990.

[6]Elena Vaitsekovskaya, "Now I Am Just Myself," *Sovietsky Sport,* 20 Oct. 1990.

Latynina today

Happy at last. After years of oppression, Vera Caslavska is honored at a meet in Germany shortly after the liberation of Czechoslovakia. With member of the F.I.G. Executive Committee, Hans-Jürgen Zacharias, she shares a private joke.

Vera Caslavska

1942 Born, May 3 in Prague.

1954 Started gymnastics at the age of 12 in the Slovan Prague club. Her first coach was Vladimir Prorok; later it was Eva Bosakova.

1958 World Championships, Moscow, July: 8th, all-around (Latynina, 1st).

1959 European Championship, Cracow, May; 8th, all-around; 2nd, vault; 1st, beam.

1960 Olympics, Rome, August: 8th, all-around (Latynina, 1st); 6th, beam.

1961 European Championship, Leipzig, June: 3rd, all-around (Latynina, 1st); 3rd, floor.

1962 World Championships, Prague, July: 2nd, all-around (Latynina, 1st); 1st, vault; 5th, bars, beam; 3rd, floor.

1964 Olympics, Tokyo, October: 1st, all-around (Latynina, 2nd); 1st, vault; 5th, bars; 1st, beam; 6th, floor.

1965 European Championship, Sofia, May: 1st, all-around (Latynina, 2nd); 1st, vault, bars, beam, floor.

1966 World Championships, Dortmund, September: 1st, all-around (Kuchinskaya, 2nd); 1st, vault; 4th, bars; 2nd, beam; 1st, floor.

1967 European Championship, Amsterdam, May: 1st, all-around; 1st, vault, bars, beam, floor.

1968 Signed "Manifesto of 2,000 Words."

1968 Olympics, Mexico, October: 1st, all-around; 1st, vault, bars; 2nd, beam; 1st, floor (tie–Petrick).

1968 Married Josef Odlozil

1968–1975
Unemployed. Out of favor with Czech government.

1975–1979
Coach at Sparta Club, Prague

1979–1981
Coach of Mexican national women's team.

1981–1992
Coach at Sparta

January 1990 to July 1992
Adviser to Czech President Vaclav Havel on matters of health care and welfare.

September 1992
President of Czech National Olympic Committee.

Vera Caslavska's is, perhaps, the greatest story of achievement thus far in the history of women's gymnastics. It is a story of happiness and bitterness; of love; of joy and sadness; of hope and despair; of emptiness; and finally of fulfillment and happiness again.

From modest beginnings in communist Czechoslovakia, she twice became Olympic champion, a national heroine; then she became a political outcast, a non-person, shunned even by her friends; and finally she was personally honored by the President of the Czech Republic. She is now President of the Czech National Olympic Committee.

The outline of her life can be gleaned from the chronology. During the first part of her life, she had an enormously successful gymnastic career, one that spanned ten years on her national team, from the 1958 World Championships to the 1968 Olympics. During the first half of her career, she was the chief rival of Larissa Latynina; during the second half, her rivalry was with Natalya Kuchinskaya. Her major achievements are described elsewhere in this book. If nothing else had happened, she might have simply retired from competition and become a coach and a judge. But something else did happen, and it is that which makes Vera Caslavska's life so special.

On June 27, 1968, Ludvik Vaculik, a life-long communist and a candidate member of the Central Committee of the Czech Communist Party, published a manifesto entitled *Two Thousand Words.* Initially signed by seventy scholars and scientists in Czechoslovakia, the manifesto expressed concern about conservative elements in the party (and condemned outside interference in Czech affairs, meaning by the Soviets). It enumerated specific democratic and liberal measures for immediate implementation. The Presidium of the Czech Communist Party disavowed and denounced the manifesto—which over 40,000 persons signed within weeks—but by this time the Soviet Union had become thoroughly alarmed by the direction and tempo of events. The Soviets had already issued warnings and these warnings were repeated.[1]

Vera Caslavska was one of those who signed the manifesto. Her signing reflected the yearning of the Czech people for freedom to run their own affairs; her action reflected the social atmosphere that existed which had resulted from the more liberal policies of Prime Minister Alexander Dubcek which were instituted during what was known as "The Prague Spring." Although thousands of people had joined her in signing the manifesto, it was nevertheless an act of defiance, especially by one who was already a prominent figure in the country as the result of her 1964 Olympic victory and her subsequent World and European victories. Remembering the Soviet invasion of Hungary twelve years earlier under similar circumstances, she well knew what the consequences for her might be. Her signing was, therefore, an act of courage. The worst fears of the Czech people were realized on August 20, 1968, when Red Army tanks crashed into Prague and the Soviets occupied the whole country.

The events of her story have been described by two correspondents who were able to interview her. One of the correspondents was Michael Janovsky of *The New York Times,* excerpts from whose article from the issue of April 9, 1990 are quoted below. (Copyright ©1990 by The New York Times Company. Reprinted by permission.)

> At the time, the Olympic gymnastics team was training in Moravia (a region of central Czechoslovakia). What happened next, Caslavska said, she has never before disclosed.
>
> A friend warned her that she might be imprisoned if the authorities found her. So he helped her escape into the tiny town of Sumperk in the Jeseniky Mountains, where she stayed for three weeks.
>
> She grew disconsolate, aware that the Soviet gymnasts, her fiercest rivals, had already traveled to Mexico City to adapt to the climate and altitude. She, meanwhile, was stuck in Sumperk, with the most rudimentary of training opportunities.
>
> As the Games approached, she rejoined her teammates by permission of the authorities. In Mexico City, she won the all-around, three other gold medals and two silvers.
>
> A day after her final event, she married a Czechoslovak 1,500 meter runner, Josef Odlozil (who had won the silver medal in this event in Tokyo), and returned home to start a family and complete her autobiography. But she found that the government had not forgotten she had signed the manifesto.
>
> She could not get her autobiography published, no doubt because 140 pages were devoted to how Czechoslovakia's sport system worked and how government officials treated athletes and sports administrators. In time, she had it published in Japan, but without the sections deemed unacceptable by the Czechoslovak authorities.
>
> On January 3, 1970, she began another fight. She asked the Sports Minister, Antonin Himmel, for a job with the national girls' gymnastics team. He refused, saying: 'Come back next year. This is not a suitable time yet.'
>
> For five years, every January 3, she appeared in the same office, asking for the same job.
>
> "For the fifth year, I was supposed to apply again, but I knew it was necessary to change my way of negotiating," she said. "So I dressed in an aerobics suit, high in the neck, very tight. I am quite a conservative person, and it was hard for me to dress like that, but I had to look for my courage."
>
> "Mr. Himmel looked at me and measured me with his eyes. He asked me: 'Vera, what have you got on? Are you crazy?' I answered him: 'No, but

I was supposed to come back on the third of January and apply for work, and now I'm here, dressed for work. And I'm not leaving until you give me a team and a gymnastics hall in which to work.'

He was not able to decide such a thing alone. He called all of his advisers into the room. A full 20 men stared at me. They finally decided I could get a team, but it had to be done in a very secret way.

To save face with their superiors, the sports authorities allowed Caslavska only to work with the current coaches. She could not be allowed to travel outside the country. In time, the authorities offered to loosen their grip if she would deny publicly that she had signed the manifesto. She refused.

Her absence from view lasted another five years, until 1979, when Czechoslovakia was trying to improve ties with Mexico. The Mexican President, José Lopez Portillo, remembered her from the 1968 Olympics, and asked the authorities if Caslavska would be permitted to come to Mexico to work with young Mexican gymnasts.

"I don't want to say I was exchanged for oil," Caslavska said, with a laugh. But she was allowed to go and spent the next two years there.

Even after her return, however, the authorities tried to keep her hidden. On a 1984 visit to Czechoslovakia, the president of the International Olympic Committee, Juan Antonio Samaranch, asked to see her and Emil Zatopek, the distance runner who won three gold medals at the 1952 Helsinki Olympics. Samaranch was told that Zatopek was ill and that Caslavska had family problems.

A year later, Samaranch returned and insisted upon presenting Zatopek and Caslavska with the Olympic Order, in silver.

This time, the authorities relented and from that point on, they were unable to deny her existence any longer. She was allowed to join the European Gymnastics Union as a representative of the country and become a full-time coach with the national team preparing for the Seoul Olympics.

A year later, when the Communists were ousted from control of the government, she began serving as an adviser to President Havel on matters of health care, human rights, physical education and sports.[2]

In an interview with *Equipe-Magazine*, republished in *Sovietsky Sport* in 1990, Caslavska told more about the story of her misfortunes.

Upon my return from the Mexico Olympics in 1968, I was among a group of people who signed what was known as "The Manifesto of 2000 Words." . . . With this, it all began. They threw my husband out of the army; they denied me any kind of work whatever. The most difficult problem turned out to be something else, however. It was the constant pressure whose aim was to change my mind about signing the manifesto. (They wanted her to say she had not signed it.) Several people did this. But I never went back on my word and did what I believed best.

The most difficult time began later, in 1970. My friends, spotting me in the street, crossed to the other side so that we would not meet on the same sidewalk. They were afraid for themselves.

Did the thought of leaving Czechoslovakia not occur to you?

I drove it out of my mind. This is my country, where my parents and children live, where I grew up.

Were you not afraid of having a breakdown?

Many times. One day—and I will always remember the date, the 7th of January 1971—they invited me to drop in at my own club, Red Star. I went there with my heart beating hard from anxiety, sure, however, that they were finally going to offer me some work. I went into the office and said, "Hello." Nobody answered. Nobody invited me to sit down. But the president of the club announced a summons for a preparatory meeting to discuss the expulsion of Vera Caslavska—27 voted "yes"; nobody voted "no." I was speechless. After several days, they expelled me from the federation.

Did the pressure continue?

It continued, but as before I stood my ground and refused to sign anything. One evening I noticed that a car of the type used by employees of the security service had stopped by my house. Two men knocked on my door, demanded that I should dress. I woke up my son and took him with me. They took me to the Ministry of Internal Affairs. We went along long, very long corridors. At each corner, there were policemen. And suddenly, I felt that I was a prisoner and I cried. Around Martin's neck was a small, orange scarf. I wiped my tears on the end of it. Again, as I had before, I told the functionaries that I was not changing my ideas.

And when this interview ended?

I wrote Gustav Husak, who was the future president of the republic and who was at that time general secretary of the party. He received me. He is a very intelligent man. He explained to me that he had to do many things that were not popular but that this was his duty. Then he asked me what I was doing. I answered that I was not doing anything. I said everything that was on my mind.

Until 1975, nothing changed. Each January, I met with Antonin Himmel, chairman of the Czech union of physical culture, and each year he would tell me to wait a little longer. In 1975, I put on an extremely low-cut T-shirt under my coat and went to meet him. He asked me: "what's the reason for your appearance?" I answered that it was my working appearance, my working clothes. And I added: "give me work or I will tell my story to all the world, to all foreign journalists." Thus, I became a coach at "Sparta." You see what a long story it is.

Then came your trip to Mexico?

In 1979, Mexican President Portillo asked me to be head coach of the national gymnastics team. The heads of the communist party agreed: in Mexico I was less dangerous than in Prague. I returned after two years, having lost in that time my brother, then my father, and soon my mother.

The Japanese adore you and the Mexicans cannot forget you. That is what Olympic medals mean.

That's correct. Not accidentally in 1985 President Samaranch of the IOC came to us and declared that I was an example not only in Czechoslovakia but in all the world. That was very important for me. And in Moscow, "Izvestia" and "Komsomolskaya Pravda" published interviews with me. Thus, little by little, my name began to return to the newspapers of the country. I came out of the shadows.

The interviewer asked her where she was when the revolution suddenly started.

I have a small house in the north in Moravia. There I was resting with my children: Martin, who is fourteen years old and Radka, who is twenty-one (as of 1990). Radka did not go to her studies because the students were on strike. We returned to Prague. The next day, the kids were out in the streets all day. In the evening, on television they showed the mass demonstration (in Wenceslas Square). "Something unexpected was about to happen," I thought. And then in my mind the first lines of my declaration were beginning to form.

Which said. . .

That our children helped us to raise our heads up and that now we should help them. That we of the older generation have too long lived in an atmosphere of fear, that we were already on the threshold of revolution. I went to the premises of the newspaper *Free Word*. There I met Havel. I read my text to him, commenting after I had done so that it was too wordy. "If each word in this declaration is important to you, then it cannot be too long," Havel said in answer. Then and there I understood what democracy is: here is a text which nobody had corrected or shortened; and I read this declaration from the balcony. I said that we had set our sights on the marathon distance, that we had only just begun and that victory would not be easy or simple.

Had you known Havel for a long time?

I first saw him in 1986 at a small students' theatre.

Is it true that after his election he offered you very important posts?

Yes. Minister of Sports Affairs, Ambassador to Japan and candidate for Mayor of Prague. I declined all these offers. To become Minister of Sport? We talked it over for a long time; but, in my opinion, this is a post a for experienced politicians or administrators and, in any case, not for a woman. Besides, managing sport at the highest levels, with its problems of money and drugs, was not my sort of work.

But Japan?

I have remained unbelievably popular there since the day of my Olympic victory in 1964. The president supposed that this might facilitate making contacts in the financial world, for the writing of contracts. But to be so far from my homeland at this moment, here where so much that was important was going on, such as victory in the general election in June, I decided to remain as an adviser. That's my job.

What did the revolution do for sport?

First of all, renewal—of people, of systems. We needed to do everything over again, to reconstruct everything. Of course, this will take some time but we must resolve the accumulated problems. And to let the sportsmen themselves move sport forwards: nobody else.

Did it fall to you, in your capacity as an adviser to the President, to take upon yourself the problems of sport?

There remained such an inheritance from the past that in the first instance we needed to resolve problems of industry, economics, education, medicine and international relations. Only then, sport. I do not mean to say that we remembered sportsmen at the last minute, but that sport would have to come later

Do you love sport as much as ever?

It will be with me all my life. Until now I have been coaching young children. It is my basic job because I am not paid for being adviser to the President. I coach three times a week and I insist on keeping my coaching job because I remember how hard it was for me to get it.[3]

She became President of the Czech national Olympic committee in 1992. With this paid job, she no longer coaches at Sparta and she has ceased to be an adviser to President Havel on matters of health care and welfare. People continue to call her for help, however, and she still tries to help them.

Three years earlier in an interview with *Sovietsky Sport,* Vera Caslavska talked more about herself.

What was more difficult—the road to Olympus or that which came after sport?

It was much easier to win the world championships and the Olympics than to bring up a child properly, even one child.

Vera, you are now a coach. What parting words do you give your student when she stands at the threshold that separates sport and ordinary, personal, non-sporting life?

Most likely I will say: "Forget flowers, medals, glory. Forget you are a champion, if, of course, that happens. Remember your bruises after a fall, your leotard wet from sweat as you leave the gym and begin all over again." Yes, I will say just that. But I will also say that nobody can forget his past, especially something so bright as sport. Day after day, evening after evening, we are sentenced to return to our past, full of hope and the expectation of happiness.

What is your strongest impression of sport?

All impressions in sport were strong.

What minutes, hours or, perhaps, days do you remember as the happiest of your life?

When my girls complain that they are deadly tired, that they have no more strength, I say to them, "Time passes and you will remember these workouts as the very greatest happiness, the greatest joy in your life. Why? Simply because everything is ahead of you, because it is still only morning and you do not know what the day will bring. But morning is surprisingly sunny, fresh and from it you live in expectation of happiness, of a miracle."

You have devoted your life to sport. But if you found yourself again confronted with the choice: sport or. . .

A long time ago, I excluded from my vocabulary the words, "what if."

But just the same.

If I had had sufficient talent, I would probably have tried to become an artist.

Is that only a dream?

I really do paint. Countrysides. In oil. I did a lot of painting in Mexico when I worked as coach of the national team. There are bright colors there, rich colors. Not to take up the brush is simply a sin. In spite of everything, however, I am slavic and my spirit is closer to our quieter, low countryside—the milk of fog, spilling about the fields, rain by the edge of the forest. I am not such a big artist that I should talk about it.

Vera, what tournament was the most difficult for you?

The 1967 European Championships in Amsterdam. Kuchinskaya was performing. A year before at the world championships in Dortmund, she had won three gold medals in the apparatus finals, even though at that time I was in good shape. Before the European Championships, however, things were not going well for me. My coach and I decided to change our program completely, to make it more difficult, to renew it. Nobody believed I would win, nor did I. Yet that was not the most important thing. Kuchinskaya . . . in Dortmund everybody loved her. But, oh, how it was in Mexico! Do you remember? The name of Natasha was on everybody's tongue. The Bride of Mexico. Yet I had many times beaten her. Everyone wants a new champion. It is natural.

Kuchinskaya and Caslavska. Caslavska won on the podium; Kuchinskaya won the hearts of the spectators. Vera won in Amsterdam; Kuchinskaya did not hold up: she fell landing her vault. In spite of that, Natasha was the prima donna of Mexico, the bride of Mexico, although Caslavska won the all-around gold. With Caslavska's victory, there was always a bitter-sweet taste. Like a good piece of news long delayed; like a love that came late.

Vera when did you finally decide to leave sport?

That happened long before the beginning of the 1968 Olympics. The first time I thought about leaving was when Kuchinskaya appeared on the world podium for the first time—so young, so beautiful. It seemed to me that I could not compete against her. But then I felt a certain impulse: I wanted to beat just such a multi-faceted rival.

It is important that a sportsman should leave at the right time, to decide exactly when, to do it when one is in flight, to break off one's sporting song on the very highest note. I remember how they persuaded my good friend and my coach Eva Bosakova (7th in Melbourne, 1956; 10th in Rome, 1960) to stay in gymnastics a while longer. She had wanted to leave the podium after the Rome Olympics. I witnessed her difficult decline. She worked out frantically, she exhausted herself, but her lightness and confidence did not return. In my opinion, it was pointless self-torture. Then and there I made a solemn promise not to give in to any persuasion a coach might make for me to continue.

Much has changed in the past twenty years of gymnastics; difficulty has spiraled upwards. There is a huge distance between your gymnastics and the gymnastics of today. What do you think has been added and what has been lost?

It is difficult for me to be impartial because I was a member of the former generation. Our sport has become much more complicated, more risky, more technical. Technique has grown to heights that were unimaginable for us. Probably there is beauty in the difficulty of gymnastics but I am sorry for that gymnastics which has gone. It was more inspired, more feminine. You can't make progress go backwards; still and all, it's a pity. I will say I was happy that in the gymnastics that I have been seeing in Moscow there were not just tiny gymnasts. That's a good sign.

What qualities in your opinion should a contemporary gymnast possess? Should she be acquainted with a feeling of fear?

I can assure you that everyone without exception is acquainted with the feeling of fear. Do not believe anyone who says the opposite. The qualities of a gymnast? Probably the same ones which any contemporary woman should possess—decisiveness, intellect, will . . . femininity.[4]

Vera Caslavska now works in an office in the old part of Prague, on Narodnyy Street, a few blocks off from Wenceslas Square towards the Vlatava River. Though it is in the interesting part of the city that has changed little over the years, it is by no means a fancy office. She has a personal secretary and about three other assistants. From this small establishment, she has to run the Czech Olympic program. She still receives delegations from Japan, as well as many other visitors. Her days are full, in fact, hectic. Yet her days of fear are gone. With a clear conscience, knowing that she did not kneel to the oppressor, she can enjoy the gift of freedom.

References

[1]The American University, Czechoslovakia, a country study, 1989.

[2]Michael Janovsky, "A Czechoslovak Hero Gets Luxury of Choice," *The New York Times,* 9 Apr. 1990.

[3]O. Polonskaya, "'Vera', Hope, Love," *Sovietsky Sport,* May, 1987.

[4]Editorial Staff, "I Did Not Kneel," *Sovietsky Sport,* 7 Apr. 1990.

Natalya Alexandrovna Kuchinskaya

1965 East Bloc Tournament of Friendship: 1st, all around.
1966 USSR National Championships: 1st all-around.
1966 World Championships, Dortmund, Germany, September: 2nd, all-around; 3rd, vault; 1st, bars, beam, floor.
1967 European Championship, Amsterdam, May: 9th, all-around; 5th, vault; 2nd, beam; 2nd, floor.
1967 Spartakiade, Moscow, July (USSR National Championships): 1st, all-around.
1967 Mexico, pre-Olympic Tournament, October: 1st, all-around.
1968 USSR National Championships: 1st, all-around.
1968 Olympics, Mexico, October: 3rd, all-around; 1st, beam.

"We fell in love with Natasha! It was impossible not to love her." So, in her memoirs, said Larissa Latynina, the senior coach of the Soviet women's team from 1968 to 1976. Indeed, it seemed all Mexico was in love with her in 1968. "Natasha, the bride of Mexico" was on everybody's lips.

I remember my first conversation about Natasha. It was in the winter of 1965, when 15-year-old Larissa Petrick had already won the USSR Championships. (Latynina was still a member of the team.)

"Why not put her on the national team?" we asked one of the team coaches.

"We are planning to," he answered. "On the other hand, she doesn't have much future. She's inclined to plumpness. Besides her character . . . ."

And Kuchinskaya, "who doesn't have much future" became in 1966 the national champion. She then won three gold medals in the 1966 Dortmund World Championships, taking second all-around. In the 1968 Mexico Olympics, she was the leader of the team.

What was the reason for Natasha's popularity in Mexico? Was it, perhaps, in Natasha's successful performances in preliminary competitions in Mexico in 1966 and 1967? Perhaps her smile and her charm had their effect upon Mexicans. To this day, I don't know. One thing I will say: the role of the bride of Mexico which was fastened on her seemed very difficult for her in the face of her responsibilities toward the competition. Clearly the leader, she drew people to her.

A strong team brings out a strong leader and she gives special coloring to the whole team. In Mexico, we competed with just such a team and we won. And not only did we show that the team was strong, but Zina Voronina took second all-around and Larissa Petrick won gold in floor exercise. And the leader? Natasha fell from bars and lost a whole point but, even so, took third place all-around and won a gold medal on beam.

It was the first victory after Dortmund and the last performance of Natasha Kuchinskaya in big-time gymnastics. She fell ill and we were left without a leader. It is bitter but more to the point to say that we lost a leader. And if already the word "bitter" is said, we must say we lost her not only from sickness. Now we recognize she did not have good luck with coaches.

I know these words will raise shame in their minds. And the question, "did we not win with her?"

Coaches. They teach girls much about gymnastics. But of life? We think of them in that moment when Natasha answered the question—are you happy? She thought and then said, "I was happy but not now".

Coaches cannot answer for the fate of athletes throughout their lives, but there are moments when much is in their hands. Were they responsible for Natasha's wretchedness? Certainly her departure was a misfortune—and for me, too. In March 1969, Natasha became twenty. Under blue spring evening skies, we celebrated Natasha's first birthday as an adult. And although the feast was not big and not noisy, she felt shy and only when she heard something about her future did she look up.

"You must understand that for several years I very much wanted to stay in this situation, so that everyone would love me and would forgive me. That's a childish wish. Right? But childhood is already gone, once and for all." said Natasha wistfully.

(She did not leave right away but trained for the national championships of 1969 in Leningrad. Latynina continues:)

We all waited for Natasha in the gym. When she came, she watched the competition and said: "I am not afraid of not being first. But then what? Who needs it?" And she did not begin to compete. Natasha came to the team as the leader, and as leader she left.[1]

For many years afterwards, her fans hoped for a miracle, that they would once again see her fascinating performances on their television screens. In an interview with *Sovietsky Sport* correspondent, Natalya Kalugina, she answered:

Unfortunately, this was not possible. I was very tired, I felt spiritually wasted. At that time I was going through a reappraisal of my values. When I performed, I felt like a young girl, a schoolgirl. Sport seemed to me like youthful enthusiasm, to which I gave my wholehearted strength.

When I finished competing, I was prepared to occupy myself with whatever I pleased, only not sport. So I dreamed about journalism, then I studied psychology, then I was carried away by the stage. I even prepared an acrobatic number for the circus. It seemed to me that sport for adults was not a serious occupation. When, however, I decided to become an actress and was ready for it, I remembered my sporting past, that when I competed I thought not of my success in front of the spectators but of the honor of the country. It dawned on me that sport is a most important social sphere of human life. I wanted to return to sport, and I went to the central children's sport school in Kiev, where I work and now teach young gymnasts.

When asked if she liked her work, she replied,

Very much, though to put it all together was not simple. For a long time I was not able to understand what it was these little kids needed from me. They would run into the gym and, with wide open eyes, look up at their coach. I came to the school, honestly worked the necessary hours but ran home, trying to forget my problems at work as quickly as possible. To tell you truly, I derived very little pleasure from my work.

Then occurred some kind of an inner revolution. I began to run not from work but to work. I wanted to see my kids constantly and teach them everything that I was able to do and that was being demanded by contemporary gymnastics. I came to love them and now cannot imagine myself without them. Perhaps it's a family tradition: my father, mother and sister are all coaches.

About her most important task, she said,

To bring up children as good people! In sport, especially with young people, you have problems besides gymnastics. Children must train many hours to achieve results on a high level. These hours cut out time for studies, the theatre and socializing with friends. With some of them, a sort of sporting fanaticism develops. This I fear most of all. While our students are young and locked into their sections, they do not understand the many-sided outside world. And this is not all bad—at least they are not out in the street. But children grow up and it comes time for them to leave gymnastics. They leave behind many people of their own age. Their education is less and they know little of life. They may be twenty years old. To catch up is much more difficult than if they had kept pace with others.

I want my kids to be honest and whole, but I cannot assume full responsibility. You understand, big sport is, in once sense, cruel. When you are riding high, when you are achieving results worthy of note, then everybody needs you; but when you leave the sporting arena, then they forget about you. In gymnastics, this blossoming out happens at 15 or 16 years old, when the girl is not yet fully formed as a person. Her head has been affected by applause, flowers and articles written in her praise. From this there is formed in girls I would say a complex of their own exclusiveness, which appears as egoism. At 20 years, she finishes performing and attention to her evaporates, as if she did not exist. She becomes like everyone else, only a bit worse because the book that everyone has read she has not read—she had to hurry off to training; the film everyone has seen she has not seen—she was at a competition; about her future occupation or profession, which others have already selected, she has not thought.

It is not that I am against big-time sport, but I think you must try to safeguard children against its costs—serious injuries, excessive psychological pressure. **It is necessary in the first place to preserve the person in the child while creating the gymnast.** Then perhaps it will soften the blow that awaits them in the future when they move apart from sport. How to do this, I do not know.[2]

A few months later, Natalya Kalugina wrote her own impressions about Natalya Kuchinskaya.

If you asked me would I give my child to gymnastics, I would answer "yes" but with this reservation: if she could be in Natalya Kuchinskaya's group. Not at all because she was a famous gymnast from the Olympics. Quite the contrary, Kuchinskaya is just an ordinary children's coach, of which we have in our country thousands (in 1988). She has not trained one single champion.

Did I write "ordinary children's coach"? Why then, knowing about the constantly evolving complexity of gymnastics, about how much strength a gymnast expends while becoming a master, do I confidently say: I would give her to Kuchinskaya? What is special about this delicate woman with the typically short stature of a gymnast? Why do I believe in her more than in others?

Once I went with Kuchinskaya from Kiev to Moscow. We enthusiastically discussed the future of our women's gymnastics team in the upcoming world championships (Rotterdam, 1987). In the end, a neighbor in our compartment could not bear not to ask: "Forgive me, where do you work? You are talking all the time about sport."

Without mentioning anything about myself, I replied, "My friend is Olympic champion, Natalya Kuchinskaya, the 'Bride of Mexico'."

Natasha's reaction was completely unexpected.

"Don't. So much time has passed since then. . . . Consider that that never happened. I am a gymnastics coach. I teach the youngest children how to move."

Only later when I got to know Kuchinskaya better, did I understand how organic to her was her answer: not a particle of posing—only the truth, until it hurts, the simple truth—that what was has passed, and now she is a children's coach.

Does that mean Natasha stopped being a leader? In no way. I sat with her during a workout. The gymnasium was full to overflowing—about three hundred children were training there at one time. On the various apparatus, there were lines; by the choreographer, a line. The coaches were being careful of injuries because of the overcrowding. In Kiev, there existed nine gymnasiums officially, but eight of them were in bureaucratic numbering; and only the gymnastic section where Kuchinskaya worked was prepared to accept children, as they say, "off the street."

Several times coaches brought up the question of new premises for the gymnastic school but it never got beyond the talking stage. Finally, they decided to write a letter and immediately had to confront the problem of who will sign it. There arose a hubbub, like gymnasts talking before a workout. Finally, Kuchinskaya's quiet voice was heard: "I will be the first to sign the letter—my name once meant something." Then everyone else was quiet.

Just as twenty years ago, Natasha led her team, so now she leads her colleagues. Once Kuchinskaya decided to accept responsibility, the matter was decided.

On that day, world champion Oksana Omelyanchick came to Kuchinskaya's group for a workout. For a long time, the girls had known about her coming—they waited, worried about it, prepared themselves for it. Finally, when the day arrived, the girls were unable to pull themselves together to do anything. All they could do was to look at Omelyanchick—how was she working, what was she doing? Oksana worked within herself but selflessly as if on just that workout depended the success of her Olympic season.

What about Kuchinskaya? She made Oksana the principle figure in the workout, but quietly cautioned her about her mistakes, trying to guard against future disappointments. Did Oksana understand her? In her words,

"A workout with Kuchinskaya makes one think about the future. You see, the girls cannot imagine who their coach is. They, dumb ones, spend all their time looking at me instead of trying not to miss one single gesture of

Natalya Alexandrovna. You know it is probably very difficult to forget about who one was, that even to you were sent bouquets of flowers and that you were asked for your autograph, but simply to devote yourself to the kids. I do not know if I could do it. You know, that is my future: I am studying at the Institute of Physical Culture. I shall be a coach."

Returning to Natasha, Kalugina asked, "Natasha, you are from Leningrad. Did you not ever want to return there?"

"I want to sometimes. Although, no. I cannot give them up. You know, my girls believe in me. To whom would I leave them? I stay with them."

Late evening. Besides me, there are only Kuchinskaya and her student, Lena Bandolish. They are learning a new floor exercise. The girl is terribly tired, but again and again they repeat the choreographic connection she cannot seem to get. Do you remember Mexico 1968? Out onto the podium that evening went the heroine of those Olympics—young Natasha Kuchinskaya and she charmed the hall. Now in the gym were only two people, she and young Lena. Lena was tired, but to leave the podium was impossible, as it was twenty years ago.

"Look, Lenochka," says Kuchinskaya, "you are lucky. Besides you, nobody has seen such movements for many years. Show that you are worthy of your coach . . . . There now, you've got it!"

Kuchinskaya and I go home at nighttime in Kiev.

"What do you think of Omelyanchick? Will she be a good coach?"

"She will be. I liked this girl; I liked how she trained and how she talked with my little beauties. She's a kind girl with a good and honest spirit. I am glad she came to our workout. Pray God she has success in Seoul!"

"And does she have enough strength to organize children?"

"She should have. You saw how she worked—she gave herself over completely to her gymnastics. Such attributes of character will lead others; she is that sort of person. You noticed how the kids watched her? They were afraid to take their eyes off her."

The question remains for Natasha: how do you carry the girls along every day with this tough work? For Oksana it was easy: her appearance was a holiday. For Natasha, the answer is equally simple: it is her life.[3]

In August 1994, Natalya Kalugina was able to talk with Kuchinskaya again. She had returned home after spending two and a half years in Japan as a coach. She was in St. Petersburg doing gymnastics commentary on the Goodwill Games for Channel 5. Kalugina wrote this piece, in part, for *Sovietsky Sport*.

I remember you signed a contract unexpectedly. You were not preparing to go anywhere and suddenly you flew away.

Exactly. I did not expect it myself. Do you remember that three years ago I went with the Soviet team to a competition? We were in the town of Izumisano, which is not far from Osaka. At a banquet in our honor, I suddenly and surprisingly said that I liked Japan. The mayor of the town promised they would invite me to come and work there. I returned to Kiev and forgot about the conversation. But here came an invitation and a contract for a year. Then I extended it another year and a half."

What were your responsibilities?

Everything! I was invited not by a club but by the Ministry of Education. So I conducted classes in school and aerobics for older women. I coached a modern rhythmic group and also artistic gymnastics. It was a terribly heavy schedule! The more so because of the tradition in Japan: the head person is the representative of God on earth. Whatever she says, subordinates are required to do and not to deviate one iota from the order.

It seems to me that if the head person blurts out an obvious stupidity, you have to do it?

Uh-huh.

But in artistic gymnastics this is likely to cause injuries.

And how! But here I allowed myself some cunning, some slyness. If a person in charge obviously made a mistake in methodology, I listened to her in full, bowed to her (of course, not like the Japanese who bow from the waist—I did not go that far. Simply I made a movement of the body forward) and when she left the room I organized the element properly.

And if they did not keep quiet about it?

That happened. You must understand, with the Japanese it is not considered wrong. They have a tradition: if you see that someone is disobeying an order, then he should report it. Then the head person would become angry and not speak to me for several days.

Was it forbidden to become good friends with her? So that you could explain the mistakes eye to eye?

You must be kidding! There you can be friends only with people on your level. A manager will not rub shoulders with an ordinary coach outside of work. There, things are not as they are at home, where a manager, respected for his abilities and moral qualities, can socialize without fear of losing respect.

But you were not an ordinary coach. You were an Olympic champion after all.

Oh, they emphasized that at every turn. In the town there was hardly a single banquet at which I was not so honored. But you know, that was even pleasant. Here on our team they forget about the past. But there I remembered the past.

Did they recognize you in the street?

Sometimes it happened. Only this: everything that I have been telling you up to now appears repellent, unpleasant. But after I had lived in Japan for a while, I understood: among the Japanese, their psychology is absolutely different. It has taken shape over the centuries. It is impossible to do anything about it. Either you must leave the country quickly or accept the Japanese as they are. I chose the second and was not sorry about it. I got to know a different people, a different language. In a larger sense, the Japanese people are a kind and generous people. Only they are very reserved.

In what sense?

How can I tell you? A Russian person understands the word sincerity to mean you must come to your friend, unburden yourself of everything that is bothering you and listen to everything that is bothering your friend. The Japanese consider it most important not to lose face, not to cause your friend anxiety over your own pains.

You yourself are very sincere about the Russian understanding of that word. What did you talk about then?

Let us say, we were eating dinner and there was someone there who was especially friendly with me. These conversations were psychologically very difficult for me. As sometimes they wanted to weep a few tears on your shoulder, to see a kindred spirit.

So you studied Japanese?

More or less. Would you like for me to say "flac" in Japanese? It is 'flyak-pokuteh.' I conducted workouts in Japanese.

How did they greet you in Kiev upon your return?

Beautifully. At work, they set up a table, declared a holiday.

You are a coach again?

Yes, but only in rhythmic gymnastics. There has been some sort of crisis. They did not want me to return to artistic gymnastics. Although, now when I am back among my own, I think I will return to it. From one's own people, it is difficult to be away."[4]

References

[1]Larissa Latynina, *What Is This Girl's Name?,* (Moscow: Pravda, 1974.) No. 35 in a series of booklets located in the Ogonyok library.

[2]Natalya Kalugina, "Natalya Kuchinskaya—Gymnastics Is My Love," *Sovietsky Sport,* 2 Sept. 1987.

[3]Natalya Kalugina, "Natalya Kuchinskaya—As the Brightest Light in Life," *Sovietsky Sport,* 24 Mar. 1988.

[4]Natalya Kalugina, "Natalya Kuchinskaya—'I Was an Honored Guest,'" *Sovietsky Sport,* 18 Aug. 1994.

Polina Grigorievna Astakhova

Astakhova and Olga

1956 Olympics, Melbourne, November: 17th, all-around.
1958 World Championships, Moscow, July: 7th, all-around, 3rd, bars.
1959 European Championship, Cracow, Poland, May: 7th, all-around; 1st, bars, beam.
1960 Olympics, Rome, August: 3rd, all-around; 1st, bars; 2nd, floor.
1961 European Championship, Leipzig, June: 2nd, all-around; 1st, bars, beam; 2nd, floor.
1962 World Championships, Prague, July: 8th, all-around; 4th, bars; 4th, floor.
1964 Olympics, Tokyo, October: 3rd, all-around; 1st, bars; 2nd, floor; 4th, beam.
1966 World Championships, Dortmund, Germany, September: 13th, all-around; 5th, bars.
1967 Spartakiade, Moscow, July (USSR National Championships): 4th, all-around.

Millions of television viewers who watched the Munich Olympics will remember Astakhova as the blonde-with-a-pony-tail coach who walked out with the Soviet women's gymnastics team. Because she is tall (for a gymnast), stands erect, has light skin and blonde hair, she is known among her friends and fans as "the Russian birch tree." After a highly successful career as a gymnast, she became a coach. She was appointed to be the walk-on coach for the Soviet ladies in 1972, 1974, 1978 and 1980. Latynina herself was the walk-on coach in the 1976 Olympics. Astakhova's hometown is Kiev, where she coaches beginning girls.

Natalya Kuchinskaya, who was a teammate of Astakhova's in Dortmund and also lives in Kiev, had these reminiscences of her friend:

> She is amazing and has a sense of humor. I remember once when I "collided" with her in training. We were both working on one beam, I on one end and she on the other. We came together in the middle. According to an unwritten law in gymnastics, the younger gymnast is supposed to give way. I wanted to jump off in order to wait for Astakhova, but she jumped off herself and I continued my combination. It was awkward! Astakhova came up to me and said: "Why are you embarrassed? It was convenient for me to dismount."
>
> As a teammate and coach, Astakhova was someone around whom we very young girls could warm ourselves. She was always peaceful, well-wishing. If she felt you were becoming nervous, she would come up to you, touch you on the shoulder, look you in the eye and say something calming. Your worries would disappear. She lived for the team. She remembered all the little things, the trifles. With her, things always went well and easily.[1]

Things did not always go well and easily for Astakhova herself. At the 1960 Olympic Games in Rome, she was confidently leading in the all-around and was about to perform on beam, one of her favorite apparatuses. She began her routine brilliantly, but then fell. Later, she shed tears, but only her teammates saw them. In twenty minutes, she was up on the podium again, this time for floor exercise. It was as though there had never been any tears. She seemed to be inspired. She could not let down the team and fought on to the end.[1]

Another memory for Astakhova relates to the Dortmund, 1966 World Championships. It was the first time in many years that the Soviet Union had lost the team competition. Onto the team had come some young gymnasts—Larissa Petrick, Zinaida Druzhinina, Olga Kharlova, and Natalya Kuchinskaya. Polina Astakhova talked about it:

> Tears? No, you cannot allow that. We smiled. Sport teaches you not only how to win, but also how to lose.
>
> To lose is probably more difficult than to win. It is hard to keep up your face, not to show how it hurts. People should not see it. A woman, especially if people are looking at her, should always be beautiful.

> You understand, it was easier for us. We, Latynina and I, were adults, we fully realized our role in gymnastics, we understood what was demanded of us. For today's gymnasts, it is much harder. They are still just kids!

In answer to the question, "what is your attitude towards contemporary gymnastics?", Astakhova said:

> You should not separate past and present gymnastics. They are united, indivisible. I become upset when I see empty stands at the major championships. Perhaps not everybody likes to see difficult tricks; perhaps they come to see a beautiful sport. Therefore we should think about introducing different age groups for gymnastics. Let older gymnasts not have to leave the sport so soon. They could take part in exhibition performances. Idols of the spectators should live in the sport for a long time. People need them.[1]

In 1976, during the USSR Cup trials for the Montreal Olympic team, Astakhova had these words to say:[2]

> On the 19th of July in Montreal, the winner of the team competition will be decided. In six previous Olympiads, the gold medals for the team competition have been won by Soviet gymnasts.
>
> They are very memorable for me, those days of the Olympiads when the highest awards were handed to us. You cannot imagine our joy—the team award! **It means there were no unsuccessful members of the team,** that all members of the team gave all their strength, all their abilities for the common goal.
>
> In Melbourne, Lidia Ivanova (Kalinina) and I were of the same age. We were terribly excited, made mistakes during the competition and occupied contentedly the last places. Of course, even as debutantes we wanted to win medals in the individual competition; above all else in importance, however, was the team success. For the sake of the team victory, it was important to forget about personal interests, to throw off emotional experiences and to work for the team.
>
> Any team ought to strive for a single goal. Without real unity, without friendship, nothing can be accomplished. Believe me, these are not hackneyed, trite words. Whoever has himself gone through these most difficult Olympic tests knows the value of these words no matter how accustomed he has become to hearing them.
>
> I was lucky: in all the tournaments that I had occasion to participate in, I was a member of a team that simply could not lose. This was because our united strength helped us in the most dramatic moments of the tournament. Each answered for herself and for everyone at the same time. So it was in Melbourne, Rome, Tokyo. So it was in Munich, where I fulfilled the

role of lead-on coach and again felt gladness for our girls who had done what we coaches had done in previous Olympics.

The tough competition, the tense struggle for a place on the Montreal team has forced our gymnasts to take a qualitative step forward. We see this in the floor exercises of Turischeva, Kim, Korbut, Saadi, Gorbick and Grozdova. The creation of an original mini-spectacle out of one combination on the apparatus, where there are both an intriguing beginning and culmination to the action is a skill in which our best coaches and gymnasts succeed.

The manner of performance of each Olympic candidate is different, but the style, the creative, meaningful, contemporary direction of gymnastics is common to them all. These are the characteristics of our school of gymnastics which we must preserve.

Recently, these notes were made by Lera Mironova, correspondent for *Family* magazine in Moscow:

For a long time she has worked as a senior coach at the Ukraine state school of gymnastics. She was married to an engineer but has been divorced for nine years. She has a grandson, Sergei.

Astakhova says she will continue to work as long as she has the strength because she loves gymnastics.

References

[1]Natalya Kalugina, "A BlueWind Whispers to Me," *Sovietsky Sport,* 10 Apr. 1988.

[2]Polina Astakhova, "We Are Strong Because of the Team," *Sovietsky Sport,* 21 May 1976.

Keiko Ikeda

1933 Born, November 11th, Hiroshima prefecture.
1954 World Championships, Rome, June–July (as Keiko Tanaka): 8th, all-around; 1st, beam.
1956 Graduated from Nihon Physical Education College. Became assistant at the gymnastic seminar, NPE College.
1956 Olympics, Melbourne, November: 13th, all-around; 4th, vault.
1958 World Championships, Moscow, July: 5th, all-around; 3rd, beam, floor.
1960 A lecturer at NPE College.
1960 Olympics, Rome, August, as Keiko Ikeda: 6th, all-around; 5th, bars, beam.
1962 World Championships, Prague, July: 6th, all-around; 3rd (tie), beam.
1964 Olympics, Tokyo, October: 6th, all-around.
1966 An assistant professor at NPE College.
1966 World Championships, Dortmund, September: 3rd, all-around; 2nd, bars; 4th, beam.
1978 A professor at NPE College.

Mrs. Ikeda now resides in Yokohama City, Kanagawa prefecture. She is the Executive Director of the All Japan Junior Gymnastic Club Federation and is the owner of a gymnastics club. She has published three books.

Doris Fuchs Brause

Doris Brause has a longer history of involvement in international competition than most American gymnasts. In the ten-year period between 1956 and 1966, she was a member of the American team in two Olympics—1956 Melbourne and 1960 Rome—and in two world championships—1962 Prague and 1966 Dortmund. She won four gold medals in the 1963 Pan American Games in Sao Paolo, Brazil.

She is now coaching at Northwest Gymnastics in Litchfield, Connecticut.

The Munich New Wave

Part Two

1969 to 1974

Landskrona, Sweden, is a little town with big ideas. Situated just across the Ore Sound from Copenhagen, Denmark, it is an embarkation point for ferry boats with passengers going to Denmark and beyond in Europe. With a population of less than 40,000, it is beautifully laid out with both new and old buildings, including the Citadel, a castle built in 1549. Modern houses are adapted to houses of the 18th century

The picture of the venue shows the extent of the preparations made for this competition.

The main sports area of Landskrona is one of the largest and most complete in Sweden. The building down left is the gymnasium where the competition was held. Submerged and built as a classical amphitheatre, it has seating for 3,000 spectators.

There is a holiday settlement with about 60 cottages where gymnasts were comfortably quartered during the championships.

European Championship 1969

Landskrona, Sweden

Sports Hall

May 16th to 17th

The 1969 European Championship was eagerly watched by the gymnastics community because the competition would help determine who would succeed to gymnastics leadership after the retirement of Vera Caslavska and Natalya Kuchinskaya. Natasha had not formally retired, but she was inactive. Her future was uncertain.

The organizers were described in this paragraph from the May/June 1969 issue of *Mademoiselle Gymnast:*

> Joining the city of Landskrona as organizers for the event was the IDROTT Gymnastic Association, the city's oldest athletic association, founded in the summer of 1882 by a handful of gymnastics enthusiasts . . . . Idrott was represented even as early as the 1896 Olympics in Athens. Thus the 1969 Championships had experienced and devoted organization and both traditional and modern surroundings.

Limited to two gymnasts per country from nineteen European countries, it was a small competition compared to World Championships and the Olympics. Furthermore, the only strong gymnasts came from the Soviet Union, East Germany, and Czechoslovakia. Consequently, it was indeed simply a test of leadership. Since this two-day tournament followed the 1968 Olympics by only seven months, there would not have been time for any significant changes in routines. Results were as follows:

Olga Karasyova in chinstand on beam.

All-around

1. Karin Janz, GDR	38.65
2. Olga Karasyova,URS	38.10
3. Ludmilla Turischeva,URS	37.90
Erika Zuchold,GDR	37.90
5. Jindra Kostalova,TCH	37.30
6. Maris Lundquist,SWE	36.15
7. Hana Liskova,TCH	36.10
8. Rodica Apateanu,ROM	35.85

Vault

1. Karin Janz,GDR	19.70
2. Erika Zuchold,GDR	19.45
3. Olga Karasyova,URS	19.40
4. Ludmilla Turischeva,URS	19.15
5. Rodica Apateanu,ROM	19.00
6. Hana Liskova,TCH	18.80

Bars

1. Karin Janz,GDR	19.65
2. Olga Karasyova,URS	19.45
3. Ludmilla Turischeva,USR	19.40
4. Erika Zuchold,GDR	19.30
5. Rodica Apateanu,ROM	18.65
6. Jindra Kostalova,TCH	16.55

Beam

1. Karin Janz,GDR	19.05
2. Olga Karasyova,URS	18.95
3. Jindra Kostalova,TCH	18.75
4. Ludmilla Turischeva,URS	18.70
5. Erika Zuchold,GDR	18.50
6. Hana Liskova,TCH	18.45

Floor Exercise

1. Olga Karasyova,URS	19.45
2. Karin Janz,GDR	19.40
3. Jindra Kostalova, TCH	19.10
Ludmilla Turischeva, URS	19.10
5. Erika Zuchold, GDR	19.00
6. Hana Liskova, TCH	18.70

Olga Karasyova seems to have performed over her head, since she did not continue to be one of the Soviet Union's leaders. Floor exercise was, however, always her strong suit. Karin Janz, on the other hand, firmly established herself as a force the Soviets would have to reckon with, while Turischeva let it be known she would probably be Janz's rival.

In other 1969 events, the USSR National Championships were held in Rostov on the 18th and 19th of October. This was the event into which under-age, 14-year-old Olga Korbut had been admitted by special permission.

Results were as follows:

1. Lyubov Burda	76.150
2. Larissa Petrick	75.900
3. Ludmilla Turischeva	75.025
4. Olga Karasyova	74.625
5. Olga Korbut	74.425

Since the USGF had not by this time been established as the primary gymnastics organization, results of the various competitions did not give a unified picture of national standings in the USA. In the German Democratic Republic, the national championships held in July 1970 yielded the probable selection for the World Championships in Ljubljana. Erika Zuchold did not compete because of injury. Results were as follows:

1. Karin Janz	76.95
2. Christine Schmitt	76.20
3. Marianne Noack	75.45
4. Angelika Hellmann	75.35
5. Richarda Schmeisser	73.90

Karin Janz, holding her Europa Cup, with Princess Christine of Sweden.

Ljubljana combines old buildings, like those shown above of the Gallus Embankment and Shoemakers Bridge, with new high rise buildings, like those in the distance below. The country Slovenia prides itself on being on the sunny side of the Alps.

World Championships
1970
Ljubljana, Yugoslavia
Tivoli Sports Hall

October 22nd to 27th

Ljubljana (pronounced Lyublyana) is the capital of Slovenia, the newly independent country in the northwestern part of what used to be Yugoslavia. On the Sava river, it is about 50 miles northeast of Trieste, a port city at the head of the Adriatic Sea. It is about 100 miles northwest of Zagreb, the principal city of Croatia, another newly independent country, which has been at war with Serbia, its neighbor to the south. Slovenia is on the northern border of Croatia. The lovely mountain range of the Julian Alps stretches across the western horizon; Ljubljana is itself in a relatively mountainous area.

It is a city whose history goes back to Roman times, when it was known as Emona, chief city of the province of Carniola. After the fall of Rome, the region, which retained the name Carniola, was settled in the 6th century A.D. by the South Slavs (*Yugoslavia* means the country of the South Slavs, the word *yugo* being Russian for *south.*) In 788 it became part of the empire of the Franks, whose greatest emperor was Charlemagne. Upon the dissolution of Charlemagne's empire in 843, the region passed to the dukes of Bavaria and in 1277, it became part of the Hapsburg Austrian empire. Half of Carniola was incorporated into Yugoslavia when that country was created following the First World War; the other half was ceded to Italy. Ljubljana was made capital of Slovenia in 1946. It has a medieval fortress and several fine

The Tivoli Arena

palaces and churches. Nowadays, it is an industrial city and is the seat of the Slovene Academy of Arts and Sciences and of a university.[1]

The selection of Ljubljana as the site of the 1970 World Championships reflected the influential strength of the Eastern European countries. In them, gymnastics received government support and it was a matter of national prestige to have top-level gymnasts and to host major competitions. In Yugoslavia 1970, Mr. Ivan Ivancevic, who was for many years that country's national coach, was a First Vice President of the Men's Technical Committee of the International Gymnastics Federation; Miroslav Cerar, Yugoslavia's top male gymnast, had placed fourth all around in Dortmund. The country was thus in a strong position to make a bid.

Furthermore, these countries had had much experience hosting major gymnastic events. For example, Prague, Leipzig, Warsaw, Bucharest, and Sofia had all hosted either World or European Championships. It would not be until 1979 that the United States would feel strong enough to host a world championship. This site selection of Ljubljana made attendance difficult for westerners, especially Americans and Canadians. Nevertheless, although attendance from the West was low, interest was high. Unfortunately, such interest was limited to the community of what was then a small sport.

People today, who are accustomed to extensive TV coverage not only of the Olympics but also of numerous events throughout the year, might find it hard to believe that in those pre–Olga Korbut days, the interest of the media in gymnastics was minimal, that is, outside the Soviet Union and the strong gymnastics countries of Europe. In American newspapers and magazines, gymnastics, even in the Olympic games, was hardly more than an entry in the results pages. The World Championships barely made the news at all. Such well-known events as Chunichi Cup, Moscow News, the World Cup, and the American Cup had not yet been inaugurated. The first Chunichi Cup was in 1970, a month after Ljubljana; the first Moscow News, 1974; the first World Cup, 1975; and the first American Cup, 1976, in celebration of the country's bicentennial. Moreover, back in 1970, the media were not paying much attention to what was going on behind the Iron Curtain. Part of the reason for Olga Korbut's explosive impact in Munich was that her performances, especially on bars and beam, were totally unexpected. They were not just a surprise; they were a shock. In the Soviet Union and in Eastern Europe, however, she had been known since 1969. She was not selected for the Soviet team in Ljubljana, but she was there. She performed her famous gymnastics elements in demonstrations before the judges. In short, although Ljubljana was not widely reported, it was a world-championships event of even greater importance than Dortmund. The big change to younger gymnasts had been made; everyone expected Munich to be a much bigger spectacle than Mexico. Ljubljana was, in effect, a dress rehearsal.

Competition for a place on 1972 Olympic teams would still be intense, but the experience of the 1970 World Championships would give veterans of that event an advantage over those who had not been there. All the veterans of the 1968 Soviet team were in Ljubljana, except that Tamara Lazakovich, 16-year-old student of Vikenti Dmitriev from Vitebsk, Belarus, replaced Natalya Kuchinskaya, who had retired. The East Germans were led by Erika Zuchold and Karin Janz, as they had been in Mexico. In addition, they had Marianne Noack, a Mexico City veteran and three gymnasts who would be strong members of the East German team in Munich: Angelika Hellmann, Christine Schmitt and Richarda Schmeisser. Consequently, the East Germans were strong enough to challenge the Soviet Union for the team title. Czechoslovakia and Japan would continue their rivalry in third and fourth positions, but their team scores were so much lower than those of the Soviet Union and East Germany that they were not really in the same class. It was a Soviet Union-East Germany show, except for one person: Cathy Rigby.

A good eye-witness account[2] was written by British coach Jim Prestidge. From the archives of the International Gymnastics Hall of Fame, that account is reprinted here with permission as an introduction to this book's narrative of that event.

> Three Olympics, three World and three European Championships ought to have hardened us in the serious business of following gymnastics, but as we traveled the 50 miles by coach from Zagreb airport to Ljubljana, we members of the British contingent were bubbling with excitement like a bunch of school kids. We had already had our bonus of gymnastic pleasure, for during the few days before our departure for the world championships, the great U.S.A. team arrived in London as our guests and opponents. As guests, they were efficiently ruthless and demonstrated clearly their superiority over our gymnasts. Even so, we enjoyed those few days with the Americans and learned much from their hard-working training

Cathy Rigby

sessions and admired their inspired workouts, especially those at our own gym at Ladywell.

So, by the time we reached Ljubljana and the Hotel Union, we had already been bloodied and were set for the ordeal which was to follow.

After one such training session, we were waiting to fall, tired and hungry into the bus which would take us back to the hotel for our meal, when the next team arrived at the training hall—it was the Russians! Tiredness and hunger forgotten, we sat for the next three hours and just watched! During this our first glimpse of the Russian girls in Yugoslavia, we were most impressed. Each girl was so confident and knew exactly what was expected of her. Hardly a word had to be spoken by their coach, a sure indication that their training had reached its peak.

During this training session, we had ample opportunity to study and analyze closely the Russian technique and general behaviour. Their greatest attribute in my opinion is their ability to play the part of the perfect artist all the time. Their carriage, posture and proud feminine elegance are a joy to see in whatever they are doing. Three days later during the compulsory exercises, Tamara Lazakovich committed the crime of crimes and fell from the beam! She walked back to her seat, knowing that 8,000 people were watching her failure; yet in spite of her obvious misery, she maintained her self-control and her proud bearing throughout the ordeal. Needless to say, every one of the Russian girls who followed Tamara showed (her) nervous strain by wobbling and generally performing some very un-Russian beam exercises, proving that in spite of all I have just said, they are capable of succumbing to that bogey of all gymnasts, psychological fear.

This series of Russian failures on the compulsory beam were certainly the big shock of the first day, indeed of the entire championships. It was generally accepted that the reigning world champions, Czechoslovakia, were no longer a threat to the Soviet Union; neither were the Japanese. The U.S.A. team with its new babes was not quite within reach of the coveted team medals. The East Germans had, however, been steadily improving since their entry into world gymnastics 12 years ago. It was just conceivable that if the East Germans made no mistake and the Russians faltered, then the German girls could take the team award.

The Russian beam debacle provided just the sort of lapse that the German girls needed, and after compulsories on the first day, the team scores were: GDR, 188.65; USSR, 188.55. The U.S.A. girls at this stage were seventh with 178.40.

The American girls had also had a rough journey on the beam, but their misfortune came from some unhelpful judging. It is significant that the U.S.A. team's lowest score came from the beam compulsories and their highest score came from beam voluntaries (optionals). Just why the judges hammered them so hard on this piece is a mystery. Cathy Rigby with 9.1 for the set was one of the hardest hit, and had this score been higher as deserved, that silver might have been a gold! Yes, Rigby made a "silver" and made history for the U.S.A., for this was their first medal ever in women's gymnastics. The excitement as Cathy neared the end of her final exercise was very intense. As she completed each length of the beam without a fault and then finally finished, everyone relaxed and then let out a terrific applause. I know that I felt this thrill and happiness for her achievement just as if she were a member of my own team, and, I think, for me, this was one of the great moments of the games (championships)!

There were fewer such emotional moments in this 17th world championships. The absence of Vera Caslavska and Natasha Kuchinskaya leaves a huge gap. There were no gymnasts who could match them for sheer artistry and personality. Even the great Ludmilla Turischeva, the world champion, did not infuse deep feeling to the beholder, despite her great technical ability and skill, and the Russian team as a whole seemed far too tense to convey their usual relaxed and happy performances.

Although these championships will be remembered as the most highly organized of any and certainly the most enjoyable, there was, I feel, a dearth of great emotional moments to stamp them as the finest ever. The last decade gave us some of the greatest personalities to adorn our sport—Astakhova, Latynina, Kuchinskaya and, of course, Caslavska. They were all artists of the highest calibre, and each had her own personal charm. Their places will not easily be filled.

The Ljubljana championships were certainly not without their perfectionists: Zuchold and Janz of the G.D.R., Turischeva and Voronina of the

U.S.S.R., Vachova of Czechoslovakia, Matsuhiza of Japan and not forgetting Rigby of the U.S.A.; but I think that not one of them has yet reached the pinnacle of gymnastics artistry which so often held us spellbound at Prague and Dortmund.

The first four places are still occupied by the same four countries, the only change being the sliding back of Czechoslovakia and the rise to prominence of the East Germans. The U.S.A., thanks to Cathy Rigby and a wonderful supporting team of babes, did well to take seventh place, only 2.5 points behind the powerful Hungarians.

What will the future be? The sport becomes more and more skillful, training becomes even harder and performers are reaching gymnastics maturity much earlier. The complexity of administration, preparation and coaching is growing every year. Are we perhaps losing some of the art form in the race to be victors? I hope not. I think it was Aristotle who said 2,000 years ago, "Gymnastics is not just an art but is also a science, an anthropological science with a social purpose." The significant inference here is that it is first and foremost an art. Need I say that we all hope it remains that way.

As related by Mr. Prestidge, the standings of the leading teams after compulsories were, much to everyone's surprise, as follows:

1. GDR	188.65
2. URS	188.55
3. TCH	185.30
4. JPN	184.60

The standings of the leading individuals were:

1. Turischeva	38.25
2. Zuchold	38.15
Janz	38.15
4. Voronina	37.80
5. Hellmann	37.60
6. Matsuhisa	37.55
7. Petrick	37.50
Schmitt	37.50
9. Burda	37.45
10. Karasyova	37.40
17. Rigby	36.80
25. Lazakovitch	36.05

During the first rotation of optionals, a lot of changes in this lineup would occur, as they would later after each rotation, up to the end.

East German gymnasts with surprised expressions on their faces, perhaps watching Lazakovich's fall from beam. Left to right: Erika Zuchold, Angelika Hellmann, Marianne Noack, Christine Schmitt, and Karin Janz. Richarda Schmeisser is behind Christine Schmitt.

Optional Exercises: October 24th

First Rotation

The Soviets, being in the unusual position of second place after compulsories, started on the second apparatus—bars. In this, they did very well, having averaged 9.69 per gymnast. The East Germans on vault did almost as well, but not quite: they averaged 9.63. The difference gave the Soviet team a 0.3 edge over the East Germans and moved them from 0.1 behind to 0.2 ahead and into first place. The East Germans, by and large, were using the Yamashita vault. Three of the top Soviets on bars were Ludmilla Turischeva, 9.80; Zinaida Voronina, 9.70; and Lyubov Burda, 9.70. Their routines were as follows:

From the low bar side, Turischeva ran, jumped off the beat board, straddled her legs while grabbing low bar, made a half turn to her left above the bar with her legs still straddled *(Figure 33)* and swung down under the low bar with her legs steeply piked but still straddled. As she passed under the low bar and her legs cleared the bar, she brought them together, still in pike position, swung back in kip and caught high bar. She swung forward while hanging on high bar, straddled her legs over the low bar to rear-lying hang and kipped up to toe-on position on top of high bar, facing low bar. With her feet on the high bar outside her hands, she swung back down and up between the bars, made a half turn, released high bar and dropped, still in pike attitude toward low bar, facing high bar. She grasped low bar as her feet passed over it and made a long glide kip on low bar into a forward hip circle around low bar. As she came up at the end of her hip circle, she tucked her legs through her arms and put her feet on the bar. She stood up, reached for and grasped high bar. Pushing off low bar, she brought her feet up onto high bar outside her hands and was again in toe-on position on high bar, this time facing away from low bar. She swung down between bars. As she came up on the far side of the high bar, she initiated a twist, released her hands from the bar, made one and a half turns with her body stretched horizontally, regrasped high bar and swung forward to beat low bar. She swung back and forward again, while hanging on high bar, and straddled her legs over low bar to rear-lying hang. She then kipped on high bar until, for the third time, she placed her feet on the bar, outside her hands, in toe-on position, again facing low bar. She swung back down in sole circle and, as she came up between the bars, she stretched her body, initiated a twist and released her hands from the high bar. She made a half

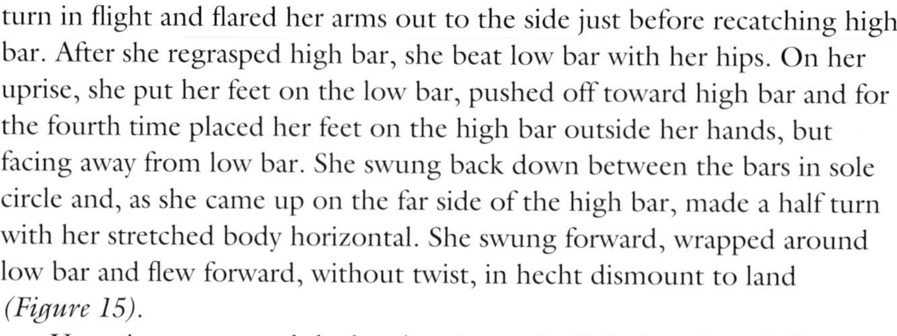
turn in flight and flared her arms out to the side just before recatching high bar. After she regrasped high bar, she beat low bar with her hips. On her uprise, she put her feet on the low bar, pushed off toward high bar and for the fourth time placed her feet on the high bar outside her hands, but facing away from low bar. She swung back down between the bars in sole circle and, as she came up on the far side of the high bar, made a half turn with her stretched body horizontal. She swung forward, wrapped around low bar and flew forward, without twist, in hecht dismount to land *(Figure 15)*.

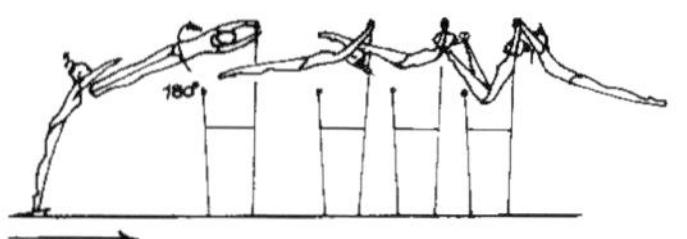
Figure 58

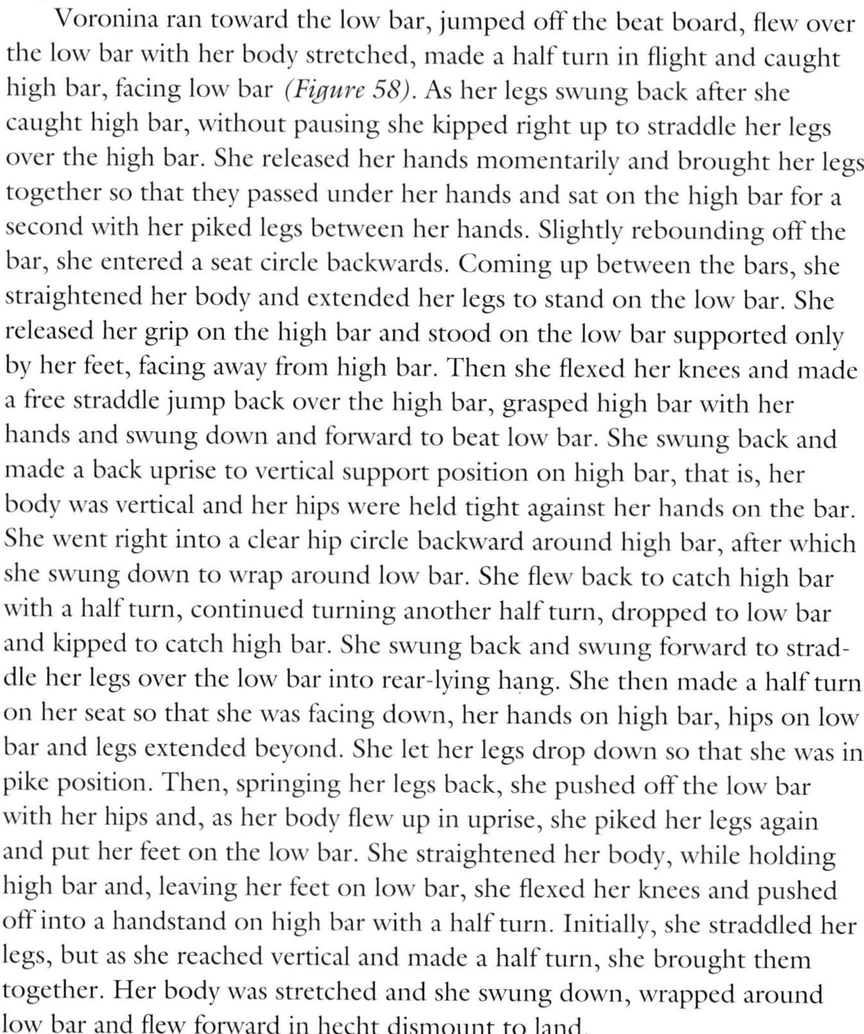
Voronina ran toward the low bar, jumped off the beat board, flew over the low bar with her body stretched, made a half turn in flight and caught high bar, facing low bar *(Figure 58)*. As her legs swung back after she caught high bar, without pausing she kipped right up to straddle her legs over the high bar. She released her hands momentarily and brought her legs together so that they passed under her hands and sat on the high bar for a second with her piked legs between her hands. Slightly rebounding off the bar, she entered a seat circle backwards. Coming up between the bars, she straightened her body and extended her legs to stand on the low bar. She released her grip on the high bar and stood on the low bar supported only by her feet, facing away from high bar. Then she flexed her knees and made a free straddle jump back over the high bar, grasped high bar with her hands and swung down and forward to beat low bar. She swung back and made a back uprise to vertical support position on high bar, that is, her body was vertical and her hips were held tight against her hands on the bar. She went right into a clear hip circle backward around high bar, after which she swung down to wrap around low bar. She flew back to catch high bar with a half turn, continued turning another half turn, dropped to low bar and kipped to catch high bar. She swung back and swung forward to straddle her legs over the low bar into rear-lying hang. She then made a half turn on her seat so that she was facing down, her hands on high bar, hips on low bar and legs extended beyond. She let her legs drop down so that she was in pike position. Then, springing her legs back, she pushed off the low bar with her hips and, as her body flew up in uprise, she piked her legs again and put her feet on the low bar. She straightened her body, while holding high bar and, leaving her feet on low bar, she flexed her knees and pushed off into a handstand on high bar with a half turn. Initially, she straddled her legs, but as she reached vertical and made a half turn, she brought them together. Her body was stretched and she swung down, wrapped around low bar and flew forward in hecht dismount to land.

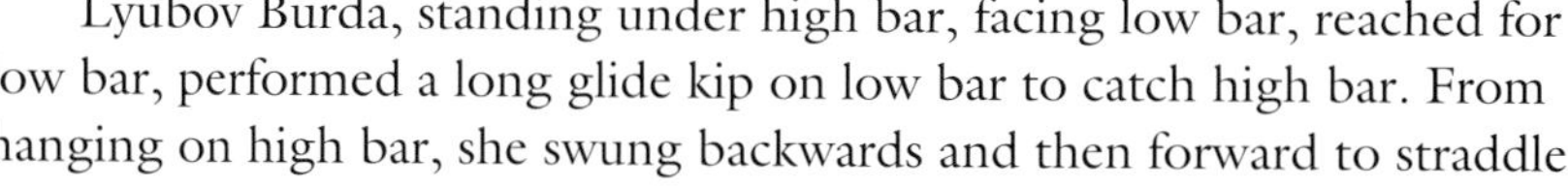
Lyubov Burda, standing under high bar, facing low bar, reached for low bar, performed a long glide kip on low bar to catch high bar. From hanging on high bar, she swung backwards and then forward to straddle

> over low bar and end in rear-lying hang. She kipped up to straddle position on top of high bar, quickly changed her grip from overgrip to undergrip and, without stopping, continued on over in straddle circle forward under the bar. As she swung back under high bar, she released her legs from pike-straddle position, extended her body, reversed her swing and swung forward to catch low bar. She did a glide and piked both legs through her arms to end in rear support on low bar and immediately reached up to grasp high bar and kip on high bar. As she reached clear support position on high bar, she piked her body and placed her feet on the bar outside her hands, swung under high bar and, as she came up between the bar, she released her feet from the bar, stretched her body, released her hands from the bar and performed one and one half turns to her right. This element has since been called the "Burda Twirl." Upon completing her twirl, she allowed her body to drop and bounce from her hips off low bar. As she came up, she piked her body, placed her feet on the high bar again, swung under high bar and, as she came up, released her feet, stretched her body, released her hands and performed a half turn while her body was horizontal. Now facing low bar, she swung forward, wrapped around low bar and flew back with a half turn to catch high bar. She made a short swing away from low bar, turned to face low bar, dropped to low bar and kipped to catch high bar. She kipped on high bar to clear support position, made a hip circle backward around the bar until her body was horizontal again, pushed with her hips off the high bar and flew forward in hecht dismount to land.

The pauses taken or not taken in these routines are interesting. Turischeva made one pause when she stood on the low bar, holding high bar, and pushed off to put her feet on the high bar outside her hands. Voronina made two pauses: one when she stood on the low bar, not holding high bar, and made a free straddle-jump back over high bar and one when she made a half turn on her hips on the low bar while holding high bar. Burda, however, made no pauses but maintained an even rhythm throughout her exercise. Her routine was, perhaps, the most graceful and the most artistic of all.

Turischeva made generous use of the sole circle, her feet on the bar outside her hands, as she swung down to enter her stretched body turns. It was not nearly so innovative a routine as that of Karin Janz, as we shall see, and was repetitious.

The Czechs on beam in first rotation did poorly; they averaged only 9.15 per gymnast. The Japanese in floor exercise averaged 9.3. Theirs was not a performance worthy of attention but was enough to move them up into third place.

At the end of first rotation, the standings and scores of the leading teams and individuals were as follows:

	Initial Score	First Rotation	Subtotal
1. URS	188.55	48.45	237.00
2. GDR	188.65	48.15	236.80
3. TCH	185.30	45.85	231.15
4. JPN	184.60	46.50	231.10
1. Turischeva *(bars)*	38.25	9.80	48.05
2. Zuchold *(vault)*	38.15	9.80	47.95
3. Janz *(vault)*	38.15	9.75	47.90
4. Voronina *(bars)*	37.80	9.70	47.50
5. Petrick *(bars)*	37.50	9.70	47.20
6. Hellmann *(vault)*	37.60	9.55	47.15
Burda *(bars)*	37.45	9.70	47.15
8. Schmitt *(vault)*	37.50	9.60	47.10
9. Matsuhisa *(floor)*	37.55	9.50	47.05
10. Karasyova *(bars)*	37.40	9.55	46.95

Second Rotation

In second rotation, the now leading Soviet team moved to beam and the East Germans to bars. Thanks to a sparkling bars routine by Karin Janz, for which she received 9.80, and other consistent scores by the East Germans, they moved back up to first place ahead of the Soviets in team competition and Janz temporarily occupied first place ahead of Turischeva in the individual all-around. The bars routines of Karin Janz and Erika Zuchold were as follows:

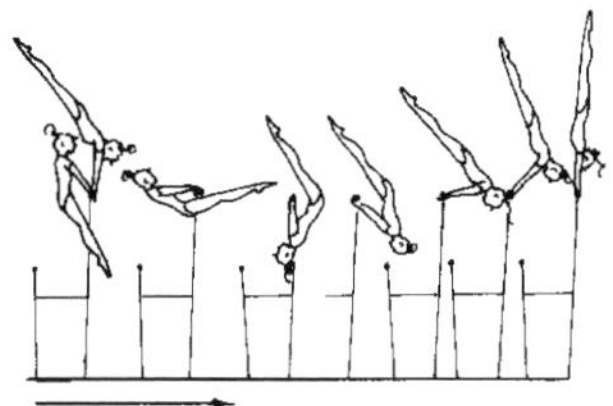

Figure 59

From the low bar side, Janz ran and jumped off the beat board up to clear support position above the low bar, her body stretched horizontally and held away from the low bar by straight arms. Keeping her arms straight, she did a clear hip circle backward around low bar up to handstand on low bar (*Figure 59* shows this element on high bar). She then let her body swing back and down under low bar, straddling her legs as they descended, and began a kip. As she came back up in her kip, she shot her legs through between her arms and pushed off to grasp high bar. She kipped on high bar to handstand, paused, made a half turn and continued on over in giant circle to wrap around low bar and fly back to catch high bar in eagle grip. She hung momentarily in eagle grip, then dropped forward to low bar. She kipped on low bar to catch high bar, swung back and then swung forward on high bar, piked her legs over the low bar and ended in rear-lying hang. She kipped on high bar, changed from over grip to reverse grip as she came up to clear support position above high bar, straddled her legs and, without

After wrap around low bar, Karin Janz flies back to catch high bar in eagle grip.

pausing, continued over and around the bar in a forward straddle circle. On the way up on the far side, however, she stopped her swing, made a quick grip change back from reverse grip to over grip, and swung forward to drop to low bar. She performed a glide, shot her legs through between her arms to rear support on low bar and reached up to catch high bar. She began to kip on high bar. She shot her legs between her arms on the side away from the low bar, extended her body from pike to stretch position, then piked her body again and began a backward seat circle around high bar *(Figure 60)*. (This is known as a reverse kip.) As she came up between the bars, she extended her body. Then, as she continued without pause on over the top and down the far side, she piked it again. Coming up between the bars a second time, she extended her body over the low bar, made half turn and allowed her body to drop to beat low bar with her hips. On her uprise, still holding high bar, she straddled her legs over the low bar while beginning her kip on the high bar. She kipped on high bar to clear support position above the bar, her body horizontal and held clear by straight arms, her feet over the space between the bars. (This was her third such clear support position.) She then let her hips drop onto high bar, performed a back hip circle and released in hecht dismount. She flew forward, on the high bar side, made a full turn and landed.

Figure 60

Janz's routine was unquestionably the most exciting of the championships. It was precise, daring, and continuous. Her mount, in which she jumped to clear support position above the low bar and then entered a clear hip circle, was unique. She used the same clear support element in the middle of her routine as she passed over high bar and used it again just before her dismount. Her clear support positions and clear hip circles, both with straight arms, were trademarks of this distinguished gymnast. Not noticeably shorter or lighter than others of her contemporaries, she was nevertheless able to bring a certain grace and lightness to her routines in comparison to which others generally appeared heavy and labored.

Erika Zuchold made a running straddle jump over low bar to catch high bar. She kipped on high bar until she could shoot her legs through between herself and the bar to assume a pike position, hanging from high bar between the bars. In a reverse kip, she swung backward and up to rear, clear support position on the high bar, facing away from low bar, her piked body held away from high bar by straight arms. From there, she released her pike, extended her body and swung in a forward seat circle around high bar until on her way up between the bars, she let go of high bar and flew to low bar to catch it in handstand facing away from high bar. She allowed her legs to swing down away from high bar and performed a clear hip circle backward around low bar with her body stretched. As she came up between the bars and passed through handstand position, she piked her legs to toe-on position on low bar, swung down and released on the way up. She flew to high bar, which she caught in crossed grip, made a half turn to face low bar and dropped forward to low bar. She kipped on low bar to catch high bar, swung forward on high bar to straddle over low bar into rear-lying hang, kipped on high bar, shot her legs between her arms behind the high bar, and swung back and up between the bars in rear seat circle (reverse kip) *(Figure 60)*. When she reached rear support position on top of high bar, she piked her legs and then proceeded to lean back slightly and lift her hips clear of the bar. In this dramatic position, facing low bar, held also earlier in her routine but then facing away from low bar, her seat was at least a foot above the high bar, her arms absolutely straight, her legs pointed vertically upward and her body tilted slightly back. She held this position for a second, then swung back and under high bar, reversed her swing and, as she came back, she kicked out of her pike to extend her body nearly vertically away from high bar. In so doing, she rotated her arms within her shoulder joints (dislocate) *(Figure 21)*. She then made a long extended swing forward to wrap around low bar and flew back to catch high bar in eagle grip. She began her kip on high bar in eagle grip, switched to normal over-grip as her legs rested momentarily on the low bar, and continued on up in her kip to make a hip circle forward around high bar which she completed in clear support position away from high bar. She swung down in hip circle backward about high bar, released and flew forward over low bar in hecht dismount, without twist, to land.

Like her teammate, Karin Janz, Erika Zuchold had her own trademark. This was the clear seat support position which she held above the bar, with her body tilted slightly back. As in Dortmund, Zuchold's routine also had many rear seat circles.

The Soviets on beam averaged 9.44, compared with 9.59 for the East Germans on bars. This difference of 0.15 in the average translated into a 0.75 difference for the five counting team scores and enabled the East Germans to move ahead. In optionals, there were no major breaks by the Soviets in performing their routines, as there had been in compulsories. Lazakovich again had lowest score, but all the others were 9.4, 9.45 or 9.5. Two leading routines were those of Turischeva (9.5) and Petrick (9.45). They were as follows:

Ludmilla Turischeva in hop with right leg elevated horizontally.

> Starting at one end of the beam, Turischeva placed her hands on the beam and jumped directly from the floor to hold herself momentarily in clear straddle support, that is to say, her body held above the beam by straight arms to her hands on the beam and her legs straddled horizontally in front of her. Then she pressed up to handstand, keeping her legs straddled on the way up, then bringing them together in handstand. She continued in walkover to stand. Then she took two steps forward and performed a dive cartwheel to her left to stand at the end of the beam, facing back the way she had come. She stepped forward, made a half turn to her left, a deep body wave *(Figure 61)* and a back handspring step-out. She made a half turn to her left, a high kick with her left leg and then leaned forward into lunge position, her left leg in front. She turned her upper body a quarter turn to the right to face across the beam. She made a full turn to her left, starting and ending in lunge position, so that as she finished she faced across the beam. She placed her hands on the beam and pressed up to

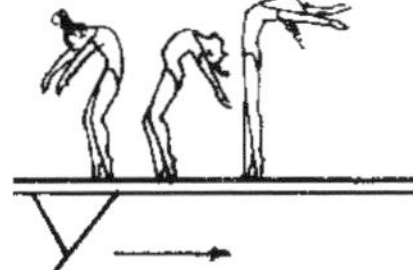

Figure 61

handstand directly from lunge position. She held the handstand for a second, made a quarter turn to her left and came back down from her handstand to stand facing along the beam in the same direction she had begun this series of moves. She stepped forward with a graceful hop with her left leg raised in front and then made a half turn to her left at the end of the beam. She ran forward and made a split leap near the end. She paused and made a squat half turn to her right. From squat position, she performed a combination that would be her trademark throughout her career: two forward rolls with her arms and hands held clear of the beam. After her second roll, she continued forward into prone position. Then, leaving her left leg in place, she raised her body a quarter turn to the left and brought her right leg up onto the beam, so that she was in splits, facing across the beam. She posed in splits for a second with her arms out to the side. She then placed her hands on the beam, made a quarter turn to her right and raised herself in clear straddle support position above the beam, the same position she had assumed during her mount. She lowered herself to sit on the beam, swung her legs down and back and flung her arms up and back for a very brief pause. Then, still leaning her body back, she brought her arms onto the beam behind her and swung her legs forward and up into vee-sit, with her straddled legs elevated 45°. Then she brought her legs together pointing vertically upward for a moment, dropped her left leg bent onto the beam and her right leg extended onto the beam. From this position and with her left hand on the beam behind her, she thrust off her left leg in valdez to stand. She made a half turn to her right, did some dance steps and a hop with her right leg raised. She posed, stepped to the end and made a half turn to her right with knees slightly bent. She posed at the end and then danced to the other end, including a stag leap. She made a half turn left and returned to the middle with dance steps. She made a half turn to her right and prepared for her dismount: a flic-flac, salto backward stretched with full twist *(Figure 62)*.

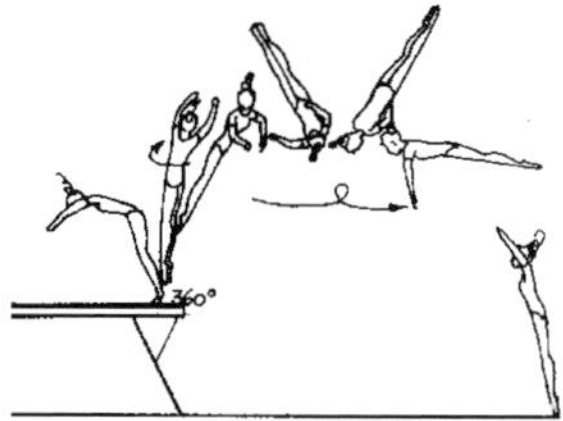

Figure 62

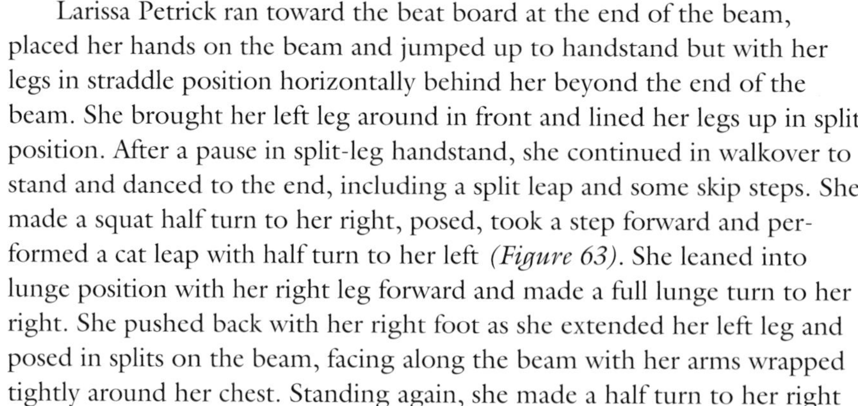

Larissa Petrick ran toward the beat board at the end of the beam, placed her hands on the beam and jumped up to handstand but with her legs in straddle position horizontally behind her beyond the end of the beam. She brought her left leg around in front and lined her legs up in split position. After a pause in split-leg handstand, she continued in walkover to stand and danced to the end, including a split leap and some skip steps. She made a squat half turn to her right, posed, took a step forward and performed a cat leap with half turn to her left *(Figure 63)*. She leaned into lunge position with her right leg forward and made a full lunge turn to her right. She pushed back with her right foot as she extended her left leg and posed in splits on the beam, facing along the beam with her arms wrapped tightly around her chest. Standing again, she made a half turn to her right

Figure 63

Zinaida Voronina in splits on beam.

and entered a beautiful scale with 180° split on her right leg, her left leg elevated to vertical, supported by her left hand, her body horizontally forward but her head up, and her right arm extended diagonally down in front of her. (See photo page 68.) She held this pose for a second and then modified it by elevating her body upward to vertical, gracefully bringing her right arm above her and twisted her hand in an elegant gesture, then letting her left leg incline slightly behind her. She held this second pose for a second and then leaned forward to perform a cartwheel to her left to turn facing back along the beam. She stepped forward, made a high kick with her right leg and dropped down onto the beam with her right knee and shin on the beam, her left foot on the beam in front of her right knee and her left knee bent, while her arms were stretched up above her. She leaned forward, placed her hands on the beam, let her left leg drop beside the beam and swung it back and up to give her the momentum needed to perform a forward walkover to stand. She stepped to the end, made a quarter turn right, posed, made an-other quarter turn to her right and danced along the beam, including a split leap. At the end, she raised her right leg and swung it back as she made a half turn to her right on her left foot. She dropped into squat, raised herself, and stepped forward into full turn to her left. She continued into a forward walkover to the end and leaned forward immediately into a standing split forward on her right leg. Her left leg was vertically above her and her head was all the way down between her right leg and her left arm, looking back along the beam *(Figure 41)*. Her hands were on the beam, supporting her. She held this position for two full seconds. She came out of it, paused while standing at the end and made a half turn to her right. She performed a chassé forward to the middle of the beam, posed, took two more steps forward and performed a gainer back handspring. She paused, stepped forward again and performed a gainer salto backward stretched to land to her left beside the beam, while steadying herself with her right hand on the beam *(Figure 25)*.

The Czechs in floor exercise averaged 9.27 and the Japanese on vault averaged 9.35. This was enough to move the Japanese into third place.

Summing up second rotation, both the East Germans and the Japanese moved ahead of their rivals and Karin Janz moved ahead into first place all around. Angelika Hellmann, the lovely East German 16-year-old who had placed fifth in compulsories in this her first world championships, continued her decline in optionals from sixth after first rotation to ninth after second. Her 9.40 on bars was not quite good enough to hold her own against other gymnasts whose scores averaged out to over 9.50.

At the conclusion of second rotation, the standings and scores of the leading teams and individuals were:

	Initial Score	Second Rotation	Subtotal
1. GDR	236.80	47.95	284.75
2. URS	237.00	47.20	284.20
3. JPN	231.10	46.75	277.85
4. TCH	231.15	46.35	277.50
1. Karin Janz *(bars)*	47.90	9.80	57.70
2. Turischeva *(beam)*	48.05	9.50	57.55
Zuchold *(bars)*	47.95	9.60	57.55
4. Voronina *(beam)*	47.50	9.40	56.90
5. Schmitt *(bars)*	47.10	9.60	56.70
6. Petrick *(beam)*	47.20	9.45	56.65
7. Matsuhisa *(vault)*	47.05	9.55	56.60
Burda *(beam)*	47.15	9.45	56.60
9. Hellmann *(bars)*	47.15	9.40	56.55
10. Karasyova *(beam)*	46.95	9.40	56.35

Third Rotation

In third rotation, the advantage shifted back to the Soviets. They went to floor, where they are always strong, while the East Germans went to beam, the more risky apparatus. In fact, the Soviets achieved a team average—9.73—which was even better than the score they achieved on bars in first rotation—9.69. During floor exercise, Ludmilla Turischeva received the highest mark of the championships—9.90. Tenth-place Olga Karasyova received a 9.80, a mark that moved her up to eighth place. The East Germans, on the other hand, averaged a dismal 9.27 on beam. Angelika Hellmann's 9.35 dropped her right down to tenth place. Far worse, however, was the fate of Karin Janz. In making her dismount from beam, she got off-center, was able only to get a partial thrust from her legs to push off the beam for her final salto, and landed on her hands and knees. For this and other errors, she received an 8.70, a score which had to count in the team average because the novice on the team, 16-year-old Richarda Schmeisser, scored 8.45. Not only did Janz's score hurt the team, but it knocked her right out of the first place all-around which she had so briefly held.

In spite of the low score she received, Janz's routine is worthy of note because it was one of the most advanced in the state of the art at that time. Furthermore, in spite of her errors in performance, it was an attractive routine to watch. It was as follows:

> Janz pressed up to handstand at one end of the beam and continued on over in walkover to stand. She made a brief pose in attitude and continued to the far end with dance steps and a high split leap. At the far end, she made a full turn to her right and then a pose and a body wave. She leaned back into handstand, paused and continued into a back straddle down to lie stretched on her back. After a pose in this supine position and while holding the beam with her hands behind her head, she piked her legs, then extended her body and her arms to raise herself backward through handstand to land first on her right foot and then her left, an element requiring great strength. She posed briefly while standing and then made a half turn to her left and posed again, standing on her right leg, her arms held out diagonally forward and back and her left leg raised behind her, bent at the knee. She stepped forward, made an assemblé with her right leg in front, a scissors jump in place and a stag jump to near the end and made a half turn to her right to squat. She jumped out of her squat into a sissone *(Figure 64)* and stepped forward into forward walkover to the end. She lifted her left leg up to horizontal in front of her, swung it back as she made a half turn to her left on her right foot, held her left leg up again in front of her for a moment, then swung it back again as she leaned forward into handstand

Figure 64

> with her legs split. She continued on over in walkover to stand, then leaned forward into handstand, which she held for a second. She moved in the same direction to roll out from her handstand and place her back on the beam with her legs piked. Then she continued her roll in the same direction into vee-sit position with her legs piked above the beam. She placed her hands on the beam in front of her and swung her legs down and back up to handstand, held it momentarily, and continued in walkover to stand. She made a step to the end, did a squat and a stretch jump with change of legs (changement) and stepped back to make a half turn to her left. She then stepped forward and performed a full turn to her right, posed and made an assemblé toward the far end. She made a half turn to her left, posed and stepped forward into a cartwheel to her right into a handstand and then stepped back down. She then posed and performed body waves and arm movements for several seconds before turning away from the far end to prepare for her dismount: a back walkover, back handspring (flic-flac) into salto backward with full twist to land.

As mentioned earlier, in landing her back handspring, she came too close to one edge of the beam: her right foot was only half on the beam. Consequently, she did not push off with full force to get high enough to complete her salto.

Karin Janz's teammate Erika Zuchold scored 9.55 on beam and placed second to Turischeva in all-around standings. Her routine was as follows:

> Zuchold ran diagonally at the beam, jumped off the beat board and landed on her hands in handstand with her legs split, facing across the beam. She made a quarter turn to her right to line up with the beam, lowered her right foot and then her left onto the beam and then sat on the beam in pose facing across the beam, with her legs bent and resting on the beam under and beside her, her left arm held vertically up. She then made a full and a quarter turn on her seat with her legs bent to pose facing along the beam with both knees bent, her feet on the beam and her left arm behind her on the beam. She pushed off with her feet and performed a valdez to stand and pose at the end of the beam. She made a sissone at the end of the beam with her left leg extended backward, danced forward, made a stag leap and continued to the end, where she kicked her right leg high in the air and made a three-quarter turn to her left to face across the beam. She did a plié while lowering and raising her arms gracefully. She then spread her legs slightly, leaned forward, placed her hands on the beam between her feet and pressed up to handstand. She held her handstand for a second, then lowered her right foot to the beam, simultaneously turning a

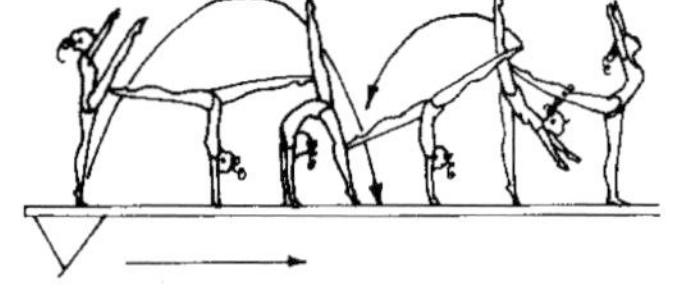

Figure 65

quarter turn to her left to face along the beam and lowered her left foot. She stood, posed, made a half turn to her left and leaned forward into a double-stag handstand, with her left leg forward. She extended her legs into split position and lowered her left leg forward to the beam. She stood, leaned forward into another handstand with her legs split, her left leg forward and then performed tic-toc *(Figure 65),* her left toe touching the beam and then her right. As she brought her right foot down, she moved it to the other side of the beam, let it drop past the beam and then sat on the beam, having turned a quarter turn to her left so that she faced across the beam, her right leg extended down and her left leg extended along the beam. She posed first with her body vertical and then leaned to her right onto her right arm on the beam, with her left arm extended over her. She held that pose only briefly, then sat up facing across the beam with her legs extended diagonally down. She rolled to her left on her seat and hips, posed and brought her feet to her left up onto the beam to stand in a lunge position, her right leg ahead but bent only half way. In this position, she made a double turn to her right on her right foot. She posed, performed a double stag leap and turn to her right at the end of the beam. She posed, did a sissone with her left leg extended back, kicked her left leg high in front and then made a running step forward into a dive cartwheel to her right. She came back immediately with dance steps and a split leap, made a half turn at the end to her left, danced forward and leaned into handstand with split legs. She performed tic-toc again, letting her left foot rest on the beam for a second, placing her weight on it and briefly raising her hands from the beam and

Erika Zuchold finishing stag leap on the beam.

flaring them to the side. Then she brought her right leg back down to the beam and stood. She made a half turn to her right and prepared for her dismount: a salto forward with half turn directly off to the side of the beam.

One final beam routine for the East Germans is included in this record in spite of a score of only 9.35. It is that of Angelika Hellmann and is given here because it was an attractive routine and because this young gymnast will be a mainstay of the East German team for the next six years, including the Montreal Olympics.

Hellmann ran parallel to the beam, jumped off the beat board near one end with her right hand on the beam to steady herself, landed on her right foot in squat position with her left leg extended, made a half turn to her right and brought her left leg up beside her right, both now in squat position. Still in squat position, she made another half turn to her right, at the conclusion of which she leaned forward to put both hands on the beam at the end, straightened her right leg to stand on it, extended her left leg vertically above herself and posed in standing split forward with her head down by her right arm and leg, her eyes looking backward. At the end of her pose, she raised her head slightly, then raised herself to stand, bringing her left foot down, and made a half turn to her right. She proceeded down the beam with a sissone and an assemblé, her long legs making short work of the distance. At the end, she kicked her right leg high, leaned forward into handstand, then back to straddle down and continue her backward movement to vee sit, her legs straddled at 45° up in front of her. Then she lowered her left foot onto the beam with her left knee bent and lowered her right leg extended ahead of her. With her left hand on the beam behind her, she did a valdez to stand and continued into back walkover. She stepped back, made a half turn to her right, stepped to the end and made another half turn to her right. She posed, stepped ahead into forward walkover and stepped to the end, where she made a half turn on her left foot with her right leg held high. She paused and posed, then made a half turn to her left and stepped back to the end. She kicked her right leg high, swung it back as she made a half turn on her left foot to her right and posed in scale on her left foot with her right leg held horizontally to her right, held up by her right hand, with her left arm extended vertically up. Then she let go of her right leg and extended both arms out to the side. Out of her scale, she made a dance step in place, then ran forward to perform a handspring forward *(Figure 66)*. She stepped to the end, did a body wave and a half turn to her left. Then she proceeded to the other end with running steps and split leap. At the end, she made a curtsy and a half turn to

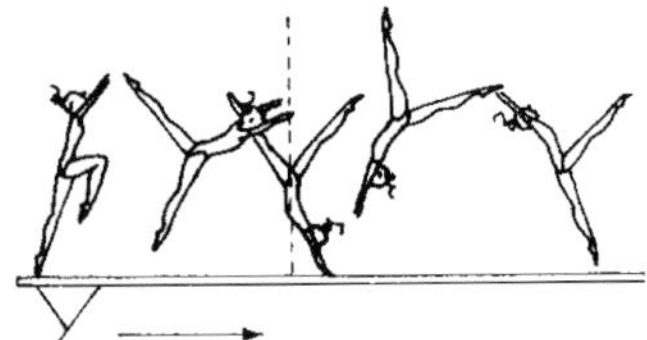

Figure 66

her right. She posed, stepped forward into handstand with her legs split and touched the beam in tic-toc first with her front left leg and then her back right leg. Standing again, she did an assemblé with her right leg extended ahead, a stretched jump with change of legs (changement) and then a high split-leg jump. Then she did a full turn on her left foot, made a step to the end, dropped into squat and made a half turn to her left in squat. Standing, she posed, leaning forward on her right leg with her right arm diagonally forward and up and her left arm back and down. She stepped forward into another pose, standing upright with her arms in similar position as in the previous pose—all this in preparation for her dismount: she ran to the end and pushed off into gainer salto backward in tuck position (*Figure 67* also shows salto with half twist).

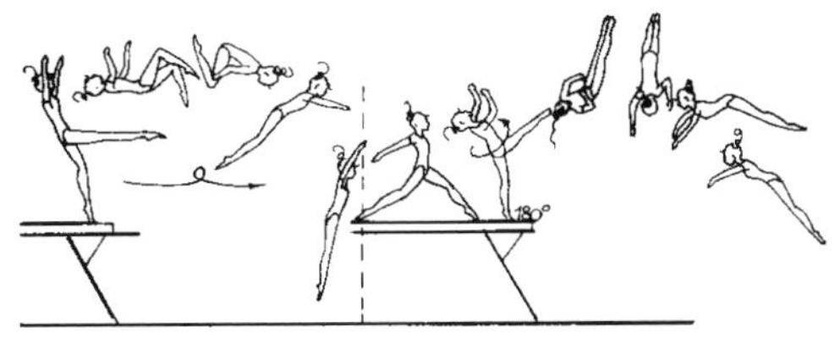

Figure 67

While the East Germans were getting their low or modest scores on beam, the Soviets on floor were demolishing the opposition: Turischeva with her 9.90, Karasyova, her 9.80, and Voronina, her 9.75. In addition, Burda scored 9.65 and Petrick, 9.55. These scores do not compare with the 9.9s and 10.00s in more recent competitions, but for 1970, they were stupendous. The leading routines were as follows:

Ludmilla Turischeva in pose in floor exercise

Turischeva started near a corner, swung her straight right arm clockwise at her side and immediately assumed a dramatic pose, standing on her right toe and leaning slightly forward on her straight right leg, her left arm and leg diagonally back and her right arm reaching up and forward. She made a full turn and performed chassé into the corner to begin her first pass: a round-off, flic-flac, arabian salto *(Figure 32)* into a round-off, flic-flac, salto backward stretched, followed immediately by a half turn to her left to face into the corner. She danced to her right along the side and made a small leap and a split leap with change of legs. She paused in the adjacent corner but did not begin her second pass. Instead, she danced along the next side and performed an aerial walkover forward. She stepped forward, squatted down and held her squat for a moment, then stood and danced toward the center gracefully, with many turns, leaps and poses. After a jump full turn, she leaned back and fell to the ground with a half turn, landed in prone position and rolled twice to her right. With her feet and hands still on the mat, she lifted her body and then pushed off into a forward walkover. Then near the middle of the floor, she turned to her left along a diagonal and immediately began a short second pass: she performed a round-off, flic-flac, salto backward tucked. Upon landing, she made a half turn to face into the corner and drop down into splits. She then stood, danced along the adjacent side to her left, turned and danced toward the middle of the floor and ended with an aerial cartwheel to her left. Upon landing her cartwheel, she dropped down to pose with her left knee and shin on the floor, her right foot in front of her with her right knee bent, her body inclined slightly back her left arm stretched diagonally down to the left and her right arm straight above her. She had a pleasing smile on her face. From this pose, she moved into two additional poses. First, leaving her left shin in place on the floor, she leaned back, supporting herself on her straight left arm behind her, extending her right arm above and her right leg diagonally to her right. Then she made a half turn to her left, placed her right knee and shin on the floor and supported herself similarly with her right arm, her left now being stretched straight above her and her left leg extended to the side, diagonally. She stood facing left, danced forward, made a full turn to her left on her left foot with her right leg kicked high, then another full turn to her left on her right foot with her left leg slightly bent. She immediately performed a double stag jump as she danced and turned toward a corner for her third pass: a round-off, flic-flac, salto backward stretched step out. After landing, she stepped back, made a full turn to her left, spinning on her left foot, and then another half turn on her left foot. As she made this half turn, she fell forward into prone position on the floor, pushed up with her arms and stood in a dramatic final pose on her right leg, her left leg just behind, her left arm at her side and her right arm flung out to her side.

Karasyova started in the middle of one of the sides, facing along the side toward a corner, stepped toward the corner, made a hop with a turn to line up with the diagonal, a side straddle jump and a full turn before starting her first pass: a round-off, flic-flac into a salto backward stretched with full twist, followed immediately by a flic-flac with half twist to land on her seat facing the corner with her legs straddled. She leaned forward between her legs to place her chest on the floor. Then she raised her body, made a graceful half turn to her left on her seat to face the center, brought her legs around in front of her, her left leg tucked under her and her right leg slightly bent in front and made an elegant gesture with her right arm around her chest. The she slowly stood up, posed in attitude and danced toward the center with long steps and sweeping arm gestures. She made a full turn on her left foot with her right leg held horizontally outward and slowly performed a cartwheel to her left. She posed as she came out of her cartwheel with her right arm and foot on the floor and her left leg and arm in the air before coming down on her left knee and making a full turn to her left on her left knee with her right leg extended horizontally behind her in the air. She then held a dramatic pose with her left knee and shin on the floor, her right leg extended diagonally onto the floor behind her, her body inclined backward, her left arm flung out to the side and her right arm pointing vertically upward. From this pose, she leaned into a forward walkover and ended in another pose in which she bent over to touch the toes of her left foot, her left leg extended slightly forward and her right leg slightly bent. Then with her hands she lifted her left leg vertically upwards in a momentary scale and danced forward into a corner with a back scissors leap and a jump half turn to begin her second pass: a round-off, flic-flac, salto backward stretched with half turn to step out into a forward walkover. Without pausing, she made a step to her right, posed in an erect attitude standing on her left toe with her right knee bent and her foot behind her, and then posed in a curtsy. She turned to her left, made a leap with a half turn to her left and performed three butterfly turns to her left. She ended in a squat full turn to her left, made a forward roll and a pose with her left knee and shin on the floor, her body inclined halfway back resting on her left arm extended to her hand on the floor and her right leg held vertically above her by her right hand. She came out of her pose with a rising left turn and began to dance in a faster tempo. She made a turning leap and a step hop, circling around toward the center on her left and performed a front handspring and a full turn before reaching a

Olga Karasyova after landing her first pass.

corner. She made a half turn and went right into her third pass: a round-off, flic-flac, salto backward stretched, which she landed on her right foot and then stepped back onto her left. She danced forward, made a full turn and assumed her final pose: she stood upright on her left leg, her right leg diagonally back, her arms flung upwards and back and her head raised.

Karsyova's was a happy exercise. She had a smile on her face much of the time and seemed to be enjoying herself; she had a lot of original poses and movements. Floor exercise is her favorite event and she made it fun to watch.

Voronina started near the middle of the floor and danced into a corner with a high scissors leap with half turn. She made a half turn to her left back toward the corner, a deep curtsy, then a half turn back toward the center for her first pass: a round-off, flic-flac, salto backward stretched with full twist. She came out of her corner with slow, straight-leg steps to her left, turned right, then left again and stopped to lean back into a back walkover down onto her right knee and shin on the floor, her hands on the floor and her left leg extended horizontally behind her. In this pose, she made a three-quarter turn to her left to parallel the adjacent side. She stood and performed a switch-leg forward walkover, bending and stretching her right leg as she landed. After standing, she posed in back attitude, then turned to her right on her left foot with her right leg lateral. She performed a back handspring and moved into the nearest corner for her second pass: a round-off, flic-flac, salto backward stretched followed immediately by a flic-flac step-out. She danced out of her corner to her left along the adjacent side and moved counter-clockwise around the floor, performing first an aerial walkover forward and then an aerial cartwheel to her right. She posed, dropped down into splits, then stood, danced, turned, and performed another split leap as she moved into a corner for her third pass: a round-off directly into a salto backward stretched. She danced forward into her final pose, her right knee partially bent and forward, her left leg diagonally behind her and her arms held out in front her in a suppliant attitude.

Lyubov Burda started in a corner, facing one of the sides, with her head down, her arms at her side and her right leg slightly bent. When the music started, she made a half turn to her right and posed, standing with her right foot slightly forward, her head raised and her arms flung out to her side. She slowly brought her arms in and wrapped them around her chest. Then she stepped back, lined herself up with the diagonal and prepared to make her first pass: a round-off, flic-flac, salto backward stretched with full twist right into another flic-flac and salto backward stretched. After a very brief pause, she began her second pass, back along the same diagonal: a round-off, two flic-flacs and a salto backward stretched stepout followed immediately by a back walkover with half twist, which she ended in a pose, leaning forward on her hands, both arms extended, her left leg extended diagonally behind her on the floor and her right leg extended ahead diagonally above her. She pushed off into handstand with legs split, made a quarter turn to her right in handstand and came forward on her right leg to stand. She then began a series of long dance steps, sweeping arm movements, turns and poses toward the middle of the floor, after which she proceeded to a corner with dance steps and a split leap with half turn *(Figure 68)* for her third pass: a round-off, flic-flac, arabian salto. She stepped out of her arabian and immediately began to dance in a long circle counterclockwise around the floor, during which she performed two split leaps and ended with an aerial forward walkover. She stepped forward, made a half turn and a walkover backward down to a brief pose on the floor, her left leg extended ahead while she sat on her right leg tucked under her. Now in a corner, she stood, posed and prepared for her final pass: a round-off, flic-flac, walkover backward with half twist into another round-off, flic-flac. After her second flic-flac, she posed and fell forward onto her knees for her final pose: her body upright, her left arm at her side and her right arm extended vertically above her.

Lyubov Burda pushing off to split leg handstand.

These floor exercises differed vastly from those today in that they depended less upon acrobatics and more on pose, gesture, expression, and choreography. The impression created was also affected by the size of the gymnasts, who averaged 2 to 5 inches taller and 10 to 20 pounds heavier than today. The lightness of today's gymnasts gives them a definite advantage in jumps and leaps as well as in acrobatics. The older, taller gymnasts of former times could, however, project grace and artistry that some commentators regard as lost.

Figure 68

The Soviet team rotating to another apparatus. Front to back: Voronina, Petrick, Burda, Karasyova, Turischeva, Coach: Sofia Muratova. Missing: Lazakovich.

The Japanese retained their third place position with a 9.47 average on bars, while the Czechs averaged 9.43 on vault.

At the conclusion of third rotation, the standings and scores of the leading teams and individuals were as follows:

	Initial Score	Third Rotation	Subtotal
1. URS	284.20	48.65	332.85
2. GRD	284.75	46.35	331.10
3. JPN	277.85	47.35	325.20
4. TCH	277.50	47.15	324.65
1. Turischeva *(floor)*	57.55	9.90	67.45
2. Zuchold *(beam)*	57.55	9.55	67.10
3. Voronina *(floor)*	56.90	9.75	66.65
4. Janz *(beam)*	57.70	8.70	66.40
5. Burda *(floor)*	56.60	9.65	66.25
6. Petrick *(floor)*	56.65	9.55	66.20
Matsuhisa *(bars)*	56.60	9.60	66.20
8. Schmitt *(beam)*	56.70	9.45	66.15
Karasyova *(floor)*	56.35	9.80	66.15
10. Hellmann *(beam)*	56.55	9.35	65.90

Fourth Rotation

In fourth rotation, the East Germans, who had suffered a grievous setback of 2.3 points in third rotation, averaged a listless 9.33 in floor exercise. Karin Janz fought back gamely and earned 9.60, but Zuchold scored only 9.35, Schmitt, 9.30 and Hellmann, 9.25. They appeared to have been pummeled into submission!

The floor exercise of Karin Janz, however, demonstrated far more complicated acrobatics than any of the Soviet floor exercises. Furthermore, it seemed to have been attractively choreographed and to have deserved more than a 9.60. Karin's fourth-place standing in floor exercise finals would be her lot again in Munich. It is probable that East German choreography just does not register so highly with the judges as that of the Soviets. Be that as it may, her Ljubljana floor exercise was as follows:

> She started in one corner, made a high kick with her right leg and began her first pass: she ran, did a front flic-flac into a salto forward piked (but with bent legs) followed immediately by a round-off, flic-flac, salto backward stretched with full twist. She danced out of her corner to her left. Then, moving toward the middle of the floor, she performed a handspring forward and continued dancing, including a stag leap, turns and poses. She turned to her right, did a step double turn to her right and then performed a cartwheel to her right into three butterfly turns to her right, clockwise around the floor, ending in a step full turn to her right. She continued in the same direction with two turning leaps to her right and a series of three step-turns to her right. She danced in place, crossing one leg over in front

> of the other, made a half turn to her left and danced to her left, making two full turns to her left. She made a half turn to her left back toward the center of the floor, ran forward into an aerial walkover forward, which she ended by sliding her right leg forward into splits. She turned her body a quarter turn to her left, leaned forward into prone position on the floor, while straightening and stretching her legs. She rolled twice to her right into a pose with her left leg on the floor but bent at the knee with her foot vertically up, her right leg extended nearly vertically up, her right arm alongside her right leg, her head up but her stomach and left arm still on the floor. She rolled to her right on her seat into a knee scale with her arms outstretched to the side. She stood and posed in a statuesque pose on her straight left leg with her right leg slightly behind her, her right arm vertically upward and her left arm diagonally out to her left. She then moved into a nearby corner to begin her second pass: a round-off, two flic-flacs and a salto backward stretched with full twist. She danced out of her corner with turns, playful dance steps and two chassés. She moved into an adjacent corner as if preparing for her third pass but first danced forward out of it with another chassé into a full turn to her right. She then took a step and made a double turn to her right, all this on her right foot. Finally, near the center of the floor, she ran forward, made a round-off, flic-flac and a salto backward stretched for her third pass. She did some dance movements in the corner and assumed a final pose, standing erect on her toes, with her left arm diagonally upward and her right arm out to her side.

For their part, the Soviets finished the competition with a creditable 9.56 average on vault. Most of the Soviet gymnasts performed Yamashitas but Burda performed her half-on, half-off. In all, they scored 3.00 points higher than the second-place East Germans in optionals and ended 2.90 points higher in combined compulsory-optional total score. In the two years since the Mexico Olympics, however, the East Germans had moved up into a solid second-place position, while Japan and Czechoslovakia began the decline from which they have not recovered. The East Germans retained this second-place standing until displaced by the Romanians in the Montreal Olympics.

Czechoslovakia finally edged out Japan for the bronze medal with a 9.45 average on bars compared to the Japanese 9.31 average on beam. Fourth rotation was an anti climax, since the Soviet team had settled matters decisively in third rotation with their stunning performance on floor. In that rotation also, Turischeva's 9.90 in floor exercise and Karin Janz's unfortunate 8.70 on beam meant there would be virtually no chance for a change in individual standings.

In the end, the standings and scores of the leading teams and individuals after fourth rotation were as follows:

	Initial Score	Fourth Rotation	Final Total
1. URS	332.85	47.80	380.65
2. GRD	331.10	46.65	377.75
3. TCH	324.65	47.25	371.90
4. JPN	325.20	46.55	371.75
5. ROM			364.50
6. HUN			362.80
7. USA			360.20
8. RDA			356.85
1. Turischeva *(vault)*	67.45	9.60	77.05
2. Zuchold *(floor)*	67.10	9.35	76.45
3. Voronina (*(vault)*	66.65	9.50	76.15
4. Janz *(floor)*	66.40	9.60	76.00
5. Burda *(vault)*	66.25	9.60	75.85
6. Petrick *(vault)*	66.20	9.60	75.80
7. Matsuhisa *(beam)*	66.20	9.45	75.65
Karasyova *(vault)*	66.15	9.50	75.65
9. Schmitt *(floor)*	66.15	9.30	75.45
10. Hellmann *(floor)*	65.90	9.25	75.15
15. Rigby			74.45

Team winners: East Germany, 2nd; Soviet Union, 1st; Czechoslovakia. 3rd.

All-around winners: Erika Zuchold, 2nd; Ludmilla Turischeva, 1st; Zinaida Voronina, 3rd

Finals on the Apparatus

It is significant that the East Germans came back to win three of the four gold medals in finals: Zuchold in vault, Janz on bars, and Zuchold on beam. Turischeva won the fourth gold in floor exercise. In addition, Janz won the silver medal in vault and placed fourth in floor exercise, while Zuchold placed sixth on bars. The East Germans were also represented by Hellmann, who placed fifth on beam and sixth in vault, with her handspring on, quarter turn off.

Far and away the most exciting, the most emotional, the most momentous event in finals was that of Cathy Rigby's silver medal for balance beam. It had repercussions well beyond the gymnastics arena in Ljubljana and the hotel rooms where the events of the evening were being discussed. Prior to

Olga Korbut's appearance in Munich, it was the one event that awoke the interest of the American media in women's gymnastics. Perhaps the most interesting circumstance surrounding this achievement was that of the low scores on compulsory beam. The unfortunate Soviet lead-off girl, the 16-year-old Tamara Lazakovich, had scored 8.00. Her fall and other errors affected her Soviet team members: Lyubov Burda scored 8.80; Olga Karasyova, 9.00; Zinaida Voronina, 9.15; Larissa Petrick, 9.25; even Ludmilla Turischeva, eventual all-around winner, only 9.15. Cathy Rigby herself scored only 9.10. Thus, the combined compulsory-optional scores going into finals were low: Erika Zuchold had a 9.50 entering average, but the next four gymnasts—Cathy Rigby, Christine Schmitt, Larissa Petrick and Angelika Hellmann—all had 9.35. Some of the big guns of the competition—Turischeva, Voronina and Burda—had even lower averages. This situation was a break for Cathy, but she still had to get a high score in finals. The fact that she did turn in a sparklingly good performance and stick her landing evoked an ecstatic, heartwarming response from the crowd, who gave her a burst of applause when she finished, as told by Jim Prestidge in his story at the beginning of this narrative. The well-known German writer on gymnastics, Dr. Josef Göhler, reported that "Cathy Rigby was the most popular woman competitor of the championships."[3] Although her routine was not characterized by elements more innovative or risky than those of other finalists, it was sure in execution and graceful.

> Cathy ran directly toward the side of the beam near one end. She jumped off the beat board, placed her hands on the beam, and raised herself to clear straddle support position, facing across the beam, with her legs straddled horizontally in front of her. She pressed up to handstand and brought her feet together in handstand. Then she split her legs, rotated her legs a quarter turn to her left so that her right leg was over the end of the beam. She lowered her right foot down onto the end of the beam and then lowered by left foot while making a quarter turn to her left with her body as she raised herself to stand. She was now facing along the beam from one end. She posed and made graceful gestures with her arms and then performed a double stag leap as she danced forward to the other end. As she reached the end, she swung her left leg up high and made a half turn to her right on her right foot. She proceeded up to the middle of the beam with poses, a squat to her right knee and steps with high kicks. Then, in sequence, she performed a forward tinsica *(Figure 24)* and a one-arm forward walkover on her left arm. She posed at the end, made a squat half turn to her left, kicked her right leg high and then slid down into splits on the

Cathy Rigby landing a double stag leap.

beam, her right leg extended in front. She posed for a second in splits, then put her right hand on the beam and raised herself, while bending her right knee, and ended in lunge position, her left leg extended behind her. She paused in a dramatic pose, her legs in lunge position, her body tilted back, her right arm extended vertically up and her left arm diagonally down behind. She raised herself to stand, posed again, then danced forward, made a deep body wave onto her right knee, then continued to the end, where she performed an elegant scale on her right leg. Her left leg was held vertically up by her left arm, her body was horizontally forward and her right arm was extended downwards. As she extended her right arm, she made graceful movements with her right hand. She came out of her scale by lowering her left leg back to the beam, took a step back and performed a one-arm back walkover on her left arm. Then she immediately entered a second back walkover. As she passed through handstand, she bent her right leg in stag handstand pose. When she extended her right leg and brought her right foot down to the beam, she remained with her hands on the beam, her arms extended, and paused for two seconds in standing split forward position, supported by her hands, her left leg being vertically upward *(Figure 41)*. Then she brought her left leg down and raised her body and arms so that she slowly passed through attitude and posed at the end of the beam. She stood on her left leg, her right knee bent with her right foot against the calf of her left leg, her right arm extended vertically upward, her left arm extended horizontally to her left and her head facing toward her left arm. Cathy then took a step forward, made a half turn to her right, stepped back to the end, posed and made a half turn to her left. Now facing along the beam, she leaned forward, put her hands on the beam and executed a forward roll onto her back. She paused for a second on her back with her legs straddled vertically above her and her arms still holding the beam behind her. Then she continued her forward motion, brought her hands from behind her head to in front of her on the beam, swung her legs down either side of the beam and on up behind her. She ended her movements in handstand. She split her legs, lowered her right leg briefly behind her and then continued forward in walkover, letting her left leg come down onto the beam followed by her right. She stood, posed and danced a step forward and then a few steps back to the middle of the beam, as she prepared for her dismount: she ran forward to the end and punched directly off into a salto forward stretched with full twist to land *(Figure 69)*.

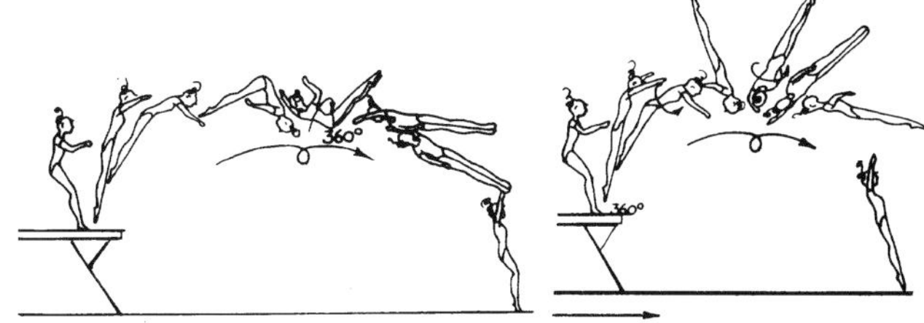

Figure 69

Cathy Rigby received 9.70 for her performance. The other 9.70 was awarded to the gold medalist, Erika Zuchold, whose routine has been previously described. The bronze medal for beam went to Christine Schmitt of East Germany. At 5 ft. 5 in., Christine was tall, even for those days. She was seventeen and weighted 48 kilograms (105.6 pounds). She received 9.55 for the following routine:

She mounted beam by running toward one end, jumping off the beat board and landing on her right foot. She took two steps forward and executed a gainer back handspring *(Figure 70)*. She took two more steps forward and posed in attitude on her right foot. She then took two more steps to the end, made a deep body wave and posed in back attitude on her right foot. She made a deep body wave and posed again in attitude, standing as before on her right foot. Still in attitude, she made a half turn to her left on her right foot. She stepped forward, made a high kick with her right leg and leaned forward into handstand, with her legs first in double stag position and then in splits. She continued on over to stand, stepped to the end and made a full turn on her left foot with her right leg kicked high in the air. At the end, she kneeled to squat, then stood and made a half turn to her left. She took two steps along the beam, did a sissone, took another step and made a split leap. She took a final step to the end and made a half turn left with her right leg kicked high in the air. She stepped forward into a cartwheel to her left which she ended in attitude, paused and performed a back handspring to the end. She stepped forward to near the middle of the beam, posed and made a half turn to her right. She stepped back, lowered herself into lunge position with her right leg forward at the middle of the beam, then let her left leg slide back as she extended her right leg and lowered herself into splits, her body facing across the beam and her left foot near the end of the beam She posed in splits, leaning forward with her arms stretched out to her side. Then, turning her body a quarter turn to the

Figure 70

> right, she raised herself to stand, facing along the beam at the end, posed and made two half turns her right. She lowered herself to squat, then stood and assumed a beautiful scale on her right foot, her left leg held vertical by her left hand and her right arm extended gracefully in front. She came out of her scale, took two steps forward and made a high split leap with change of legs to the other end, where she paused while kicking her right leg horizontally to the side and throwing her arms up overhead. She made a half turn to her left, posed, stepped forward, did an assemblé and came down into squat position. She stood up briskly into attitude on her right leg with her arms thrown up over her head. She then stepped forward into a round-off and punched off in salto backward stretched to land.

Christine's beautiful routine, which included two back handsprings—unusual for that era—was marred by several instances of loss of balance and a big hop back upon landing.

The exercises of the finalists on the other apparatuses—vault, bars, and floor exercise—have already been described. There are two routines on bars, however, that deserve mention—namely, those of Cathy Rigby and Angelika Hellmann. Although Rigby's routine was not exceptional in terms of originality, it had two elements that were both risky and not widely performed.

> From standing about six paces away from high bar, Cathy ran under high bar toward low bar, jumped off the beat board, wrapped forward around low bar and flew back in a salto forward (a "Brause" or "Radochla") *(Figure 36)* to catch high bar facing low bar. She dropped forward to low bar, kipped on low bar to catch high bar, swung back, swung forward and piked her legs over low bar to rear-lying hang. She kipped on high bar and cast back to place her feet outside her hands on top of high bar. She swung back down until, coming up between the bars, she stretched her body, made a half turn to her right and let her body drop to bounce off low bar on her hips. On her uprise from low bar, she released high bar, made a full turn to her right and, instead of bouncing off low bar a second time, she dropped to catch it with her hands. She kipped on low bar and cast back to place her feet onto the bar in stoop position facing high bar. She stood up, jumped off the low bar over the high bar with a half turn, her legs straddled, grasped high bar and swung down to wrap around low bar and fly back with a half turn to catch high bar with crossed grip, facing away from low bar. She made a half turn hanging on high bar to face low bar, dropped to low bar, performed glide, half turn, glide kip and performed a front hip circle around low bar until she could place her feet on top of low bar in stoop position. She paused, reversed direction and performed a back sole

circle on low bar one full revolution until she was on top of the bar again, this time in squat position, still facing toward high bar. Then she stood, reached for high bar, paused, pushed off low bar and pressed up to handstand. She made a half turn in handstand and swung back down to wrap around low bar, release and fly forward in hecht dismount with full turn to land.

The two elements that stood out in this routine were her salto forward ("Brause") going from low bar to high bar early in her routine and her drop to low bar after her full turn horizontally above it, after which she went immediately into her kip on low bar. Cathy did not make finals on the uneven bars because of a low score in compulsories and she only received 9.55 for the above routine in optionals. It was more exciting, however, than some of those that scored higher.

Angelika Hellmann's routine on bars scored only 9.40 in optional team competition and she did not make finals. Her routine is recorded here, however, because, as mentioned earlier, Angelika will be competing for six more years and readers may want to compare her routines in various competitions.

From the low bar side, Hellmann ran at the low bar and wrapped around it in forward hip circle up to clear front support position over the bar, her body horizontal. Then she made a long glide on low bar and piked her legs through her arms on the side away from high bar to hang on low bar. She made a partial seat circle forwards and upwards back of low bar until she could extend her inverted body vertically. She then performed a backward seat circle around low bar to rear support position (reverse kip). She moved her body backward so that the bar moved from under her seat to the under side of her knees. She then threw her body backward in a circle around low bar hanging just by the backs of her knees. (This is called a hock swing.) As she came up between the bars, she reached up and grasped high bar while releasing her knees from the bar and made a half turn. She was now facing low bar. She swung back, swung forward, and straddled her legs over low bar in rear-lying hang. She kipped on high bar until she could bring her legs up over the high bar outside her hands in straddle position. She made a straddle circle backward around high bar until, as she came up between the bars, she stretched her body horizontally over the low bar and made a half turn to her left. Now facing downwards, she allowed her stretched body to drop and bounce on her hips off low bar. On the uprise from bouncing off low bar, she made a full turn to her right this time and bounced again off low bar. After her second uprise, she made a long glide kip on high bar until she could place her feet on top of the high bar outside

Ludmilla Turischeva in vault pre-flight.

her hands, facing away from low bar. She swung back down between the bars and up on the far side, released the bar, made a half turn to her right with her stretched body horizontal and recaught the bar. She swung down, wrapped around low bar and flew back to catch high bar in eagle grip. She hung momentarily on high bar, dropped forward to catch low bar and kipped on low bar to catch high bar. She kipped on high bar to clear support position back of high bar, made a clear hip circle backward about high bar, swung forward to wrap around low bar and flew forward in hecht dismount with full twist to land.

Except for her rearward circle about low bar hanging only on the backs of her knees, Hellmann's routine contained only the usual elements of her time. It was clean, however, and very nicely done. She received a 9.40 in optionals.

The standings and scores for apparatus finals are listed below. The average is the average of compulsory and optional scores from team competition, used as an entering score.

	Average	Finals	Total
Vault			
1. Erika Zuchold	9.750	9.700	19.450
2. Karin Janz	9.650	9.700	19.350
3. Ludmilla Turischeva	9.650	9.650	19.300
Lyubov Burda	9.650	9.650	19.300
5. Marcela Vachova, TCH	9.625	9.650	19.275
6. Angelika Hellmann	9.575	9.500	19.075
Bars			
1. Karin Janz	9.750	9.800	19.550
2. Ludmilla Turischeva	9.750	9.700	19.450
3. Zinaida Voronina	9.650	9.650	19.300
4. Marianna Nemethova, TCH	9.575	9.700	19.275
Lyubov Burda	9.625	9.650	19.275
6. Erika Zuchold	9.600	9.600	19.200
Beam			
1. Erika Zuchold	9.500	9.700	19.200
2. Cathy Rigby	9.350	9.700	19.050
3. Christine Schmitt	9.350	9.550	18.900
Larissa Petrick	9.350	9.550	18.900
5. Angelika Hellmann	9.350	9.500	18.850
6. Miyuki Matsuhisa, JPN	9.475	8.650	18.125
Floor Exercise			
1. Ludmilla Turischeva	9.800	9.850	19.650
2. Olga Karasyova	9.725	9.800	19.525
3. Zinaida Voronina	9.625	9.750	19.375
4. Karin Janz	9.500	9.700	19.200
5. Miyuki Matsuhisa	9.475	9.600	19.075
6. Lyubov Burda	9.525	8.700	18.225

Miyuki Matsuhisa of Japan

Thus ended this prelude to Munich. There would be one other important pre-Munich competition—the 1971 European Championships in Minsk, USSR—but Ljubljana set the stage. Furthermore, judges in Munich would, willingly or not, have what they saw in Ljubljana in the backs of their minds as they watched the competition in Munich.

Summing up his thoughts on the 1970 World Championships, Dr. Göhler, the well-known German commentator on gymnastics, wrote these comments about the Soviets and East German women gymnasts: "Those graceful Soviet girls (were) a pure delight. How to combine the hard and difficult sport of Olympic gymnastics with so much grace and beauty may remain a secret carefully kept in Moscow, Kiev, Minsk and Leningrad . . . . The GDR girls' progress has become more marked still. Karin Janz is the best gymnast in the world as to technique. Without half slipping off the beam before her dismount, she might have become all-around champion. The Olympic team victory is within their reach in 1972 if the present rate of progress continues."[3]

Larissa Petrick

References

[1] *The Columbia Encyclopedia*, 3rd ed., s.v. "Ljubljana."

[2] Jim and Pauline Prestidge, *Mademoiselle Gymnast*, Jan./Feb. 1971: 6–7. (Now *International Gymnast*)

[3] Dr. Josef Göhler, *Olympische Turnkunst* , Dec. 1970: 14

Descriptions of routines by individual gymnasts are taken from video tapes made from films taken by Frank Endo, Fred Turoff, and l'Institut National du Sport et de l'Education Physique (France).

Larissa Petrick as a commentator. With her is her husband Viktor Klimenko, Munich Olympic Champion on the pommel horse.

Larissa Leonidovna Petrick

1965 USSR National Championships; 1st all-around (at age 15).
1966 World Championships, Dortmund, Germany, September: 6th, all-around; 3rd, beam; 4th, floor.
1967 Spartakiade, Moscow, July (USSR National Championships): 2nd, all-around.
1967 Mexico, pre-Olympic Tournament, October: 3rd, all-around.
1968 Olympics, Mexico, October: 4th all-around; 3rd, beam; 1st, floor (tie–Caslavska).
1969 USSR National Championships, Rostov, October: 2nd all-around.
1970 University Games, Turin, Italy, August: 1st, all-around.
1970 Ljubljana World Championships, October: 6th, all-around; 3rd, beam.

Born in the Ukraine, Petrick moved at an early age to Sakhalin, a big island in the Soviet far east, just north of the Japanese island of Hokkaido. Her father, an Army officer, had been transferred there. Later, the family moved back to European Russia and settled in Vitebsk, a major city in Belarus. She took up ballet at the age of seven but was encouraged to switch to gymnastics by Vikenti Dmitriev, who became her coach. (A later student of Dmitriev was Tamara Lazakovich.) A writer for *Sovietsky Sport* said of her:

> Petrick was a surprising gymnast. You looked at her exercises and were able to tell that she created from her heart, from her spirit. Larissa did not want and was not able to be a rational performer. She never repeated an exercise on the podium exactly. Larissa Latynina described her as "the great improviser."
>
> She loved the public. The noise of the hall excited her, set her on fire and the famous "Little Gypsy" brought indescribable delight even to the judges. It was in floor exercise that Petrick opened herself up completely: ease of movement but more than anything, in her gymnastic études, she created charming images by means of her passionate outbursts. (The story of how the "Little Gypsy" came about is described in the narrative of the 1968 Olympics.)
>
> In the 1970 World Championships in Ljubljana she . . . experienced the joy of being captain of the gold-medal-winning team. In the following year (at the national championships), she experienced the pain of defeat. She

> wanted to compete and felt her strength undiminished; but already a new wave had flowed over the podium with courageous girls who dared with their prodigious tricks. Since she did not want to play a secondary role, she decided to leave the scene.[1]

Larissa quit gymnastics in 1971 at the age of 21. Six years later, she talked about her life with correspondent Natalya Kalugina:

> For six years (after leaving gymnastics) I worked for Rossconcert as a variety actor. Director Sergei Andreevich Kashtelyan and I made up a number on the beam on the theme of my beloved Carmen. We built a beam which, of course, resembled gymnastics only in a very small way: in the first place in was higher and in the second place it was wider. We took the melody "Habanera" and staged an étude. From the audience it seemed that Carmen was dancing on the edge of a knife. We wanted to personify as deeply as possible the image of the heroine in this number. We thought for a long time about the design and decided on the possibility of staying away from outside effects. I tried to embody Carmen by the fluidity of my movements.
>
> The number lived for six years. A renewing of the contract was not expected and the traveling life of an artist did not suit me. I was drawn to the family, to home. Yet I understood I must look for something. At that time preparations were going forward for the Moscow Olympics and some former athletes were invited to study at the journalism school of Moscow State University so they could work as commentators at the Games. I was among those invited.[2]

Petrick began her work as a commentator at the 1978 World Championships in Strasbourg, where, incidentally, she was very much impressed by the Americans—Marcia Frederick, world champion on bars, Kathy Johnson with her interesting program in floor exercise, and Rhonda Schwandt with her highly successful performance in vault.

In an interview in the Soviet magazine *Physical Culture and Sport* a few months before the Moscow Olympics, she talked about possible candidates for the Soviet team and reminisced about herself.

> Nelli Kim came from the gymnastics of Korbut and Turischeva, but she did not stay put in one place. In love with that gymnastics, brought up in those traditions, she, like Comaneci, did not feel deeply the success of the gold medals she had won in Montreal and so ought to try again. In Montreal 1976, her double salto backwards in floor exercise and her Tsukahara with twist vault satisfied her wish, but the evolution of difficulty is unending. Kim is doing the double salto backward stretched, an element

of the highest difficulty, but at 22, she is getting older. That is why, disregarding the lure of medals, I very much hope for success for Nelli.

Why do I relive Kim's past? Simply because memories wash over me. I left gymnastics just when experience and the real ability to control my body had come to me. Only at 20 did I understand how to prepare myself. Yet there was now this matter of difficulty. Of course, I could learn from the new gymnastics another two elements but no more. In addition, even mastering them, I would be betraying myself. Kuchinskaya did simple exercises on the beam, but they made my flesh creep. This is where it begins: if a gymnast's head does not keep up to what her body can do, it is not gymnastics.

Nelli Kim—may she have still another moment of inspiration such as I had in Mexico on the 25th of October 1968. An enormous amount of energy, as if accumulated in my whole sporting life, filled me to overflowing and carried me under the gypsy melody in that floor exercise to the happiness of the temperamental public, to their love of Larissa Petrick. That is what I wish for Nelli Kim.[3]

Petrick married gymnast Victor Klimenko after the 1972 Olympics and moved to Moscow. They have a son and a daughter. The family is now in Rome, where Victor is coaching an Italian club.

References

[1]V. Yasterov, "Larissa Petrick Did the Gymnastics Commentary," *Sovietsky Sport,* 29 Mar. 1981.

[2]Natalya Kalugina, "I Always Searched for Inspiration," *Sovietsky Sport,* 10 July 1987.

[3]Y. Darakhvelidze, "Wonderful World of Gymnastics," *Physical Culture and Sport,* 1980.

Young gymnasts having fun.

Zinaida Voronina

1966 World Championships, Dortmund, Germany, September (as Zinaida Druzhinina): 10th, all-around; 3rd, floor.

1967 European Championship, Amsterdam, May (as Druzhinina): 2nd, all-around; 5th (tie) vault; 4th, bars; 3rd, beam, floor.

1967 Mexico, pre-Olympic Tournament (as Voronina): October: 5th all-around.

1968 USSR National Championships, Leningrad: 2nd all-around.

1968 Olympics, Mexico, October: 2nd, all-around; 3rd, vault, bars; 4th, floor.

1970 USSR National Championships, Minsk, May: 2nd, all-around.

1970 World Championships, Ljubljana: 3rd, all-around; 3rd, bars, floor.

Zinaida Voronina and Tamara Lazakovich are the two Soviet gymnasts whose lives were extremely unhappy after they retired from gymnastics. Voronina herself was so talented that she could easily learn new elements; after the birth of her son, Dimka, she was able to get back into shape quickly and become a member of the 1970 World Championships team. In 1967, between Dortmund and Mexico, she married Mikhail Voronin, world champion in Dortmund. Zinaida Voronina and Olga Karasyova, who had been together on the Soviet team since Dortmund, tried to make the team for the 1972 Munich Olympics but were replaced by Olga Korbut and Tamara Lazakovich. Her life since then has been well described by Natalya Kalugina in an article for *Sovietsky Sport* dated February 4, 1990.

> I turned a letter to Zinaida over in my hands. Then, with her permission, I read it. A fan from Estonia begged for a her autograph. Almost twenty years had gone by since she carried the women's team on her shoulders to first place in the Mexico Olympic Games and seventeen years since we had, if you like, some official news about her.
>
> We could write about Zinaida Voronina if only because she was an Olympic champion. Whoever has even once come close to the podium knows what a titanic job it is even to become "simply" a master of sport, let alone winning an Olympic medal.
>
> We should, however, write about Zinaida Voronina for still another reason. There were in her life frightful days when an alcoholic fog clouded

her eyes. But this delicate woman was able to pick herself up and overcome it herself. And it was, I think, a victory no easier than her most crucial competitions.

To find Voronina seemed like a difficult task. To the appointed meeting at the Valashihinsky mechanical foundry where she was working Zinaida did not come, and when I appeared at her home, she asked me: "Could we go over all this tomorrow? I am not ready now." When the next day came, I went to her house, but I was worried.

Zina, why is it you do not like us, journalists?

Well, it's this way. Understand, I have been frightfully ashamed. You know what they say—in gymnastics, there are only two good-for-nothings, Voronina and Lazakovich. I was afraid you would be checking up on me: had I become the person they talk about? Now I am not afraid. Ask what you want.

To tell you the truth, it was not an interview in the strict sense. I asked about something, Zina made inquiries about her friends on the team. Her heart yearned for them and for her happy sporting youth. And so, little by little, we stretched out a woman's conversation about a difficult life.

Less than a year after Mexico, I was waiting for Dimka (her child). Two weeks after his birth, I ironed my leotard, got out my gym shoes and went to the workout. Of course, they were waiting for me; but nobody knew whether I would be able to show results quickly. Yet four months later, I competed in the national championships and took second place. Again I returned to the team. Then I went to the world championships in Ljubljana; that was in 1970. There, young Ludmilla Turischeva went by me in the all-around; I was third. Incidentally, I always admired her. Her love of work was astonishing. Her coach said: "Do it ten times." So that's how many times she did it. For me, everything came more easily: after the second or third time, I had it. I loved victories, the attention of the spectators. I loved gymnastics, but not fanatically. Not so Lyuda. It is now, when I look at my medals or how gymnasts go out onto the podium, that my heart winces. At that time, my friends and my favorite person, my husband, were more important than anything else in my life; but it turned out that all my friends were not friends. I was young, kind of dumb, and did not realize it.

Well, no matter. After Ljubljana, Olga Karasyova and I began to prepare for the Olympics in Munich, but Lazakovich and Korbut were put on the team instead of us. After Munich, I trained again but with less enthusiasm. Gradually, I left. I was then twenty-seven. I tried to work as a coach but I could not. My husband and I separated.

Why were you not able to be a coach?

I was impatient. I wanted the girls immediately to perform what I told them and showed them. When they didn't get it, I felt nervous, I became irritated. I could not work with young kids.

But you loved gymnastics . . .

I loved to train and to perform, but to be a coach was not my vocation. And a love for gymnastics . . . ? I always said that when I finished gymnastics, I would be a simple worker. Well, that's what happened.

Zina, are you not ashamed?

What for—that I am a simple worker? No, I'm ashamed for another reason. You see, I gave everything I had to gymnastics. When I left, did anybody remember me? Did anybody need me? Nobody took an interest in how I felt or how I was living. And if I went to the Sport Committee, they said: "Zina, you're a grown woman now. Look after yourself." For me to live was not easy. But in such a life as mine was, it's true, I was guilty.

Now they give Olympic pensions.

Yes, but it's not money I need. Money I earn myself. I put in two shifts, so my income is not bad. And I'll have a good pension—132 rubles. Understand, then I wanted simple human attention, kind words. And now it's OK. I left gymnastics so let it forget me. Sometimes I even wish that nobody knows that I am an Olympic champion. Yet not long ago, I was walking along the street and there a very old lady was standing. She was afraid to cross. I went up to help her and she said: "Zina?! Druzhinina?!" She cried and I cried, as memories washed over me.

Would you like to see your old friends on the team?

As much as ever! Olechka Karasyova, Larissa Petrick and Natalya Kuchinskaya. But, no. I'm afraid. They will not believe, will not understand that my life has become normal. Yes, it's a shame. Everything has turned out for them, they have good work. How much I went through before I found out how to live as a person! Even so, yes I would love to see them again. We did quarrel and did offend one another, but I only now remember what a friendly team we had.

What is your work now?

At the time of pouring into the mold, I must prepare the earth. I oversee this work. In principle, the work is not complicated. I press the button—that's all. But as you stand gaping, the earth begins to fall down, then it happens you have to forge with the spade. Sometimes the whole machine.

But that's not woman's work!

Yes, I'm a carrier. I can drag along the whole bale. In sport it was not any easier.

Are you satisfied with this work?

In general, yes. At the factory we have a big sport complex and there is gymnastics there. We are selecting a group. Any kids, even those without any talent. We train. I would like to be closer to sport, to gymnastics.

Zina, but the past, not necessarily your gymnastic past, but other parts of it. Couldn't you go back to it?

No. Not for any reason. That was some kind of a delusion. Now that is past. Everything. It is enough.

I turned the letter over in my hands. Then with her permission I read it. The fan from Estonia had remembered Zina Voronina all these years, but we had forgotten her, had left her alone with her unhappiness. Alone she had overcome it. I believe that, for Zina, everything is now ahead of her. I believe she will overcome her fear and, in the spring, with her head proudly lifted up, will enter the Olympic sport complex for the *Moscow News* tournament. There she will get together with all her friends. She will have nothing to be ashamed of but can be proud of herself and continue her life.[1]

Four years later, Natalya Kalugina again interviewed Voronina and wrote this supplement to the former article.

Foreigners have difficulty understanding what life is like in remote, out-of-the-way places in Russia. Confused by the large number of different populations in the country, they suppose they are normal towns but with all their own peculiar cultures. Alas, they are wrong. Authentic Russian life exists only in Moscow and St. Petersburg. Out there, on the periphery, people morally deteriorate. They drown in drunkenness and have family fights in a frenzy of intoxication. Arguments are settled by a blow with a knife or an axe. In breaks from these fights, they try to earn a living—whoever can. (80% of crime in Russia takes place in the family.)

In such a province, in the town of Uoshkar-Ola, Zina was born in 1949. She does not remember her father. Her mother worked as a cook in the town canteen and sometimes suppressed her troubles with vodka. And, probably, Zinaida was destined for such a life if she had not been richly endowed with physical abilities or if nobody had noticed her gifts. Thus, Zina Voronina found herself in artistic gymnastics.

It was a stroke of luck for her that Yuri Shtukman, Lyubov Burda's coach who had formed the first sports school specializing in gymnastics, had begun to open other gymnastics schools besides the one in Voronezh. Thus such schools were opened in Moscow itself, Alma Ata, Yaroslavl and Uoshkar-Ola.

Her first victories soon appeared and with them her summons to Moscow in the group at the Dynamo Sports Club. Coach Peter Shelkovnikov brought her there. Life for the fifteen-year-old girl developed differently from her peers. Model Moscow girls who led upright lives lost to her. Although she became familiar with all the establishments around her where she could buy champagne, nevertheless she became stronger and stronger in gymnastics.

Sometimes when I think about Zinaida Druzhinina-Voronina, I associate her with Edith Piaf in the first stages of her life. They were both girls of the street, both unusually talented. But how differently their lives ended! (Edith Piaf was a French singer who was born in a poor area of Paris. She earned her living by singing in the streets and was befriended by the owner of a cabaret. He gave her the name Piaf, which is French for sparrow because of her diminutive size and chirpy appearance, and built her into a star. After a career which spanned nearly twenty-five years, her health began to fail and she died at the age of 48. Her most famous song was "La vie en rose.")

Now in a moment of sobriety, Zina says:

"You understand, I am not a champion, not a gymnast. I am from among unskilled workers and I did not need glory. Like my mother, I wanted to be a cook. You know how tastefully I cook shchee (a Russian soup)? The girls needed their glory, but I did not. If it had not been for sport, my life would probably have been more normal."

Frankly speaking, I do not believe such assertions. Not only because at the end of the nineteen-sixties and the beginning of the nineteen seventies, Zinaida Druzhinina was among the top gymnasts of the world but also because such an achievement demanded enormous willpower. Gold Olympic medals are not won with talent alone. I do not believe it because the more I know Zinaida, the more she asks about her friends on the team, the more I see her cutting clippings from the newspapers which tell of the doings of the Mexico champions. She greedily seizes each word which tells about them and their husbands and how the children are growing up. But to the question, why do you not get in touch with them yourself? she answers:

"Their lives are in order. But what have I become? They will look upon me as on some wild animal in a zoo."

I know that when a friend of coach Peter Shlkovnikov called her, she agreed to a meeting but again had a bout of drinking. When one wants not to talk about the past, one does not behave oneself in such a way. Normally, the past does not arouse emotions; about it one simply forgets. Zinaida wanted to talk about the past but was afraid to.

After her departure from sport in 1972, Druzhinina, who was then already Voronina, having married the strongest gymnast of that time, Mikhail Voronin, tried to work as a coach but could not. She remembers those times.

"I was young. I knew gymnastics, of course, but I could not busy myself with small children. My son was very young. Therefore I had no experience in handling six-year-olds. To teach beginners correct gymnastics seemed very boring to me. If they had offered me a group of masters of sport, whose performance I could just polish, with whom I could show in what I was talented, then perhaps I would have remained as a coach. But just to explain how to point your toes was something I could not do. My mind was occupied with complicated acrobatics."

Around Dynamo, where Zinaida worked at that time, there were people who liked to be acquainted with stars of sport. They tried to drink with sport stars in order to brag that they had drunk with such and such a star.

Zinaida did not shun the temptation. The more she heard unpleasant words from her colleagues because her work did not go well, the more in drinking she became the queen she once was. Now in my opinion, she regrets it sincerely enough. But it's late. Her sickness is almost incurable. She finally lost her work and her family. Because of her drinking she was denied family rights. Because of being a parasite she was sent, by decision of a judge, out beyond the first hundred kilometers from Moscow.

How she lived in exile, God only knows. Although I am the only journalist with whom Zinaida Voronina will confide since the day of her return to the outskirts of Moscow, I did not hear how she lived. She does not like to talk about it.

"Well, what are the first hundred? There people also live, but not as you live here."

With a big effort, Zinaida succeeded in returning to the Moscow suburbs. There was no question of thinking about work in sport. She arranged to work in Balashikha at a foundry working in farming equipment. As she explained to me, her work consists of regulating the amount of earth in the steel kilns. Voronina once again plunged into the same life as in the provinces where she was born. Her name is only remembered by people connected with gymnastics. But even then she did not find peace.

She became very ill and went to the hospital. She had three operations on one part of her body. When she was about to die, she suddenly heard the words which she had waited to hear all these years. The doctor who did the operations, understanding that he was taking a big professional risk, muttered:

"Be patient, Zinochka. Be patient, dear girl. I will do everything I can for you. I remember the name Zinaida Voronina."

The hospital was pitiful. There were not enough nurses or hospital attendants. There was nobody to carry the dying from the wards. And Zinaida helped the only nurse. At first, they persuaded her that it was harmful for her to carry heavy burdens, but she replied:

"I am a gymnast. I know how to control my muscles. I know which group to strain, which to relax. It is nothing; I can manage."

Actually, she did manage. After eight months, Voronina was released from the hospital. Hardly had she gone back to work than her mother fell ill. In four months she had died.

All this time, Voronina did not work. She did not think about getting documents from the hospital to explain her absence. She lost her work.

"I now have a dream—to return to work at the factory. I am accustomed to it; I have friends there. Yes, they do not forget. They say it will be difficult here, but we will help you. Only I am afraid they will not be able to understand what is really my difficulty. You know, for me what is difficult is not the same as for them. All my life I have been able to work with my hands. For me it is difficult when I remember gymnastics. When I see the podium on television, it is as though something passes by me. Then I begin to cry and I don't want to see anybody."

Thus life flies past the great gymnast Zinaida Voronina. It torments her.[2]

References

[1]Natalya Kalugina, "Zinaida Voronina: A Faded Flower Returns to Life," *Sovietsky Sport,* 4 Feb. 1990.

[2]Interview by Natalya Kalugina, Mar. 1994, for this book.

Olga Karasyova

1966 World Championships, Dortmund, Germany, September: 15th, all-around, as Olga Kharlova.

1968 Olympics, Mexico, October: 7th, all-around, as Olga Karasyova.

1969 European Championship, Landskrona, Sweden, May: 2nd, all-around; 3rd, vault; 2nd, bars, beam; 1st, floor.

1969 USSR National Championships, Rostov, October: 4th, all-around; 1st, floor.

1970 World Championships, Ljubljana, Slovenia, October: 7th, all-around; 2nd, floor.

1971 Spartakiade, Moscow, July (USSR National Championships): 2nd, all-around.

1972 USSR National Championships, Kiev, April: 4th, all-around.

Like Elvira Saadi, who came after her, Olga Karasyova was always a strong, supporting member of the Soviet team, as evidenced by her 7th place all-around standing both in the Mexico Olympics and the Ljubljana World Championships. Her highest achievement came in the 1969 European Championships, where she placed second all-around behind Karin Janz. As with Saadi, Karasyova had a beautiful floor exercise. She won the gold medal for floor exercise in the European Championships and the 1969 National Championships; she won the silver medal for floor exercise in the Ljubljana World Championships.

Commenting on the 1969 USSR National Championships, Larissa Latynina wrote:

> I witnessed a competition in which Olga Korbut was a rival of Olga Karasyova, an Olympic gold medalist and the reigning European champion (in floor exercise). The rapturous expression with which the little girl watched Olga Karasyova is something I shall remember for a long time.
>
> "Like it?," I asked her.
>
> "Very much," she replied. "When I look at her, I can hardly keep my feet still. I'll try to do as well,"[1]

Olga Karasyova and Zinaida Voronina, both veterans of the 1970 World Championships, tried to make the team for the 1972 Olympics but were replaced by Olga Korbut and Tamara Lazakovich.

Karasyova graduated from the Moscow Teacher's College having majored in foreign languages. She worked for a time for the USSR Sport Committee, where she reviewed material from the International Gymnastics Federation, but was let go in a reduction of sport committee staff. Now she is at home, mainly looking after her mother, who is not well. Her husband is a businessman; they have no children.[2]

During the Moscow Olympics, she worked as an interpreter for the organizing committee.[3]

References

[1]Larissa Latynina, "A Determined Little Girl," *Soviet Union,* Jan. 1973: 36–37.

[2]Notes by Lera Mironova of the Russian magazine, *Family.*

[3]Dr. Josef Göhler, "Russian National Championships," *International Gymnast,* Jul. 1977: 51.

Ludmilla Turischeva's great after-flight in Yamashita vault

European Championship

1971

Minsk, Belarus

Sports Palace

October 16th to 17th

The most important event in 1971 was the European Championship, held in Minsk, Belorussian Republic, now Belarus. It was the steppingstone from Ljubljana to Munich. Considering how few international competitions there were in those days, the European Championships had great prestige. In Minsk, forty-two gymnasts representing twenty-one countries participated.

An eye-witness account, written by Mr. Carl Haberland for Gymnast magazine, is reprinted here in part, courtesy of the International Gymnastics Hall of Fame.[1]

> The competition took place in the beautiful Sports Palace opposite the modern Yubileinaya Hotel where the competitors were housed. Minsk, although in existence for 800 years, has few older buildings, since most of the city was destroyed in the second world war. The city is now composed of a number of modern flats, parks and very wide boulevards.
>
> (On the first day of competition) the forty-two competitors were placed in four groups . . . . Within a group, the first competitor would rotate to next-to-last for the following event. The competition took roughly four hours. Optional exercises were presented, so this competition will give a good indication of what to expect in Munich in 1972.

Tamara Lazakovich on beam, having recovered completely from her experience in Ljubljana.

Ludmilla Turischeva and Tamara Lazakovich tied for first place honors with scores of 38.85. Turischeva had 9.9 on floor (even though her routine has been enriched since the World Championships at Ljubljana, where she also had 9.90) and got 9.8 for a Yamashita which had to be one of the all-time classics in this event. Erika Zuchold of East Germany was third with a score of 38.80. Unfortunately, she had several bobbles on the beam which led to a score of only 9.4. Tied for fourth place were the Hungarian Ilona Bekesi and the Czech, Sonya Brazdova.

(The evening of the second day of competition) saw the six top girls in each event compete for the final event championships. Turischeva won gold medal in free exercise and vault, while Lazakovich took bars and beam. Zuchold took third place on all events except bars for which her teammate Angelika Hellmann got the bronze medal.

Just to let the rest of the world know that they still have a few promising young gymnasts left, the meet was brought to a close with exhibitions by three fine young Russian girls 12 to 14 years old. Their routines would get 9.0 plus in my book.

Notes:

1. Lots of good, high tumbling on the floor. Turischeva's mount is now round-off, flip-flop back $1/2$, round-off, flip-flop, full.

2. On the bars, one of the young Russian girls stands on the high bar and throws a layout back catch the high bar, wrap around low bar. (Korbut)

3. Lazakovich works the beam with great forcefulness and precision. Tack-tack-tack!

4. On the vault, Turischeva's Yamashita seemed destined to take her into orbit. Such after-flight!

Ludmilla Turischeva

All-around

1.	Turischeva, URS	38.85
	Lazakovich, URS	38.85
3.	Zuchold, GDR	38.30
4.	Brazdova, TCH	37.65
	Bekesi, HUN	37.65
6.	Hellmann, GDR	37.30

Vault

1.	Turischeva	19.60
2.	Lazakovich	19.55
3.	Hellmann	19.50

Bars

1.	Lazakovich	19.35
2.	Turischeva	19.20
3.	Hellmann	19.00

Beam

1.	Lazakovich	19.20
2.	Turischeva	19.15
3.	Zuchold	19.00

Floor Exercise

1.	Turischeva	19.65
2.	Lazakovich	19.60
3.	Zuchold	19.25

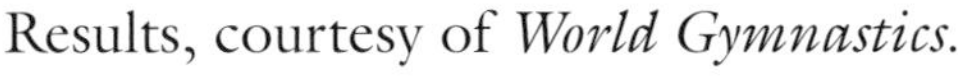

Results, courtesy of *World Gymnastics*.

There are other important events that should be noted.

Minsk

U.S.A. vs. U.S.S.R.

Penn State University
University Park, Pennsylvania: February 5th and 6th

Under the direction of Penn State coach Gene Wettstone, a full house of 7,200 spectators each night saw American gymnasts competing against the world champions from Ljubljana. It was a unique occasion because the Soviets had brought the cream of their crop, including four Ljubljana team members—World Champion Ludmilla Turischeva; bronze medalist all-around Zinaida Voronina; veterans from Dortmund, Mexico and Ljubljana Larissa Petrick and Olga Karasyova; and Rusudan Sikharulidze, the number one reserve at Ljubljana. (They brought only five gymnasts.) It was also one of the last meets for Larissa Petrick and Zinaida Voronina, who would be fading from the scene as Munich approached.

The American team consisted of Wendy Cluff, Mexico veteran; Cathy Rigby, Mexico and Ljubljana; Joan Moore and Adele Gleaves, Ljubljana; and future Munich team members, Roxanne Pierce and Kim Chace.

The great former champion, Larissa Latynina, was most impressed by Cathy Rigby and said, "Cathy Rigby is a splendid gymnast, confident in all the exercises, and simply matchless on the beam, which everyone thinks is the trickest piece of apparatus. Cathy is unquestionably the ace of the American team; the only contender, I believe, who can hold her own against European and Japanese opposition."[2]

Unfortunately, in this meet, Cathy had some problems on bars (8.35). Kim Chace had some problems on beam (8.40), but Joan Moore earned special distinction in floor exercise.

Results were as follows:[3]

	Vault	Bars	Beam	Floor	Total
1. USSR	37.90	37.70	37.30	38.25	151.15
2. USA	37.50	36.75	36.55	38.10	148.90
1. Ludmilla Turischeva, USSR	9.60	9.65	9.40	9.70	38.35
2. Zinaida Voronina, USSR	9.50	9.40	9.40	9.55	37.85
3. Rusudan Sikharulidze, USSR	9.30	9.35	9.45	9.35	37.45
4. Olga Karasyova, USSR	9.40	9.30	8.90	9.65	37.25
5. Wendy Cluff, USA	9.35	9.05	9.15	9.45	37.00
Joan Moore, USA	9.20	8.95	9.25	9.60	37.00
7. Cathy Rigby, USA	9.40	8.35	9.65	9.50	36.90
8. Larissa Petrick, USSR	9.40	9.25	9.05	9.05	36.75
9. Roxanne Pierce, USA	9.50	9.40	8.50	9.20	36.60
10. Kim Chace, USA	9.25	9.35	8.40	9.55	36.55

Other important events in 1971:[4]
Spartakiade of the Russian Federation, May, in Rostov:

1. Lyubov Burda	75.95
2. Zinaida Voronina	75.35
3. Ludmilla Turischeva	75.30

Spartakiade of the Belorussian Republic, now Belarus, in Minsk:

1. Olga Korbut	75.50
2. Tamara Lazakovich	74.75

Spartakiade of the Soviet Union, Moscow, July:

1. Tamara Lazakovich	75.20
2. Olga Karasyova	75.05
3. Antonina Koshel	74.60
4. Ludmilla Turischeva	74.40
Olga Korbut	74.40
6. Rusudan Sikharulidze	73.95

References

[1]C. Haberland, "European Gymnastic Championships for Women," *Gymnast,* Jan. 1972: 15–17.

[2]Lyn Moran, "Cathy Rigby—Gymnast, Coach, Celebrity," *International Gymnast,* Oct. 1978: 32–48.

[3]*Mademoiselle Gymnast,* Mar./Apr. 1971: 6

[4]*Olympische Turnkunst,* Sept. 1971: 21–23.

Soviet team at Penn State, left to right: Voronina, Petrick, Sikharulidze, Karasyova, Turischeva's coach Vladislav Rastorotsky, Larissa Latynina, Turischeva.

Olympics 1972 Munich, Germany Sporthalle

August 27th to September 1st

There is no more exciting word in all the history of gymnastics than "Munich." The 1972 Olympics in Munich, Germany, was the spark that set off the explosion of interest in women's gymnastics throughout the world.

Munich's effect was felt not just by the gymnastics community but by all the hundreds of millions of people who were watching the Olympics on television. This effect resulted from the emotional impact of what those millions of people saw. It was not just admiration for the athletic achievement that coincided with watching a swimmer win seven gold medals. The emotional impact came from the joy of seeing an adorable young woman perform unbelievable feats on the apparatus, followed by the anguish of seeing her stumble on the very apparatus that had first given rise to that joy and then the joy again of seeing her vindicate herself on the last day. She attracted all who watched so that they became completely involved in what she was doing. They exulted with her on the first occasion, cried with her on the second, and exulted with her again on the third. Nothing like it had happened before; nothing similar has happened since.

Newsweek magazine summed it up well in the following paragraphs:

> She enthralled the crowd in Munich's bright little Sporthalle the moment she entered, 88 pounds of charm and magnificent skills. Some had come to the gymnastics competition to view Cathy Rigby, the Californian

> who had stolen the Mexico City show when she was only 15; others were pulling for the East German favorite, Karin Janz. But Rigby didn't even qualify for the final night of competition and Janz proved talented but colorless, and soon the scene belonged to tiny 17-year-old Olga Korbut.
>
> Like her sister Russian gold medalist, Ludmilla Turischeva, gymnast Olga belied everything about the widely-held image of strapping, manly Soviet female athletes. She was pure femininity as she swirled and twisted through her routines: she was a children's-story heroine in peril as she slipped heartbreakingly on the uneven bars.
>
> When she finished, Olga had captured three gold medals and one silver, just surpassing the total of her rival Janz, who took two gold medals, two silver and one bronze; but the numbers mattered less than the impression she created. In fact, all the angry words and judges' decisions and medals totals seem far less meaningful than the images etched in Munich: Olga, slipping, faltering, recovering, as the crowd exhales in relief; Mark Spitz, holding his gold medals and studying them hard, as if he was just beginning to realize what he was accomplishing; Shane Gould (Australian swimmer) raising her stuffed kangaroo mascot on the winner's platform or Beverly Whitfield (Australian swimmer) hurling herself aloft in giddy triumph. Now track and field offers a whole new range of images, all framed against the sculpted grandeur of the roofed Olympic stadium—and all destined to add to the brilliance of an already dazzling Olympics.[1]

There had been a reasonably large build-up by the media. Everyone knew the 1972 Olympics in Munich was going to be a much bigger affair than the 1968 Olympics in Mexico. There was much publicity about the advanced architectural design of the stadium where the athletic events would take place. The innovative design of the Olympic village had caught the public's attention, not only for its uniqueness but also for the prospect that the buildings would be converted to apartments once the Olympics were over. Such matters as electronic timing, communications equipment, accommodation, and food for the athletes were expected to be on the highest possible scale. It was, in short, going to be West Germany on parade.

The two bell towers of the 15th century Liebfrauenkirche (Church of Our Lady)

The Munich Olympics took place two-thirds of the way through a year that had already been eventful. In February, President Nixon had gone to China with his National Security Adviser, Dr. Henry Kissinger, for talks with Mao Tse-tung and Prime Minister Chou En-Lai. It was a momentous occasion, a diplomatic breakthrough that captured the attention of the world. In May, President Nixon and Dr. Kissinger had gone to Moscow for talks with General Secretary of the Communist Party, Leonid Brezhnev. The Moscow trip generated less enthusiasm than the China trip, but people hoped it would reduce tensions and create better relations between the United States and the Soviet Union. It did for a short while, but unfortunately by September relations had chilled and had gone back to normal: the Soviets were exhibiting their customary suspicion and xenophobia. The chill in Moscow would unexpectedly be replaced by the exuberance and warmth of the world's reaction to Olga and the other Soviet Olympians. In Munich, the world received a different view of the average Russian.

On June 17th, five men were arrested for breaking into the offices of the Democratic National Committee in the Watergate apartment complex in Washington, D.C. The scandal over political espionage erupted and displaced all other news in importance. President Nixon and the Republican party survived it temporarily and the Democratic Presidential candidate, George McGovern, suffered a devastating defeat in the November elections. The Watergate break-in and subsequent cover-up, however, eventually led to Mr. Nixon's resignation.

Throughout the year, peace talks between the United States and North Vietnam were being held in Paris, led by Dr. Kissinger. At the end of October, the negotiators revealed agreement for a ceasefire in the Viet Nam war.

In the United States, the Olympics came as a sort of respite between Watergate and the onset of the climax to the Presidential campaign. In the rest of the world, interest was centered on how the technologically superior West Germans would hold the Games and on athletic performance that people expected would exceed that of previous Olympics. In gymnastics, they were not to be disappointed. Munich was a time of great change, not only in the nature of the sport itself, as we shall see, but also in the way competitions were conducted.

At the time of the 1972 Olympics, the rules and organization of women's gymnastics competition were still in a state of evolution. The structure of competition has developed and stabilized since then, although organizing committees and the technical committees of the International Gymnastics Federation continue to experiment with changes in format and execution in order to eliminate biased judging, prevent any one team from having an advantage over the others because of favorable competition time and, in general, to make the competition more fair. At the time of this writing, the International Federation is conducting world championships in new ways.

Most importantly, Munich was the first Olympics with a separate individual all-around competition. In Mexico and other previous Olympics and world championships, the all-around winners were those who had scored highest in team competition, that is, those who had the highest total scores from compulsory and optional exercises. This procedure allowed a gymnast to receive two medals—team and individual—from the one team competition. Since Mexico, the International Olympics Committee had decreed that no athlete could win two medals from one competitive performance. Hence, the new all-around competition in gymnastics was instituted. In Munich, the gymnast would have to perform in this separate competition to win an all-around medal. His or her total score would be made up first of an entering average from team competition, that is, the compulsory and optional totals added together and divided by two; this score would then be added to that achieved in the all-around to make up the combined total. This all-around competition would not affect the final competition on the apparatus, however. In other ways, the gymnastics competition in Munich was different from what it is today.

♦ Judging was much more biased than it is today. There has always been a temptation for a judge to favor a gymnast from her own country or from a country of the same political persuasion. Since then, measures have been introduced to eliminate or at least reduce political bias. In 1972, however, biased judging was blatant.

♦ Women's optional competition took place on the day immediately following compulsories. There was no day of rest in between as there is today.

♦ The field of competition was more crowded than it is today. There were nineteen teams in Munich. Nowadays, the preceding world championship qualifies the teams and only the top twelve are allowed to enter the Olympics.

♦ In Munich, only one woman coach per team was allowed on the floor. Now it is customary to have two coaches, one man and one woman.

♦ The compulsory exercises were less uniform in Munich than they are today, or even than they were before Munich. Nowadays, and in previous competitions, compulsory exercises are and were rigidly specified: each gymnast had to perform exactly the same routine or vault. In Munich, as an experiment, only required elements of the exercise were specified by the

International Gymnastics Federation. Teams could incorporate the elements as they wished into routines that they made up themselves, but all members of a team had to perform the same exercise. They were allowed to select their own music for floor exercise. (In vaulting, of course, all gymnasts performed the same vault.) This experiment did not last beyond Munich, primarily because it was too hard on the judges. It was too difficult for them to determine whether all the required elements were being included when they were presented with nineteen different versions of what was supposed to be the same exercise.

♦ In Munich, gymnasts were not allowed to do stretching and warm-up exercises while awaiting their turns on to the apparatus. Such warming up is now permitted. Perhaps one reason for the modification of this rule was that it was more rigidly enforced on western countries than it was on eastern bloc countries.

♦ As the gymnastics competition began, the efficient West Germans dispatched both the men's and women's compulsory exercises in one day, with five sessions of women and three of men. This difference in number was possible because men's teams can compete simultaneously on the six apparatus whereas only four women's teams can compete simultaneously on the four apparatus. Nowadays, compulsory exercises are stretched out over a period of two or more days.

View of the Olympic site from the television tower.

The Compulsory Exercises

Competition 1a: August 27th

As in Ljubljana, the competition in Munich was primarily between the Soviet Union and East Germany. These two top teams competed in the last group of the evening, always the most favorable time because the judges are more in a better mood for their job than they are in the early morning. Also, they know that the best teams are on the floor, teams that are expected to get the best marks, so they get them. After the last evening performance, the Soviets finished 1.85 points ahead of the East Germans in compulsories, but the East Germans were 5.15 points ahead of the third-place Hungarian and Czech teams and 5.20 points ahead of the United States. The two leading teams were thus in a class by themselves.

In compulsories, the Soviets started on bars. Korbut and Turischeva, who had come in to the Olympics in first and second positions, respectively, as a result of their standings in the USSR Cup selection trials, each scored 9.60. Until then, only Ilona Bekesi of Hungary had scored so high on bars; she had been in the previous group. Tamara Lazakovich scored 9.55.

The East Germans started on beam, a difficult apparatus to begin on. The scores of the leaders were remarkably low: Karin Janz scored 9.35 and Erika Zuchold, 9.25. The East German team as a whole, however, scored only 0.10 less than the Soviets would on beam, 45.80 to 45.90. The American girls, incidentally, had scored 45.60 in a previous group. This total would put them 0.2023 ahead of the Hungarians, who had scored 45.40.

When, in second rotation, it came to the Soviets' turn on beam, Olga Korbut scored 9.25, but Ludmilla Turischeva scored only 9.05. Tamara Lazakovich, however, scored a strong 9.40, the highest score for compulsory beam in the Olympics. Lazakovich, who had fallen from beam in the 1970 World Championships, had worked hard since then and had performed excellently on that apparatus in the 1971 European Championships in Minsk.

While the Soviets were on beam, the East Germans were on floor. There, Janz and Zuchold scored higher than they had on beam—9.50 and 9.40. Angelika Hellmann also scored 9.40.After these two rotations, Lazakovich was the surprise leader at 18.95; Korbut and Janz followed at 18.85 and Turischeva and Zuchold were at 18.65.

During third rotation, with the Soviets on floor and the East Germans on vault, the Soviets showed their real strengths. Turischeva scored 9.80,

Lazakovich, 9.70, Korbut, 9.60, Burda, 9.50, Saadi 9.40 and Koshel, 9.35, for a remarkably high team total of 48.00—far and away the highest of any team total on any event in compulsories. These high scores were due not only to the traditional excellence of Soviet floor exercise but also to the concept in force, which allowed teams to make up their own floor exercise. This concept enabled the Soviets to make use of their own choreography, the superiority of which has its roots in the long Russian tradition of ballet.

Meanwhile, the East Germans on vault scored creditably but not outstandingly. Janz and Zuchold each scored 9.45, while Hellmann, number three on the East German team, scored 9.40.

In the final rotation—the Soviets on vault and the East Germans on bars—Janz and Zuchold had their chance to score high on their favorite apparatus. East Germans are always strong on bars and Karin Janz had been European Champion on this apparatus in 1969. When her turn came, Karin scored 9.85—by far the highest score in compulsory bars—and Erika Zuchold scored 9.70, the second highest score on this apparatus. The Soviets did well in vault. Turischeva and Lazakovich scored 9.60, Burda, 9.50, and Korbut, 9.45.

At the conclusion of compulsories, Tamara Lazakovich continued to be the surprise leader at 38.25, followed by Karin Janz at 38.15, and Ludmilla Turischeva at 38.05. Olga Korbut was fourth at 37.90, Erika Zuchold was fifth at 37.80 and Hellmann was sixth at 37.50. At 36.85, Cathy Rigby of the United States was ahead of everyone on all the other teams but behind the Soviets and all but two of the East Germans. She was thus in eleventh position.

In team total, the Soviets at 189.15 and East Germans at 187.30 were decisively ahead of the Hungarians and Czechs at 182.15 and the United States, only 0.05 back at 182.10. In turn, these second-ranked teams were comfortably ahead of Japan at 179.10 and Romania at 179.00.

In compulsories, the United States women were not treated badly by the judges, as they would be in optionals. Their scores might have been higher had they competed in the last group of the evening instead of the second group of the morning. One writer observed, however, that "the compulsory scores appeared within reason based upon the scoring observed in the first group." He went on to say, "it was felt that if the judging were to continue on the same level, the U.S. women should place quite high."[2]

At the conclusion of compulsory exercises, the standings and scores of the leading teams and individuals were as follows:

1. URS	189.15
2. GDR	187.30
3. HUN	182.15
TCH	182.15
5. USA	182.10

1. Lazakovich	38.25
2. Janz	38.15
3. Turischeva	38.05
4. Korbut	37.90
5. Zuchold	37.80
6. Hellmann	37.50
7. Burda	37.45
8. Saadi	37.20
9. Schmeisser, GDR	37.00
11. Rigby	36.85
12. Nemethova, TCH	36.75

The Optional Exercises

Competition 1b: August 28th

In optional exercises, the placement of the teams according to group depended not on a draw, as it did in compulsories, but on the teams' standings in compulsories, with some exceptions. As a courtesy, Mexico, host of the preceding Olympics, and Canada, host of the succeeding Olympics, were placed in the last evening group. (Munich was the only Olympics in which this was done.) Thus, the last group consisted of the Soviet Union, East Germany, Mexico, and Canada. The next-to-last group contained Hungary, Romania, Czechoslovakia, and Norway. For some reason, the United States, which had placed fifth in compulsories and should have been in this group, was left out of it. The United States was assigned to the first of the three evening groups with Japan, West Germany, and individual gymnasts from countries that did not have teams. This placement was a setback for the Americans. Being with lesser teams contributed to lower scores; furthermore, since they were not in the same group, the American gymnasts could not be compared directly with their chief rivals—the gymnasts from Hungary and Czechoslovakia. Judging in the optional team competition was a source of bitter controversy for the Americans. In particular, Hungary was the beneficiary of biased judging: they ended optionals with a score of 186.10 compared with the United States' 183.80. This was an enormous difference of 2.3 points, an average of 0.575 per apparatus for the team or 0.115 per gymnast on each apparatus. Actually, on floor exercise, the United States was 0.05 ahead. Therefore, these differences were concentrated on the other three apparatuses: 0.85 on vault, 0.70 on bars, and 0.80 on beam. It was the consensus that the Hungarians were simply not that much better, if in fact they were better at all.

The East German big three leaving the floor after warmup in compulsories. Left to right: Angelika Hellmann, Karin Janz, and Erika Zuchold.

Impartial West German observers commented strongly on the judging. Ms. Liesel Neimeyer of the Deutscher Turner Bund press department wrote, "Never did a U.S. women's team perform at Olympic or world (championship competition) as convincingly as the 1972 team did in Munich. This tribute was paid to them before entering into details because they had every reason to be dissatisfied with their overall scores. More than any other team, they were handicapped by bad luck in belonging to the second of the five compulsory competition groups, and there were ever so many cases of underscoring."[2]

Dr. Joseph Göhler, editor of *Olympische Turnkunst* magazine, wrote: "If there was anything to complain about, it was the scoring. One of the reasons for unfair scoring always provoking the shrill whistling of the 12,000 spectators was the deplorable fact that some judges, male and female, were not able to discard national prejudice, and another more frequent reason being the slackening of judging standards in the course of competitions. Scores in the evening were milder than in the morning, with competitors that had to perform early losing

USA team rotating to a new apparatus. Front to back: Cathy Rigby, Nancy Thies, Kim Chace, Linda Metheny, Joan Moore, Roxanne Pierce, Muriel Grossfield (coach), Art Maddox (accompanist).

valuable tenths. The U.S. girls were among those luckless, thus narrowly missing the bronze medal, though experts were unanimous that they were better than the Hungarians . . . ."[2]

The adversity of the Americans was in sharp contrast to the stunning success of the Soviet team and the rapturous applause given to their stars—Korbut, Turischeva and Lazakovich. The crowd warmly applauded Burda and Saadi, as they did also the East Germans—Janz, Zuchold and Hellmann. The audience in the arena had by now determined that the leading Soviets and East Germans were the people they wanted to watch. Everything else had been a kind of preliminary. The unfortunate Canadians and Mexicans who competed at the same time suffered the indignity of being virtually ignored.

The competition devolved into questions, such as: Would Lazakovich maintain her lead? Would the East Germans' Janz and Zuchold beat Korbut and Turischeva? Already the crowd had taken to the diminutive and unknown

Olga Korbut but had no idea of what was in store for them. Nothing they had seen in the performances of the earlier groups had prepared them for the spectacle they were about to see. It was in these optional team exercises that Olga Korbut first made her impact upon the world.

The excitement over Olga gradually increased during the evening. Although nowadays the number one team in each group starts on vault and works its way through the competition in the normal order of events—vault, bars, beam, and floor—in Munich the order was decided by draw: the Soviets started on floor. Thus Olga's famous tricks on bars and beam did not come until later on in the evening. Floor exercise did, however, serve to introduce to the spectators, the TV audience, and the TV commentators (who were also unprepared for what they were about to see) the qualities in Olga for which she would be remembered: her charm, the impish choreography of her floor exercise, and, yes, that much over-used word, her charisma. These qualities, when added to her solid gymnastics performance, drew people to her, made them feel part of what she was doing, and made them love what they saw. She received the highest score of all for her floor exercise—9.75—and went on to receive a strong 9.60 for a high Yamashita vault.

It was in her uneven bars routine, however, that she first shocked the world. Her back flip from standing on the high bar to regrasping the high bar caused the crowd to gasp in astonishment. An excited Jim McKay of ABC-TV told his audience that "she defied gravity." She had other important elements in her routine, but her back flip was the one people remember. It was replayed many times on TV and its magnitude and the relative slowness of its execution made it understandable to people who do not know gymnastics. Many other equally difficult or more difficult elements (like a triple twist) are not appreciated because they happen so fast that most people do not see them. The back flip to recatch high bar, however, was something people could understand and they loved it. Olga received a 9.70 for her bars routine, a score equalled only by Karin Janz. (Olga's routine is described in detail in third rotation of the all-around.)

Then, in the beam event, the world was stunned again. At the end of her routine, Olga actually performed a salto backward tucked on the beam. For the world as a whole, this was the first time it had ever been done. It was a back salto (somersault) in tuck position from a standing start, immediately preceding her salto forward to dismount. Such a trick was so much more spectacular, so much more sensational than anything people had seen so far in the gymnastics competition that it was almost difficult for people to believe what their eyes had, in fact, seen. What made it an emotional as well as a spectacular happening was the sight of this young woman standing beside the beam after her dismount, an irresistible grin going from ear to ear, as if to say, "how about that?!" (Her routine is described in detail in fourth rotation of the all-around.)

People could not resist and almost cried in their delight. Olga's beam routine, for which she received a 9.75, capped her evening of triumph, but she had no way of knowing the extent of her impact around the world. She only knew she had scored a triumph in Munich's Sporthalle.

Olga was not alone, of course, in her success. The crowd appreciated Ludmilla Turischeva, even though her personality was reserved. She lacked Olga's ability to communicate with the audience, and it was widely known among the knowledgeable German audience that she and Olga were rivals. They loved Olga but they respected Ludmilla, the world and European champion; they gave her the applause she deserved. In particular, they liked her floor exercise, set to Slavic music, which gave the audience an occasional chance to clap in rhythm. Her exercise also included a salto backward stretched with double twist, the element with highest difficulty on floor at that time. She received 9.70 for this routine.

Olga and Ludmilla were tied in their scores for optional exercises, but Ludmilla had a slight overall advantage (0.15) from her higher score in compulsories. Tied with Ludmilla for first place after team competition was the capable and determined Karin Janz. Tamara Lazakovich, who was in the lead after compulsories, dropped to fourth place after optionals and Erika Zuchold, who was fifth after compulsories, remained fifth after optionals. Angelika Hellmann, who was sixth after compulsories, dropped to seventh and Lyubov Burda, who had been seventh, moved up to sixth.

It was an exciting evening altogether, in which there followed consecutively the disapproval over the scores given the American gymnasts, the build-up in interest as the eastern bloc countries performed and, finally, the climax as the two leading teams clashed. It was expected that the Soviet team would win, as they did, and everyone knew that Karin Janz was out to win the all-around gold medal; but nobody, nobody at all, was prepared for the intoxication, the thrill, and the emotional appeal of Olga Korbut. It was a day that would remain in the minds of those who saw it as long as they lived.

At the conclusion of optional exercises, and with them the team competition, the standings and scores of the leading teams and individuals were as follows:

	Compulsories	Optionals	Total
1. URS	189.15	191.35	380.50
2. GDR	187.30	189.25	376.55
3. HUN	182.15	186.10	368.25
4. USA	182.10	183.80	365.90
5. TCH	182.15	182.85	365.00
6. ROM	179.00	181.70	360.70
7. JPN	179.10	180.65	359.75
1. Turischeva	38.05	38.80	76.85
Janz	38.15	38.70	76.85
3. Korbut	37.90	38.80	76.70
4. Lazakovich	38.25	38.15	76.40
5. Zuchold	37.80	38.20	76.00
6. Burda	37.45	37.90	76.35
7. Hellmann	37.50	37.80	75.30
8. Saadi	37.20	37.45	74.65
9. Bekesi, HUN	36.75	37.65	74.40
10. Rigby	36.85	37.40	74.25

Team winners. Second, East Germany. Left to right: Christine Schmitt, Angelika Hellmann, Irene Abel, Richarda Schmeisser, Erika Zuchold, Karin Janz. First, Soviet Union: Polina Astakhova, Elvira Saadi, Lyubov Burda, Tamara Lazakovich, Ludmilla Turischeva, Antonina Koshel, Olga Korbut. Third, Hungary: Fourth from left, Ilona Bekesi; second from right, Monika Csaszar.

Ludmilla Turischeva in vault pre-flight.

Ludmilla Turischeva in Yamashita post-flight. For a view of her post-flight one second later, *see page 194.*

The Individual All-Around

Competition II: August 30th

After being awakened in the optional competition to the excitement of women's gymnastics in general and to the amazing developments in Munich in particular, the world watched—riveted—as the women's all-around began. The number of competitors had been filtered down to thirty-six in four groups of nine gymnasts each. While there would be some also-rans in each group, the top gymnasts would command attention. A spectator could watch them and ignore the rest. Since the four events ran simultaneously, one of the better gymnasts would be performing most of the time. Hopefully, there would not be many occasions when two top gymnasts would be competing at the same time.

The four groups marched in to shouts, cheering and the catchy, rhythmic music used for entrances and rotations between events. The group containing Ludmilla Turischeva went to vault; Lyubov Burda, Elvira Saadi, and Ilona Bekesi went to bars; Karin Janz, Angelika Hellmann and Cathy Rigby went to beam; and Olga Korbut, Tamara Lazakovich, and Erika Zuchold, went to floor exercise.

First Rotation

In vaulting, Turischeva received 9.65 for her Yamashita and also for her second vault, consisting of a handspring onto the horse followed by a full twist off in after-flight. On bars, Lyubov Burda received 9.50, Elvira Saadi received 9.40, and Ilona Bekesi received 9.55. Bekesi's score, when combined with the 9.60 she received in compulsories, would gain her entrance into finals in uneven bars. Her short, quick, lively routine was as follows:

> From the low bar side, she ran, jumped off the beat board, pushed off the low bar with her hands and performed a salto forward with her legs straddled between the bars to catch high bar in normal grip *(Figure 71)*. She made a half turn, dropped to low bar, immediately kipped to catch high bar and swung back on high bar. As she swung forward and up between the bars, she performed a salto backward with her legs straddled and dropped to catch low bar. She immediately kipped on low bar to catch high bar, swung back on high bar and swung forward to rest her feet against the low bar, her legs approximately horizontal, while she was hanging by her hands from high bar. She paused for a second in this position, pushed off with her

Figure 71

Ilona Bekesi mounts with salto roll forward between bars.

feet and hoisted herself up to a vertical front support position against high bar. That is to say, her body was vertical and held at waist height against the bar by her hands. This was the only clumsy-looking element in an otherwise exciting routine. She had to bend her arms to push herself up. From this front support position, she pushed off with her hands and arms (cast) and made a vertical turn in the air, recaught the high bar *(Figure 72),* swung down and wrapped around low bar. She flew back with a half turn to catch high bar in crossed grip. With her crossed grip, she made a half turn back to face low bar, dropped to low bar, kipped to catch high bar and kipped on high bar to clear support position back of high bar. She swung down, wrapped around low bar and flew forward in hecht dismount with full twist to land.

Ilona Bekesi: from hang on high bar, she swings forward to perform salto roll backward to hang on low bar.

Figure 72

Bekesi's two saltos between bars were well executed and showed her willingness to take risks. It is unfortunate that her coaches included that clumsy-looking press up to vertical support position in the middle of her routine. Without it, she would surely have scored higher.

Among those on beam in first rotation, Cathy Rigby received 9.35 for her routine. She had been directed to leave out her aerial walkover during team competition but restored it during the all-around. She received the same score in both competitions. Also on beam in first rotation was Angelika Hellmann, who received 9.25. The principal gymnast on beam in first rotation was, of course, Karin Janz. Although she was one of the contenders for the all-around gold medal, her score on balance beam was only 0.05 higher than Rigby's. She received 9.40 for the following routine:

Karin Janz on beam.

Janz ran diagonally toward the middle of the beam and jumped off the beat board into split-leg handstand in line with the beam. Without pausing, she slowly continued on over to stand, immediately performed a flic-flac straddle down *(Figure 73)* and continued her backward movement until she lay supine on the beam with her hands on the beam behind her. Then she piked her legs, extended her body and her arms to raise herself back through handstand to land first on her right foot and then her left. She posed briefly at the end of the beam, standing erect with her right leg slightly back and her arms extended vertically upward. Then she made a deep squat, jumped up into double stag sissone, danced forward, made an assemblé and a stretched jump. She made a half turn to her left at the other end of the beam, stepped forward and made a full turn to her right. She paused and posed, then stepped forward and made a series of half turns and poses as she stepped past the middle of the beam. She performed a cartwheel to her right into handstand at the very end of the beam. She then rolled forward to place her back on the beam with her legs piked vertically upward. She continued her roll in the same direction into vee-sit position with her legs straddled at 45° above the beam and her arms extended parallel to her legs. She placed her hands on the beam ahead of her and swung her legs down and back up to handstand, held it momentarily and continued in walkover to stand. She then went into a scale forward, standing on her right leg, with her left leg extended horizontally behind. She raised her body to upright position while squatting down on her right leg, swung her left leg forward and allowed it to go down straight beside the beam. As she sat down on the beam, she raised her stretched left leg ahead of her to about 45° above the beam while her right foot was on the beam, her right knee bent. Then she stretched her right leg ahead of her and raised it, while lowering her left foot onto the beam, with her left knee bent. Then she bent her right knee and brought both feet close in front of her, her feet being a few inches above the beam. She made a

Figure 73

Karin Janz in beam dismount.

three-quarter turn to her right on her seat so that she faced across the beam with her legs extended downwards. She posed briefly, moved a quarter turn to her right, brought her legs up slightly elevated above the beam, her left leg extended, her right knee bent and right foot resting on her left knee. She posed again, then stood, did a three-quarter turn to stand facing across the beam with her feet separated, posed, made a quarter turn to her right to face the end, a half turn back to face along the beam and then danced forward. Near the end, she performed a split leap. She made a half turn to her left, danced forward to the middle of the beam and made a full and a half turn to her right on her right foot. She then executed a back walkover to the end of the beam. She danced forward and performed a front handspring to the other end of the beam. She made a half turn to her right, stepped forward and made a forward walkover. She paused, made a cartwheel to the end of the beam where she punched off into a salto backward stretched with full twist to land.

Karin's routine was attractively choreographed and well executed, but it had no aerial walkovers or aerial cartwheels and no back salto. Consequently, it did not receive a top score.

During first rotation, there were two top performers in floor exercise—Tamara Lazakovich and Olga Korbut. It was a chance to see graphically illustrated the difference between the past and the future. At 5 feet, 3.5 inches and 112 pounds, Tamara, lovely as she was, represented the past; at 5 feet, 0.5 inch and 83.5 pounds, Olga represented the future. None of the other gymnasts could compete against the lightness and sprightliness of Olga's routine. Nevertheless, Tamara's routine was attractively choreographed and delightfully performed.

Standing a few paces away from a corner and one of the sides, facing across the floor to the opposite side, Lazakovich started toward that side with slow, sensuous steps, her arms out to her side. She gradually speeded up her steps until, by the middle of the floor, she was almost running. Halfway between the middle of the floor and the opposite side, she performed a full and a quarter turn to her right to face the adjacent side to her right. She took a big step toward that side and punched off into a full and three-quarter jump turn to her left. During the first half of her jump, her left leg was hanging straight down and her right leg was held up, bent at the knee; during the second half of her turn, her right leg hung down and her left knee was held up. She landed facing away from the corner along the diagonal. She paused and posed with her left leg diagonally back and her right leg forward, her knee partially bent, made body turns left and right with her arms alternately crossed in front of her. She ended posing with her body tilted back and both arms stretched diagonally back above her. Then she made a half turn to her right to face the corner, took two steps in slow rhythm into the corner, made a half turn back to her right and posed again as she prepared for her first pass: a round-off, flic-flac, salto backward stretched with full twist into a flic-flac step-out. She posed, leaning back with her arms thrown up diagonally behind her, turned to her right and did a sissone with bent rear leg. As she landed on her right foot, she quickly stepped across in front with her left leg in plié to face the center of the floor. She made a half turn to her left to face the side and a side step to her left. She turned to her left, danced along the side again and did a scissors jump with quarter turn. She stood and posed, with her feet spread apart and, after a slow full and a half turn, executed her unique pose: a deep curtsy, squatting down with her left knee and leg on the floor, her right knee deeply bent, her body leaning over her right knee and her arms out to the side. She stood, turned to her left to face a far corner, made an aerial forward walkover toward it, a few more dance steps and another one of her deep curtsies, this one including a full turn. She stood, turned toward the corner and pushed off into a handstand. Without pausing, she made a half turn to her left in handstand and came down on her hands and right knee and leg to sit facing sideways. She posed on the floor with her legs and feet out to the side, turned to her right on her seat and drew her knees up in front of her. She posed for a second, stood, turned toward the corner and prepared for her second pass: a round-off, flic-flac, salto backward stretched with full twist. She posed, standing again with her arms thrown up diagonally behind her, stepped forward, raised her left knee high and crossed her left foot over in front of her right. She made a three-quarter turn to her right and danced along the adjacent side with quick steps, and rhythmic changes. Near the corner, she made a deep body wave and full turn. After more turns and poses, she backed into the corner to begin her third pass: a round-off, flic-flac, salto backward stretched. She stepped forward, made a quarter turn to her right and stood erect, her legs together, her right arm raised vertically above her and her left arm extended horizontally to her side.

It was one of the most graceful, artistic, and tastefully choreographed routines that existed before the advent of the small, light, super tumblers in the late 1970s and early 1980s. Tamara received a score of only 9.65, but it was enough to move her from fourth to third place. Her routine was sensuous, almost voluptuous, and quite slow-moving. In contrast, the one that followed was entirely different. Set to a faster pace, it was distinguished by the quickness of the actions of hands, legs, or body and was characterized by playful movements and laughing facial expressions. The routine was that of Olga Korbut.

Olga Korbut's floor exercise was one big smile from beginning to end.

Standing in the middle of one of the sides, she immediately assumed a pose in attitude, elevated on her right toe and facing across the floor to her right. She ran along the side, took a hurdle step as before a vault: that is, she swung her arms up in front of her, over her head and down behind her, and brought her feet together. She then punched forward from both feet and dove forward and diagonally upward with her arms straight up in front of her. Then she arched her back, threw her head back and flung her arms out to her side. These actions, which all took place in a fraction of a second, resulted in a swan dive pose. It began with her legs horizontal and her back and head arched slightly above the horizontal. It then became even more beautiful as her chest began to drop and her legs began to point upward. She quickly brought her arms forward to break her fall, tucked her head under, landed on her shoulders and rolled out onto her back. She jumped upwards, landed on her feet, which were spread apart, put her hands behind her on her seat, turned her head to her left and posed with a smile on her face, as if to say, "how's that!" It was, in fact, a spectacular beginning.

She made some playful—but also graceful and artistic–turns, hops and poses in the corner before beginning her first pass: she ran, made a handspring forward, taking off from one foot, a salto forward tucked into a round-off, flic-flac, salto backward stretched. Upon landing, she posed with her right knee bent, her left leg straight and extended behind her, her arms thrown up and back and her body arched backwards. She brought her feet together, extended her arms out to her side and moved her bent knees from side to side playfully. She then ran parallel to the side on her left with her body leaning forward and her legs kicking up behind–all in keeping with the projection of her personality. She made a few such steps parallel to the side, turned to her right and went past the middle of the floor with dance steps, a jump full turn to her right and a side split leap. She made another full turn to her right. As she came out of this full turn, she leaned back, made a half turn with her right leg straight, fell onto her seat and rolled on her back over into a pose resting on her right knee and leg, her left leg elevated vertically above her and her hands on the floor, supporting her with straight arms. She held this pose for a second. Then, leaving her right knee and leg on the floor, she made a half turn to her left, brought her left foot down onto the floor in front of her, her left knee bent, and assumed this pose for a second with her left hand on her left knee and her right arm held vertically upward. She stood up out of this pose, advanced to the nearby corner with measured steps, her left arm vertically up and her right arm down at her side. She changed and put her right arm vertically up and her left arm down at her side. Then she put both arms down at her side, her hands together on her seat, an impudent smile on her face. She then made a half turn to her right, a little jump step forward and then back and began her second pass: a round-off, flic-flac back dive chest roll, that is, she punched off from her feet as if entering a flic-flac but instead of pushing off with her hands as she landed, she used her hands just to break her fall, landed on her chest and rolled out until just her hips and straight legs were on the floor, her back was steeply arched upwards and her arms thrown diagonally up back. The first part of this element was a beautifully high flic-flac; then, as she landed, she seemed to delay bringing her legs down onto the floor, so that momentarily her chest and hands were on the mat, her head was held high and her feet were over her head, so much was her back arched. She dropped her head and chest forward as her legs reached the floor, turned to her right and sat up in pose with her legs in straddle on the mat in front of her. She bent her knees and brought them up to her chin as she bent her head

forward. Then she kicked her legs upward together in pike and lowered them once again in straddle on the floor. She posed with that same smile on her face, sitting with her legs straddled, her arms extended horizontally to her sides while she looked along her left arm. She stood, faced along the side to the right of the diagonal she had just left, posed on her left leg her right foot slightly back, her left arm extended out to her side, her right arm across her chest pointing to the left in line with her left arm and her head turned left as she looked along her left arm. She took a big step to her right, still looking to the left, took a couple of little tiny steps and kicked her left leg up high behind her, flung her arms up above her, arched her back and threw her head back in a momentary exaggerated arabesque.

She did a chassé into a hurdle, performed an aerial forward walkover, leaned forward into a chest stand with her legs split, touched the floor in front of her head with her left foot, brought her legs together over her head, split them again and began a half turn to her left. She settled down onto her right knee and leg on the floor, her left knee bent with her left knee in front of her and her left foot on the floor, her arms out to her side. She continued turning to her left, at the same time rising in one continuous motion until she faced the nearby corner and began to move toward that corner. She took one step and paused, standing with her right arm stretched diagonally down to her

> right and looking to her right, took another step and made another pause looking to her right, her right arm diagonally down to her right, then she took two more steps into the corner with both arms raised vertically above her. With each step she waved her hands, one forward the other back alternately. Finally she reached the corner, made a half turn to her left and began her third pass: a round-off, flic-flac, salto backward stretched. Upon landing, she stood for a second with her left leg diagonally back and her arms stretched diagonally back above her. Then she danced along the adjacent side to her left a short distance, made a three-quarter turn to her left to face across the floor and paused. She stood with her legs spread, her right leg diagonally to the right, her arms stretched out to her side and looked to her right. Then she brought her right leg in next to her left and assumed her final pose: she bent both knees slightly, kept her left arm stretched out to her side and brought her right arm around in front of her, still stretched. She was still looking to her right. Then, in one final, foxy motion, she twisted her right arm at the elbow so that her right forearm and handwere in front of her, twisted her right arm at the wrist in a graceful little gesture and threw her head back, cocked to her right with a laughing smile on her face.

Olga received a 9.80 for her routine. Considering the overall excellence of her gymnastics and the thunderous applause she received from the crowd, the judges really had no choice. Her score moved her ahead of Turischeva and Janz into first place.

At the end of first rotation, the standings and scores of the leading individuals were as follows:

	Initial Score	First Rotation	Subtotal
1. Korbut *(floor)*	38.350	9.80	48.150
2. Turischeva *(vault)*	38.425	9.65	48.075
3. Lazakovich *(floor)*	38.200	9.65	47.850
4. Janz *(beam)*	38.425	9.40	47.825
5. Zuchold *(floor)*	38.000	9.60	47.600
6. Burda *(bars)*	37.675	9.50	47.175
7. Hellmann *(beam)*	37.650	9.25	46.900
8. Bekesi *(bars)*	37.200	9.55	46.750
9. Saadi *(beam)*	37.325	9.40	46.725
10. Rigby *(beam)*	37.125	9.35	46.475

Second Rotation

In second rotation, Korbut, Lazakovich, and Zuchold moved on to vault; Turischeva went to bars; Saadi, Burda and Bekesi went to beam; Janz, Hellmann, and Rigby went to floor exercise. Korbut, Lazakovich, and

Zuchold all performed Yamashita vaults. Lazakovich received 9.55; Korbut, 9.65 and Zuchold, 9.70.

On bars, Olga's arch rival, Ludmilla Turischeva, received 9.65 for her routine. Since both received the same score, Olga's standing remained number one. Turischeva's routine on the uneven bars had the same general characteristics as her routine in Ljubljana.

From the low bar side, she ran, jumped off the beat board, grasped low bar in clear straddle support, made a half turn to her left above the bar, still in clear straddle support (*Figure 33),* and swung back down under the low bar. As she passed under the low bar and her legs cleared the bar, she brought them together, still in pike, swung back in kip and caught high bar. She kipped on high bar, straddling her legs over low bar as she did so, and swung up to toe-on position on top of high bar. With her feet on the high bar outside her hands, she swung back down and up between the bars, stretched her body at about a 45° angle above the horizontal over the low bar and was able to make one and a half turns before her body dropped onto the low bar on her hips. She bounced up off the low bar, straddled her legs and swung forward in a long glide kip. She kipped on high bar up between the bars, made a forward hip circle about high bar up to handstand. She held her handstand for a second, spread her legs to straddle and brought them down to toe-on position on high bar outside her hands. She swung back down between the bars and up to the side away from low bar and once again stretched her body. She made one and a half turns, starting from just above the horizontal. She recaught high bar after her turns, swung down and beat low bar. She swung back

Ludmila Turischeva performs $1^1/_2$ turns off high bar.

> and, as she came up after passing under the high bar, she released her grip on the bar and made a full turn with her body vertical. After her full turn and regrasp of the high bar, she dropped to low bar, kipped on low bar, bringing legs together between her arms and over the low bar as she did so, caught high bar with her body in rear-lying hang, and kipped up to toe-on position for the third time, her toes outside her hands. She swung down and up between the bars again, made only a half turn this time with her body stretched but executed a quick flare with her arms, that is, she flung her arms out to her side and recaught high bar. After recatching high bar, she let her body drop and bounce on her hips off low bar, made a short uprise, brought her feet down onto the low bar, pushed hard off the low bar with her legs and pressed up through handstand on high bar. As she went through handstand, she made a half turn and swung down to wrap around low bar. As she came up on her wrap, she pushed off with her hips in hecht dismount and made a full twist to land.

Ludmilla Turischeva flares her arms before regrasping high bar and dropping to bounce off low bar.

This routine was vintage Turischeva: she performed no extraordinary or original elements but performed with smoothness and precision a routine that fulfilled difficulty requirements.

On beam, Ilona Bekesi received 9.3, Lyubov Burda and Elvira Saadi both received 9.4. In floor exercise, Karin Janz received 9.7, one of the high scores for that apparatus. Angelika Hellmann and Cathy Rigby both received 9.55. Janz's and Rigby's routines will be described in this section; Hellmann's routine will be described in the section on apparatus finals.

> Karin started near the middle of one of the sides, danced in a long semi-circle counter-clockwise over to an opposite corner for her first pass: she ran, performed a handspring forward, followed immediately by a salto forward tucked into a round-off, flic-flac salto backward stretched with full

twist. She made a three-quarter turn to her left. Now near the same position from which she had started her routine, she went along the same semi-circle she had started on with running dance steps and a jump full turn before reaching the diagonal crosswise from the one on which she had made her first pass. She turned to her left along this diagonal and executed a free (aerial) walkover forward. She turned left again, executed a jump full turn to her left, coming down nearly to splits, then stood with her legs separated longitudinally, her left foot forward, turned out, her left arm at her side and her right arm raised straight above her. She gracefully lowered her right arm to her side with her hand turned upward and paused in a well photographed pose. (See page 258.) She then stepped to her right and made a full turn to her right. She executed a cartwheel to her right and three consecutive butterfly turns to her right and danced into the corner from which she had started her routine and her first pass to begin her second pass: a round-off, flic-flac, salto backward stretched followed immediately by two more flic-flacs and a salto backward stretched step-out. She danced forward, made a full turn and leaned back into a bridge pose, that is, her feet were on the floor, hands were on the floor out to her sides, her head was thrown back nearly touching the floor and her body was arched between. She lowered her seat to the floor, posed while sitting with her right leg tucked under her, raised herself on her right knee and made a full turn to her left in knee scale *(Figure 74)*. She stood, took a few steps forward and made a triple turn to her right on her right foot, her first turn being in forward scale position and her next two turns being upright. Then she performed a tuck jump and a stag leap, paused and posed, and

Karin Janz

continued with dance steps circling to her right to reach the corner on the cross diagonal from which she began her third pass: a round-off, flic-flac, salto backward stretched step-out. She danced back along the same diagonal into her final pose: her left knee and leg on the floor, her right foot ahead with right knee bent, her body and head inclined far back, her right arm stretched horizontally back and her left arm out horizontally forward.

Figure 74

Karin's routine was set to a fast pace, which slowed down only during her pauses. It had superior acrobatics with good gymnastic connections. The judges may have felt it lacked the kind of personality exhibited by Korbut and Turischeva during their exercises. Her 9.7 score maintained her position among the leaders, however.

Cathy Rigby, long before she came to Munich, was aware of the importance of projecting her personality. In floor exercise, particularly, the judges are sensitive to the audience. If a gymnast can win the hearts of the spectators, their loud approval has an effect upon the judges. Olga Korbut had given convincing proof of this doctrine during her own floor exercise. Cathy, therefore, came up onto the podium with a cheeky little smile on her face and maintained throughout her routine a cocky, fresh-little-kid demeanor, similar to that which Olga had so skillfully employed. Cathy's themes were fun and good humor, played off against the music of "Roll out the Barrel."

Cathy Rigby

She began by dancing about near one of the corners for several seconds before performing an aerial cartwheel into the corner to begin her first pass: a round-off into a salto backward stretched with full twist followed immediately by a back walkover. She turned to her left and danced along

> the side of the floor into the adjacent corner to begin her second pass: a round-off into half twist into a salto forward (arabian salto) into a cartwheel to her right and a walkover backwards. She danced to her left out of the corner, performed a forward roll into a handstand with split legs, stood and performed an aerial walkover. Now near the middle of the floor, she performed a cartwheel, an aerial cartwheel and another cartwheel into a corner from which she started immediately into her third pass: a round-off into a whip-back salto into a flic-flac with half twist to land on her seat and fall forward onto her stomach with her legs split to the side. She immediately brought her legs together so that she was lying prone, face down. She made a full turn to her right, while lying prone, and then stood up on her toes to assume her final pose: she was standing erect with her left leg slightly forward, her knee slightly bent and her left hand on top of her leg; her right leg was straight and her right hand was held high above her. On her face was the same laughing smile that had been there so many times in her routine.

Cathy at that time was 4 feet, 11 inches tall and weighed 89 pounds. Like Olga, she was distinctly smaller than most of the gymnasts. She was one of the crowd's favorites and received loud and prolonged applause after her routine. The severity of the judging against her during team competition kept her out of apparatus finals, but she was still in tenth place all-around as the second rotation came to a close.

At the conclusion of second rotation, the standings and scores of the leaders were as follows:

	Initial Score	Rotation	Total
1. Korbut *(vault)*	48.150	9.65	57.800
2. Turischeva *(bars)*	48.075	9.65	57.725
3. Janz *(floor)*	47.825	9.70	57.525
4. Lazakovich *(vault)*	47.850	9.55	57.400
5. Zuchold *(vault)*	47.600	9.70	57.300
6. Burda *(beam)*	47.175	9.40	57.575
7. Hellmann *(floor)*	46.900	9.55	56.450
8. Saadi *(beam)*	46.725	9.40	56.125
9. Bekesi *(beam)*	46.750	9.30	56.050
10. Rigby *(floor)*	46.475	9.55	56.025

Third Rotation

In third rotation there occurred one of the best remembered accidents in the history of the Olympics. It was a minor slip, but it led to one misfortune after another. It occurred during Olga Korbut's bars routine. Before describing the mistakes she made in this all-around competition, let us first look at the routine itself and describe it in detail, as performed during the optional competition.

After wrap from low bar, Olga flies back to catch high bar in eagle grip. For her back flip from high bar, see page 324.

Standing under high bar, facing low bar, Olga jumped forward to catch low bar, kipped on low bar to catch high bar, swung back and then swung forward to straddle her legs over low bar She then kipped on high bar until she could place her feet on the high bar between her hands, with her knees bent and her body in squat position on top of the bar. She paused in this position for a second to get herself ready and then thrust upward with her legs off the high bar. She flung her arms up and back, arched her back as steeply as she could and came around in a tight back flip to recatch high bar *(Figure 75)*. She swung down under high bar, wrapped backwards around low bar and flew back to high bar, which she caught in eagle grip. She hung on high bar for a second, dropped to low bar, then kipped on low bar to catch high bar. She kipped on high bar, keeping her body close to the bar as if entering a forward hip circle. As she came over the bar, she leaned forward and stretched her body so that it was horizontal above the bar. Then she pressed her hips upward and piked her legs until she could pass her feet between her straight arms over the bar. She then passed through a position where her body was extended vertically and supported by straight arms, her hands holding the high bar behind her. Facing low bar with her feet hanging down, she dropped forward onto the bar on her hips and wrapped forward around it, that is, in a direction away from the high bar. As she came up between the bars, she raised her hips while extending her arms and spreading her legs in straddle until her hips were up level with the high bar. Her body was now parallel to a line between the bars, her straddled legs still hanging down below the high bar. Then she brought her legs above the bar and together, extending beyond the high bar, gave one final push off the low bar, released it and allowed her legs to drop until her body was horizontal, at the same time flinging her arms out to the side and slightly back to assume a momentary swan dive pose–excellently calculated to be the subject of millions of photographs. From

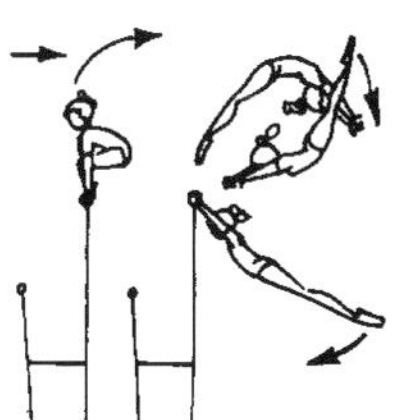

Figure 75

Olga in her dismount.

> this pose, she threw herself forward and around the high bar, beginning a free hip circle, grasped the bar as her body was inverted vertically, continued on up into handstand, made a half turn in handstand and allowed her body to drop down and bounce off low bar on her hips. From her uprise, she initiated a kip on high bar. As she came up between the bars, she piked her body and placed her feet on the high bar outside her hands. She continued forward around high bar in sole circle. As she came up between the bars, she thrust off backwards with her feet and legs and made a salto backward stretched over the low bar to land.

Since Munich, there have been many routines on the uneven bars with far more difficult elements and combinations of elements than those of Olga's routine. Yet it remains original and exciting. These days, when routines on the uneven bars are all very similar, the uniqueness of Olga's routine is refreshing.

Now let us look at what happened during third rotation of the all-around competition. On the day of the all-around competition, the situation just before Olga's routine was as follows: Tamara Lazakovich had just finished her bar routine and had scored 9.70. She was within 0.65 of Karin Janz, who had scored 9.65 on vault; at 67.175, Janz was the new leader. Olga Korbut, at 57.80 after two rotations, would need only 9.375 to tie Janz or 9.40 to go slightly ahead. Having received 9.70 on bars in team optionals, Olga may well have thought she could do equally well now and give herself a commanding lead. She walked up to the apparatus confidently, with a little smile on her face.

> As before, she stood under the high bar, facing low bar, jumped forward to catch low bar and began her kip. Hardly had she begun her kip, however, than the soles of her feet rubbed against the floor. They rubbed against the floor so firmly that they almost stopped her forward motion. This was a major break right at the very beginning of her routine. She

paused, stepped back and began her kip again. She kipped on low bar to catch high bar, kipped on high bar, straddling her legs over the low bar as she did so. She continued her kip up to where she could put her feet on the high bar between her hands, with her knees bent and her body in squat position. She paused in this position for a second to get herself ready and then thrust upward with her legs off the high bar. She flung her arms up and back, arched her back as steeply as she could and came around in a tight back flip to recatch high bar. She swung down, wrapped around low bar and flew back to high bar, which she caught in eagle grip. After catching high bar in eagle grip, she dropped to low bar and kipped on low bar to catch high bar. She kipped on high bar, keeping her body close to the bar as if entering a forward hip circle. As she came over the bar, she leaned forward and stretched her body so that it was horizontal above the bar. Then she pressed her hips upward and piked her legs until she could pass her feet between her straight arms over the bar. She then passed through a position where her body was extended vertically and was supported by straight arms, her hands holding the high bar behind her. Facing low bar with her feet hanging down, she dropped forward onto the bar on her hips and wrapped forward around it, that is, in a direction away from high bar. So far, she had been doing her routine well and might have been able to minimize her loss on that initial break. Unfortunately, her real troubles were about to begin. After wrapping around low bar, she was supposed to raise her hips, extend her arms, spread her legs in straddle to clear the high bar, bring them together, and rest her hips on top of the high bar. She was then to push up with her hands and arms from low bar until her body was horizontal, momentarily balanced on her hips in swan dive attitude.

In this instance, however, when she came off her wrap and pressed up to handstand, her body was vertically upward instead of slanting in a line parallel to an imaginary line joining the bars. In fact, she had gone slightly past vertical, away from high bar. She had misjudged the force needed to achieve a $^3/_4$ handstand and overshot her goal. There was no way she could get her legs and hips back to the high bar. Realizing her predicament, she quickly made a half turn in handstand on top of the low bar and swung down away from the high bar to initiate a kip on low bar in order to get back up to the high bar and start over again at the point where she got into trouble. On swinging down under the high bar to begin her kip, she hit her feet on the floor again, this time very hard. Her legs had been only partly straddled and her knees were bent. She had apparently not regained her composure after the surprise of not completing the earlier element of pushing her legs and hips over the high bar. Nevertheless, after this second major break, she continued her kip on low bar, passed her feet over the low bar between her arms and pushed off to catch high bar. She began her kip

Olga being comforted by Astakhova after her disaster on bars. Erika Zuchold at right.

on high bar, swung forward and placed her hips up close to the high bar with her legs piked and pointing vertically upward. As she came back on her kip, however, she must have suddenly lost strength in her arms, because she swung clumsily backward. Her feet hit the low bar and then her legs and then her seat slid down against it; her body was slightly piked. She made a big effort and swung forward again, her hands still holding the high bar. Then she heaved herself up to front support position, that is, her hips were against high bar and her body was vertical, supported by straight arms. She lifted her feet up and put her toes on the high bar just outside her hands. Now, at least, she was in a position to execute her dismount. With her hands and toes on the bar, she executed a sole circle forward, that is, in a direction away from low bar. As she came up between the bars, she thrust off backwards with her feet and legs and performed a salto backward stretched over low bar to land.

"Oh well. I suppose it could be worse."

Somebody sends her flowers; she smiles and waves and everybody smiles and claps, including the band. Joan Moore is at right, in black

With a stunned expression on her face that seemed to express her disbelief that anything like that could happen to her, Olga faced the judges and then walked off the podium. Coach Polina Astakhova gave her a pat on the back as she came off the stairs and then sat down next to her to comfort her as Olga fought back the tears and realized that her dreams had come crashing down. Her score of 7.50, soon posted, was proof of what she already knew. From being in the lead after two rotations, she dropped back to tenth place after third rotation. Furthermore, she now had to pull herself together and get a good score in fourth rotation on beam.

Olga's misfortune on bars opened the door for her arch rival, Ludmilla Turischeva who, after second rotation, had trailed Olga by 0.075 points. As we note in her biography, Olga had won the USSR Cup selection trials held in Minsk a few weeks before the competition and had, therefore, come to the Olympics as captain of the team. This had been a bitter pill for World Champion Turischeva to swallow. Winning the all-around title in Munich would be sweet revenge. Her opportunity was now at hand and she was on beam. She had a two-tenths advantage over third-place Karin Janz. With a good score on beam, she would move into the lead.

> Standing at one end of the beam, Turischeva placed her hands on the beam and jumped directly from the floor to hold herself for a second in clear straddle support. She pressed up to handstand, keeping her legs straddled on the way up, then bringing them together in handstand. She split her legs and continued in walkover to stand. She kicked her right leg up in front of her, took two steps forward and performed a diving cartwheel to her left to stand at the other end of the beam. She stepped forward, made a half turn to her left on her right foot and then a back handspring step out. She made a high kick with her right leg, a half turn to her left on her left foot, then a high kick with her left foot. She leaned forward in lunge position, with her left leg in front and turned her body a quarter turn to her right to face across the beam. Then she made a full turn to her left in lunge position, so that as she finished, she again faced across the beam. She placed her hands on the beam, pressed up to clear straddle support, made a quarter turn to her left but retained her clear straddle support position, supported by her hands on the beam, her arms straight and her legs straddled 45° on either side. She then sat on the beam and allowed her legs to swing down and back on either side of the beam and extended her arms up and back behind her. Then she placed her hands on the beam behind her, brought her feet up onto the beam with her knees bent, released her hands, leaned forward and stood up. She stepped to the end, made a half turn to her left, danced along the beam and performed a split leap. At the end, she paused and made a squat half turn to her right. From squat position, she performed two consecutive forward rolls with her hands and arms clear of the beam, her trademark combination. After her second roll, she continued forward into prone position for a second. Then, leaving her left leg in place, she raised her body with her hands and arms, turned it left a quarter turn and brought her right leg up onto the beam so that she was in splits facing

> across the beam. She posed in splits for a second and made graceful gestures with her arms. She then placed her hands on the beam, made a quarter turn to her right while raising herself into clear straddle support above the beam again. She lowered herself to sit on the beam, swung her legs down and back and flung her arms up and back for a very brief pause. Then, still leaning her body back, she placed her hands onto the beam behind her and raised her legs up vertically together into vee-sit. She lowered her left foot onto the beam with her knee bent and extended her right leg ahead of her on the beam. Then, leaving her left hand on the beam behind her and extending her right arm upward, she performed a valdez to stand and face in the same direction. She stepped forward to near the center of the beam and made a half turn to her right. She danced forward, performed a split leap, continued to the end and made a half turn to her right. She danced toward the other end and performed a stag leap just before she reached the end. She made a half turn to her left and stepped rapidly along the beam in preparation for her dismount: near the end, she made a round-off and punched off into a salto backward stretched to land.

In her routine, Ludmilla was definitely playing it safe. More than anything else she wanted to avoid having any breaks. Her leaps, therefore, were low and lacking in extension. She suffered a loss of balance after her back handspring step out on her first return along the beam and was unsteady as she stood after the first time she sat on the beam with her legs and arms extended backward. She took a step back on landing. This lack of boldness and her one or two bobbles caused her to receive only a modest score—9.40. It was sufficient to keep her in second place but not enough to withstand the attack of Karin Janz, who scored 9.65 for her Yamashita vault and moved past Turischeva into first place, by 0.05. The showdown between these two would take place in fourth rotation when each would be on her favorite apparatus—Karin on bars and Ludmilla in floor exercise. Meanwhile, another top contender, Erika Zuchold, was performing on bars.

> The first part of Erika's routine was identical to the one she performed in Ljubljana. To mount, she made a running straddle jump over low bar to catch high bar. She kipped on high bar until she could pike her legs and shoot them between herself and the bar. She stretched her body for a second, then piked her legs again and swung back down between the bars and up to rear, clear support on the high bar, facing away from low bar, her piked body being held away from high bar by straight arms. From there, she released her pike, extended her body and swung down in a seat circle forward around high bar until, on her way up between the bars, she let go of

the high bar and flew to low bar to catch it in handstand (see photograph page 236), facing away from high bar *(Figure 20)*. (This element has been named for Zuchold in the Code of Points). She allowed her legs to swing down in a direction away from high bar and performed a clear hip circle backwards around low bar with her body stretched. She continued up to handstand. She swung down and performed a second hip circle–this time not a clear hip but with her hips against the bar–made a hecht release off her hips at the top of her circle and flew forward to catch high bar in eagle grip. She hung for a second in eagle grip, then swung back, made a half turn in flight and dropped to low bar. She kipped on low bar to catch high bar, swung back and swung forward to straddle her legs over low bar into rear support. Then she kipped on high bar to clear support position off high bar on the side away from low bar and performed a clear hip circle backwards around high bar up to handstand. She continued in the same direction to swing down, wrap around low bar and fly back to catch high bar in eagle grip. She swung forward to straddle her legs over low bar and come to rear support position, changed her eagle grip to normal grip and kipped on high bar up to clear support on the side away from low bar. From this clear support position, she performed a hip circle backwards around high bar, released when her body became horizontal above it and flew forward over low bar in hecht dismount to land.

Erika Zuchold in clear, rear support.

Erika Zuchold just before grip change to grasp low bar.

Erika received 9.65 for this exercise. She, too, moved ahead of Olga into fourth place but remained close behind third-place Tamara Lazakovich. Other scores in third rotation were 9.65 for Lyubov Burda in floor exercise, whose routine will be described in the section on apparatus finals, and, also on floor, 9.55 for Saadi and 9.50 for Ilona Bekesi. Angelika Hellmann received 9.50 and Cathy Rigby 9.40 in vault.

An interesting observation: two of the elements in Olga Korbut's routine on the uneven bars, started with take-off from both feet. These were her back flip and her dismount. Either to discourage such elements or because nobody is doing them now anyway, the section entitled "Elements with take-off from both feet" has been eliminated from the Code of Points. The drawing of the Korbut flip shown in this book is taken from the 1979 edition.

At the conclusion of third rotation, the standings and scores of the leaders were as follows:

	Initial Score	**Rotation**	**Total**
1. Janz *(vault)*	57.525	9.65	67.175
2. Turischeva *(beam)*	57.725	9.40	67.125
3. Lazakovich *(bars)*	57.400	9.70	67.100
4. Zuchold *(bars)*	57.300	9.65	66.950
5. Burda *(floor)*	56.575	9.65	66.225
6. Hellmann *(vault)*	56.450	9.50	65.950
7. Saadi *(floor)*	56.125	9.55	65.675
8. Bekesi *(floor)*	56.050	9.50	65.550
9. Rigby *(vault)*	56.025	9.40	65.425
10. Korbut *(bars)*	57.800	7.50	65.300

Fourth Rotation

By the time fourth rotation began, Olga was out of the individual all-around competition. Looking ahead, her 7.50 on bars will not apply to her entering score in apparatus finals. This score will be the average of her compulsory-optional team score. Consequently, she will have a good chance for medals in the apparatus finals competition. Meanwhile, what she wants now is a good score on beam to move her up out of tenth place in the all around.

Fourth rotation excitement revolved about two aspects of the competition: one was the chance to see Olga's beam routine again, with its concluding salto backward tucked; the other was the battle for first place between Ludmilla Turischeva and Karin Janz. It would be especially exciting because, as mentioned earlier, each would be on her favorite apparatus—Janz on uneven bars and Turischeva on floor. They would both be capable of achieving high scores. If anything, the advantage lay with Turischeva, because floor exercise appeals to the emotions and generates more applause than the uneven bars. Besides, Turischeva had received 9.90 in Ljubljana; the judges would remember.

As it happened, Janz made a few small mistakes and received 9.70. This was a pity because she had created an entirely new routine with one original element and some risky ones, including a salto forward between bars. Her routine was as follows:

> From the low bar side, Janz ran and jumped off the beat board, made a half turn as she flew over the low bar with her body stretched and caught high bar facing low bar. Using the momentum gained from her run, she let her body swing back and pressed right up to clear support position behind the bar, her body actually being elevated at an angle of 45°. Then she initiated an entirely new element: first, she entered a hip circle backwards from her clear support position, came up between the bars and stopped for a fraction of a second in a position on top of the high bar where her stretched body was horizontal, her head on the low bar side and her feet on the high bar side. Then, in a hecht release, she sprang with her hips off the high bar and made a one hundred and eighty degree lateral turn, with her body still beautifully stretched horizontally, so that she was now oriented with her feet over the low bar and her head just above the high bar. As she did so, she grasped high bar and let her body drop to bounce off low bar. As her hips contacted the low bar, she let her legs drop down in pike position behind the bar so that, in her uprise, she was able to combine the upward flex of the bar as it rebounded with the upward thrust of her abdomen as she stretched her body. The combined vertical force threw her upward and enabled her to release her hands from the high bar and drop them to grasp

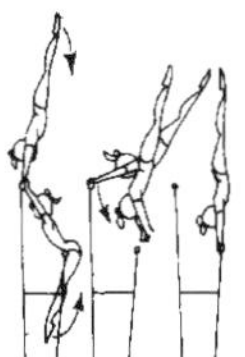

Figure 76

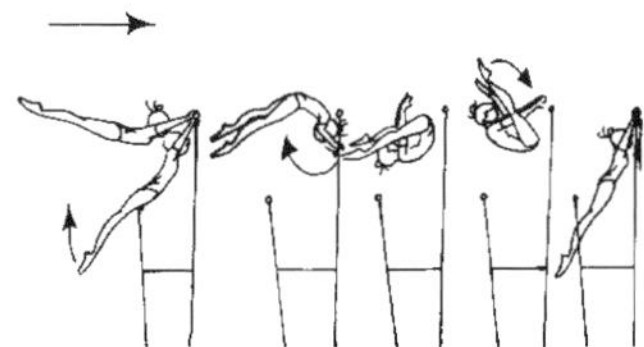

Figure 77

low bar, her body now absolutely straight in handstand on low bar, facing away from high bar *(Figure 76)*. She swung down away from high bar in clear hip circle around low bar, passed through handstand, straddled her legs and began a kip on low bar. She shot her legs through her arms and reached for high bar. She began a kip on high bar and shot her legs between her arms and pumped up to extension as she hung on high bar on the low bar side–a favorite East German element. She hung inverted for a second, then piked her legs and performed a back kip down between the bars. As she came up on the far side, she was now upright but holding the bar behind her. She released the bar, made a quick half turn to grasp the bar in front of her and dropped to low bar. She kipped on low bar to catch high bar and kipped on high bar right up to handstand. She made a half turn as her body dropped and bounced on her hips off low bar. Again, using the same technique, she got a strong uprise. This time, she released high bar, straddled her legs and performed a salto forward between the bars to catch high bar *(Figure 77)*. (This combination is known as the "Janz.") After catching high bar, she swung forward and kipped back up to clear support position, her body now over low bar. She then performed a hip circle backwards around high bar. As she came up on the far side, the released high bar with her hips and flew forward (away from low bar) in hecht dismount with full twist to land.

Karin Janz in bars dismount.

Karin's routine was a joy to watch. All elements were executed with maximum amplitude: that is, they were taken to the fullest extent the body would allow. She would well deserve the gold medal in finals. In the all-around, however, she would have to be content with the silver. Ludmilla Turischeva did, in fact, earn 9.90 in floor exercise and with it the gold medal all-around. This was her routine:

She started along a side a few paces to her right from a corner. From standing stiffly at attention, she jumped up, spread her legs briskly to the side, turned sharply to her left, danced to the corner, made a three-quarter turn to her left, as she made a sweeping gesture in a deep bow with her body, and began her first pass: a round-off, flic-flac salto backward stretched with double twist. She danced slowly with big steps away from the corner in a direction parallel to the side to her left and then ran forward to perform a front handspring. Upon landing, she made a half turn to her left, spread her legs halfway down in splits and made a further half turn of her body to the left to lean on her left arm. She then continued turning, leaning first with her left hand and then her right hand on the floor, and made a full turn to her left to pose with her right knee and leg on the floor, her left foot in front with her left knee bent, her arms making graceful gestures. Now near the middle of the floor, she stood, made a quarter turn to her left, danced toward the opposite side and made a split leap with change of legs as she neared the opposite side. Near it, she made a quarter turn to her left and posed, facing along the side, then made a half turn to her left to face along the side in the opposite direction. She proceeded along that side with dance steps and a forward aerial walkover. She then very slowly and gracefully did a deep body wave down to squat, stood with a half turn to her right and slowly entered a pose in which she stood on her straight right leg, her leg diagonally back, her left arm at her side and her right arm extended vertically upward. By now she was on the diagonal across from that on which she performed her first pass, about half way between the corner and the middle of the floor. She advanced along the diagonal toward the opposite corner with long steps, turns and sweeping arm gestures to pose in the middle of the floor on her right leg, her left leg being extended horizontally behind her, her left arm stretched out in front and her right arm stretched back parallel to her left leg (Arabesque) *(Figure 78).* After this pose, she began to dance more rapidly along the same diagonal toward the corner, made several turns and poses, stepped into the corner and made a half turn back to prepare for her second pass: a round-off, flic-flac, take off with half twist into a salto forward tucked (arabian), round-off, flic-flac into a salto backward tucked. She danced out of her corner along the diagonal with long

Figure 78

Ludmilla Turischeva as she makes great strides with high kicks in rhythm to the solid beat of a Russian folk dance.

> steps and arm gestures sweeping from side to side, then turned to her right parallel to the side and made slow, great strides with high kicks with her arms first raised high above her and then stepping down firmly and plunging her arms down to her side, all in rhythm to the solid beat of a Russian folk dance. She made three such big steps, did a full turn to her left and executed a cartwheel to her left. She posed in a pose that she likes: one knee and leg on the floor, the other foot in front, her leg bent in a right angle at the knee, one arm to the side and the other elevated vertically. She turned back to the corner, posed again, standing statuesquely erect, turned to face along her first diagonal and prepared for her final pass: a round-off, flic-flac, salto backward stretched with full twist. She ended her third pass several steps in from the corner, made two full turns as she stepped toward it, leaned back to sit on the floor in her final pose: her right leg was extended in front, her left knee was steeply bent with her left foot resting on her right knee, her left arm diagonally behind with her hand on the floor and her right arm crossed over in front, her right elbow resting on her right knee and her right hand pointing toward her left shoulder.

In its own way, Turischeva's was a beautiful routine, perhaps the most beautiful of the entire Olympics: it was performed to a variety of music—some popular, some slavic; it was a happy routine, in that she smiled throughout and appeared to be enjoying herself; and it emphasized the artistry possible in a gymnastic floor exercise when the choreography is superior and the gymnast has the ability to dance.

Turischeva was the arch-typical exponent of the classical style of gymnastic floor exercise. Bouncy infantilism, as exemplified by later Romanians, was not for her; nor did she have anything to do with what one correspondent from a national publication used to call "kiddie porn." That also came later. Ludmilla made the most of what she had: grace, a severe beauty and for her time, unequalled gymnastic ability. Such acrobatics as double saltos backward would not be introduced for four years (by Nelli Kim in Montreal) and would not become standard practice for another eight years. Furthermore, she did not try to be what she was not or do what she could not do. Her personality could not compete with that of Olga; her acrobatic skill was not as technically advanced as that of Karin Janz. In the all around, she made mistakes, as did the others. They made more mistakes, however, so, in the end, she came out ahead.

While this drama on bars and in floor exercise was unfolding, the world's best performers on balance beam were displaying their virtuosity. Tamara Lazakovich earned 9.75 and with it the bronze medal all-around. Olga

Korbut proved her ability to overcome adversity. She somehow put bars behind her and performed a brilliant routine to earn 9.80. In so doing, she moved up from tenth to seventh place. This victory over herself was a remarkable achievement, the sort of thing we expect to see from a true Olympian. Erika Zuchold earned 9.50, the third highest score so far on beam. Her routine was so much like the one she used in Ljubljana that it will not be repeated here. Tamara Lazakovich's routine was as follows:

Tamara Lazakovich

> In line with the beam, Lazakovich ran, placed her hands on the end of the beam, jumped off the beat board and pressed up to handstand, her legs going from straddle on the way up to split at the top, with her right leg over the beam. She continued on over to stand, danced forward and performed a dive cartwheel to her left to the end of the beam. She danced back, performed a sissone and continued to the end where she made a half turn to her left. She danced forward and posed briefly in lunge position, stood and performed a back walkover. Half way through her back walkover, she paused briefly in vertical split, her right leg on the beam and her left leg vertical, both hands on the beam. She completed her walkover and stood back at the same end she had just left. She stepped forward, made a full turn to her left, then danced on to the other end, including two hitch-kicks, one forward and the other back. She posed at that end in a quick scale forward, then performed a back handspring. She returned to the same end with two steps during which she kicked first her right leg than her left horizontally upward. She made a half turn to her left and danced along the beam to the other

end with skip steps and little dance steps, crossing one leg over in front of or behind the other. At the end, she made a half turn to her left, danced forward a few steps, made a half turn back to her right, returned to the end and entered a split-leg handstand. She made a half turn in handstand, came back down to her feet, made a half turn to her left and posed again in a scale forward. She then performed a cartwheel to her left, posed near the middle of the beam, stepped forward, made a half turn to her right, posed and performed a back straddle down to sit on the beam, her right leg out straight in front and her left leg in front but her knee bent. With her left hand on the beam behind her, she pushed off in valdez to stand at the end of the beam. She posed, took a long, slow step forward and posed again, standing facing half way to her left. Then she stepped forward purposefully, made a round-off and punched off into a salto backward stretched to land.

Olga Korbut after she hopped up to side splits in her mount.

Tamara's routine was in no way original; it contained only those elements common to her era. Compared with today's routines, it was elementary. Yet it was artistically and gracefully executed.

Now here is Olga's routine, an exercise for which she would become as famous as for her routines on bars and floor.

From the side of the beam, near one end, Olga hopped from the beat board up to side splits. She extended her arms out to her sides in a graceful but definite, forceful gesture and held them there as she posed for two seconds in side splits. Then she placed her hands on the beam in front of her, lifted her seat up clear of the beam and brought her legs from split position around to straddle, that is, at 45° on either side of her, held up horizontally. She made a quarter turn to her left so that she was in clear straddle support, facing one end of the beam. She sat down, allowed her legs to swing down and back, while she kept her hands on the beam. After a brief pause, she brought her legs forward until they were level with the beam and then thrust them down and up, at the same time extending her arms until her body was nearly vertical. Near handstand position, she let her right leg drop down so that she could place it on the beam to support her while she brought her left leg down onto the beam, raised her body and stood. She immediately performed a back walkover, letting her right foot come down onto the beam first. (Photo OK 1 shows Olga at the beginning of her back walkover. For photo OK series, see pages 244–245). As her left leg came down, she let it swing down past the beam and up onto it, giving her forward momentum, so that as she put her foot on the beam, she was already moving forward. She stepped forward, did a sissone, stepped to the end and made a half turn to her left. She danced forward, did a tuck jump with her right knee bent and her right foot extended back to land on her left foot, immediately pushed off her left foot to land on her right foot with her left leg extended back and then moved forward to perform a cartwheel to her left to the end of the beam. Now facing back along the beam she danced forward, did some skip steps and a stag jump to the other end. She posed at the end of the beam, her body erect but tilted slightly backwards, her left leg straight up and down about a foot back from the end and her right leg extended forward, slightly diagonally, with her toe pointed and touching the end of the beam. Both arms were extended horizontally in front of her and she gracefully moved them up and down. She made a slight body wave and tap with her right foot and performed a back walkover. After landing, she stepped back with her right foot and made a deep body wave. Then she brought her right foot

Olga getting ready to perform her Korbut.

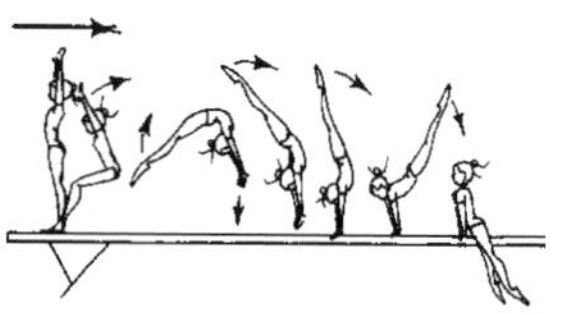

Figure 79

forward again and stood for a moment, preparing for her next move: she made a high backward dive to straddle down (an element known as a "Korbut") *(Figure 79)* (photo OK 2), continued in roll onto her back, piked her legs, brought them over her head, put her knees and shins onto the beam, raised her body, put her hands on the beam, straightened her arms, raised her hips, straightened her legs and stood up—all this in one continuous motion since her back straddle down. She leaned back and passed through a near vertical planche position—her straight arms supporting her on the beam, her legs straight and separated about half way to straddle, her back arched and her head raised (photo OK 3). She finished in straddle down at the end of the beam, once again allowing her legs to swing forward so that she could thrust them back and up. She came back up in two motions: first, she swung her legs back and up until her body was about 45° above horizontal, supported by her straight arms on the beam. Second, she lowered her right leg and placed her right foot on the beam while swinging her left leg down and forward. She thrust her left leg back and up. Its momentum enabled her to move her body up and forward into her famous stag handstand, her right knee the one bent (photo OK 4). She held her handstand for two seconds, extended her right leg, then came back

OK 1

OK 2

OK 3

down on her feet to stand at the end of the beam, her left leg straight, her right leg forward, her right knee bent. She stepped forward, made a full turn to her left, performed a forward walkover and danced near to the end with a chassé. About a foot back from the end, she posed with her left leg slightly bent and her right leg extended ahead, her toes, pointed and touching the end. Then she swung her right leg back diagonally behind her, her foot touching the beam, her toes pointed. Her arms were extended horizontally, right arm in front, left arm behind. With her feet slightly separated, she made a half turn to her right. She did a few dance steps, a high split leap (photo OK 5) and more dance steps to the end. At the end, she made a quarter turn to her left, a body wave with bent knees and another quarter turn to her left. She stepped forward toward the middle of the beam and did an assemblé. She made two body waves, each deeper than the one at the end. During these body waves, she rotated her arms from overhead to down behind and up in front of her, then to down in front and up behind her, as she performed her second body wave, all the while getting ready for her dismount: starting with her feet together and her arms over her head, she swung her arms down in front and up behind her while flexing her knees, then swung her arms down behind and up in front of her

OK 4 *OK 5* *OK 6*

Olga at the beginning of her back tuck.

while she thrust off with her legs. She executed a salto backward tucked (photo OK 6) to land with both feet at the same time and straighten her body to stand with her head and arms thrown back in a triumphant pose. Then she immediately executed a salto forward tucked to land beside the beam on the left side, her right hand on the beam as she landed to steady herself. Once again, she flung her arms and head back in a triumphant pose, then stepped back to her left with a big smile to receive the wild applause of the crowd.

From the point of view of the crowd's interest, Olga's beam routine was the high point of fourth rotation. She left the podium happy that she had redeemed herself but still emotionally crushed that her dreams of becoming all-around Olympic champion had been dashed by what must have seemed to her a stupid blunder on bars, something she had never done before. She knew she would have to face the press and a lot of criticism at home. She was afraid of what her coach might have to say.

Her coach, Renald Knysh, surprised her, however. He had not been brought along as an official member of the Soviet gymnastics delegation but had come on his own as a tourist to see his star pupil perform. When finally he was able to catch up with Olga the following morning by one of the gates to the Olympic Village, he did not berate her or even criticize her. Instead he congratulated her on the sensation she had caused. He had known all along that Olga would be a sensation when she got to Munich. Olga had simply verified his predictions; she had lived up to his expectations.[3] As to the trouble on bars, he brushed that aside: he knew she would perform up to her usual standard during finals on the apparatus. And this, of course, as everyone knows, she did.

At the conclusion of fourth rotation, the final standings and scores in the individual all-around competition were as follows:

	Initial Score	4th Rotation	Final Score
1. Turischeva *(floor)*	67.125	9.90	77.025
2. Janz *(bars)*	67.175	9.70	76.875
3. Lazakovich *(beam)*	67.100	9.75	76.850
4. Zuchold *(beam)*	66.950	9.50	76.450
5. Burda *(vault)*	66.225	9.55	75.775
6. Hellmann *(bars)*	65.950	9.60	75.550
7. Korbut *(beam)*	65.300	9.80	75.100
8. Saadi *(vault)*	65.675	9.40	75.075
9. Bekesi *(vault)*	65.550	9.40	74.950
10. Rigby *(bars)*	65.425	9.50	74.925

All-around winners: Turischeva, Janz, Lazakovich. Man at right, clapping, is Arthur Gander, President and founder of F.I.G.

Finals on the Apparatus

Competition III: August 31st

Finals on the apparatus were awaited with great anticipation. The crowd's emotions had been wrung out by the excitement of Olga Korbut's triumph and tragedy, but their emotions would well up into tears of joy as they watched her turn tragedy once again into triumph. They were eager to cheer her on and live this moment of their lives to the utmost. There was other excitement. Karin Janz, who had narrowly missed winning the gold medal in the all-around, was now ready for her second chance at a gold medal and Turischeva wanted to win for herself the two medals that Korbut so desperately coveted.

Vault

Roxanne Pierce, USA, in vault pre-flight.

Right away, Karin won vault with her handspring onto the horse followed by a pike off and then a full turn, that is, a Yamashita full twist; she scored 9.90. Erika Zuchold won the silver medal with a 9.70 for her Yamashita and Ludmilla won the bronze with 9.60, first on a Yamashita and then on a handspring followed by full twist off. (In Munich, the gymnasts performed two vaults, the highest one counting. As in all finals on the apparatus, the total score is the score in finals combined with the average of compulsory and optionals in team competition.)

Lyubov Burda scored 9.70 on her second half-on, half-off vault, but her 9.525 entering average allowed her only fourth place. Similarly, Olga Korbut placed fifth because of her 9.525 entering average, although she scored 9.65 on each of two Yamashitas. Tamara Lazakovich was sixth with 9.60 for two Yamashitas and her entering average of 9.45.

The final standings and scores for vault were as follows:

	Entering Avg.	Score in Final	Total
1. Karin Janz	9.625	9.90	19.525
2. Erika Zuchold	9.575	9.70	19.275
3. L. Turischeva	9.650	9.60	19.250
4. Lyubov Burda	9.525	9.70	19.225
5. Olga Korbut	9.525	9.65	19.175
6. T. Lazakovich	9.450	9.60	19.050

Uneven Bars

On bars, Karin Janz scored another 9.90 and won her second gold medal. (Her routine has previously been described.) This 9.90 and her 9.775 entering average meant that her final score of 19.675 was 0.225 ahead of Olga Korbut and Erika Zuchold, who tied for second place. The considerable difference between Janz's score and that of Korbut and Zuchold was an indication of just how good Karin Janz was on bars. Olga Korbut's silver was her first medal of the evening. Fourth and fifth places went to Turischeva and Bekesi, whose routines, like those of Korbut and Zuchold, have previously been described. In sixth place was Angelika Hellmann, the popular and attractive gymnast from East Germany who made her 1970 debut in Ljubljana. This was Angelika's routine:

> From the low bar side, she ran, jumped off the beat board, straddled over low bar and caught high bar. She kipped on high bar until she could straddle her legs over the high bar. Continuing in the same direction with her legs straddled over the bar, she entered a circle around and under the bar (stalder forward). As she came up between the bars, she stretched her body and let it drop to bounce on her hips off the low bar. On her uprise, she made a full twist to her left and bounced again off the low bar. On her second uprise, she straddled her legs and swung forward under the high bar to initiate a second kip. She kipped up to clear support position over the low bar, then executed a partial clear hip circle back under high bar and up to handstand. She made a

Karin Janz in vault post-flight.

Kim Chace, USA, in turn off high bar.

half turn in handstand and swung back down in giant circle to wrap around low bar. She flew back toward high bar, which she caught in eagle grip. She hung for a second from high bar, then dropped to low bar. She kipped on low bar to catch high bar, kipped on high bar up to clear support on the side away from low bar. She then executed a clear hip circle backwards down on the side away from low bar. As she came up between the bars and then passed over the top in clear support, she went right into a salto backwards tucked on the side away from low bar to land *(Figure 80)*. She took two little steps back on landing.

It was a stock routine except for her unusual dismount. Her two steps back on landing necessitated a deduction in her score, but she executed the rest of her routine with her usual clarity of form.

The final standings and scores for bars finals were as follows:

	Entering Avg.	Final Score	Total Score
1. Karin Janz	9.775	9.900	19.675
2. Olga Korbut	9.650	9.800	19.450
Erika Zuchold	9.650	9.800	19.450
4. L. Turischeva	9.625	9.800	19.425
5. Ilona Bekesi	9.575	9.700	19.275
6. A. Hellmann	9.550	9.650	19.200

Balance Beam

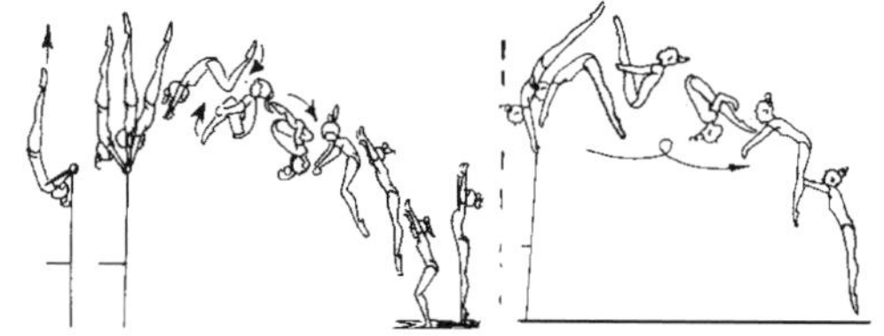

Figure 80

During the second half of finals, irresistible Olga Korbut came into her own and scored 9.90 on beam. With her 9.50 entering average, this gave her 19.40 for a total score and her second medal of the evening, this one a gold. Lazakovich was only 0.25 behind: her 9.80 in finals with her 9.575 entering average gave her a 19.375 total. Interestingly, these two scores were the only high ones in finals. Karin Janz scored only 9.55, but her 18.975 score—0.4 less than that of Lazakovich—was good enough for the bronze, her third medal of the evening.

In fourth place was a gymnast who had not been a leading contender in previous competitions—Monica Csaszar of Hungary. She had placed twelfth in preliminary (team) competition and fourteenth in the all-around. She scored 9.60 for the following routine:

> Csaszar ran at the beat board, placed at one end of the beam, jumped off, put her hands on the beam and pressed up to handstand, straddling her legs on the way up and bringing them together in handstand. She paused in handstand and continued in walkover to stand. She danced forward until just past the middle of the beam, where she posed, standing erect, her right leg in front, her arms out to the side but inclined slightly back, and her back similarly inclined backwards. She stepped forward, made a stag leap and a half turn to her right. After a pose, she executed a forward walkover, posed, made a quarter turn to her right, posed again, turned back to her left and entered a standing split forward on her right foot, her left leg vertical supported by her left hand, her right arm stretched forward. From her split, she leaned forward into handstand with her legs split and performed tic-toc, touching the beam first with her left foot. As she came back to touch the beam with her right foot, she continued down onto her right knee and leg, her left leg elevated horizontally behind, her body just above horizontal and her hands on the beam. In this knee scale, she posed, then swung her left leg forward, stood and made a half turn to her left. She danced forward until just beyond the middle of the beam, paused, posed and performed a back handspring. Then she leaned back into a stag handstand, which she held briefly, then continued on over to stand right at the end of the beam. She danced forward, did a split leap and a series of three half turns and poses, then came back with a walk-over forward with

Erika Zuchold

> alternate hand support (a tinsica) to the end of the beam. She stepped back slowly, posed in arabesque and then performed a back walkover. She made a deep body wave down to squat and danced back to the end, where she posed and made a half turn to her right. After a pause to get herself ready, she executed a front aerial walkover, stepped to the end and dismounted with a salto forward stretched with full twist.

Her dismount was the same as that used by Cathy Rigby in her silver-medal-winning routine in Ljubljana. Cathy's preliminary average in Munich was 0.05 below Czaszar's. Their compulsory scores were the same (9.25) but the difference came in optionals (9.35 and 9.40), where the American gymnasts had received such a hammering from the judges. Interestingly, Rigby's preliminary average of 9.30 was the same as that of Zuchold, but she was not selected for finals because of the limitation to six competitors in finals and because Zuchold's all-around placement was higher.

Fifth and sixth places went to Turischeva and Zuchold, whose routines have already been described. The balance beam standings and scores in finals were as follows:

	Entering Avg.	Final Scores	Totals
1. Olga Korbut	9.500	9.900	19.400
2. T. Lazakovich	9.575	9.800	19.375
3. Karin Janz	9.425	9.550	18.975
4. Monica Czaszar	9.325	9.600	18.925
5. L. Turischeva	9.400	9.400	18.800
6. Erika Zuchold	9.300	9.400	18.700

Floor Exercise

The last event in finals on the apparatus allowed the world to see this most beautiful event of the beautiful sport. It was one that would gradually build in excitement and come to a joyous conclusion for the thousands of spectators in the Sporthalle and the millions of television viewers around the world. It began with the two gymnasts who were tied for fifth place going in, with an entering average of 9.50, Lyubov Burda and Angelika Hellmann. As it happened, they both received the same score of 9.60 in finals and so remained in fifth place. Their routines were as follows:

> Burda's exercise was similar to the one she had used in Ljubljana. She started in a corner, standing facing a diagonal, turned to her right to face parallel to one of the sides and took a step forward with her right foot. She posed in a statuesque attitude on her right leg, her left leg diagonally behind, her head thrown back and her arms flung out diagonally to her

sides. She wrapped her arms around her chest, then extended them out again one at a time but this time slowly and gracefully. She turned left to face along the diagonal and begin her first pass: a round-off, flic-flac, salto backward stretched, right into another flic-flac, salto backward stretched step-out. After a very brief pause, she began her second pass, back along the same diagonal: a round-off, flic-flac, half turn into salto forward tucked (Arabian), which she ended in a pose leaning forward on her hands, both arms extended, her left leg extended diagonally behind with her foot on the floor and her right leg extended diagonally forward above her. She pushed off into handstand with legs split, made a quarter turn in handstand to her right and came forward on her right leg to stand. She then stepped forward, made a half turn back toward the corner from which she had started her routine and stood posing for at least two seconds, while she brought her arms down slowly and gracefully to her side and then drooped her head forward. After this long pause, she began a series of long dance steps, sweeping arm movements, turns and poses as she proceeded toward the middle of the floor. From there, she proceeded with dance steps toward the corner to the right of the one from which she had started. She performed a split leap into the corner, did a half turn and began her third pass: a round-off, flic-flac half turn into a front handspring followed by a dive cartwheel to her left. She stepped back from her cartwheel and began to dance in a long circle counterclockwise around the floor, during which she performed two split leaps and ended with an aerial forward walkover. She made a tour jeté to a scale, a back walkover with half turn, stepped into the next corner and posed, preparing for her fourth and final pass: she ran forward, performed a split leap and then a round-off directly into a salto backward stretched, in which she came down on her left foot and then stepped back with her right. She stepped forward onto her left foot, her right foot remaining behind her, arched her back and flung her arms out to the side, slightly above horizontal in her final pose.

Angelika Hellmann had an unusual beginning. She started several steps in from one corner, but instead of beginning her first pass from there, she danced along the entire diagonal performing the following elements: she did a plié preparation into a full turn and finished in a lunge. Then she did a high kick followed by a chassé and a jump kick. She stepped into a stag jump and another chassé and then did a half turn into a flic-flac followed by a few steps back into the corner and a full turn to her left before beginning her first pass: a round-off, flic-flac into a salto backward stretched with full twist. She danced in a full turn and then circled off to her right with bold, marching steps, with her knees raised high, and energetic arm movements, with her elbows fully bent. When she reached the center, she turned again to her right toward the corner one corner clockwise from where she had

> started her first pass, and went toward it with a cartwheel to her left and a back walkover followed by a half turn to her left to face the corner. Facing the corner, she made a half turn to her right, leaning on her right hand outstretched to the floor and supported also by her right foot on the floor, and then began her second pass: a round-off, flic-flac, salto backward stretched followed by another flic-flac into a salto backward tucked. She stepped back after her back tuck, then stepped forward, returning along the same diagonal, and made a full turn to her right on her left foot with her right leg held high. She turned slightly to her left, continued forward and performed a split leap with change of legs and with a half turn to her left to face toward the center. She made another half turn to her left and posed briefly in attitude, facing the corner to the right of the one she had just left. She turned to back her right towards the center, danced forward, made a full turn and stepped forward to kick her right leg up almost vertically in front of her and extend her arms up above her parallel with her right leg. She leaned back, kept her left leg straight, crossed her right leg over her left and continued leaning back until her seat and straight left leg touched the floor. She continued her backward movement until her back was on the floor and stretched her arms out to her side. As her back touched the floor, she elevated her legs in a wide straddle above her and then rolled to her right a half turn, bringing her left leg over her right and letting her right leg slide under her so that she finished in side splits with her arms out to the side. She slowly rolled a half turn and brought her straight legs together, then rolled a turn in which she brought her legs from stretched to tucked and finally a full turn on her seat with her knees bent so that she ended sitting with her knees bent, her feet under her seat as pushed forward into a standing split on her right leg with her left leg vertical and both hands on the floor supporting her. She held this pose for barely a second before bringing her left leg down and standing. She made a series of poses, turns and dance steps while she proceeded to the corner on her left for her final pass: a round-off, flic-flac, salto backward stretched step-out. She ran straight forward along the same diagonal, executed a high split leap with both legs stretched absolutely horizontally and dropped down into squat upon landing. She stood, made a full turn to her left on her right foot and assumed her final pose: she was up on her toes, her right foot slightly ahead and her arms out to her side, just above horizontal.

Because of its grace and artistry, Hellmann's was a routine truly deserving to be in floor exercise finals. Her stretched saltos were executed with her body absolutely stretched, her split leaps all had 180° leg separation, and her movements were all taken to the maximum. It is hard to know where the deductions came from.

Hellmann's routine was followed by those of Lazakovich, Janz, and Turischeva, who each received 9.80, whose routines have previously been described, and whose total scores were 19.450, 19.400, and 19.550 respectively. Finally, the time came for the climax of the evening: the floor exercise of Olga Korbut. In this event, her entering average was 9.675; this was 0.075 less than Turischeva's 9.750. Olga would need a 9.90 to achieve a total score of 19.575 and win the gold medal. Everyone knew this because the scoreboards prominently displayed the challenge for all to see.

Olga's routine, previously described, began with her standing at the middle of one of the sides. She hopped up into her pose in attitude and held it for barely a second. She ran along the side, performed her lovely swan dive-roll and ended standing with her feet apart, her hands behind her seat, her head thrown back, and her winning "How's that?!" smile on her face. She already had the crowd in the palm of her hand. From then on, she went from element to element, one refreshingly–Olga pose after another and made no mistakes that were evident to the untrained eye. When at the end of her routine, she assumed her playful, teasing, final pose, the crowd burst into thunderous, shouting applause. There was some delay in the scoring, but the cheering persisted and, in the end, a 9.90 was posted. The volume of the cheering was such that the judges really had no choice. Olga had won her second gold medal in finals to go with her silver on the uneven bars and her gold for team competition. She was once again the little heroine of team competition. The tears of the all-around made the results in finals all the more joyful, not only for her but for everyone else.

Thus, this last event ended as the crowd hoped it would. The standings and scores for floor exercise finals were as follows:

	Entering Avg.	Finals Score	Total
1. Olga Korbut	9.675	9.900	19.575
2. L. Turischeva	9.750	9.800	19.550
3. T. Lazakovich	9.650	9.800	19.450
4. Karin Janz	9.600	9.800	19.400
5. Lyubov Burda	9.500	9.600	19.100
6. A. Hellmann	9.500	9.600	19.100

Olga's collection of medals had the highest value: she won gold for team competition and for beam and floor exercise finals. In addition, she won a silver medal on bars. Karin Janz had her gold medals for vault and bars, her silver medal for the all around, her silver medal team award, and her bronze medal on beam. Turischeva had her team and all-around gold medals, her silver on floor, and her bronze medal in vault. Tamara Lazakovich had her gold

Olga Korbut with the smile that conquered the world.

team award, her silver on beam, and her bronze for all-around and floor exercise. Erika Zuchold had her silver team award, her silver on vault, and her bronze on bars.

One gymnast who has not been mentioned so far is Joan Moore of the United States, four-time U.S. National Champion who placed 21st all-around. Her name is now Joan Moore Rice. She is mentioned because, in floor exercise, she was the only gymnast besides Ludmilla Turischeva to open with a salto backward stretched with double twist. This acrobatic element was then at the highest level of difficulty. Now it is considered an element of difficulty level C, well below difficulty levels D and E, in which are such elements as double saltos and double saltos with twist.

> Joan Moore performed a beautiful floor exercise, although she did not qualify for finals. Her music included portions of Rachmaninoff's second piano concerto. As already mentioned, she opened with round-off, flic-flac salto backward stretched with double twist. Her second pass was a front handspring into a salto forward stretched (another current C-element). Following this, she danced and performed two cartwheels into a flic-flac and a stag jump. Then after more dance steps, she started a back walkover, dropped down onto her elbows, split her legs, reversed direction, fell backward, stood and made a full turn. After proceeding parallel to one of the sides, she performed a front handspring followed by another front handspring in which she rolled out onto her shoulders (a dive roll). Her final pass was round-off, flic-flac, whipback, salto backward stretched followed by a flic-flac into her final pose.

Having watched Olympic-level gymnastics for six days, the world was temporarily sated with the sport but not with Olga. People the world over were frantic for information about her and eagerly read every bit of news. So it was with joy they found out that she and her teammates would make exhibition performances. These began within a few weeks when she returned to West Germany for an exhibition in Frankfurt. In March 1973, she made an extensive tour of the United States, the first of six she and her teammates would make before the 1976 Olympics in Montreal. She made many tours also in other countries. Among her most adoring fans were the British, who sold out all exhibition performances and who enthusiastically supported the 1973 European Championships and the 1975 World Cup, both held in London.

In gymnastics, the history of Munich and its participants was destined for a long life. The competition ended before the terrorist attack the following week. Its memory, therefore, was not sullied by that tragic event.

References

[1]Peter Axthelm, "The Olympics: New Faces of '72," *Newsweek,* 11 Sept. 1972: 70–71.

[2]Dick Criley, "Olympic Report," *Gymnast,* Nov. 1972: 19.

[3]Olga Korbut, *My Story: The Autobiography of Olga Korbut,* (London: Century, 1992), 59.

Descriptions of the routines of most gymnasts are taken from video tapes made from films taken by Frank Endo and Fred Turoff. Descriptions of Olga Korbut's uneven bars routine in Competition II and the floor exercises of Cathy Rigby and Joan Moore were taken from the video tapes of ABC–TV. With their kind permission, these were viewed at the ABC New York office. Scores were taken from *Gymnast,* October 1972.

Ludmilla Turischeva

Lyubov Burda

Karin Janz

Karin Janz

1952 Born, February 17.

1966 East bloc "Tournament of Friendship": 1st , all-around (at age 14).

1967 European Championship, Amsterdam, May: 4th, all-around; 3rd, vault; 2nd, bars.

1968 Olympics, Mexico. October 6th, all-around; 2nd, bars; 4th beam (tie–Metheny).

1969 European Championship, Landskrona, Sweden, May: 1st, all-around; 1st, vault, bars, beam; 2nd, floor.

1970 World Championships, Ljubljana, October: 4th, all-around; 2nd, vault; 1st, bars; 4th, floor.

1972 Champions All, London, April: 1st, all-around.

1972 Olympics, Munich, August: 2nd, all-around; 1st, vault, bars; 3rd beam; 4th, floor. Height at Munich: 156 cm (5' 1"); weight 45 kg (99 lbs.)

1972 Chunichi Cup, Japan, November: 1st, all-around.

I had the pleasure of meeting Karin Janz at the Forum Hotel in the former eastern part of Berlin in October 1993. During a phone call to her after I had arrived in Berlin, I immediately detected something unexpected: I heard her laugh—not a loud laugh but a light, happy, musical laugh. I thought to myself, "This is Karin Janz?" My reaction resulted from never having seen a picture of Karin with anything but a stern expression on her face. I had expected the real person to resemble her photographic image.

In the course of a most enjoyable dinner with her and a man she was seeing now that her marriage was breaking up, I became acquainted with someone who in her social intercourse was prone to laughter, was easy to talk to and seemed at ease with herself and her companions.

Her relaxed attitude in a social environment might be the result of confidence in herself from her many achievements and the intensity of her daytime activities. She is head of the Kaulsdorf Orthopaedic Clinic in Berlin. As such, she not only has administrative responsibilities but also regularly performs surgical operations that last from one or two to seven hours.

Karin Janz, one year and four months old, with her father.

She arrived at her intention to become a doctor at an early age.

> I was as young as 10 when my father asked me which profession I would like to choose. I would like to become a dentist or an interpreter, I answered then. Two years later, I decided to become a doctor, as I was too small to work as a dentist."[1]

If she decided upon a medical career at an early age, her gymnastics career was decided upon equally far in advance of its actual starting. In fact, she undoubtedly set a record for beginning gymnastics—six months! There was some kind of a bar across her crib. Her father has a picture of baby Karin with her hands on the bar, trying to pull herself up!

Her father was a gymnast in the 1930s and 1940s, so it was natural for young Karin at least to consider gymnastics. In fact, she had a career that lasted 13 years. She began at age 7 and was 20 when she competed at the Munich Olympics. Her gymnastics has been fully described in this book on the pages devoted to the major competitions. That the apparatus on which she achieved her greatest success was the uneven bars is due partly to the circumstance that her coach at the Sports Club Berlin was Jurgen Heritz. This famous coach not only coached Janz to gold medals on bars at the 1969 European Championship, the 1970 World Championships, and the 1972 Olympics but also coached Annelore Zinke to her gold medal on bars in the 1974 World Championships and Maxi Gnauck similarly in the 1979, 1981, and 1983 World Championships. In addition, he was Angelika Hellmann's coach.

In an article for *Sports in the GDR*[2], Karin Janz said, "He certainly has a special talent precisely for that apparatus." Annelore Zinke added, "It's also essential whether or not you are at home with an apparatus, whether you have the required physical preconditions and in how far you are able, with the trainer's help, to develop ideas and put them into practice." The youngest of the three, Maxi Gnauck, said, "What I appreciate most about Jurgen Heritz is his expertise, his untiring effort, and his constant encouragement to improve performances. Sometimes he gets a bit loud in the process, but that's part of the game."

The same article noted that all three girls had equally good physical and psychological prerequisites for that apparatus, being not too tall, but strong and at the same time flexible in the shoulder joints, courageous, and ready to take a risk.

Karin Janz's name is now associated with an element in the gymnastics "Code of Points." Called the Janz-Salto or Janz-Roll, it is "cast from front lying hang to salto forward to hang on high bar," as illustrated *(Figure 77)*.

Karin later said, "Admittedly it no longer forms a part of the top-class gymnast's repertoire. More visually attractive flight elements of greater amplitude have asserted themselves."[4]

Nevertheless, perhaps Bela Karolyi might have got some ideas from the Janz-Salto for his own Comaneci-Salto (see page 4). In any case, it was used as a model for the later Jaeger-Salto on the men's horizontal bar, invented by the GDR gymnast Bernd Jaeger.[1]

In spite of her own technical prowess, Karin compared what she did in 1972 with what Maxi Gnauck had done in 1979 and said, "My difficult Olympic exercises in 1972 would no longer be enough to reach the world championship final."[2] Yet in her day, Karin was in the forefront of women's gymnastics in its development of difficult elements. She had tried a new and more difficult dismount from beam in the 1970 World Championships and had fallen. This fall was perhaps the biggest disappointment of her career. It cost her the all-around championship in Ljubljana, a title won by Turischeva. About Turischeva, Karin graciously said, "I have always been in awe of one of the world's biggest gymnastic stars, Ludmilla Turischeva. She possesses the most valuable attribute for any athlete—the ability to get it all together at the right moment and push hard till the very end. I feel this is the main reason for Ludmilla's long and successful career in the sports arena."[5]

The two of them had parallel careers. Both began their major international competitions as 16-year-olds in the 1968 Mexico Olympics; Janz won the 1969 European Championship in Landskrona, while Turischeva placed third; Turischeva won the 1970 World Championships while Janz placed fourth; Turischeva won again in 1972 Munich, where Janz placed second; then, taking her final bow, Janz won the 1972 Chunichi Cup and Turischeva placed third.

A personal article on Karin provided by *Panorama DDR* noted that when Janz, then 21, withdrew from sports, she had been asked whether it was really true that she wanted to finish her active career. She had then answered:

> Gymnastics have been and will remain my passion, but a continuation after the success in Munich would have become really significant only if I had decided to participate once more in the Olympic Games in Montreal 1976. This way, however, would have been too long for me.[3]

She had, in fact, enrolled in the famous Humboldt University in Berlin in 1971, a year before the Munich Olympics. Because of the intensive preparations required for the Olympics, she had to interrupt her course. She made up for this time and by 1978, she had completed her training and was admitted to the general practice of medicine. Her area of practice later became orthopaedics, which is defined as "the branch of surgery dealing with the treatment of deformities, diseases and injuries of the bones, joints muscles, etc." Her specialty became endoprosthetics, *prosthetics* being defined as "the branch of surgery dealing with the replacement of missing parts . . . artificial substitutes" and *endo-* being a combining form meaning "inner." Thus, her operations frequently include hip replacements and replacements of the knee.

Her particular contribution to endoprosthetics, however, has been the development, with another doctor, of an artificial intervertebral disc, that is, an artificial disc to replace one that has been destroyed. This process relates to the disc-shaped part between vertebrae which enables the vertebrae to move relative to each other easily and without pain. The endoprosthesis is performed in the lumbar vertebra region, that is, in the lower back. It is an experimental process of which there are three models of discs. Between 1987 and June of 1993, there have been 740 implantations of Model III in Germany, France, the Netherlands, Great Britain, Italy, Switzerland, and Argentina. A team of the Texas Back Institute in Plano, Texas, is working to get permission from the F.D.A. in the United States.

Karin Janz's training for this work has, of course, been extensive. After graduating in 1978 from the School of Medicine at Humboldt, she started her training as a specialist for orthopaedics in the School of Medicine of Charité Hospital, Humboldt University of Berlin. In 1981, she became resident physician in the pediatric ward and in 1985 in the endoprosthetics ward. In 1982, she took her doctor's degree on diagnosis of knee joint lesions, especially in competitive sportsmen. In 1983, she got the approbation as specialist in orthopaedics.

After having been head physician in the ward for endoprosthetics at the Department of Orthopaedics, Charité Hospital, she was appointed medical superintendent at the Orthopaedic Clinic of the District Hospital, Berlin

Kaulsdorf, in March 1990. This clinic has 70 beds and a staff of 12 medical doctors, including doctors in training.

Karin, who should more properly be referred to as Doctor Janz, has lectured at numerous international scientific events. In 1987 as a member of a delegation of the European Society for Knee Surgery and Arthroscopy, she travelled to the United States for education and lecturing and became on this occasion an honorary member of the American Orthopaedic Society for Sports Medicine. Within the framework of research on the development of implants, especially in cooperation with the firm Link/Hamburg, she carried out guest operations in several western European countries, together with one other doctor. She has had over 200 articles published, either as author or co-author and has made video films on intervertebral endoprosthetics and different diseases of the hip, the knee and ankle joints and the shoulders, including traumatic as well as tumerous lesions.

The transition of Karin Janz, the Olympic champion, to Dr. Janz, orthopaedic surgeon, seems to speak well of the former German Democratic Republic in this particular aspect of its political and social life. The GDR did not simply forget about its former athletes as the USSR did. Dr. Janz has said: "Our state provides all opportunities for everybody to learn. It depends on the individual how much he can grasp this opportunity. It is a matter of attitude to work and profession, whether he wants to work at more than the minimum requirements."[1]

An article in the *GDR Review* describes how the gymnast Karin Janz took advantage of her opportunity. "Many a quality which she has always had and which, through hard gymnastic training, she further developed, now stood her in good stead in her new career. For example, the healthy urge gradually to achieve perfection. Commenting on this, Karin Janz said, 'Once I finished gymnastics, I determined that I would also be a good, successful doctor.'" She made a comparison: "'Behind my sporting successes lay long periods of training. However, the exercises with which I won the medals lasted at most one and a half minutes. In medicine, things are more drawn out. We recognize that curing patients and restoring body functions are processes to which one must devote great patience.'"[4]

With her daily work and the further development of the artificial disc, Dr. Janz "maintains her zest, drive and pleasure in solving a medical problem. 'The reason for this,' she explained, 'is simple—namely, the patients. Can you imagine how a doctor feels when a person who has endured severe pain for years suddenly shows clear signs of improvement?'"[4]

Karin rents a house in the southeastern part of Berlin, not far from her Kaulsdorf clinic. Her son Eiko is now 14.

References

[1]Andreas Götze, "Formerly 'Miss Uneven Bars'—Now a Doctor," *World Gymnastics,* 1984/2, No. 19: 18–19.

[2]Wolfgang Richter, "The Girls of the GDR," *International Gymnast,* Sept. 1980: 20–21.

[3]"Karin Janz and Erika Zuchold Today," *Panorama DDR,* Artikel Kommentare 6-V-141/9.4.

[4]Birk Meinhardt, "From Somersault to Scalpel," *GDR Review,* 8/86: 57–59.

[5]*Sport in the USSR,* 1978: No. 5

Erika Zuchold

1947 Born, March 19, as Erika Barth, in the little village of Lucka/Breitenhain near Leipzig, Saxony.

1959 Began gymnastics at local sport school, age 12.

1961 Entered boarding sport school, age 14.

1963 First international competition: member of Leipzig college team that competed against Budapest college team in Hungary.

1963 Became member of national team and performed in exhibition in China.

1964 Competed in the Soviet Union, Romania, and Bulgaria. Became first person to perform flic-flac on the beam in competition in Berlin against Soviet Union.

1964 Qualified for Tokyo Olympic team but had to withdraw because of injury.

1965 to 1969
Studies in Institute for Teacher Training in Leipzig: subjects, sport and music.

1966 World Championships, Dortmund, September: 4th, all-around; 2nd, vault.

1967 European Championship, Amsterdam, May: 5th, all-around; 2nd, vault; 6th beam.

1968 Olympics, Mexico, October: 4th, all-around (tie–Petrick); 2nd, vault; 5th, bars; 6th, beam.

1969 European Championship, Landskrona, Sweden, May: 3rd, all-around (tie–Turischeva); 2nd, vault; 4th, bars; 5th, beam, floor.

1970 World Championships, Ljubljana, Slovenia, October: 2nd, all-around; 1st, vault beam; 6th, bars.

1971 European Championship, Minsk, Belarus, October: 3rd, all-around; 3rd, vault, beam, floor; 5th, bars.

1972 Olympics, Munich, August: 4th, all-around; 2nd, vault; 2nd (tie–Korbut) bars; 6th, beam.

1972 to 1976
Studies of Art Education at Karl Marx University in Leipzig.

1977 to 1980
Leipzig Sport Museum. Set up department of art and sport. Collected pictures, graphics, and sculptures with sport motifs from GDR artists and organized exhibitions in GDR and Poland. Initiated painting and drawing contests in Sri Lanka and Philippines.

Since 1980

Self-employed for painting and graphic art with permanent exhibitions at home and in Iraq, Spain, and Switzerland, except for period 1984 to 1987 when she was an entertainer.

1990 to 1993

Studied at Johannes R. Becker Institute for Literature at Leipzig University.

Erika Zuchold is another former East German gymnast who made a successful transition to life after gymnastics following her gold and silver medal-winning career. Today, she is an extremely good-looking, personable woman. She has not only weathered her own transition from gymnastics but also her country's transition from socialism to capitalism. Her marriage and her interest in art were her keys.

Erika began drawing while still a gymnast. She found that drawing helped overcome her nervousness both before and during competitions. She has an affinity for art that goes beyond talent. "In phases of exhaustion or moods of depression, she found work with the drawing pencil relaxing. With it she learned to overcome disappointments—for her successful sports career was often interrupted by injuries."[1]

A most devastating disappointment hit her early on in her career. She had risen quickly in East German gymnastics. In 1963, four years after she began her serious gymnastics training, she was a member of a college team in a Leipzig–Budapest competition that took place in the Hungarian capital. She was then 16. In 1964, in another competition, she was the first gymnast ever to perform the flic-flac (back handspring) on the beam in competition.[2] It was as time when everything was going well for the young gymnast. Later that year, she qualified as a member of the GDR team for the 1964 Olympics in Tokyo. German gymnastics experts confidently expected her to win the gold medal on beam. Then she tore an Achilles tendon and lost her place on the team.

During her recovery, "the flowers sent to comfort and encourage her became the objects of her battles against depression. Each time her drawings of the flowers were more successful. She wanted to try more."[1] That she was able to pick herself up and compete again is proved by the full extent of her achievements in gymnastics, which are described in the sections of this book devoted to competitions.

Her injury in 1964 was not her only one.

> In 1968 at the Olympic Games in Mexico City, I performed with a half-ruptured meniscus on my right knee. For two years, until 1970, I did gymnastics in pain. My achievements were stagnating; I lost courage; I

> could not increase my exercises with new elements. Involuntarily, I decided to stop my career. I was very sad it was over. Many doctors had tested me without success. I went to a last doctor; it was my last chance. I had luck: the doctor knew my injury. In February I was operated on and in October I performed at the World Championships in Ljubljana."[3]

This story does indeed have a happy ending, for Ljubljana was the scene of her biggest success.

Between 1966 and 1972, she competed in three European Championships, two World Championships, and two Olympics. She won at least one individual medal in each of these major, international competitions and contributed strongly to the GDR team performance. Her best achievements were at the 1970 World Championships in Ljubljana where she won two gold and two silver medals, one of them for the team award. At that time, she was twenty-three years old. After these world championships achievements, she was named "Sportswoman of the Year" in a nation-wide vote among East German sportswriters. She distinguished herself again the following year in Minsk with four third-place showings in the 1971 European Championship and in Munich in 1972 she closed out her career with three silver Olympic medals, one of them for the team award.

A glance at her chronology shows that vault was her strongest event: she won an individual medal in vault in every one of her major competitions. This was, perhaps, because "she always felt like trying something new, to find elements and sequences of exercises which had not been done before. When told that Mr. Yamashita of Japan had 'invented' a new jump over the long horse, she felt challenged to try it over the women's transversely-placed horse."[5] She thus became one of the first women to do the Yamashita and perfected her performance of it over the years.

Her career on the GDR team spanned nine years. During this time, her gymnastic successes, her blonde, nordic good looks, her smile and pleasing personality made her a favorite among the East German people. Her successes and her personality encouraged her younger sister Monika to take up gymnastics. Monika had a brief, successful career but a shoulder injury forced her to give it up.

Life has been good for Erika. Since 1966, she has been happily married to Dieter Zuchold, a champion cyclist. When he retired from sport, he got a good job with the Ernst Thälmann heavy machinery company and rose to become public relations manager. Erika herself wasted no time. She immediately enrolled in a course of art education at the Karl Marx University in Leipzig and studied there from 1972 to 1976, when she received her teaching credential. Thereafter, she taught art at a newly-constructed school on the eastern outskirts of Leipzig.

For a few years in the 1980s, she left her teaching job and organized a variety show, called "Erika Introduces Herself," which toured the country. She had learned to dance and performed different dances; one was a number in which she wore top hat, white tie, long pants, and a short jacket. Sometimes, well-known singers and actors joined the troupe. It was, however, only moderately successful. Its end came with the fall on the Berlin Wall, when there was no money for art and culture and when members of the troupe went on to other things.

The fall of the Berlin Wall affected her life as it did the lives of all former East Germans. Employment at Dieter's company soon dropped from 30,000 to 5,000. Fortunately, he had reached retirement age of 55, so he was retired and not let go. His retirement pay is their primary support.

They live in a modest house in Leipzig. An extension to the house is a room which she has made into a gymnasium. In it she has a low beam, an exercise mat and a mirror. Outside is a lawn on which she can do her exercises in good weather.

Her primary activity is her art, including watercolors, oil, acrylic, and sculpture; she has had a number of exhibitions. In 1992, her art was included in an exhibition for the Olympic Games in Barcelona. In 1993, she had exhibitions in St. Gallen, Switzerland and again in Barcelona. Her pictures generally sell for 200 DM; the highest price she has received is 2,000 DM. Her art is a source both of income and satisfaction.

She did not greet the fall of her country's government in 1989 with enthusiasm. Many social problems arose. In this continuing period of adjustment, she looks back with nostalgia to the time when everyone's existence was provided for, when everyone had a job. Like other athletes, she had to spend as much time on her studies as on her training. In this way, the East German government assumed a certain responsibility toward its athletes for their lives after sport. In her gymnastics days, her mornings were devoted to her studies; she trained for five hours in the afternoon.

The East German government rewarded its athletes in another way: every year top athletes of each sport were invited to a celebration in Berlin. This was a happy time for them and enabled them to maintain friendships.

Judging from her exhibitions in Spain and Switzerland it is obvious that she appreciates the chance to travel. As before, when she immediately took up art to fill the void left by her departure from gymnastics, so now she is not idle. In the fall of 1993, she began an intensive course to improve her ability in English, which was already at a level where she could speak and write with considerable competence.

For Erika, her gymnastics began at an early age. She seemed naturally able to do the gymnastics elements which her father had taught her. Often when visitors came to her parents' house in the little village where they lived, furniture was pushed back so there would be room in the middle of the living room. There the little girl performed some handstands, side splits, and arabesques. It was meant for play and a pastime, nothing more. In the course of time, however, it became evident that the little girl was extraordinarily gifted for gymnastics.[5] Her father put her into a children's sport school, and there she became a very enthusiastic young gymnast. Nevertheless, it was hard for a shy country girl to warm up to the big city of Leipzig, to get up at five in the morning, to walk a kilometer around the fields to the station and to take the train to the city for school and workouts. Often she did not get home before ten o'clock at night. It became easier when she turned 14 and was able to go to boarding school.[4] Even there, her father kept on encouraging her, telling her: "You must do better than the others if you want to get to the top."[1]

Erika has never regretted her gymnastics. Her sport made harsh demands in training and required a regimen of discipline. Yet it also gave her something, "Joy, for example, in her performance and her potential for increasing it . . . as well as the happiness of offering to her millions of fans her gymnastics ability combined with her charm and grace."

Now she dresses her slender and graceful figure in clothes that are both sporty and feminine. Her tastes are simple and practical; she loves harmony in her selection of colors. To be with Erika is to be with a woman who has matured, who is at home with herself.

References

[1]Siglinde Freitag, "Erika Zuchold—Young Lady on the Move," *GDR Review*, 2/82: 32–35.

[2]Dr. Josef Göhler, "International Report," *International Gymnast*, May 1982: 30.

[3]Letter from Erika, 16 Jan. 1994.

[4]*Army Soldier* (GDR), No. 5, 1979.

[5]Karl-Heinz Friedrich, "Flip-flap on the 4-inch Beam," *Mademoiselle Gymnast*, Nov./Dec. 1970: 22–23.

Linda Metheny Mulvihill

1948	Born, August 22.
1961	Began gymnastics, age 13.
1963	Junior AAU National Championships: 1st all-around. 1st, vault, bars, beam and floor.
1964	Tokyo Olympics, October: 10th beam (team competition).
1965	Wembley Games, London: 1st, all-around.
1965	Cup of America, an F.I.G. meet hosted by Canada: 1st, all-around.
1967	Pan American Games, Winnipeg, Canada: 1st, all-around. 1st, vault, beam and floor; 2nd, bars.
1967	University Games, Tokyo: 2nd, all-around 1st, beam and floor; 2nd, vault and bars.
1968	Olympics, Mexico. October: 28th, all-around; 4th, beam.
1969	Cup of America, hosted by Mexico: 1st, all-around.
1971	Pan American Games, Cali, Columbia: 1st, beam.
1971	AAU National Championships: 1st, all-around, for fifth time since 1966.
1971	USGF National Championships: 1st, all-around (tie–Joan Moore.)
1972	Olympics, Munich August: an injury prevented good results.
1972	Retired. Together with husband Dick, opened National Academy of Artistic Gymnastics in Eugene, Oregon.
1975	Appointed to President's Council on Physical Fitness.
1975	Coached first U.S. team to compete in communist China.
1979	Head coach of U.S. team in World Championships, Fort Worth, Texas.

As Linda Metheny until after the 1972 Olympics, she grew up in the mid-West and attended the University of Illinois. There she was a James Scholar in her post-graduate studies and received an M.S. degree in both Dance and Human Anatomy and Physiology.

She began her gymnastics when she was 13, an age when today's gymnasts are competing for a place on the national team. She made up for her late start by working 6 to 7 hours, 6 days a week and 3 to 4 hours on Sunday. Consequently, she won the Junior AAU National Championships two years later and in three years was a member of the Tokyo Olympic team. Thereafter, she was a leading member of U.S. teams until her retirement after the Munich

Olympics. She and Muriel Grossfeld are the only American women gymnasts to compete in three Olympics.

As noted in the chronology, her coaching career included being coach of the U.S. team in the 1979 World Championships in Fort Worth, Texas.

During the 1980s, she contributed to the training of many top American gymnasts, including Tracee Talavera, Julianne McNamara, Tanya Service and Yumie Mordre, as well as gymnasts from Brazil, Japan, England, Finland, Mexico, Switzerland, and Portugal.

She has twice composed the national age group compulsories in floor exercise. She is an F.I.G. brevet judge as well as an NCAA judge. She has done commentary at gymnastics competitions for ABC, NBC, and CBS.

She and her husband Dick have three children—Donijo, David, and Matthew—who are all engaged in sports activities.

Information supplied by husband Dick Mulvihill

Cathy Rigby McCoy

1952	Born, December 12.
1963	Began gymnastics.
1968	Olympics, Mexico, October: 16th, all-around.
1970	U.S. National Champion.
1970	World Championships, Ljubljana, Slovenia, October: 15th, all-around; 2nd, beam.
1971	U.S.A.-U.S.S.R. competition, Penn State University: 7th, all-around; 1st, beam.
1971	International Meet, Riga, Latvia, against USSR and East Bloc countries. 3rd, all-around; 1st, beam; 3rd, bars; 6th, floor.
1971	Ranked seventh all-around in the world.
1972	U.S.A.–Japan competition: 1st all-around.
1972	U.S. National Champion (tie–Joan Moore Rice).
1972	Olympics, Munich, August: 10th all-around.

Cathy Rigby McCoy is a survivor. She survived not only the pressures of Olympic competition and the requirements of a demanding coach but also her eating disorder and her not being prepared for life after gymnastics.

Her life in gymnastics began at the age of ten, when she joined the Lakewood, California, city recreation program. The gymnastics portion of the program was run by her future coach, Bud Marquette. From there she moved with Bud to his newly established club, the Southern California Acro Team, the Scats, whose workouts took place in the basement of St. Stevens Lutheran Church in Long Beach. Her tiny body earned her the nickname "Peanut," but her size, her natural ability, and her fearlessness soon proved she was a girl of promise in the sport of gymnastics. Reflecting on it a few weeks before Munich, coach Marquette said, "Cathy's main factor is that her fear factor is absolutely minimal. (This is what) makes her so great. If I were to ask her to throw a double back, you'd better be ready to catch her."[1]

By the age of 14, Cathy had set her sights on the Olympics. She had progressed so much now that everyone saw what could lie ahead. Never before had an American girl placed higher than 28th in Olympic competition. Was Cathy the one who could brighten up the gloomy days of international competition for the American team?[2]

As it turned out, Cathy, who was then 16, placed sixteenth in the Mexico Olympics, October 1968, well ahead of another 16-year-old debutante, Ludmilla Turischeva, who placed twenty-fourth. But in 1969, after the Mexico Olympics, a problem began for Cathy that was to affect her for the next 12 years. She hit puberty and began to gain weight. " . . . all of a sudden . . . the sport that was validating my very being was doubting me because I had gained weight . . . so I was terrified and went on a starvation diet."[3]

For an entire week Cathy ate nothing and she lost the weight. And once more people said she looked great, and she felt like a champion. "So at that point . . . I thought I am never going to gain weight again. I learned how to perfect the technique of bingeing and purging. It went like that throughout my gymnastics career. I don't know whether I could have done better, but I know that if I had not been in that frame of mind, possibly I could have learned more, been stronger and possibly had more endurance. Who knows? I know it wasn't good for me."[3]

Bingeing and purging and anorexia are unnatural ways of losing weight. Anorexia is simply not eating. Constantly starving oneself is so difficult that people resort to bingeing and purging, which is a matter of eating and then inducing vomiting. Both habits have extremely undesirable consequences.

As Cathy personally explained it, "Women gymnasts become involved in eating disorders because they want to get their thinness back, to get their weight down. They do this because their coaches say they would perform better if they were lighter and because they are going through a natural stage in life when they gain weight. Their eating disorders result also from a lack of knowledge about nutrition, about how to maintain a low weight without starving themselves.

"Eating disorders are about control," Cathy continues, "and result from being out of control in most areas of your life. The only things you can control are your weight and your food. They're a sort of rebellion, especially if you have a domineering and controlling coach. A high level of competition and the perfectionist nature of the sport add to the stress."[4]

Cathy managed to stay healthy in spite of her eating disorder and to train and to grow in her gymnastics, so that two years after Mexico, she and her fellow Mexico debutante, Ludmilla Turischeva, met again in the 1970 World Championships held in October in Ljubljana, Slovenia. Turischeva became world champion and Cathy won the beam silver medal, America's first medal at this level of competition. They met again in February 1971 at a dual meet at Penn State University, which Turischeva won. Cathy had trouble on bars but won beam. Her victories on beam in Ljubljana and Penn State caused Soviet coach Larissa Latynina to comment, "Cathy Rigby is a splendid gymnast, confident in all the exercises and simply matchless on the beam, which everyone thinks is the trickiest piece of apparatus. Cathy is unquestionably the ace of the American team."[2]

In the spring of 1971, Cathy placed third in the Riga Cup, a major competition in Riga, Latvia, in which the USSR and East Bloc countries participated. Again she won beam. By this time she was ranked seventh in the world by Dr. Josef Göhler, West German gymnastic writer.[5]

In 1972, the year of Munich, the volcano of women's gymnastics erupted in enthusiasm for the sport all over the world. Cathy was in the middle of this and had to compete in the decisive all-around competition at the same time as Olga Korbut, whose every performance was greeted with a storm of applause, and at the same time as such precise and polished gymnasts as Karin Janz and Ludmilla Turischeva.

It was not a happy time for her. After her silver medal win on beam in Ljubljana, the media expected her to win one in Munich. As part of the media build-up, she had suffered the indignity of being photographed in the nude on beam for a double-page spread in a pre-Olympic issue of *Sports Illustrated.* There was dissension among the coaches before and during the competition. She was ordered to leave out an aerial walkover on beam that was one of the elements she was counting on to win her an extra point from the judges. She had to try to explain this omission to Jim McKay on TV as "in the best interests of the team." She had to put up with being compared to the top Soviet and East Germans when she was not achieving the same results they were getting, although her all-around result was the highest—10th place—that any American woman had won in Olympic competition.

Commenting on Munich, Cathy said:

> Yes, there was a lot of dissension among the coaches and I frankly I don't know if it's any better these days. I feel as I look back on the Munich Olympics that we really did an incredible job there. We did hit our routines. The aerial walkover in my routine should not have made any difference because there were very few people, if I can remember back that far, who did aerials. And, therefore, it should not have mattered whether I put the aerial in or not. We went up very early in the morning in compulsories and that made a big difference. Everybody basically hit their routines, but we just didn't get the scores, especially compared to the Hungarians. If you remember, Madame Nagy (from Hungary) was the head of the women

judges at that point and was really pushing for the Hungarians to win a medal. So there was a lot of politics going on. There was a lot of emphasis on this because the media needed a story to tell and because Bud was so dramatic at that time talking about the injustice of the scoring. So really there was this whole tornado going on around all of us gymnasts, but frankly we were very pleased with our performance and how well everybody stuck together.

Concerning the *Sports Illustrated* picture, I did not want to do it but was coerced into doing it. I'm not trying to sound like a victim, but I was only nineteen years old—and a very young nineteen at the time—and was under the thumb of my coach who strongly encouraged me to do that. It was a very difficult thing to do. If I knew what I know now as an adult, I certainly would not have done it and would not as a parent let my child do it.

I think that with the build-up of the media and the expectations and the pressure, the fact that the United States placed fourth as a team is very important. Remember that all the top teams were competing. At that time, there were no boycotts and if you think about my placement—tenth—in the all-around, back then if you were from the Soviet team or if you were from the East German team, it didn't matter whether you had three girls or six girls. If six girls made it to the finals, they all competed. So really, we were competing against more people, more top people, than today. If there had been only three from each country competing, as it is today, I certainly would have placed higher in the all around.[4]

In an article for *Parade,* Cathy amplified her comments on her Munich experiences.

"I couldn't wait for the '72 Olympics to be over. You cannot imagine the pressure. My family had made many sacrifices for me. I had a coach who had dedicated so much time and effort to me, almost neglecting his own family. There had been a lot of media hype, saying I was going to win a medal. To have your whole career come down to this one moment is frightening. I performed very well, but I didn't win a medal. I was apologetic about it for a long time."[6]

"There's a great need for athletes to be accepted," she added, "and you work harder than anyone else in order to prove yourself. But you've got to learn the difference between what you do and who you are. If your whole personality is determined by your performance, you're going to crumble along the way . . . .

"Now I realize that just getting there and pursuing a sport makes you a winner . . . Being in the Olympics is about individual human spirit and effort. You cannot always judge yourself by others . . . .

"How many times have we seen people receiving medals who are really losers in life? . . . ."[6]

Cathy's unhappiness in Munich was soon transformed. Because of her dainty figure and strikingly attractive features, (she) was inundated with invitations to appear at state fairs, to guest on television specials, and eventually to appear in a seven-month tour of the very successful stage show, *Peter Pan*.[2]

Along with these activities, Cathy had to begin to make up for the lack of education she had been receiving during her high school years. The explanation for this neglect lies in the philosophy of her coach, Bud Marquette: "I say this most emphatically: It is impossible to be a top-flight international gymnast and still go to school."[1] Similarly, Olga Korbut's coach, Renald Knysh, had said: "Your school is of no interest to me."[8]

The situations of Cathy Rigby and Olga Korbut in this respect are in stark contrast to that of Karin Janz, who had so kept up with her studies—and had been encouraged to do so by her coach and the gymnastic authorities—that after Munich she went directly to medical school.

What Cathy did was to embark on a new and different career. It turned out that her invitation to appear in *Peter Pan* pointed her in the direction of future study. In her first *Peter Pan* production, all she had to do was lip-synch the prerecorded words and songs. "Fortunately," Rigby recalled, " someone in the show said to me, 'If you really like this, why don't you take voice lessons?'"[6]

Cathy accepted the suggestion and devoted much time during the next seven years to taking lessons and studying voice and acting. She took intensive, private courses in theater not only in voice and acting but also in art history and history of the theater. She studied psychology in order to understand people. She has continued to train herself and get as much education in this area as she could during her acting career and during the years she spent doing commentary for ABC. Her ABC career, incidentally, included the 1976 and 1984 Olympics and the 1985 and 1987 World Championships.

The success of her career on stage and in television means that in the over twenty years since Munich, she has more than made up for her lack of education before Munich.

She had married Tommy Mason, a former pro-football player, a few months after Munich and had two sons, Bucky and Ryan. In 1981, facing problems in her marriage, she divorced Tommy and made her stage debut in a summer-stock production of *The Wizard of Oz*. She played the role of Dorothy and was well-received by the critics. "A genuine theatrical talent!" wrote *Variety*. During the summer, she fell in love with a member of the cast, Tom McCoy. They were married a year later. After her second marriage, Cathy found herself able to begin to cope with her eating disorder.

Cathy said she was able to stop denying that her eating disorder was life-threatening and to find professionals who could help her overcome it. After having dealt with it on her own for twelve years, it was a long, hard process. It was also an educational process, that of understanding herself, understanding this disorder and going out and talking about it with other people. "Once you get control your eating disorder," Cathy says, "it's as though you come out of a fog: you are much more able to focus on your family and your career. You are much happier because of it. It's as though a light came on.

"It's not that you have complete control of your life," she continues. "We can't control everything that goes on in our lives. When you go through the healing process, however, you come out with more confidence to deal with different aspects of your life, to say 'no,' and to make decisions in your life. Coming from a sport where all the attention is on you, you begin to look outside of yourself; you're not so narcissistic; you begin to focus on how others are feeling; you step into their shoes for the first time and understand. In short, you're not so busy taking care of yourself that you can't look to somebody else and have a little compassion about situations."

It took 12 years—from 1969 to 1981—but Cathy, now Cathy McCoy, was no longer afflicted with her eating disorder. She was performing either by herself in a production by another company or in one of their own productions. They have four children: Bucky and Ryan, by her former husband, and Theresa and Kaitlin. She was also active in helping to expose the problems of anorexia and bingeing and purging.

The career that began for her in 1981 has been many-faceted. As everyone in gymnastics knows, she has been part of the ABC-TV team doing commentary on major events. She has appeared on television in the after School Special *Hard to Read* and the telefilms *The Great Wallendas* and *Triathlon*. She has also been a special guest on such episodic series as *Policewoman*, *The Hardy Boys*, and *Six Million Dollar Man*. She has headlined in Las Vegas and in 1974 she won the George M. Cohan Award for Best Specialty Act.

With her husband, Tom McCoy, a noted producer, Cathy also produces legitimate theatrical productions, videocassettes, and special events. Among the many productions created by McCoy Rigby Entertainment are the historical all-star concert prior to Pope John Paul II's Celebration of Mass at the Los Angeles Coliseum; an award-winning video on eating disorders entitled *Faces of Recovery*, and the 35th anniversary national tour and Broadway production of *Peter Pan*.

It is in her role as Peter Pan that Cathy is, perhaps, best remembered, having performed it not only in the 1974 production in which she lip-synched the words, but also in the 1986 production by the Long Beach State Opera and then in the 1989–1990 national tour that she and her husband produced. She feels close to the role of Peter Pan because it's the story of a boy who did not want to grow up.

"I grew up in a sport that didn't allow you to grow up. There was always the threat of younger competition. So you had to maintain the image of youth.

"When you're on the Olympic team at 15, you don't do anything else. There's no normal social development, and your decisions are made for you .

"With all the tremendous pressure, you stuff a lot inside and the result is denial—like Peter Pan who can be heartless and self-absorbed. He puts his fingers in his ears and cuts people off when there's something he doesn't want to hear."[7]

Peter Pan has traditionally been played on stage by a woman. Sir James M. Barrie's creation has been a handy metaphor for eternal youth and a model of escapism since its first theatrical incarnation in 1904.[7] "I won't grow up," Peter sings.

"I wouldn't go so far as saying I traded my childhood for a gold medal," she said, "but there were times when I wanted to plug my ears and say, 'I can't do this!"

"My background has given me an incredible understanding of Peter Pan. I really identify with him. I know what it means to be afraid of growing up, to be self-centered and feel the need to prove yourself all the time," she said. "When those emotions come out in my performance, they are very real. It's like an incredible therapy session for me."

It also help to look the part. Five feet tall, weighing less than 100 pounds, it isn't difficult to pass for "boyish," she said, even at the age of 37.

" . . . and my daughter tells me that when she grows up, she wants to be a boy just like me."[9]

Between her 1981 debut in *Wizard of Oz* and her later productions of *Peter Pan,* Cathy also performed in *They're Playing our Song, Meet me in St. Louis,* and *Paint your Wagon*. The McCoy-Rigby production of *Peter Pan,* which was twice on Broadway, was nominated for two Tonys—one for the show for best revival and one for her as best actress in a musical.

"Really, Broadway is the Olympics of theater, so this was a great honor. It was kind of acceptance by my peers in this area."

The McCoy Rigby production was a tribute to Mary Martin on the 35th anniversary of the 1954 production devoted to her, which is considered the classic song-and-dance adaptation. It is, perhaps, also a celebration of Cathy Rigby McCoy's own release from the captivity of not growing up.

She has now spent twice as much time in the theater as she did in gymnastics. Her whole theater background is very important to her. "It's something I took just as seriously as I did my gymnastics," she says, "and probably enjoy more because I can keep it in perspective a little bit better. I'm not white-knuckling it every time I go out on the floor. Yes, I do it for the audience, but I also feel great joy in just singing, performing and relating to other people on stage. I'm not so concerned about what everybody else thinks."

Since *Peter Pan,* she has played the role of Annie Oakley in a national tour of *Annie Get your Gun,* which was very successful with the critics, and has been on the road with *South Pacific*. That was not a national tour but did play in some big markets, where it did well critically.

As of this writing, she and her husband Tom are producers at the La Mirada (California) Theater for the Performing Arts, a beautiful 1,200-seat theater. There they will be producing four shows a year

The future looks bright for this popular gymnast turned actress who is also wife and mother. She is an example of a person who did her best and came out a winner.

References

[1]Richard Flood, "Interview with Bud Marquette," *Gymnast.* Aug./Sept. 1972: 36–37.

[2]Lyn Moran, "Cathy Rigby—Gymnast, Coach, Celebrity," *International Gymnast,* Oct. 1978: 32–48.

[3]Glori Stifler, "America's First Gymnastics Heroine," *International Gymnast,* Aug.1986: 56–61.

[4]Comments from Cathy on audio tape made summer 1994.

[5]Dr. Josef Göhler, "International Women's All-Around Rankings," *Mademoiselle Gymnast,* Sept./Oct. 1971:8.

[6]Sheryl Flatow, "It's Okay to Grow Up," *Parade,* 26 May 1991: 4–5.

[7]Alvin Klein, "Cathy Rigby's 'Peter Pan': Real Wish Fulfillment," *The New York Times,* 25 Nov. 1990: Theatre Section.

[8]Olga Korbut, *My Story: The Autobiography of Olga Korbut,* (London: Century, 1992), 83.

[9]Sharon Randall, "Cathy Rigby Can Relate to Peter Pan," *The Sunday Herald* (Monterey County), 12 Aug. 1990: 17A.

Tamara Lazakovich

1954	Born, November 3.
1968	At age 14, became the USSR's youngest Master of Sport.
1969	East Bloc Tournament of Friendship: 1st, all-around.
1970	USSR National Championships, Minsk, May: 3rd, all-around.
1970	East Bloc Tournament of Friendship: 1st, all-around.
1970	World Championships, Ljubljana, October: 21st, all-around.
1971	Spartakiade, Moscow, July (USSR National Championships): 1st, all-around.
1971	European Championship, Minsk, Belarus, October: 1st, all-around (tie); 1st, bars, beam; 1st, floor; 2nd, vault (both ties–Turischeva).
1972	USSR National Championships, April, Kiev: 1st, all-around.
1972	USSR Cup, Minsk, July (Olympic selection trials): 3rd, all-around; 3rd, vault, bars, beam.
1972	Olympics, Munich, August: 3rd, all-around; 6th, vault; 2nd, beam; 3rd, floor.

After her disastrous falls from beam in Ljubljana, where she scored 8.00 on that apparatus, Lazakovich made a brilliant comeback the following year in the European Championships. There she tied Turischeva for first place all-around and in floor exercise, and she won bars and beam herself. Her experience on beam in Ljubljana was an aberration for Tamara, as her other results show and as is explained in this excerpt from an article on her in the August 1972 issue of *Soviet Life* magazine.

> Tamara Lazakovich is 17 (at the time of Munich). She first walked into a gym nine years ago. At 14, she became the youngest Master of Sports in gymnastics, and in 1968 she won the junior championship of the Soviet Union.
>
> Tamara Manina, a leading Soviet gymnast and winner of many competitions, said at the time: "She has everything I like to see in a gymnast of her age—good proportions, purity of lines, an athletic look and not a hint of stiffness."
>
> Tamara won her first adult championship on the beam . . . in 1970 . . . .Thus far, 1971 has been her peak year: she won three gold medals at the National Summer Games, became the all-around champion of the Soviet Union, and in the autumn shared first place with her teammate Ludmilla Turischeva at the Eighth European Championship in Minsk.

Tamara lives in Vitebsk, Belarus—a town that has produced many famous gymnasts.

She met her present coach, Vikenti Dmitriev, in 1964. Dmitriev made a name for himself by training 15-year-old Larissa Petrick, who in 1965 became the youngest USSR champion in the history of the sport. Quite naturally, Tamara, who was 10 at the time, tried to copy Petrick and insisted on doing everything the older girl could do. Even then, she showed her characteristic stubbornness and persistence.

Her natural plasticity, mastery of the most difficult elements of gymnastics and doggedness combine to give her a unique image. Outwardly she appears rather withdrawn, but inwardly everything seems to boil. Every turn of the head is deliberate, yet impulsive. Every movement of the arm is precise, yet soft and inspired.

After finishing secondary school, Tamara enrolled at a physical education college.[1]

The program produced by Fabergé for the Soviet 1973 American tour[2] had this to say about Lazakovich:

> Throughout all the gymnastics competition at Munich, one unheralded Soviet performer kept popping up, going through her routines in a most business-like manner and capturing high marks. She was Tamara Lazakovich. With all the fuss over Olga Korbut and all the praise for Turischeva, Miss Lazakovich went about making quite a haul—one gold, one silver and two bronze.
>
> (Her) style, grace and precision made it seem as if Lazakovich was a 20-year veteran. The fact that she was only 18 at the time never came to light.

A cloud hung over Lazakovich, however. In her book, *My Story: The Autobiography of Olga Korbut*[3], Olga describes what took place during one of the times the Soviets got their team together for training at the Black Sea resort of Leselidze:

> I was on reasonably friendly terms with the other girls, but I had hoped to make lots of friends right away. When I became a veteran myself, I understood their attitudes. New girls come to the team as your eventual replacements. In gymnastics, a five- or six-year career is considered a long one. So the footsteps echoing from behind sound especially loud.
>
> Tamara Lazakovich was the most friendly, and mischievous, of the old girls. She was very much a corrupting influence, teaching the "greenhorns" to smoke and drink. "Let's drink some wine," she said one day, when we were on our way to work out.
>
> "What?" I was shocked. "Before training? Besides, I'd rather have some ice cream."

> We came to two booths: one sold ice cream, the other wine. I watched in astonishment as Tamara helped herself to some wine. Then, half an hour later, I was even more horrified as I saw her sweating profusely and working on the beam. I still don't know how she kept from falling. As I got to know her better, I would be amazed to see her drink as much as a full bottle of cognac at night and then perform perfectly the next morning.

The Lazakovich story has an unhappy ending. She died in November 1992 from alcoholism. She was married twice, the second time to a forester with whom she lived in the country. After finishing her gymnastics, she got involved with criminals, was brought to trial on a charge of larceny, and served several years in prison. She had a daughter by her second husband.[4]

References

[1]Lev Kuleshov, "Gymnast Tamara Lazakovich," *Soviet Life,* Aug. 1972: 62–65.

[2]Program for the 1973 Soviet tour in the United States, underwritten by Fabergé and published by Spencer Marketing Services.

[3]Olga Korbut, *My Story: The Autobiography of Olga Korbut,* (London: Century, 1992), 39.

[4] Notes by Lera Mironova of the Russian magazine, *Family.*

Lyubov Victorovna Burda

1967 Spartakiade, Moscow, July (USSR National Championships): 3rd, all-around (at age 14).
1968 Olympics, Mexico, October: 25th all-around.
1969 USSR National Championships, Rostov, October: 1st, all-around.
1970 USSR National Championships, Minsk, May: 1st, all-around.
1970 World Championships, Ljubljana, October: 5th, all-around; 3rd, vault; 4th, bars; 6th, floor.
1970 First Chunichi Cup, Japan, November: 1st, all-around.
1972 USSR National Championships, Kiev, April: 5th, all-around.
1972 USSR Cup, Minsk, July (Olympic selection trials): 4th all-around; 2nd, vault; 2nd, floor.
1972 Olympics, Munich, August: 5th all-around; 4th, vault; 5th, floor.
1973 University Games, Moscow, August: 2nd, all-around.

> Her admirers will long remember that hot summer day in 1967 when the frail-looking and relatively unknown girl from Voronezh stepped on to the winner's rostrum, having gained third place in the USSR National Games.[1]
>
> At the gymnastics tournament of the 1967 Spartakiade, Yuri Edwardovich Shtukman, who was already called "master," for he had trained Olympic Champion Tamara Lyukina (Rome 1960) and World Champion Irina Pervushina (Prague 1962), walked across the podium and screwed up his eyes: that meant he had prepared a surprise. And so it was that tiny, thin, frail-looking Lyuba Burda performed a prodigious turn. (Known since as the Burda twirl, it was underswing to one and a half turns to hang.) It seemed then like a miracle.[2]

To talk about Burda, it is necessary to include a word about her famous coach. As related in the 1985 fiftieth anniversary book describing the achievements of the Spartak Sports Club[3], the first sport school specializing in gymnastics was opened in 1962 by Yuri Edwardovich Shtuckman in Voronezh, a city about 400 miles south of Moscow. He was an innovator, an inventor of new elements, a "philosopher of gymnastics." Shtuckman created a real center for the making of masters. He gathered around him a group of like-minded people but remained the chief theorist and chief expert of the Voronezh school.

Lyubov Burda with her handsome bridegroom, Nicolai Andrianov, and Saadi holding her train.

Yuri Shtuckman developed not only beautiful champions but also young coaches. One of these was Gennady Korshunov, who became Shtuckman's right-hand man but eventually left to form his own club. One of his students was Elena Davidova, who became the 1980 Olympic champion.

Before starting his own club, Shtuckman had already coached two champions, but perhaps his greatest achievement came with Lyubov Burda. In 1968, she and Ludmilla Turischeva became the two debutantes on the Soviet Olympic team in Mexico.

Burda married Olympic Champion Nicolai Andrianov after the 1972 Olympics and moved from her home town of Voronezh to his town of Vladimir (about 100 miles east of Moscow). She likes Vladimir, an old town, which has treasures of art and beautiful cathedrals. In the middle ages, it was the most important town in Russia. Both Lyubov and her husband coach in the sport school there. They have two boys.

In a 1987 article in *Sovietsky Sport*[4], Lyubov Burda spoke about her life as a coach. The following are excerpts from that article.

> My girls are my joy. They are different—happy and reserved, fidgety and obedient. When I came into the gym for the first time and had my first intake of students, I was strict. The girls began to be afraid of me. What do you think! Our coach is an Olympic champion! I thought that with strictness I would impart more responsibility and would teach gymnastics better. My group turned out to be strong: it included Sveta Mironova, who in 1985 at a major international meet in Kosice, Czechoslovakia took 4th place. I worked with a great desire, literally day and night. But, perhaps, I tried too hard. Now I understand that's not the way. It's as if I enchained the will of my students, their temperament. They are very dependent upon their coach. They did not reveal themselves as kids until the end.
>
> It's quite often that children come from broken or unfortunate backgrounds, from unhappy families. Some come from single mothers busy with the management of their own affairs, or what is worse—drunk women. But children are children. You need to caress them again and again and talk with them from your own life's experience. Sport should straighten them out, help them to become real people. I grew up with my children. When I came into the sport school, I was 23; they were about five. With the years, my attitude toward them changed. Now we are friends. The children grew up. In time they needed purely woman's advice. Even simply to chat or to discuss fashions of clothes. To whom can some girls go to talk, to pour out their souls if not their coach?
>
> Here I remember the wise lessons of my coach, Yuri Edwardovich Shtukman. He was a surprisingly patient person. I was a difficult, cocky

student. He knew that at home they were always training me toward work, that come what may I had to do my assignments. It happened once in a while that I would come to work but would not go to the apparatus. Yuri Edwardovich would sit next to me on the bench and be quiet. He did not scold me or reprimand me; he would just sit quietly. So I sat that way the whole workout. But on the next day, I worked twice as hard. I did everything Shtukman had mapped out for the week and maybe a little bit more in two days.

I have worked as a coach for almost ten years; in all these years I have hardly had any holidays. Of course, they do give me a holiday when I want it. And so with my students and my sons I am going off to the south, to a children's camp. We will swim, become tanned and train. Many people ask me: why do I have to do this? I can give them thousands of explanations, but the most meaningful will be one: I am interested in my girls, I love them. I know that the journey will bring them joy. Many kids will remain in the city all summer, knock about in the streets, not get any rest. We, on the other hand, will go away all together. The children will return refreshed, with new impressions. Furthermore, on trips like these, you can create a group, strengthen friendships. I always remember my coach who was for us an example, and that means I have to become an example for my own children. Shtukman taught me to work wholeheartedly and to try to teach that to one's children. I must say they are very responsive to this lesson.

If formerly our Vladimir school was known only for men's gymnastics (from which came Nicolai Andrianov, Yuri Korolev, Vladimir Artemov), now our girls are announcing themselves. In the competitions of the republic, they will have to take us into consideration. Those who competed recently in the championships of the republic were my first students. I am afraid to sound immodest, but I think this is due to all the time and effort I have put into their training. If our gymnasts do not raise themselves higher, I shall consider myself responsible. If their development does not continue, the reason will be my inexperience, a too strong wish to insist on my own way, to compel them to do what I want. Well, from mistakes you learn. Now that I have more experience, I have changed. We will work further . . . .

(Burda had some criticisms about the emphasis on acrobatics at the expense of artistry and about judges not giving credit for artistry during performances in competition. To a certain extent, decisions made by governing bodies in the past six years have lessened the causes of her criticisms.)

In gymnastics there are many problems that wait for their solution. I want very much that my gymnastics, which gave me so much happiness when I was performing and continues to give me happiness now when I look into the wide open eyes of my students, should become again the most popular, best-loved sport, that the competition halls should again be filled to the ceiling with spectators, that more girls should come into the sport, girls who want to become both daring and feminine.

(Note: it is interesting that at a time when the stands are full of spectators in the United States, they are relatively empty in Russia. This situation is, of course, partly the result of economic conditions. Perhaps there are other reasons.)

References

[1]Lev Kuleshov, *Gymnast,* Apr. 1974: 20.

[2]Introduction to item 4 below by Vladimir Golubev and Natalya Kalugina.

[3]*Fiftieth Anniversary Book,* Spartak Sports Club.

[4]Lyubov Burda,"I Look Into the Eyes of My Girls," *Sovietsky Sport,* 1 Nov. 1987.

Domes and crosses over the 17th century Church of the Deposition of the Holy Robe, Kremlin

The Soviet team at the time of the University Games. Women in front row: Antonina Koshel, Lyubov Bogdanova, Olga Korbut. Back row: Ludmilla Turischeva, Lyubov Burda, Elvira Saadi, Tanya Shegolkova.

European Championship

1973

Wembley, London

and Other Important Events

February – November

The most important competition of 1973 was the European Championship. There were some other events that took place this first post-Olympic year, however, that must be recorded.

Considering the burst of enthusiasm for women's gymnastics that resulted from Munich in 1972, it was to be expected that 1973 would be a busy year. By the end of 1972, the struggle between the A.A.U. (American Athletic Union) and the U.S. Gymnastics Federation for control of gymnastics in the United States ended in favor of the U.S.G.F. by decision of Arthur Gander, President of F.I.G., the International Gymnastics Federation in Switzerland. Armed with new authority, the U.S.G.F. set about organizing the first tour by the Soviet gymnasts.

It began in March at the Astrodome in Houston, went on to Buffalo, Los Angeles, Miami and Philadelphia and ended in New York at Madison Square Garden. Angry at being left out, Chicago Mayor Richard Daley sent a telegram to Soviet Prime Minister Alexei Kosygyn. In it he requested that the tour be extended to Chicago and demanded that Olga Korbut be included in the delegation. His request was granted and on the day of the Soviets' arrival, Mayor Daley proclaimed it "Olga Korbut Day." He further stipulated that the designation be perpetual. The day was so remembered but only for a few years because Soviet custom would not permit Olga to come to be so personally honored.

Before the Soviet tour, American gymnasts competed in February against teams from Hungary and Romania. Enterprising coach Gene Wettstone of Penn State University organized the official meet against Hungary, which the Hungarians won. They were led by Munich veterans Ilona Bekesi, Krisztina Medveczky, and Monika Csaszar. All-around results were:

1. Ilona Bekesi	38.30
2. Krisztina Medveczky	38.00
3. Kim Chace	37.45
4. Monika Csaszar	37.35
Joan Moore Rice	37.35
6. Nancy Theis	37.30

In the following week, a competition took place against Romania in the Harmon Gym at the University of California, Berkeley. Fifteen-year-old Debbie Fike of the U.S.A. won a surprising third place behind Munich veterans Alina Goreac and Elena Ceampelea. All-around results were:

1. Alina Goreac	37.90
2. Elena Ceampelea	37.80
3. Debbie Fike	37.20
4. Kim Chace	36.95
Nancy Theis	36.95
6. Anca Grigoras	36.85

Champions All International Tournament

Empire Pool, Wembley London: April 14th

1. Elvira Saadi	37.70
2. Angelika Hellmann	37.05
3. Anca Grigoras, ROM	36.25
4. Uta Schorn, RDA	35.20
5. Agnes Banfi, HUN	35.15
6. Patrizia Bazzi, SUI	34.90
7. Avril Lennox, GBR	34.60

World University Games, Palace of Sports

Lenin Central Stadium Park, Moscow: August 16th to 19th

The first competition of the year to achieve worldwide attention took place in August in Moscow: the 1973 World University Games. They were almost like the Olympics. So much effort did the Soviet government expend on staging them that they obviously had an eye on the 1980 Olympics, the decision for which would be made by the International Olympic Committee in 1974. In gymnastics, it was a Soviet show, because the Soviets merely imported members or alternates from the Munich team, whereas the United States, for example, gave bona fide university students a chance to cap their careers by participating in a competition of this magnitude. The only notable American achievement was that of 23-year-old Terry Spencer, a senior at Southern Illinois University, who placed fourth in floor exercise.

Interesting impressions of the leaders of the competition were written by Gail Chimielenski, then of the University of Connecticut, for the October 1973 issue of *Gymnast* magazine.[1] They are reprinted here by courtesy of the International Gymnastics Hall of Fame.

> For the next few hours each performer took her turn on each . . . apparatus and seemed to exhibit her very individual gymnastic style. Olga mounted beam, did a couple of passes and her back somie. Though her movements were smooth and polished beyond what I had seen in New York or had remembered even from the Olympic films, they were kiddish and simple. There were no innovations in her routine since Munich. The floor routine was again the same. And so the unevens. Each had its intermittent moment of thrilling difficulty yet the childlike activities in between were less than satisfying. I had come to Moscow to witness the growth and maturity of a gifted athlete and found instead the "Good Ship Lollypop." I began to wonder if this could pull the scores of Munich.
>
> It was time to concentrate on what the others had to show. Lyubov Burda performed a lovely exercise on the beam and another in floor exercise. Her movements were fluid, lyrical, and utterly flawless in their execution. Aerial and single-handed moves were done with the precision of a fine Swiss watch. The exercise was minus the sudden thrill of difficult passages, but rather consistent and in complete control of every body segment. If you could be stirred by a leaf floating on currents of air or a gull riding the wind to the strains of Prokofiev's "Romeo and Juliet," you couldn't help but be a fan of Burda. In the finest tradition of Turischeva, she is a beautiful gymnast.

Olga and Bogdanova in opening ceremony parade.

Elvira Saadi mounted the balance beam with a one-arm walkover to a back lying on the beam. Her arm movements were strong though intensely feminine. Her carriage was deliberate and a determined expression encompassed her face. Unlike Burda, Saadi does aerial tricks with a fierce kind of grace and amplitude. She reflected what my impression was of the proud Russian character though totally sensuous in her delivery. She was overwhelming in her bearing on the apparatus. Off of it, she was into herself, not conscious of distractions.

The last of the four, and I must admit my favorite, was Lyubov Bogdanova. Lyubov always had her coach nearby while in both practice and competition. There seemed to be a warm rapport between them and it didn't take long for me to see why he stayed so closely with her . . . So difficult were the elements and combinations in her routines that without perfect concentration and execution we'd probably be speaking of her in the past tense. There was probably no single thrill greater than watching Bogdanova perform the . . . Tsukahara, unless it was her layout back to regrasp (Korbut) to body bounce low bar, or perhaps her round-off, back handspring to double twisting back. There was little doubt in my mind that this was the most brilliant gymnast appearing in the University Games and maybe any other competition.

There can be no argument that that at this point in time the Russian gymnasts are far superior to others in the world. The only question remaining to be answered is which of the Russians will be labeled champion. You know how I feel!

Results were as follows:

All-around

1. Olga Korbut	77.65
2. Lyubov Burda	76.45
3. Elvira Saadi	75.45
4. Lyubov Bogdanova	75.30
5. Agnes Banfai, HUN	73.05
6. Ilona Bekesi, HUN	72.60

Vault

1. Lyubov Bogdanova	9.75
2. Elvira Saadi	9.70
3. Olga Korbut	9.55
4. Lyubov Burda	9.50
5. Nobue Yabe, JPN	9.40
6. Agnes Banfai	9.30

Bars

1.	Olga Korbut	9.75
2.	Lyubov Burda	9.55
3.	Fusami Hajasida, JPN	9.25
4.	Jennyfer Diachun, CAN	9.20
	Erzebet Bellak, HUN	9.20
6.	Agnes Banfai	9.10

Beam

1.	Olga Korbut	9.70
2.	Lyubov Burda	9.45
3.	Elvira Saadi	9.35
4.	Lyubov Bogdanova	9.30
5.	Fusami Hajasida	8.90
6.	Erzebet Bellak	8.85

Floor Exercise

1.	Olga Korbut	9.80
2.	Elvira Saadi	9.70
3.	Lyubov Burda	9.60
4.	Terry Spencer, USA	9.25
5.	Fusami Hajasida	9.20
6.	Ilona Bekesi	9.20

Olga was as much loved at home as abroad.

9th Women's European Gymnastics Championship

Empire Pool, Wembley, London: October 26th and 27th

As mentioned previously, the most important gymnastic event of 1973 was the women's European Championship. The Soviets dominated this competition as they had the University Games. This time, Olga and Ludmilla represented the Soviet Union because only two gymnasts per country are allowed in the European Championship. As in Minsk in 1971, there were 42 gymnasts from 21 countries.

Two gymnasts from East Germany—Angelika Hellmann and Kerstin Gerschau—and two from Romania—Alina Goreac and Anca Grigoras—did provide some competition. These four gymnasts, who were veterans of Munich, provided leadership for their countries in the 1974 World Championships in Varna, but only Gerschau survived the shakeout of leadership that took place in 1976 in Montreal.

Ludmilla Turischeva followed the example of Larissa Latynina in 1957 in Bucharest and Vera Caslavska in 1965 in Sofia and in Amsterdam in 1967: she won all five gold medals. Olga Korbut won the silver medal, all-around, but had to drop out of finals after an aborted first vault. Her many-times injured left ankle flared up and forced her withdrawal. The atmosphere during the competition was well described by Peter Shilston in his story for the December 1973 *Gymnast*.[2]

> In the second half, all eyes and applause were for the Russians, to the obvious discomfort of many of the other competitors. As soon as Ludmilla Turischeva began her floor exercise, one was made aware of the yawning gulf between high talent and surpassing genius. She looked incapable of making mistakes. Not only did her 9.6 put her straight in the lead, but her gamesmanship was formidable—totally ignoring the other competitors, the crowd and even the scoreboard, and spending every spare moment on some ferocious limbering up. Only one thing mattered from this moment onwards—could Olga Korbut prevent the contest from becoming a massacre?
>
> Olga stepped onto the mat with her left ankle heavily strapped. She looked pale and hollow-eyed, from tears or lack of sleep. The audience cheered her on, but something was missing. The gaiety seemed forced; she was no longer held up by levitation on the leaps and somersaults. She shook her head sadly and took 9.45. While Ludmilla warmed up, she sat in unhappy silence, staring blankly in front of her, removing and replacing bandage, demanding massage, drinks and pain-killing sprays. She knew she wasn't going to win and it was breaking her heart.

Another writer for *Gymnast,* Carl Haberland,[3] wrote:

> There was not too much new shown at Wembley. Korbut did a full twist on, handspring off vault, and very nicely.
>
> Turischeva and Goreac both showed Tsukahara vaults. Goreac's was more or less piked, while Turischeva's was more-or-less tucked. However, Turischeva (as is her style) gained great height on the touch.

Regardless of the outcome, the London audience went mad with enthusiasm for their guests, especially Olga and Ludmilla. London soon became the favorite city for visiting Soviets. For their part, the adoring British spectators already began to look forward to the first World Cup which would be held in Wembley in 1975. Prime Minister Edward Heath followed President Nixon's example. As Nixon had invited Olga and Ludmilla to the White House, so Heath invited them to 10 Downing Street.

Results of the 9th European Championship follow.

Olga sympathizes with her friend as Prime Minister Sir Edward Heath cracks a joke and Ludmilla wishes she were somewhere else.

All-around

1.	Turischeva	38.10
2.	Korbut	37.65
3.	Gerschau	37.40
4.	Goreac	37.30
5.	Hellmann	37.10
6.	Uta Schorn, RFA	36.90
7.	Csaszar	36.75
	Sonya Brazdova, TCH	36.75
9.	Grigoras	36.60
10.	Medveczky	36.15

Vault

1.	Turischeva	18.85
	Hellmann	18.85
3.	Schorn, U.	18.70
4.	Goreac	18.55
	Gerschau	18.55
6.	Brazdova	18.50

Bars

1.	Turischeva	19.30
2.	Hellmann	19.25
3.	Goreac	18.95
4.	Csaszar	18.90
5.	Gerschau	18.15
6.	Grigoras	18.10

Beam

1.	Turischeva	19.10
2.	Goreac	18.85
3.	Grigoras	18.75
4.	Csaszar	18.65
	Gerschau	18.65
6.	Schorn	17.40

Floor Exercise

1.	Turischeva	18.90
2.	Gerschau	18.80
3.	Goreac	18.75
4.	Hellmann	18.65
5.	Brazdova	18.45
	Schorn	18.45

Olga admiring the Europa Cup . . .

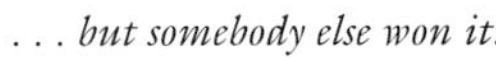

. . . but somebody else won it.

Angelika Hellmann shows perfect form in an aerial cartwheel, European Championship.

Chunichi Cup

Nagoya, Japan: November 24th and 25th

All-around

1. N.Kim	38.00
2. E. Saadi	37.45
2 A. Hellmann	37.45
4. T. Schegolkova, URS	37.40
5. I. Abel, GDR	37.30
6. I. Hanke, GDR	37.20
7. K. Medveczky	37.10
7. S. Brazdova	37.10
9. M. Matsuhisa	36.80
10. J. Moore Rice	36.80
10. J. Hayashida, JPN	36.80
12. M. Csaszar	36.75
13. Z. Dornakova, TCH	36.70
14. D. Dunbar, USA	36.65
15. A. Oshida, J PN	35.80

Results courtesy of *Olympische Turnkunst,* Mar. 1974: 29.

References

[1]Gail Chimielenski, "Visions of Four," *Gymnast,* Oct. 1973: 12–15.

[2]Carl Haberland, *Gymnast,* Dec. 1973: 22.

[3]Peter Shilston, *Gymnast,* Dec. 1973: 23.

Angelika Hellmann in floor exercise.

Golden Sands Arena

World Championships

1974

Varna, Bulgaria

Golden Sands Arena

October 21st to 27th

By 1974, Olga Korbut and Ludmilla Turischeva were at the peaks of their careers. Since the Munich Olympics, Olga had won the 1973 World University Games, held in Moscow in July. In November 1973 in London, Ludmilla and Olga had placed one-two in the European Championship. They had participated in many exhibition tours and special events in Europe and North and South America, as well as occasional exhibitions in other parts of the world, such as, Australia and New Zealand. Their dominance in women's gymnastics was absolute and would remain so until Nadia Comaneci presented the first real challenge to them in the spring of 1975. Even then, Ludmilla and Olga would take the top two places in the 1975 World Cup held in London in October.

So it was primarily in the anticipation of seeing these two gymnasts that spectators traveled the long way to Varna, Bulgaria, an ancient town on the coast of the Black Sea. The 1974 World Championships were originally scheduled to be held in Munich, where the Sporthalle, made famous by the 1972 Olympics, was ready to receive them. Behind-the-scenes scheming within the International Gymnastics Federation by the European countries of the old East Bloc, however, finagled a change of venue to a place under their own control.

What kind of a place is Varna? Like many European cities, it has a long history. According to the 1963 *Columbia Encyclopedia,* it was "founded in 580 B.C. as Odessus, a Greek colony . . . and . . . passed to the Roman Empire in the first century A.D. Here in 679, the Bulgarians defeated the Byzantine emperor, Constantin IV. Varna passed to the second Bulgarian kingdom in 1201, was captured by the Turks in 1391 and became an active seaport under their rule. In 1444, the Turks under Murad II here won a decisive victory over an army of crusaders led by Ladislaus III of Poland and Hungary, who was killed in the battle. The battle of Varna was the last major attempt of the Christian nations to stem the Ottoman tide. Varna was in 1854, the chief naval base of the British and French forces in the Crimean War. There are ruins of an old basilica (5th century) and of a 6th century Byzantine fortress. From 1949 to 1956, the city was named Stalin."[1]

It is now a "major seaport and an industrial center; it has shipyards and machine, metallurgical and textile industries. It is also a noted summer resort. Varna has a university (founded 1920), a polytechnic institute and an archeological museum."[1]

Interestingly, the city and the area reflect French influence. It is evident in the architecture of the buildings, in the street signs and the general flavor of the place. Furthermore, the road from Varna to the coast passes many attractively terraced vineyards. The road is actually a modern, four-lane, divided highway, part of the government's program to develop the major resort on the coast, known as the Golden Sands. At this resort, there were, at the time of the 1974 World Championships, more than a dozen modern hotels in a landscaped, hilly area leading down to the miles and miles of beautiful beaches. It is truly a riviera. At the time of the world championships, it was hard to believe one was in a communist country.

The sports palace where the gymnastics competition took place is situated on the outskirts of the city of Varna, on the highway to the Golden Sands. Unfortunately, it is a small arena, capable of seating only 4,000 people. In spite of the remoteness of Varna for westerners, many tourists, principally from Europe came. There were loud and lusty cheering sections for the East and West German teams.

The primary significance of the 1974 World Championships is that it led to the rule established by the International Federation of Gymnastics that only three gymnasts per country could participate in the individual all-around competition and only two per country, in apparatus finals. It was the success in Varna of the Soviet and East German gymnasts that brought about this rule.

In the all-around, five of the top seven places were won by Soviet gymnasts. It would probably have been six out of the top eight or nine if Nelli Kim had competed, but she did not because of an injury which her coaches wanted her to rest. East German gymnasts won five of the remaining top fourteen places

In the apparatus finals, three Soviets competed in vault and two on bars; but on balance beam, the top four finishers were Soviet and in floor exercise, the top five. In floor exercise, only Angelika Hellmann of East Germany sneaked in to sixth place. For Hellmann, incidentally, her bronze medal all-around and her sixth-place finish on beam and floor were the pinnacle of this attractive gymnast's career.

Angelika Hellmann

Presumably, the purpose of the above rule was to give gymnastically developing countries a better chance to participate in finals, that is, to keep them from being completely dominated by the Soviet gymnastics colossus. Whether the rule has, in fact, done much good is open to question.

Two other factors were significant in these championships. First was the continued biased judging which worked to the detriment of American gymnasts in general but to that of Olga Korbut in particular. She suffered from preferential treatment given Olympic champion Ludmilla Turischeva throughout the competition and by what she considered pressure by the East German superior judge on bars on behalf of Annelore Zinke in bars finals. The judging of the American girls was considered to be almost an organized effort to retard American progress.

The other more long-lasting significance of these two factors was the emergence of Nelli Kim. That she should have been there at all was testimony to her guts and competitive spirit. The book, *Nelli Kim,* published by *Physical Culture and Sport* magazine in 1979, related how Nelli fought her

Nelli Kim

way onto the 1974 Soviet World Championships team: "That summer in the USSR Cup in Vilnius, Lithuania, Kim was in thirteenth place after compulsories; in the end, she turned out to be in second place, squeezed in between Korbut and Turischeva, for the first time. 'No one before had ever had such a wonderfully consistent level of performance in the all-around competition,' commented the newspaper, *Sovietsky Sport* on the optional exercises, making this highly significant conclusion: 'Kim is, of course, a fighter.'"[2]

Due, perhaps, to her relative inexperience, she was in sixth place on the Soviet team after team competition, but in apparatus finals, she won bronze medal on beam. Her experience in Varna served her well: in 1975 and 1976, she would come into full bloom as a great gymnast and the chief rival to Nadia Comaneci.

The only other development of a personal nature that was unexpected was the debut of the East German gymnast, Annelore Zinke. Not only did she win the gold medal on uneven bars, but she placed sixth all-around, second behind Hellmann on the East German team. Her promising career was short-lived, however. After placing third behind Comaneci and Kim in the 1975 European Championship, with a silver medal on bars, she was severely injured and had to retire before the 1976 Olympics.

As the competition opened, there was keen excitement everywhere and a feeling of great anticipation. This was the first major competition involving whole teams and all the stars of the world since Munich two years earlier. Though it was late October, the sun was shining and it was comfortably warm during the day at this Black Sea resort. There was serious business at hand and disappointment ahead for many people, but at the time of the opening, the atmosphere was festive. The opening ceremonies took place in the Varna Sports Palace, Sunday evening, October 20. All the teams marched into the arena, formed up on the podium in columns behind their standard bearer, and were presented. This part of the ceremony at each world championships is always a stirring tradition. There was a gymnastics display by many young people and an exhibition of rhythmic gymnastics. An interminable speech by President Fodor Zhivkov of Bulgaria nearly put everyone to sleep, especially since not many people understand Bulgarian. (He had been President already since 1954 and would remain so until deposed by the people in 1989.) When he finally finished, a well-organized fleet of buses took people back to their hotels by the beach. Correspondents, coaches and fans stayed up late, going over and over the likelihood of this or that result, while gymnasts tried to get some sleep before the first day's competition began.

Compulsory Exercises

Competition 1a: October 21st

The strength and depth of the Soviet team were decisively demonstrated during compulsory exercises. Their team score of 190.80 was more than 4.5 full points ahead of the second-place East Germans, whose score was 186.20. The average per Soviet gymnast was 9.54, compared to 9.31 for the East Germans. Turischeva led Korbut 38.95 to 38.65, but East Germany's Angelika Hellmann was in third place at 38.00. Not only was the Soviet's execution obviously more precise, but they put more expression into their prescribed floor exercise than any other team. In fact, their expressiveness was so intense they appeared to be on fire with their zeal in floor exercise. Korbut was especially notable in this regard.

This observer has a personal remembrance of the evening of compulsories that will be etched in his mind forever. It is the memory of those few moments when the door at the far end of the arena opened and all the Soviet team marched onto the floor for the first time. Led by Turischeva and Korbut, all the members of this famous team walked out onto the floor in their beautiful, new leotards with the self-assurance of the leaders they knew they were. Their expressions were serious at first, but then they smiled and waved at their loud and enthusiastic supporters, principally a group from the Soviet Union in one corner of the stands who stood and waved red flags. The excitement their appearance generated was of an intensity that few other experiences have matched.

In contrast to this initial feeling of excitement at seeing the Soviet women gymnasts was the dismay aroused by the scores for the American gymnasts that averaged 9.00 in compulsories. Scores of 8.85, 8.95, 9.05, and 9.15 came up one after the other. Only one reasonably high score was posted, that of Joan Moore Rice in floor exercise. She scored 9.45. Debbie Fike was next with 9.25 on floor.

Joan Moore Rice, leader of the American team

In an article published later, the coach of the U.S. women's team, Muriel Grossfeld, made these comments: "Our women had some trouble with falls and misses in the compulsory routines which, combined with the overall feeling of being generally underscored, put a damper on the morale of the entire women's team, but each day was a new experience and low feelings can quickly be lifted."[3]

At the conclusion of compulsory exercises, the standings and scores of the leading teams and individuals were as follows:

1. URS	190.80
2. GDR	186.20
3. HUN	184.25
4. TCH	182.80
5. ROM	180.85
6. USA	180.30
7. JPN	180.05
8. FRG	178.35

1. Turischeva	38.95
2. Korbut	38.65
3. Hellmann	38.00
4. Kim	37.65
5. Dronova, URS	37.55
Medveczky, HUN	37.55
7. Sikharulidze, URS	37.50
8. Czaszar, HUN	37.45
Saadi, URS	37.45
10. Schmeisser, GDR	37.40
11. Dornakova, TCH	37.00
Zinke	37.00

Optional Exercises

Competition 1b: October 23rd

During optionals, there were not many changes in the standings of the teams and individuals as they existed at the conclusion of compulsories. The United States slipped to seventh place as Japan moved up to sixth. There were a few notable changes in individual standings as one gymnast made more improvement than another in optionals in comparison with scores in compulsories.

Turischeva's average for the four optional events was a tenth higher, Korbut's was 0.12 higher and Hellmann's 0.113. Elvira Saadi, however, had an optional average 0.213 higher and jumped from eighth place to fourth; her teammate, Rusudan Sikharulidze, averaged 0.175 better and moved up from seventh place to fifth. Alina Goreac of Romania jumped from 13th place among all gymnasts up to seventh place with a big improvement in her average score of 0.3875. Annelore Zinke, the other big improver, went from eleventh place to seventh, with an improvement of 0.3625.

The big loser was Nelli Kim. She dropped from fourth place after compulsories to ninth place after optionals. The interesting cause of this big drop was an 8.60 in vault. She scored 9.60 on bars and beam and 9.55 on floor, but she came to grief in one of the events for which she would receive the gold medal two years later in the 1976 Montreal Olympics.

Two aspects of optional exercises were most noteworthy. First was the joy and excitement of seeing the optional exercises of the leaders, especially Turischeva and Korbut. Second was the continuing battle of the American women for recognition in the face of the hostile attitude of the judges. The evening came to a climax with a vehement protest by the entire crowd at one of the scores awarded. In her article, previously referred to,[3] U.S. women's coach Muriel Grossfeld described the situation. It took place while the American women were on vaulting.

> Anne Carr was the fifth American up and did a round-off back (Tsukahara), which was good but not up to her best, as she had bent her knees and had less height than usual. She got the usual pep talk and proceeded with her second vault. Second time up, she gave it everything and the crowd went absolutely beserk. It was a beautiful vault and the audience acknowledged it. The score was posted, 9.4, and the crowd couldn't believe it. The spectators from all the countries in the stands watching would not allow anything to happen after that. They whistled, shouted and stamped their feet and refused to accept the score. The pianist could not play for the

> floor exercise competition because he couldn't hear the piano and the girl was forced to stop her performance. Diane Dunbar was the next American vaulter up and couldn't begin her vault because the crowd simply would not settle down. The superior vaulting judge stated that the American team would be penalized unless Dunbar began. Frank Comiskey (American men's judge) lodged a protest and finally the judges agreed to give satisfaction. Some 45 minutes later the meet was allowed to continue. Carr's final score was 9.40.

The other incident related to floor exercise. It had an even more significant effect on the competition than the incident just mentioned because it affected one of the apparatus finals. It took place, however, in a judges' conference and the public was not aware of it. In an article published later,[4] this observer wrote:

> During the optional floor exercise, Nina Dronova received a score that would have caused her to tie Joan Moore Rice (of the U.S.A.) and that would have admitted Rice to the finals. Superior Judge Demidenko of the Soviet Union actually called one of the judges and instructed her to raise Dronova's score. She did so and thereby knocked Rice out of the finals. Delene Darst of the United States, floor exercise judge, witnessed this incident firsthand:

Joan Moore Rice

> "The scores, which came from the four judges, were fed into the machine, which computed them and flashed the totals on the superior judge's scoreboard. After Nina Dronova's scores were in, there was a delay and Superior Judge Demidenko of the Soviet Union asked the Japanese judge to come to the head table and bring her score with her. The Japanese woman put her hand down on the table and made some marks with her pencil. Shortly thereafter, the average to Dronova's routine appeared as a 9.7. Now for Dronova to get a 9.7, she would have had to get a 9.6 and 9.8 averaged together. The Swiss judge scored her a 9.6, as had I. The Japanese judge had originally scored a 9.7, she later told me, but the superior judge made her come up to a 9.8. It is strictly illegal to call in a single judge to make a score change under these circumstances. The effect of the change was to keep Joan Moore Rice out of the finals, since she and Dronova had been tied for sixth place going into the floor exercise event."

The Ann Carr and Joan Rice incidents had a depressing, demoralizing effect upon the young American team. Fortunately, Varna was the nadir, the lowest point in the history of biased gymnastic judging. In succeeding years, the fairness of judging would slowly improve. Judging got better as the American team got better. Ironically, it also improved as the political and economic conditions in the communist countries declined.

The judging in Varna was a major topic in post mortem discussions not only during the championships but also within the American gymnastic community at home. In another article, published later,[5] U.S. coach Muriel Grossfeld said that "A certain 'closeness' existed between certain judges antagonistic to the USA, because of their fear the USA team might place as high as third and a certain antagonism because the USA had opposed the return to Varna." She commented that the authorities were "using F.I.G. gymnastic rules to defend poor and unfair judgements while breaking these same rules for 'vested interests' of the Technical Committee Leaders." Much criticism was leveled at Madame Valerie Nagy (pronounced "Narzh") of Hungary, who was not only President of the Women's Technical Committee but Hungarian national coach. Madame Nagys had devoted her life to women's gymnastics and had worked for the International Federation of Gymnastics for thirty years. She had been President of the Women's Technical Committee from 1972 to 1976.[6] As Ms. Grossfeld noted,[5] she "was constantly on the telephone to the judges on their scoring of Hungarian gymnasts. It seemed to have the desired effect." Under her protection, the Hungarian teams placed third in both the 1972 Olympics and the 1974 World Championships. After she retired in 1976, the Hungarian standings were never again so high.

As the American team's group left the floor, the Soviet team came out in the last group of the evening. As noted earlier, their scores in optionals were slightly higher than those in compulsories, with the exception of Nelli Kim. Their routines, for the most part, will be described in the section devoted to the all-around competition, with the exception of Ludmilla Turischeva's floor exercise. Ludmilla performed a different floor exercise, in the all-around than she did in team optionals. Accordingly, her routine in optionals will be described here.

This observer has a special respect for Ludmilla in that she did indeed perform different floor exercises in optionals and the all-around. She even had a third routine prepared for apparatus finals but chose to perform again her routine from optionals because it made such a favorable impression. Her varied floor exercise performance in Varna is a far cry from that of the vast majority of gymnasts who subject spectators to the same routine time after time—first in optionals, then in the all-around and then again in finals. Repetition on the other apparatuses is understandable, but in floor exercise a little variety would be appreciated by spectators and might even be rewarded by the judges. Ludmilla's routine was as follows:

Ludmilla Turischeva

> Standing erect, she started on a diagonal, facing a corner, two steps away from it. When the music started, she began to move with an exaggerated step: she threw her shoulders forward, then she pulled them back while moving her right foot forward, her right knee deeply bent. After a body wave, she took another step forward, more normal this time, made a quarter turn to her right and kicked her left leg up to the side. She made a second quarter turn to her right while

making little hops first on one foot than the other and prepared for her first pass: a round-off, half twist into a salto forward piked (Arabian) *(Figure 32)* and stepped out into a round-off, flic-flac, salto backward tucked. Upon landing, she assumed a pose with her right foot forward, knee bent, her left foot well back and her body tilted diagonally back with her arms thrown up and back. Leaving her feet in place, she threw her head and body horizontally forward then pulled it sharply back, her arms going from extended above her head down to her side, with her elbows bent, her hands by her shoulders, palms facing forward. Then, after a slight upper body turn to her left, as she straightened her right leg and brought her left leg together to her right, she ran forward three steps parallel to the adjacent side to her left, turned right to face the center of the floor, spread her legs, while at the same time reaching down with her left hand to touch her right toe. She raised her upper body and circled her arms around above her, brought her hands together in front of her with her elbows bent, and bent her knees slightly as she leaned forward. She then threw her arms up and back to pause for a fraction of a second in spread-eagle pose. Then she brought her hands together in front of her and made a full and a quarter turn to her left. She made two little steps forward, parallel to the side, lifting her heel off the floor each time but barely lifting her toes off the floor. Then suddenly thrust her right foot forward and her left foot back and ran with a big step, a skip step and another step toward the corner, made a half turn to her left and stepped back into the corner while turning more to her left to face along the diagonal and begin her second pass: a round-off, flic-flac, salto backward stretched then piked with her arms out to her side. Upon landing, she assumed a pose similar to that after her previous pass, but this time facing to her left across the diagonal. Her feet were still on the diagonal, legs separated and with her right knee bent. She slowly bent her upper body down and back with her arms extended above her, then stood up, brought her feet together, turned to her right to face parallel to the adjacent side and began to walk with strutting steps, raising her knees high and moving her right arm from side to side expressively across in front of her. After three such steps, she quickly turned a quarter turn to her left, ran toward the center of the floor and executed an aerial forward walkover. Upon landing, she posed for a second with her feet together, her knees bent and her arms extended in front of her, her hands together. She made a quarter turn to her right and posed for a second, with her left knee slightly bent, her right leg straight but extended diagonally out to her side, her left arm at her side, her right arm extended diagonally out over her right leg and her head facing along her right arm and leg. Then she turned another quarter turn to her right to face across the floor and made a playful jump in which her knees were together and her feet were splayed out to each side, her arms also out to her side, bent, with her elbows above her hands. Finally, in this series of poses, she stood with her hips pushed out to her right, her upper body back, her right arm extended vertically upwards and her left arm at her side. She took a step back, turned to her right to face into the corner, made a double turn to her left and performed a cartwheel to her right toward the corner. She ended her cartwheel in a crouch—her knees and shin on the floor, her seat on the backs of her feet and her body bent forward so that her forehead touched the floor. Separating her knees but leaving them on the floor, she raised her upper body and posed, having flung her left arm out in front of her and her right arm up and back. She put both hands on the floor in front of her, kicked her left leg up behind her and extended her right leg. In so doing, she raised her seat but kept her hands on the floor. She lowered her left leg and placed her left foot behind her on the floor so that her feet crossed. She raised her upper body and made a full upper body turn to her left so that her feet uncrossed, stepped forward and posed, standing erect with her straight arms stretched above her. She then ran forward and performed a high split leap with change of legs, ran again and performed a second split leap with change of legs. Upon landing, she performed a jump half turn to her left and came down into a pose with her right foot on the floor, her right knee fully bent, her left leg extended behind her, her upper body bent forward over her right knee and her hands at her side on the floor. She held this lunge pose for a second, made a creeping step forward with her left leg and then ran with little steps forward as she gradually stood up. She ran toward the middle of the floor and stood with her feet widely separated and performed some wild, crazy motions, moving her arms from side to side and in circular motion and turning her head left and right. She turned to her left along a diagonal, ran toward a corner and performed an aerial cartwheel to her left. Upon landing, she fell back, to lie supine on the floor but with her right knee raised. Her arms were behind her on the floor. She lay there for a second, extended her right leg vertically in a kick, sat up suddenly while at the same time elevating her left leg, straddling her legs and holding them for a second at forty-five degrees above the floor. In a continuous motion, she leaned her upper body forward, let her legs drop to the floor and leaned far forward to touch the floor with her right hand, inside and ahead of her right foot. Then, placing her left hand on the floor and leaving it there, she raised herself and circled counter-clockwise around it a full turn with tiny little running steps, dropped down again with her left knee on the floor, her right foot in front of her with her right knee bent, her head and body bent forward over her right knee and her arms and hands loosely draped down to the floor slightly ahead. She stood and posed, having thrown her arms up and back while preparing her last pass: a round-off, flic-flac, salto backward stretched. Upon landing, she threw her upper body back and let her arms flop down to her side, again with her legs separated, her right foot forward and left foot back. She stepped forward, leaned her body forward and let her arms hang down and swing back and forth like a limp rag doll. She finally moved energetically into her final pose: she stood with her straight legs widely separated, her hips moved laterally over her right leg, her upper body tilted slightly forward and to the left, her left arm extended horizontally to the side, her right arm pointing vertically upward and her head tilted back.

Turischeva justly received 9.90 for her routine; she also received 9.90 on beam. These scores contributed to her total scores' in compulsories and optionals being slightly higher than Korbut's and thereby increased the challenge for Olga in the all-around.

Team winners, left to right: East Germany (front row: Zinke, Schmeisser, Hellmann); Soviet Union (front row: Dronova, Korbut, Sikharulidze, with Turischeva looking on); Hungary (second Hungarian from left is Krisztina Medveczky.)

The only other 9.90 in optionals was that of Annelore Zinke of East Germany. She surprised everybody with a routine that included the Korbut back flip from high bar. Her routine will be described later.

At the conclusion of optional competition, the standings and scores of the leading teams and individuals were as follows:

1. URS	384.15
2. GDR	376.55
3. HUN	370.60
4. ROM	369.30
5. TCH	368.45
6. JPN	362.90
7. USA	362.50
8. FRG	361.00

1. Turischeva	78.30
2. Korbut	77.80
3. Hellmann	76.45
4. Saadi	75.75
5. Sikharulidze	75.70
6. Dronova	75.55
7. Goreac	75.25
Zinke	75.25
9. Kim	75.00
Medveczky	75.00
11. Schmeisser	74.95

The unfortunate consequence of this result for the United States was that the American women's team, now in seventh place, would have to qualify for the 1976 Olympics, under a new F.I.G. rule which stated that only the top six from world championships would be admitted to the Olympics without further qualification. (This rule was later modified to read that the top twelve teams in the world championships next before the Olympics would be the teams qualified.)

A general observation on the optionals relates to team support by the spectators. In the beginning, there was only scattered applause for the American girls because of the small number of Americans present. Toward the end, however, as people realized the effect of the cheering, West German fans started cheering for the Americans, when their own team was not involved, and both the Americans and the West Germans started cheering for the Japanese, who also had very few people present. There was strong cheering for the East Germans and, when the Soviet girls were on the floor, almost all the cheering was for them. It cannot help but have had a telling effect.

Individual All-around

Competition II: October 25th

Ludmilla Turischeva and Olga Korbut were so far ahead of the field as the individual all-around began that only a disaster, such as befell Olga in Munich, was likely to shake one or the other of them out of her lead. Olga was certainly not going to let that happen again. On the contrary, she desperately wanted to move up to become champion and was constantly frustrated by the extra tenths that kept being awarded to her rival. It seemed to her that she was constantly coming up against a stone wall. Her nervous agitation was extreme. It was reported that she walked back and forth along the corridor at night, unable to sleep. She at least had the sympathy of observers this writer spoke to, who believed she was being underscored.

Years later, her husband, Leonid Bortkevich, who after ten or more years of married life with Olga had become a perceptive observer of the gymnastic scene, had this to say: "I am persuaded that in several competitions they (the judges) came to an agreement on the distribution of places in the table of ranks. I'm not talking about subjective scores; in gymnastics this is unavoidable, although objective criteria exist. In the 1970's, an international judging 'corporation' gave preference to the more traditional gymnastics of Ludmilla Turischeva, to which the judges were more accustomed, instead of the cheeky style of Olga Korbut."[7]

As the individual all-around began, the standings and averaged scores from team competition of the top ten gymnasts were as follows:

1. Turischeva	39.150
2. Korbut	38.900
3. Hellmann	38.225
4. Saadi	37.875
5. Sikharulidze	37.850
6. Dronova	37.775
7. Zinke	37.725
8. Goreac	37.625
9. Medveczky	37.525
10. Schmeisser	37.475

First Rotation

In vaulting during first rotation were Elvira Saadi, who scored 9.40; Alina Goreac, 9.45 and Krisztina Medveczky, 9.40. Saadi's vaults were Yamashita with full twist; Goreac performed a Tsukahara pike for her first vault and then one of a half turn onto the horse followed by a half turn off.

Ludmilla Turischeva beginning half turn before dropping to low bar.

Ludmilla Turischeva led the group on bars, which included Rusiko Sikharulidze and Richarda Schmeisser of East Germany. Turischeva scored 9.80 for her familiar routine.

> Standing under high bar facing low bar, Turischeva first threw her hands up above her head with her arms extended, brought her hands back down to her side and made a big jump forward to begin a glide on low bar. The momentum of her jump caused her to make her glide on low bar one of big amplitude as she swung under the bar. She piked her legs between her arms and swung up to rear support position on low bar. She reached up to grasp high bar and kipped on high bar up to toe-on position on top of high bar. From her toe-on position on high bar, her routine was identical to the one she performed in Munich.

Richarda Schmeisser of East Germany was one of those reliable gymnasts who, like Elvira Saadi of the Soviet Union, was never a star and never received an Olympic or world championships individual medal. Just as Saadi backed up Korbut and Turischeva by being fourth individually in team competition and fourth also in the all-around, so Schmeisser backed up Hellmann and Zinke. Her standings were lower (eleventh and ninth), but, like Saadi, she was the number three gymnast on her team. Her routine on bars was as follows:

> From a position several steps away from the low bar on the low bar side, she ran, jumped off the beat board, made a half turn in flight and flew backwards over the low bar to catch high bar, her body hanging in piked position with her legs pointing vertically upwards between the bars.

Without pausing, she kipped back up to clear support position, her stretched body just above horizontal, held away from high bar by straight arms. She performed a clear hip circle backwards down under high bar and up between the bars to handstand. From handstand, she allowed her body to drop toward low bar, executing a half turn to her right to face low bar as she did so, and bounced on her hips off low bar. In her uprise, she kept her legs together and piked her body as she passed over the low bar and then stretched it as she began a long kip on high bar up to handstand. In handstand, she made a half turn to face away from low bar and swung back down under high bar to bounce her hips against the low bar. She swung back, released high bar and performed a full turn to her left with her body vertical. She recaught high bar, dropped to low bar and kipped on low bar to catch high bar. She swung forward on high bar and performed a salto backward with her legs straddled to catch low bar. She immediately began a kip on low bar to catch high bar. She swung back and swung forward to straddle her legs over low bar and bring them together in rear-lying hang. She kipped on high bar back up to clear support position away from high bar, her body well above horizontal. She performed a hip circle backward down under high bar and up between the bars. In so doing, she allowed her hips to rest against the bar. As she came up between the bars, her body was slightly piked. As she neared the top of the high bar, she energetically straightened her body and pushed with her hips off the bar. She flew forward over low bar in hecht dismount with full twist to land.

Richarda Schmeisser in turn off high bar, an element she left out of finals, from which our routine was taken.

It was an artistic and gracefully performed routine, worth more in this observer's opinion than the 9.50 she received.

Angelika Hellmann

On beam in first rotation were Angelika Hellmann, who received 9.60 and Annelore Zinke, who received 9.50.

Nina Dronova was one of the leaders who performed floor exercise during first rotation. Hers was an elegant exercise, full of dramatic and expressive gestures. "Her floor exercise was so distinctive that she had been referred to as the 'Mozart of Gymnastics' in her own country."[8] Her routine, for which she received 9.65, was as follows:

> Nina started in the middle of the floor, standing erect with her arms at her side. In a series of puppet-like moves, she sharply extended her right foot to the side, raised her right arm to her side and then her left, in jerky motions. Finally, she raised both arms smoothly and stretched herself upward, made a nearly three-quarter turn to her right to face a corner, ran into it and made a cat leap half turn to her left to face along the diagonal and begin her first pass: round-off, flic-flac high salto backward stretched with double twist *(Figure 81)*. Upon landing, she posed with her legs spread forward and backward and her arms stretched overhead. Then she dropped straight down into squat position, with both knees fully bent, her arms at her side with her fingers extended onto the floor and her head and body bent forward over her knees. She slowly and expressively raised herself up to stand on her toes and slowly made a half turn left on her toes to face the corner. Then she made a hop turn to her left and ran parallel to the side to the left of her first pass diagonal She made a jump half turn, made another half turn upon landing

Figure 81

and continued toward the adjacent corner. Near it, she dropped down into another squat pose, similar to her last one. She stood in the corner, turned right to face along the diagonal and made a short pass along it. She ran, performed an aerial forward walkover and a split leap with change of legs. Upon landing, she posed in a half lunge position, her left knee partially bent. She turned a quarter turn to her right, fell forward on her knees and, without pausing, made a full turn to her right on her knees. She finished in a dramatic lunge pose—her bent right knee forward, her left leg diagonally back and her body leaning forward over her knee. He left arm was diagonally forward and down and her right arm was diagonally up and back. She made a full turn to her left in lunge attitude and then another full turn down on both knees (a knee spin). She slowly stood, bent forward and circled and extended her arms backwards, downwards, forwards and upwards to end with her hands at her chest and her elbows bent. She kept her head down and allowed her body to express herself. She made two steps with a half turn, stepped backward with three steps on her toes with a soft plié (photo) and finished with a small leap onto her left foot. She stepped back on her right foot, lifted and circled her left leg up and back and lowered herself down to her seat. She settled back onto her back, brought her legs vertically upward in straddle position, turned them slightly to the left and brought them together as she stood. She stepped toward the corner, made a deep body wave with sweeping gestures of her arms and a turn to her right to face along the diagonal. For her second pass, she performed round-off, flic-flac into a half twist salto forward stretched (Arabian) to land facing the corner.

Nina Dronova in photo taken in 1974 Champions All, which she won.

She ran the few remaining steps into the corner, made a half turn to her left and posed with her arms outstretched above her. She then made a wide semi-circle from that corner, around to the one on her right. She danced, paused in the middle of the floor to make a full turn on her right foot, her right knee partially bent, her left knee fully bent and raised up near her, and her body bent forward over it. She danced again toward the corner and performed an aerial cartwheel to her right into it. She paused only briefly before beginning her final pass: a round-off, flic-flac, salto backward stretched. She stepped forward, dropped her right knee to the floor and placed her left foot on the floor ahead of her. Over her bent left knee, she lowered and lifted her torso while bending and stretching her arms. She slowly stood and gracefully entered her attractive final pose: her body erect, her right foot on its toes behind her left foot, her left arm was at her side and her right hand was by her right shoulder, her elbow bent. She was looking ahead and straight up.

Olga Korbut

One distinguishing characteristic of Dronova's floor exercise is that of frequently changing and varying the levels on which she performed—sometimes on her knees, on her seat, on her back, or on her toes—and of often going back and forth between these levels.

The other competitor in floor exercise was Olga Korbut. Except for a few minor changes, Olga's floor exercise was identical to the one she performed in Munich. It had the same playful charisma. That she only scored 9.70 was, perhaps, for the very reason that it was the same exercise the judges had so often seen before in Munich, in exhibitions, and now already in team competition. Judges expect to see something different in Olympics and World championships, especially in floor exercise. It is interesting that the most daring change in floor exercise was made by that gymnast who had so steadfastly refused to change her exercises on the uneven bars or balance beam—namely, Ludmilla Turischeva.

At the end of first rotation, the standings and scores of the leading gymnasts were as follows:

	Initial Score	1st Rotation	Subtotal
1. Turischeva *(bars)*	39.150	9.80	48.950
2. Korbut *(floor)*	38.900	9.70	48.600
3. Hellmann *(beam)*	38.225	9.60	47.825
4. Dronova *(floor)*	37.775	9.65	47.425
5. Sikharulidze *(bars)*	37.850	9.50	47.350
6. Saadi *(vault)*	37.875	9.40	47.275
7. Zinke *(beam)*	37.725	9.50	47.225
8. Goreac *(vault)*	37.625	9.45	47.075
9. Schmeisser *(bars)*	37.475	9.50	46.975
10. Medveczky *(vault)*	37.525	9.40	46.925

Second Rotation

In second rotation, Olga Korbut moved from floor exercise to vault, as did Nina Dronova. This time Olga did not receive so high a score as she had in optionals of team competition (9.70) or as she would later in finals (9.85). For her innovative vaults, full turn on with either handspring off or full turn off, she scored 9.55 and 9.45. Dronova scored 9.50. On bars, Saadi, Goreac, and Medveczky scored 9.70, 9.55 and 9.60 respectively. On balance beam were Turischeva, Sikharulidze, and Schmeisser. Ludmilla Turischeva's beam routine was identical to the one she had performed in Munich in 1972. It will not be repeated here. Suffice it to say that she performed it well and scored 9.80. Both Sikharulidze and Schmeisser continued to perform well. Sikharulidze scored 9.70 and Schmeisser, 9.60.

Ludmilla Turischeva

Angelika Hellmann and Annelore Zinke, both from East Germany, were the two competitors in floor exercise among the leaders. Hellmann's

Annelore Zinke

routine was beautifully executed, was traditionally choreographed and was set to classical music. Both Hellmann and Zinke scored 9.65.

At the end of second rotation, the standings and scores of the leaders were as follows:

	Initial Score	2nd Rotation	Subtotal
1. Turischeva *(beam)*	48.950	9.80	58.750
2. Korbut *(vault)*	48.600	9.55	58.150
3. Hellmann *(beam)*	47.825	9.65	57.475
4. Sikharulidze *(beam)*	47.350	9.70	57.050
5. Saadi *(bars)*	47.275	9.70	56.975
6. Dronova *(vault)*	47.425	9.50	56.925
7. Zinke *(floor)*	47.225	9.65	56.875
8. Goreac *(bars)*	47.075	9.55	56.625
9. Schmeisser *(beam)*	46.975	9.60	56.575
10. Medveczky *(bars)*	46.925	9.60	56.525

Third Rotation

Third rotation brought the two East Germans, Angelika Hellmann and Annelore Zinke to vault. Hellmann scored 9.60 for her vaults of handspring on followed by full turn off and half turn on followed by half turn off. Zinke scored 9.50 for two vaults of handspring on followed by full turn off.

Olga Korbut led the group on bars. With her was her teammate, Nina Dronova. Olga's routine was the same as her famous routine at the Munich Olympics except for two modifications. In her original routine, after kipping from low bar to high bar and kipping on high bar up to toe-on position on top of high bar, her body piked with her hands outside her feet, she paused, and pushed directly off into her back flip. In Varna, from her toe-on position on top of high bar, she performed a sole circle forward down between the bars and up again on the far side, keeping her toes on the bar. As she came up on the far side, she continued her upward momentum and thrust immediately off into her back flip.

The other modification affected her dismount. In Munich, near the end of her routine as she was preparing her dismount, she made a sole circle forward around high bar and then thrust off backward, that is to say, in the opposite direction, into her salto backward stretched to land; in Varna, on the other had, she made her sole circle backward and then thrust off in the same direction for her salto backward dismount.

In Varna, Olga received 9.80 for her bars routine. Remember that it was in the same all-around competition in Munich that she had had her famous disaster. Dronova received 9.70.

Olga Korbut (Confusion over the appearance of the apparatus results from men's parallel bars in the background.)

Elvira Saadi, Alina Goreac, and Krisztina Medveczky were the competitors on beam among the leaders in third rotation. Saadi scored 9.70, Goreac, 9.60, and Medveczky, 9.45. Goreac's routine did not seem to have enough difficulty to earn a really high score, but it was artistically and cleanly executed. It was set to quite a fast space. It was as follows:

She ran toward the end of the beam, jumped off the beat board from her left foot and landed on the beam on her right foot. She stepped forward to the middle of the beam and made a body wave down to squat position. She stood, made a high kick with her right leg and skip-stepped forward to the end. After some dance steps in place, she performed a back walkover. She paused and posed, then performed a back handspring to near the end of the beam. After more posing and body waves, she stepped forward past the middle of the beam and performed a stag leap. She danced to the end, kicked her right leg up almost vertically, held it with her right hand and made a half turn to her right on her left foot with her right leg still vertical. She posed, stepped forward to the middle of the beam, lowered herself down to squat position and executed a forward roll with her arms out to the side. She stood and stepped to the end. She made a half turn to her right, a deep body wave and stepped forward. Near the middle of the beam, she made a jump in which she kicked both feet up behind her but kept her body straight. After she landed, she turned a quarter turn to her left to face across the beam, bent her right knee and extended her left leg along the beam. In this lunge position, she made a full turn to her right, then straightened her right leg and slid her left along the beam until she was in side splits posi-

Alina Goreac

tion. She made an attractive pose with her arms out to the side, each arm elevated to about 45° above horizontal. She put both hands onto the beam, raised her body, brought her right leg around, bent under her, and posed with her upper body elevated diagonally off the beam, supported by her right arm, her left leg still extended along the beam, now over her right leg. She posed again sitting on the beam, her body now upright, her right leg in the same position but her left leg now also bent and resting on her right. She posed a third time, briefly reclining on her right side along the beam, with her right arm extended along the beam. During these second and third poses, she was gesturing expressively with her left arm. She turned to her right on her seat to face along the beam and stood. She made two quarter turns to her left, while making side body waves and gestures with her arms. Then she stepped forward and performed a forward walkover. She continued with a step to the end, made a half turn to her left to face back along the beam and skip-stepped to the middle of the beam where she posed and prepared for her dismount. She performed a round-off into a salto backward stretched with a full and three-quarter twist. She was possibly trying to make a double twist but did not get all the way round. She had to take a big step to her right on landing.

When it came time for floor exercise, the audience was treated to two notable routines—those of Turischeva and Rusudan Sikharulidze. Turischeva's routine was notable in that it was not the same routine she had performed two days earlier.

Sikharulidze's was memorable because of its expressiveness and the uncommon eye contact she maintained with spectators. This observer had a good seat in the middle of the stands not many rows up; it seemed to him that Sikharulidze was looking right at him several times during her routine. Her ability to maintain eye contact is in contrast to that of those many gymnasts who are so busy with what they are doing that they forget to look at the audience. Sikharulidze's floor exercise has received another accolade in that it is one of the favorites of Larissa Latynina, the matriarch of Soviet women's gymnastics. Years later when asked about her favorites in floor exercise, this was the first one she mentioned.

Rusudan Sikharulidze

Music evoking the fiery nature of Spanish people is often used in gymnastics and figure skating, Bizet's *Carmen* having some of the most popular melodies. For her routine, Sikharulidze chose the Spanish dance, "Malaguena."

Starting in the middle of the floor, her arms down at her side, she slowly raised her arms up to her side until they were outstretched 45° above horizontal and then snapped her head back in a gesture of finality. She then ran forward, made a hop on her right foot with her left leg raised behind her, crossed her left leg over her right and ran to her right two steps. She turned left to pose dramatically with her right foot forward, her right knee bent, her straight left leg diagonally back and to her right, her left hand on her hip and her right arm extended horizontally to her side. She looked first to her left and then moved her head sharply to the front. She then slowly turned to her left, looking over her right arm directly at the audience, keeping her arm straight and letting it turn as her body turned. She continued her turn nearly a full turn until she faced a corner, posed on her right foot with her left leg next to her right, her left knee bent, her left shin horizontal with her left toes pointed, her arms at her side and, again, her head pointed toward the audience and her eyes making contact. She ran toward the corner and performed an aerial cartwheel to her left toward it. Not pausing after her cartwheel, she turned left toward the corner, stepped into it, and posed, looking steadfastly at the audience, standing with both arms extended in front of her, while preparing for her first pass. She made a half turn to her right, ran and performed a round-off, flic-flac, salto backward stretched with double twist into an immediate back handspring. She posed in the corner with her legs separated to the side, making energetic movements with her arms, pointing them ahead and looking ahead, then bringing her arms down to her sides while raising herself on her toes. She hopped up and danced off to her right with poses and a high assemblé, followed by a sissone with a bent rear leg which she ended in a pose bending down over her bent right knee with her right foot on the floor, her left knee on the floor beside her, her left foot back and her hands on the floor. She raised her body slightly off the floor, made a half turn to her left while extending her left knee into lunge position, bent over it, and stretched her right leg out onto the floor behind her. She then lay down on her left side on the floor, her bent left knee in front of her, her left leg on the floor. She rolled to her left over onto her back and rolled a full turn on her back and shoulders, straddling and scissoring her legs above her as she turned. She made another full turn to her left, getting up first on her right knee, then both knees and then coming down on her seat as she finished her turn, with her knees drawn up in front of her. She stood, advanced into the nearby corner and made a half turn to her right to begin her second pass: a round-off, flic-flac, half twist into forward salto stretched (Arabian) that she landed facing the corner. Without stopping, she stepped into the corner, posed, kicked her right leg forward, kicked her left leg up backwards, turned and ran back toward the middle of the floor in a shallow semi-circle to her left, nearly parallel to the side of the floor. Part way along this side, she paused and posed, her feet separated forwards and backwards, left foot forward with toes on the floor, her left hand on her hip and her right arm crossed over so that her right hand was near her left. She looked over her left shoulder at the audience with a challenging expression, befitting the character of a Spanish dancer. She took two steps forward, pausing each time in the same pose with the lead foot alternately having its toes on the floor. She ran a few more steps forward, made a quarter turn to her right to face across the floor, ran forward and performed a forward aerial walkover. Upon landing, she turned a quarter turn to her left, came down on her left knee with her hands on the floor and pushed off with her right foot into a momentary

> stag handstand. She sat back down, facing back toward the center of the floor, made a three-quarter turn on her seat to her left to face the opposite side, ran toward it, performed a split leap and continued running, turning slightly into the corner. When she reached the corner, she turned left to face along the diagonal to prepare for her third pass: a long run, followed by a round-off into a salto backward stretched stepout. Upon landing, she stepped forward, kicked her right leg up high, crossed her right foot over in front of her left, made a full turn, bent her knees and sat back into her final pose: her shoulders and right foot were on the floor and her body was arched in a bridge between them. Her left knee was bent and held high, with her left foot on her right knee. Her left arm was at her side and her right arm was extended up at right angles to her body. She was looking straight up.

For this exercise, Sikharulidze was awarded 9.75. She maintained her fourth-place standing. Richarda Schmeisser, who also performed floor exercise in third rotation, scored 9.60.

Turischeva's second floor exercise, which she performed during this all-around competition, was set to the music of Tchaikovsky's famous first piano concerto. It was conventional, in contrast to her routine in team optional competition, which was certainly unconventional. It was, as was customary with her, beautifully performed. She received another 9.90.

At the end of third rotation, the standings and scores of the leaders were as follows:

	Initial Score	3rd Rotation	Subtotal
1. Turischeva *(floor)*	58.750	9.90	68.650
2. Korbut *(bars)*	58.150	9.80	67.950
3. Hellmann *(vault)*	57.475	9.60	67.075
4. Sikharulidze *(floor)*	57.050	9.75	66.800
5. Saadi *(beam)*	56.975	9.70	66.675
6. Dronova *(bars)*	56.925	9.70	66.625
7. Zinke *(vault)*	56.875	9.50	66.375
8. Goreac *(beam)*	56.625	9.60	66.225
9. Schmeisser *(floor)*	56.575	9.60	66.175
10. Medveczky *(beam)*	56.525	9.45	65.975

Olga Korbut had dropped from 0.25 behind Turischeva to 0.70 behind. Her chances of overtaking her great rival were dim, but she had a comfortable lead of almost 0.90 over third-place Hellmann. There would not be many changes in fourth rotation, but Annelore Zinke would continue to make a name for herself.

Fourth Rotation

All Turischeva needed now was a 9.35 in vaulting to win the championship. Even if Korbut got a 10.00 on beam, she would still be 0.5 behind. As it was, Ludmilla got a 9.70 and then a 9.80 for her Tsukahara tuck vaults, that is, a half turn onto the horse followed by a salto backward off in tuck position. Rusudan Sikharulidze scored 9.55 and 9.60 for her two Yamashita with full twist vaults.

The most exciting performances in fourth rotation were on bars, where the East Germans are always strong. First to perform on the East German team was the lovely Angelika Hellmann.

> Starting from the high bar side, several steps back from under high bar, Hellmann ran, jumped up to catch high bar and kipped up to clear support position off high bar on the side away from low bar. In doing so, she straddled her legs over low bar as she began her kip, cleanly brought them together in the middle of her kip, with her legs piked up between the bars, and then held them together throughout her kip and when her was body stretched in her clear support. In this position, her body was horizontal with her straight arms holding the bar. She did a clear hip circle back down under high bar and up between the bars to handstand, then another clear hip circle in the same direction up to handstand. From handstand, she slowly allowed her body to fall and bounce on her hips off low bar, while performing a half turn as her straight body was falling. On her uprise, she straddled her legs over low bar and performed a long kip on high bar and brought her legs together. As she came up between the bars and above the high bar, she straddled her legs again and piked her body so that her toes were just above the bar outside her hands. She continued forward and around high bar with her legs still straddled and on up between the bars to a momentary position over the low bar where her body was stretched horizontally facing low bar. She dropped onto low bar again and bounced off from it on her hips. On her uprise, she made a full turn to her left, dropped and bounced a third time off low bar. On her uprise, she straddled her legs over the low bar and, for the second time, performed a long kip on high bar while bringing her legs together. She kipped to clear support position off high bar, her body being just above horizontal over low bar, but instead of dropping to bounce off low bar this time, she performed a clear hip circle back down between the bars and up to handstand on high bar. Her body was absolutely straight as she made her hip circle and was held away from high bar by straight arms. In handstand, she was facing low bar. She made a half turn to face away from low bar as she began a giant circle back down

Figure 82

> from handstand to wrap around low bar and fly back to catch high bar in eagle grip. She hung for a second from high bar with her hands widely separated on high bar and dropped to low bar. She swung forward, piked her legs between her arms, swung back up to rear lying hang on low bar, having released her hands from low bar and reached up to grasp high bar. She kipped on high bar up to clear support position in back of high bar, widely straddling her legs over low bar as she did so. From her clear support, she performed a clear hip circle back down under high bar and up between the bars to clear support position again. She immediately pushed off and performed a salto backward tucked to land *(Figure 82)*.

For her excellent performance, Angelika received 9.80, easily good enough to maintain her bronze medal standing.

Annelore Zinke had already caused a sensation when she scored 9.90 on bars during optional team competition. Her other exercises were not strong and she was a long way from stardom in Varna. There was a general feeling there, however, that in a short time this 15-year-old would be among the top contenders. Her routine on bars was as follows:

> Standing facing low bar on the high bar side, Zinke grasped low bar and kipped to catch high bar. She swung forward, straddled over low bar into rear lying hang. She kipped on high bar up to squat position on high bar, facing low bar, her toes on the bar between her hands. Directly from squat position, she pushed off backwards and performed the Korbut back flip to recatch high bar. She swung down under high bar, wrapped around low bar and flew back with half turn to catch high bar in crossed grip facing away from low bar. She made a half turn back to face low bar, dropped to low bar, performed a glide, piked her body to shoot her legs between her arms, swing up to rear support and reach up to grasp high bar. She kipped on high bar and cast right up to handstand, facing away from low bar. She held her handstand for a second, then slowly allowed her body to fall toward low bar, executing a half turn

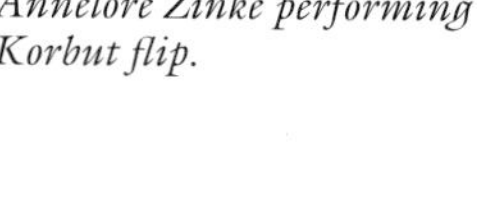

Annelore Zinke performing Korbut flip.

> as she did so to face low bar. She bounced off low bar and, on her uprise, let go of the high bar with her hands, performed a salto forward between the bars, her legs straddled, and recaught high bar. She made a long kip on high bar up to clear support position above high bar, her stretched body being supported by straight arms, her hips over high bar and her legs over low bar. From this position, she let her hips drop down onto the high bar and performed a hip circle backwards, her hips against the bar and her body piked. As she came up on top of the bar, she energetically straightened her body. This action exerted pressure downward on the bar and pushed her body up off the bar. Her momentum carried her forward in hecht dismount and she flew forward with her arms out to the side to land.

Zinke's form was excellent throughout and she stuck her landing. It was a beautiful routine, for which she received 9.95. Her 9.95 moved her from seventh to sixth place, just ahead of Nina Dronova. Her total score in the all-around was 38.6, for an average of 9.65, which is considerably less than the scores achieved by top gymnasts today. Nevertheless, her appearance in Varna provoked a lot of excitement.

On beam in fourth rotation we had a chance to see Olga Korbut's already famous routine. We had had

Annelore Zinke performing salto forward.

a preview of it in July at the Expo (World's Fair) in Spokane, Washington, where she had performed for five consecutive days. Ahead of Olga in the starting order was Nina Dronova, the one Soviet gymnast who did not win an individual medal, although her performance on the whole was excellent: she was fifth individually after compulsories, sixth after team optionals, and seventh in the all-around. She made finals on beam with the following routine:

Nina Dronova

She ran toward one end of the beam, jumped off the beat board with both feet, while placing her hands on the beam, and pressed right up to handstand. She straddled her legs on the way up, held them together for a second in handstand, then split them forwards and backwards, her right leg being in front of her, extending beyond the end of the beam. She lowered her right leg back down to the end of the beam and stood. She danced forward, performed a high split leap as she passed the middle of the beam, danced to the end and made a half turn to her left. She posed at the end, made a body wave down to a position where her left knee was almost fully bent, nearly touching the beam, her right knee bent past 90° and the toes of her right foot on the beam ahead of her. She then stood, kicked her left leg just above horizontal behind her and leaned forward in a unique scale in which she extended both arms to her left side, her left arm pointing upward, her right arm across her chest. After her scale, she kicked her right leg up high in front of her, stepped forward and executed a forward aerial walkover just past the center of the beam. After a pause, she stepped ahead to the end, made a half turn to her left and a body wave. She danced along the beam with a chassé and a hop to the other end and made a half turn to her right. She danced back along the beam a few steps and assumed a pose in which she squatted down onto her toes. Her feet were pointed so that only her toes touched the beam, her right foot being forward and her left foot under her. Her hands were extended to the side. She stood, danced forward, made a big hop and more dance steps and poses. She made a quarter turn to her right and posed in body wave facing across the beam. She made another quarter turn to her right to face along the beam, danced forward and made a second high split leap as she passed the middle of the beam. She squatted down, began a full turn to her right and raised herself to stand during her turn. Without pausing after her turn, she took a step to near the end with her right foot, made a half turn to her right on her right foot and stepped forward. She took another step forward and performed a forward walkover in which one hand is placed well ahead of the other in the take-off phase (tinsica). She stood and paused, took a few steps to the end, paused again in pose, then made a half turn to her left. She danced forward along the beam and posed in lunge position, her left knee bent and her right leg extended behind, her left arm extended diagonally back and her right arm extended vertically above her. In lunge pose, she made a full turn to her left and then made another half turn as she brought her knees together, simultaneously straightening her legs to stand. Now near one end of the beam, she stepped forward and made a full turn to her right on her right foot. She took another step forward and paused as she prepared for her dismount: a flic-flac into a salto backward stretched.

It was a graceful routine in which she emphasized her ability to pose and hold steadily on her toes. She had rhythmic fluidity—that is, she moved smoothly from one element to the next. With her aerial forward walkover and her high level dance combinations, she deserved better than the 9.50 she received.

While Olga's routine on the uneven bars was almost a repetition of her routine in Munich, her beam routine was a rehearsal of the one she would perform in Montreal. There would be certain differences, however, so we will present her routine in full.

Her mount was the same as it has always been, that is, from standing on the floor at the side of the beam near one end, she hopped up onto the beam into side splits, facing across the beam. She turned to her left and stretched both arms toward her left foot, then turned back to face across the beam and stretched her arms out gracefully on each side. Equally gracefully, she brought her hands down onto the beam in front of her and lifted herself into clear straddle support position while making a quarter turn to her left to line up with the beam. She lowered her body to sit and let her legs swing down beside her and slightly back. She put her hands on the beam behind her and elevated her legs to a wide straddle position just above the beam, that is, her legs were out to her sides away from the beam, as in side splits position. She brought her legs together and pointing vertically upward in front of her, as in a vee sit, then brought her right foot down onto the beam and extended her left leg in front of her. She straightened her right leg to stand and danced forward. She made a little assemblé and a stag leap as she approached the end and made a half turn to her left. She skip-stepped toward the middle of the beam, paused and performed her salto backward tucked. Then she leaned back to pass through handstand position with her legs together, separated her legs and let them swing down on either side of the beam and up until they were horizontally in front of her. As she did this, she sat down onto the beam. She swung her legs back down and up behind her until she could place her right foot on the beam, with her knee bent. Her left leg was extended upwards. She allowed her left leg to swing back down until it was hanging down beside her, then thrust it back up in an arc while pushing off with her right foot. She went through handstand position and paused with her legs extended horizontally forward, the back of her legs facing the beam, her steeply-arched body held up by straight arms angled back to maintain balance. She bent her knees so that her feet and shins pointed down, held this position for a second, then straightened her legs let

Olga Korbut

Olga Korbut

her toes come down to touch the beam. With her toes on the beam, she bent her arms and lowered her chest onto the beam. She grabbed the underside of the beam with her hands and extended her legs in front of her horizontally. Then she lowered them slightly until the soles of her feet were just above the beam. She held this famous chest scale with horizontal leg hold for at least two seconds. (Incidentally, this element is not included in the Code of Points.) After this, while keeping her legs together and straight with her toes pointed, she elevated her legs and swung them up through vertical, back down onto the beam, so that she was lying face down in prone position on top of the beam. She pushed up with her arms, raised her body and sat back in crouch position, her shins remaining on the beam, her seat just above them. She stood, stepped forward to just beyond the middle of the beam and performed a graceful full turn to the left on her left foot with her arms out to her side, her right knee bent and her right foot momentarily resting against the calf of her left leg. She danced to the end, posed, her right foot well behind her with toes on the beam and her arms out to the side. She made a half turn to her right, danced along the beam and made a split leap. Now near the end of the beam, she leaned forward

> into split-leg handstand with her left leg in front of her, pointing in the direction she had been moving. She lowered her left leg ahead of her so that her left toe just touched the beam and held this pose for two seconds—her body inverted, supported by straight arms to her hands on the beam, and her legs split but extended so that her left toe was touching the beam and her right leg was vertically upward. She then put her weight on her left foot, brought her right leg down onto the beam and stood at the end of the beam. She did a high back handspring to straddle down and continued her rotation so that she rolled out on her back and brought her legs over her head, keeping them straight as they went over her but then bending her knees so that her knees came down onto the beam just behind her head and her shins and feet were on the beam. For a second she was in crouch position on the beam, but she raised her body and stood with her feet separated, her right foot ahead. She leaned slowly back into back walkover, splitting her legs as she passed through handstand and coming down first onto her right foot, to stand near the end of the beam. She posed with her left foot back and her right knee bent, her hands and arms moving alternately and gracefully from up above her to down at her side. She danced forward, made a little hop and posed at the middle of the beam while making a body wave and gestures with her arms and hands. From standing, she performed a back handspring, paused and performed a salto forward, tucked, to dismount beside the beam. She placed her right hand on the beam for support as she touched down.

Olga's routine contained difficult elements, such as her salto backward tucked, and original elements, such as her famous chest scale. Equally important, her routine was characterized by grace and artistry. She performed everything she did in a way that made her body movements seem effortless, almost sensual. She instilled a bit of magic into each of them. Her score of 9.70 seemed unjust to many spectators, who whistled and jeered as the score was posted. Olga had matured since Munich but was still not getting the recognition from the judges that many thought she deserved.

While Olga and Nina Dronova were performing on beam, floor exercise was in progress. Medveczky scored 9.50, Goreac, 9.7, and Elvira Saadi, 9.75, for an exotic, seductive routine to the music of Rimsky-Korsakov's *Sheherezade*. Her routine was as follows:

> Saadi started her floor exercise about a third of the way along one of the sides, a few steps in. She began her routine with slow, measured dance steps, some turns and poses, seemingly designed to create an aura of mystery. She proceeded a few steps parallel to that side until she came near the

adjacent side she had been facing. There she made more turns and dance steps, some in place, took two long sideways, sliding steps away from the side, turned toward the nearby corner and advanced into it to begin her first pass: a round-off, flic-flac, salto backward stretched with double twist. She turned back toward her corner and ran backwards out of it with many, small running steps in a semi-circle toward the middle of the floor. There she turned toward the corner to the right of the one where she had just finished her first pass. She proceeded toward that corner with a full turn, a split jump, another full turn, a high kick with her right leg and a forward aerial walkover into a pose in which she stood with her right leg forward bent at the knee and her left leg diagonally back. She leaned forward into a quick scale with her left leg vertically upward and her right arm diagonally down and forward; her body was leaning slightly below horizontal and her left arm was extended upward parallel to her left leg. She turned back toward the center of the floor, lay down on her back, kicked her right leg vertically upward, straddled both legs, then rolled over to her right and began to stand facing the corner. She stepped into it, posed, did a body wave and made a half turn to her left to face along the diagonal and prepare for her second pass: a round-off, flic-flac, salto backward stretched into another flic-flac, salto backward stretched. She stepped forward into a pose in which she stood in a statuesque fashion, her left foot forward, her left hand on her hip, her right arm thrown vertically upwards and slightly back, and her face looking up and to her left. She then made exotic dance steps from side to side and some partial turns with her knees bent and together in the same slow tempo with which she had begun. She ended in a full turn to her right on her left foot with her right knee bent so that her shin was horizontal. She continued into a second full turn to her right on her left foot, this time with her right leg kicked up high in front of her. She posed with her left foot forward and her

Elvira Saadi

Figure 83

left knee bent, her right leg diagonally behind her, her body slightly tilted back and her head facing down to her left foot. She made a three-quarter turn to her left to face toward the corner she had left, posed, made a half turn to her left to face the next corner clockwise around the floor and proceeded parallel to the side of the floor in four long, sweeping strides. Now near that corner, she turned to her left again, posed, made some dance steps in place, and then continued in her progress around the floor by proceeding parallel to the next adjacent side to her left. She performed a round-off to her left and rebounded into a half turn and a front handspring (Arabian handspring) *(Figure 83)*. Near the next corner, she turned to her right and ran parallel to the third adjacent side and made a rear-leg stag leap (split leap with a bent rear leg). Near the fourth corner, having gone three-quarters of the way around the floor along the sides, she advanced into it with many turns, poses and dance steps to prepare for her third pass: a round-off into an immediate salto backward stretched from which she stepped out into a back walkover. She danced sideways, made a full turn and assumed her final pose. She stood over her left leg, looking down, her right leg diagonally back, her left arm across her chest and her right arm vertically upward.

All-around winners: 1st, Turischeva; 2nd, Korbut; 3rd, Hellmann; 4th, Saadi; 5th, Sikharulidze (behind Hellmann); 6th Zinke.

Like the choreography of Sikharulidze, Saadi's was a finely crafted integration of expressive, seductive dance with the acrobatics of her day. Both gymnasts would be rewarded with the bronze medal in finals.

The final standings and scores of the leaders in the individual all-around competition were as follows:

	Initial Score	**4th Rotation**	**Final Score**
1. Turischeva *(vault)*	68.650	9.80	78.450
2. Korbut *(beam)*	67.950	9.70	77.650
3. Hellmann *(bars)*	67.075	9.80	76.875
4. Saadi *(floor)*	66.675	9.75	76.425
5. Sikharulidze *(vault)*	66.800	9.60	76.400
6. Zinke *(bars)*	66.375	9.95	76.325
7. Dronova *(beam)*	66.625	9.50	76.125
8. Goreac *(floor)*	66.225	9.70	75.925
9. Schmeisser *(vault)*	66.175	9.35	75.525
10. Medveczky *(floor)*	65.975	9.50	75.475

Finals on the Apparatus

Competition III: October 27th

Vault

Vault finals gave Olga Korbut her only gold medal in apparatus finals. For her two vaults, she scored 9.85. Her first vault was full turn onto the horse with handspring off; her second was full turn onto the horse with full turn off. When she received her gold medal, it was a heart-warming moment for those of us who had been pulling for her during the competition.

Ludmilla Turischeva fell forward landing her Tsukahara tuck vault and scored only 9.50 for the average of her two vaults. Her other vault was handspring onto the horse with full turn off. She won the silver medal, however, because her vaults in compulsory and optionals team competition had given her the highest entering average.

Bozena Perdylukova won the only medal for Czechoslovakia, a bronze medal with a 9.60 average for her Tsukahara pike and her handspring full turn vaults.

Of the other finalists, Alina Goreac performed a Tsukahara pike and a half-on, half-off; then, Angelika Hellmann did handspring full turn followed by half-on, half-off. Rusudan Sikharulidze twice attempted the Yamashita full twist with which Karin Janz had won the gold medal in Munich, but she fell each time. It is interesting that at Varna, the Tsukahara was first performed by

A more proudly-standing Olga takes her place among vault finalists.

women in major competition, at least by the leading gymnasts. (Nelli Kim will win the vaulting gold medal in Montreal with a Tsukahara tuck full twist.)

The standings and scores for vault finals were as follows:

	Entering Avg.	Final	Total
1. Olga Korbut	9.600	9.850	19.450
2. Ludmilla Turischeva	9.700	9.500	19.200
3. Bozena Perdylukova	9.475	9.600	19.075
4. Alina Goreac	9.475	9.550	19.025
5. Angelika Hellmann	9.450	9.400	18.850
6. Rusudan Sikharulidze	9.450	8.450	17.900

Uneven Bars

After bars finals, spectators had the unusual sight of the relatively unknown Annelore Zinke standing on the top step of the victory pedestal to receive her gold medal, with Olga Korbut and Ludmilla Turischeva in second and third positions. Zinke received 9.90 for her "Korbut look-alike" routine, which was described in fourth rotation of the individual all-around competition. Although the emergence of Zinke as a new star in the gymnastics firmament was an exciting development, this result upset Korbut. In the Russian edition of her autobiography, she said:

> About Varna—enough. I would still like to say how unjust it was that they gave 'my' gold medal to Zinke, who in ten attempts performed the back flip worse and did not ask permission (to use it)." She also reflected, "why not organize an international center of author's rights concerning gymnastic elements? If you invent it, you use it—it's yours, nobody else's." She apologized for any tactlessness toward Zinke and the judges who gave her the gold medal, but then said, "The devil take it! That's the way it seems to me!"[9]

The standings and scores for bars finals were as follows:

	Entering Avg.	Final	Total
1. Annelore Zinke	9.750	9.900	19.650
2. Olga Korbut	9.775	9.800	19.575
3. Ludmilla Turischeva	9.700	9.800	19.500
4. Angelika Hellmann	9.650	9.700	19.850
5. Richarda Schmeisser	9.600	9.650	19.250
6. Krisztina Medveczky	9.550	9.500	19.050

Balance Beam

Beam gave Nelli Kim an opportunity to come back into the competition. This apparatus was another instance where it seemed Olga Korbut beat her head against a wall. She was first up and scored 9.80; later on, Turischeva, who was last up, scored 9.85. Olga's second place finish seemed unjust to spectators. Actually, Turischeva had such a lead going into finals that Korbut would have needed a 10.00 just to tie her. These two gymnasts were far ahead of other beam competitors in final scores, but Nelli Kim achieved an electrifying 9.75 for her routine. With this result, we knew a great gymnast had arrived. Her routine was as follows:

> Nelli ran diagonally along one side of the beam, jumped off the beat board into handstand about a third of the way from the end of the beam she was facing. She continued in walkover to stand, took a small step to the end and made a half turn to her right. She danced along the beam, performed a split leap as she went past the middle and danced forward to near the other end. She squatted down and made a full turn to her right on her left foot, while extending her right leg horizontally as she made her turn. She stood, bent her left knee and let her right leg plunge down beside the beam. She sat on the beam, brought her legs together in front of her, pointing vertically upward in vee-sit, kicked her legs a few times, then

dropped her legs onto the beam and prepared for her valdez: her left knee was bent with her foot on the beam, her right leg was extended ahead, her left arm was on the beam behind her and her right arm was gesturing above her. She pushed off with her left foot to pass through handstand and continue in walkover to stand. Upon completion of her valdez, she was at the middle of the beam. She paused briefly and then performed a back walkover to stand near the end of the beam. She stepped forward, made a half turn to her left, stepped towards the end of the beam again, made a half turn to her right and stepped forward further onto the beam, making high kicks first with her right leg, then her left. All this was in preparation for her upcoming element: after a brief pause to stand and get ready, she executed a salto backward tucked. She landed it squarely and surely and immediately stood up straight with her arms thrust down at her side. She stepped forward, kicked her right leg up high and came down on it with her right foot on the beam, her right knee bent at a right angle, her left knee bent and resting on the beam, her left shin behind her. She gestured with her arms, stood, advanced a step to the end and made a half turn to her left on her left foot. She stepped forward and made a full turn to her right on her right foot. She danced to the other end with a chassé, made a half turn to her right on her right foot, stepped forward and made a high tuck jump. She stepped further ahead, paused and performed a back handspring, paused and performed a back straddle down and lie back into supine position on the beam. She sat up, put her left hand on the beam, made a half turn to the left on her left

Olga with coach Polina Astakhova.

Another study of Olga and Astakhova.

hand and her right foot with her left leg hanging down and stood, put her left foot on the beam and made a half turn to her left on her left foot. She danced forward with a little hop and continued to the end, kicked her right leg up high, swung it back to place her toes on the beam behind her and made a half turn to her right on both feet. She took a step forward, paused, then ran forward and performed a high split leap. She continued to the end, made a half turn to her right, danced a few steps forward and prepared for her dismount: she performed a back handspring to place her feet right at the end of the beam and punched off into a salto backward stretched with full twist to land.

Nelli exhibited the same sureness of execution as Dronova. Her routine contained more difficulty, however, so she scored higher in finals. She and Dronova both performed split leaps with 180° leg separation.

The standings and scores for beam finals were as follows:

	Entering Avg.	Finals	Total
1. Ludmilla Turischeva	9.875	9.850	19.725
2. Olga Korbut	9.725	9.800	19.575
3. Nelli Kim	9.450	9.750	19.200
4. Nina Dronova	9.500	9.600	19.100
5. Alina Goreac	9.350	9.550	18.900
6. Angelika Hellmann	9.525	9.100	18.625

It is interesting to note Nelli Kim's inclusion of the salto backward tucked that Olga Korbut so sensationally introduced to the world in the 1972 Olympics. There, on the advice of the top people in the Soviet gymnastic community, it was placed at the end of her routine, just before her dismount. The purpose of this placement was to give Olga an opportunity for a cover-up. If she lost balance on landing her salto, she could immediately jump forward into her dismount off to the side and so neutralize the possibility of falling. When Nelli Kim's coach, Vladimir Baidin, decided she should include that element in her exercise, he resolved that it should be in the middle of her routine as an expression of their confidence that she could do it safely. As it turned out, in this competition, both gymnasts performed the back tuck in the middle of their routines.

The only other gymnast to perform the back tuck in Varna was the American, Joan Moore Rice, about whom we spoke in the section on team competition. Her beam routine contained other elements in use at that time but deserves special mention for this particular distinction. She had scored 9.45 on beam in the individual all-around and had a total score there of 37.90. She would have placed at least eleventh all-around had she been more fairly scored in team competition. This four-time U.S. national champion and member of U.S. teams in Ljubljana, Munich, and Varna deserves to be better known.

Olga and Ludmilla

Floor Exercise

In floor exercise, Ludmilla Turischeva treated us to a repetition of the wild and crazy routine she had performed in team optionals. She scored 9.90. Olga Korbut, Sikharulidze, and Saadi all scored 9.80; Dronova scored 9.70 and Hellmann, 9.60. It should be noted that although Korbut and Turischeva were leaders and medalists in all four apparatus finals, Angelika Hellmann was the only other gymnast also to perform in all four. Floor exercise finals were really a treat for the spectators, who saw the five splendid Soviet routines and that of the charming Angelika Hellmann.

It is now appropriate to describe the floor exercise of Joan Moore Rice, the American gymnast who could have been the number six finalist if she had not been the victim of judging intrigue.

Her exercise was set to the music of "Lady of Spain." It began with a standing front aerial walkover near one corner. She danced toward the center of the floor on one diagonal, turned left on the cross diagonal and proceeded toward the corner on that diagonal. She performed a double turn, a split leap with half turn and an immediate back walkover. She made a half turn to her right out of her walkover and entered the corner leaning forward to put her right knee on the floor in a momentary pose and made another half turn to her right as she stood to face along the diagonal for her first pass: a round-off, flic-flac, whip-back, flic-flac into a salto backward stretched with full twist. She danced out of her corner along the same diagonal and entered a semi-circle to her left. She performed a split leap with rear leg bent. In the corner to her left she executed a series of turns down on one knee, similar to the one she had done before her first pass, and prepared for her second pass. a front handspring into a salto forward stretched. She danced into the corner, turned and performed some deep body waves with her legs crossed. She danced out of her corner, performed an aerial walkover forward and, as she neared the center of the floor, a full turn on her left foot with her right leg elevated horizontally. In the center, she performed a series of elements including a scissors kick with her legs up in front of her, a gainer back handspring and turns and poses. She turned toward the corner from which she had begun her first pass and performed a front handspring with bending and stretching of the legs (mounter) and a front handspring down to her knees. She posed, made a half turn as she stood and then a full and a half turn to face the nearby corner. She did not enter that corner, however, but posed and turned to her left to make a deep, sweeping semi-circle around to another corner with a side leap and a tour jeté *(Figure 84)*. As she approached the corner, she turned and without pausing began her third pass: a round-off, two flic-flacs and a salto backward stretched stepout. She danced forward and did a forward roll into her final pose, sitting on the floor with her legs tucked under her, her right arm diagonally behind her with her hand on the floor and her left arm extended vertically upward.

Figure 84

The standings and scores for floor exercise finals were as follows:

	Entering Avg.	Final	Total
1. Ludmilla Turischeva	9.875	9.900	19.775
2. Olga Korbut	9.800	9.800	19.600
3. Rusudan Sikharulidze	9.750	9.800	19.550
3. Elvira Saadi	9.750	9.800	19.550
5. Nina Dronova	9.575	9.575	19.275
6. Angelika Hellmann	9.600	9.600	19.200

The award ceremony in finals in floor exercise was followed by a ceremony in which special awards were given to certain gymnasts for some outstanding contribution. They were given to both men and women. Those for the women were:

1. To Ludmilla Turischeva for becoming world champion a second time. She also won two gold medals in finals.
2. To Olga Korbut for her vault gold medal.
3. To Annelore Zinke for the most difficulty.
4. To Nadia Chatarova of Bulgaria for being the youngest competitor. Born the second of July 1960, she was 14 years old. She was not quite 5 feet tall and weighed 81 pounds. She went on to participate in the 1976 Olympics, where she placed 47th.

Rusudan Sikharulidze and Nina Dronova did not make the Soviet team in Montreal but were replaced by Svetlana Grozdova and Lydia Gorbick, who were the reserves in Varna. At the last minute, as we shall see, Gorbick was replaced by Maria Filatova. So, four members of this wonderful Soviet team went on to Montreal, three of whom—Korbut, Turischeva, and Saadi—had been together since Munich in 1972.

Ludmilla: number one for the last time.

References

[1] *The Columbia Encyclopedia,* 1963.

[2] S. Popov and A. Srebnitsky, *Nelli Kim,* (Moscow: Physical Culture and Sport, 1979.)

[3] Muriel Grossfeld, "1974 World Championships," *Gymnasts of America,* Dec. 1974: 23–39.

[4] Minot Simons II, "A Scandal in Bulgaria," *WomenSports,* Feb. 1975: 34–50.

[5] Muriel Grossfeld, "Outrage in Varna," *The Olympian,* Jul./Aug. 1975: 5–14.

[6] *World of Gymnastics,* 1982, Vol. 4, No. 1: 37

[7]Valentina Nikkiforova, "The Stars Fade Early," *Echo of the Planet*, (Moscow, 8 Mar. 1990), 46–47.

[8]*British Amateur Gymnastics Association Awards for Gymnastics,* The Sunday Times, No. 7, Summer 1974.

[9]Olga Korbut, *Zhila Buila Dyevochka* . . . (Moscow: Molodaya Gvardiya, 1988), 152–153.

Descriptions of the routines of most gymnasts are taken from video tapes made from films taken by Frank Endo and Fred Turoff. The description of Joan Moore Rice's floor exercise is taken from a video which she supplied.

Olga Korbut

Ludmilla Ivanovna Turischeva

Ludmilla Turischeva with daughter Tanya and husband Valery Borzov, 1994

1952 Born, October 7, in Groznyy, Russia.

1963 Began gymnastics, age 11. Coach: Vladislav Rastorotsky.

1967 Spartakiade, Moscow, July (USSR National Championships): 5th, all-around (age 15).

1967 USSR Cup, November, 1st, all-around.

1968 Olympics, Mexico, October: 24th, all-around.

1969 USSR National Championships, Rostov, October: 3rd, all-around.

1969 European Championship, Landskrona, Sweden, May: 3rd, all-around (tie–Zuchold); 4th, vault; 3rd, bars; 4th, beam; 3rd, floor.

1970 World Championships, Ljubljana, Slovenia, October: 1st, all-around; 3rd, vault (tie–Burda); 2nd, bars; 1st, floor.

1971 Spartakiade, Moscow, July (USSR National Championships): 4th, all-around (tie–Korbut).

1971 European Championship, Minsk, Belarus, October: 1st, all-around, (tie–Lazakovich); 1st, vault; 2nd, bars, beam; 1st, floor.
1972 USSR National Championships, Kiev, April: 1st, all-around.
1972 USSR Cup , Minsk, July (Olympic selection trials): 2nd, all-around; 1st, vault, bars.
1972 Olympics, Munich, August: 1st, all-around; 3rd, vault; 4th, bars; 5th, beam; 2nd, floor.
1972 Turischeva and Rastorotsky families moved to Rostov and new gym.
1973 European Championship, London, November: 1st, all-around; 2nd, vault; 1st, bars, beam, floor.
1974 USSR National Championships: 1st, all-around.
1974 World Championships, Varna, Bulgaria, October: 1st, all-around; 2nd, vault; 3rd, bars; 1st, beam, floor.
1974 Elected to Central Committee of the Young Communist League.
1974 Chunichi Cup, November. Went to Japan but scratched because of injury.
1974 Graduated from Rostov Teacher's College.
1975 European Championship, Skien, Norway, May: 4th, all-around (tie–Schmeisser); 3rd, floor.
1975 Spartakiade, Moscow, July (USSR National Championships): 3rd, all-around.
1975 First World Cup, London, October: 1st, all-around; 1st, vault, bars, beam, floor.
1976 Olympics, Montreal, July: 3rd, all-around; 2nd, vault (tie–Dombeck, GDR); 4th, beam; 2nd, floor.
1976 Awarded the Order of Lenin.
1977 December, married Valery Borzov, Olympic 100 meter and 200 meter champion in Munich.
1978 Joined the Communist Party.
1978 October 30, daughter Tanya born.
1979 Defended her dissertation in postgraduate studies at Rostov College of Education. Subject: "A study of the emotional state of qualified female gymnasts."
1991 Left the Communist Party.

> One day a man I did not know came into our phys ed class. This was in 1963 when I was in fourth grade. He attentively noticed how we performed simple exercises and wrote something in his notebook. Then he proposed to several girls—of which I was one—that we seriously take up gymnastics.[1]

This is the story of how Ludmilla Turischeva became involved in gymnastics. The man she did not know was, of course, Vladislav Rastorotsky, the coach she would have throughout her career.

Soviet chroniclers of the time like to point out in rather long-winded fashion that what Rastorotsky noticed was not a physical talent for performing certain exercises but her character. This deduction follows the Soviet line of always admiring strong character. Whether a coach could determine character just from watching an eleven-year-old perform simple exercises is open to question. Perhaps he can. Nevertheless, Ludmilla's character, which in fact was one of her strong points, if not her strongest, quickly became apparent.

"Eight years ago, (1965), she did not stand out from the other girls who had come to the children's sport school, except perhaps only for her persistence, industriousness, and absolute conscientiousness. She achieved something that no one else had ever been able to do—after two years of training in gymnastics, she was taken on the national team."[2]

"I've had pupils more capable than Ludmilla," Rastorotsky recalls , "but Ludmilla has always stood out for her industriousness. I've never had to repeat anything to her. Naturally, just like everyone else, she can make mistakes. But when she understands her error, she strives hard never to repeat it. Perhaps, you can say that she has always been a girl with a very small number of errors."[3]

That she was a hard worker was universally recognized. Larissa Latynina tells us about the relationship between coach and gymnast:

"Most of the time it is . . . harmonious between Ludmilla and Rastorotsky. These two reticent persons understand each other amazingly well. If you ever happen to see them at one of their training sessions, you'll notice they hardly speak a word. Vladislav goes up to Ludmilla, explains a point, demonstrates it and steps aside. She practices independently. He stands watching her thoughtfully. Perhaps he is wondering if the move couldn't be done some other way and worked into the sequence more successfully. He notices Ludmilla doing something wrong. He goes up to her, corrects her again, watches silently from a distance. And heaven help her if she doesn't take it seriously. Angry and upset, he walks out of the gym."[4]

Latynina describes one incident when things did not go smoothly:

> Ludmilla was calmly going through her program under the critical eye of her coach. Now and again he showed dissatisfaction with the way she executed her sequences. The reproaches came thick and fast.
>
> "Are you sick of training? Go and have a rest then! Just one thing though. Who's going to perform on the day? Me or you?"
>
> I caught a hurt look on Ludmilla's face. After all to reproach her for being slack is simply a sin. You won't find a more industrious gymnast in training. But I also know that Turischeva's training with Rastorotsky gives her a vast reserve of strength and molds such qualities as endurance and self-control into her character.
>
> Rastorotsky is a demanding coach, a perfectionist. He considers that nothing less than victory is good enough. However, this policy has not

always paid off in the past and he has often suffered for it.[5] (An example of this will be described in the biography on Natasha Shaposhnikova in Volume 2.)

Ludmilla with her coach, Vladislav Rastorotsky

Ludmilla Ivanovna Turischeva was born on October 7, 1952, in the town of Groznyy, which is in the southern part of Russia in the region of Chechen-Ingush. The southern boundary of this region borders on Georgia and Azerbaijan. To the east is the Caspian Sea; to the west are the Caucasus mountains. Rastorotsky was then gymnastics coach at a children's sport school in Groznyy. She and her family moved to Rostov after the Munich Olympics when Rastorotsky moved there with his family and established his own gymnastics school. Rostov is about 250 miles northwest of Groznyy, at the mouth of the Don River, where it empties into the Sea of Azov and thence to the Black Sea. Nevertheless, the association with Groznyy remained with her because "groznyy" is a Russian adjective meaning "terrible, formidable, stern, ferocious." Tsar Ivan the Terrible was known as "Ivan Groznyy." Ludmilla was known as "the groznyy girl from Groznyy." This, of course, is a play on words. "The pun raised a smile among those who knew her, for she was a shy little girl with white ribbons in her hair."[3] Personally, I have met Ludmilla on several occasions and would say that "groznyy" describes her only in the sense of being a hard worker in training and a fighter in competition. In her personal relationships, she is anything but "groznyy."

In 1967, when she was 15, Ludmilla participated in the Spartakiade, the all-inclusive competition in all sports that takes place in Moscow in the summertime during the year before an Olympics. In her last event, floor exercise, the timer forgot to let Ludmilla know when there were only ten seconds to go. Consequently, she went a second or two over. As expected, Rastorotsky protested. His proposal to the judges, which was accepted, was: "We'll do the whole exercise over again right now!" So she did and gained great respect from the judges, correspondents and spectators who saw her pull herself together for an immediate second attempt.[6]

In this her debut among the adult group of gymnasts, "her exercises were very intricate, and all they lacked was precision and polish. As a result, the debutante remained below the top. And five months later Turischeva won the USSR Cup, one of the most cherished sports trophies in Soviet gymnastics. That is how her path to grand victories started."[7]

Thereafter she qualified for the Mexico Olympics and had her first experience in a major international competition. She had a break on balance beam but, along with Lyubov Burda, the other debutante, did her part in the Soviet team's winning the gold medal. There are no losers on a winning team.

What were the tactics that Ludmilla and Rastorotsky employed in her rise to the top and in staying up there? Simply speaking, their plan was to learn the new vaults as they were invented and as she was ready to learn them, to create and learn an entirely new floor exercise for each major competition, but only to refine and gradually improve her routines on uneven bars and balance beam. Readers of the competitions will note the similarity of her routines on these apparatuses in all her competitions from Mexico to Montreal.

Floor exercise was her favorite. Because of her love for it and for her ability to dance and to express herself, and because of the evident future she had as a leading gymnast on the Soviet team, she had the benefit of the best choreography available. Having a new floor exercise to work up almost every year must have gone a long way in overcoming the monotony of doing virtually the same exercise on bars and beam for nearly ten years.

As we know, she was selected for the European Championship in 1969 in Landskrona, Sweden. A mistake on bars dropped her to third place in the all-around, behind Karin Janz of East Germany and her teammate Olga Karasyova. Nevertheless, the experience gained made her stronger. She was among the leaders in the trials for the 1970 World Championships in Ljubljana, Yugoslavia (Slovenia) and there became World Champion for the first time.

In 1971, she and her teammate, Tamara Lazakovich, won the European Championship in Minsk; Ludmilla was considered the favorite by the sporting press to win the upcoming Olympics in Munich. On the way, however, she was upset by Olga Korbut in the 1972 USSR Cup, also held in Minsk, that served as an elimination tournament to select the Munich team. Olga Korbut placed first and Ludmilla, second. The story of this closely fought match is told in Olga Korbut's biography.

The much-coveted title of all-around Olympic champion was hers at Munich, although Olga had won the hearts of all who were watching. Olga, in fact, won two gold medals in the apparatus finals, while Ludmilla did not win any. Olga made up for her heart-breaking loss in the all-around with her golds in finals, but Ludmilla won the title she really wanted.

She went on to win a succession of first places: her second European Championship, this time in 1973 in London; the 1974 Soviet National Championships and the 1974 USSR Cup; and her second World Championships, this time in 1974 in Varna, Bulgaria. For the first time, she was named first of the top ten athletes in the Soviet Union for her performances in 1974.

"Last year was the happiest and most successful of my life," Ludmilla Turischeva of Rostov-on-Don, world overall gymnastics champion, who headed the top ten Soviet athletes of the year in the annual sportswriters poll, told our reporter. "I took first place in all the competitions I entered—the national championships, the USSR Cup and the world championships at which I won the overall title for the second time. I want to pay tribute once again to my coach Vladislav Rastorotsky. At the 17th Congress of the Young Communist League of the USSR, I was accorded the high honor or being elected a member of the YCL Central Committee. (More on this aspect of Ludmilla's life later.)

"My ambition is to enter a postgraduate course this year. I have already begun to prepare for it by working in a psychology of sports laboratory in Rostov. I hope to make a good showing in the European championships and can't wait to compete in the USSR National Games, the main competition of the year."[8]

Two circumstances were to pour cold water on these hopes for 1975, however. The first was a back injury she suffered before the Chunichi Cup in Japan, shortly after the Varna World Championships. This injury prevented her from competing in the Chunichi Cup and severely reduced the amount of time she would have to train for the European Championship. The second was the arrival upon the world scene of Nadia Comaneci. These circumstances will, of course, be major stories in Volume II.

For now, we should discuss Ludmilla's activities in the Young Communist League.

Young people in the Soviet Union were all considered members of the Young Communist League, whether they wanted to be or not. Later, a very small percentage of these people were allowed to join the Communist Party itself. So, all members of Soviet gymnastic teams were "Comsomolits," i.e., members of the Comsomol or Young Communist League. After her victory in the 1974 World Championships, she was elected (read "appointed") to the Central Committee of the Young Communist League. In 1976, after the Montreal Olympics, she was awarded the highest decoration of her country—

the Order of Lenin. In 1978, she joined the Communist Party itself. In 1991, as she relates below, she left it.

There would have been three reasons for Ludmilla to join the Communist Party. First, she believed in the ideology of communism and wanted to work through it for the benefit of the people of the Soviet Union. Second, she wanted to get ahead. In the communist system, you have to be a member of the party to get a top job. Third, both of these reasons together.

With Ludmilla, her reasons were both. Reading a speech she made to the central committee of the Comsomol, one gets the impression she believed in the ideology. Considering that her life was mainly confined to the gymnasium and that she received favored treatment, i.e., money, food, head-of-the-line privileges, her belief in the ideals of the party did not suffer from daily contact with the frustration and austerity that afflicted the lives of ordinary citizens. In addition, she was ambitious and realized the advantages of membership.

During my coverage of several world championships, I became a good friend of the TASS correspondent who covered gymnastics, Valentina Nikiforova. In 1985, at the Montreal World Championships, I asked her as we walked along a street once if she was a member of the Communist Party. She looked at me, surprised perhaps, that I should have asked a question the answer to which should have been obvious, and said, "Minot, if I were not a member of the communist party, I would not be here."

One cannot, therefore, blame Ludmilla. Since she believed in what she was doing, she was not living a lie. Furthermore, she was living a good life. She was held up in the press as a good example of the Soviet woman.

She made a major speech to the members of the Comsomol Central Committee in November 1976. In it she recalled "the order of the Lenin Comsomol, heard at the fifth plenum of the Central Committee of the Young Communist League (1975) which expressed confidence that in the upcoming Olympics, our Olympians will demonstrate the best qualities of Soviet patriots, will show courage, self-confidence, stoicism and will give the motherland in the year of the 25th Congress of the Communist Party of the Soviet Union a new, clear Olympic victory."

She continued, "And today, it gives me special joy to report to the Central Committee of the Comsomol in the name of all Soviet Olympians: the order of the Lenin Comsomol was fulfilled." She went on to enumerate all the medals won.

Later she said: "Not long ago in the Kremlin, I was awarded the highest decoration of the country—the order of Lenin. In those unforgettable minutes, I felt with special strength the paternal care of our party for Soviet youth, Soviet sportsmen—pupils of the Young Communist League. This highest award for our modest work obliged me to think not only about victories and records, meters and seconds, but to bear responsibility for the education of Soviet youth and to generate in them a conscientious attitude to their studies and to socially useful work."[9]

She concluded by urging her listeners to work for the success of the 1980 Moscow Olympics. It is a pity that such idealism and such energy as Ludmilla put into her work was directed toward an ideology that did not work.

In an addendum to an interview conducted by Lilya Kovalyova (see below), she summarized her relationship with the Communist Party.

> A large part of my youth was spent during a time when communist ideology in the USSR was very strong. People believed in communism because for the many people in the Soviet Union, there was no alternative. It was like a tale, like a dream. And in 1978 I joined the ranks of the Communist Party even though I did not fully understand my role in it. When the truth about communism was revealed, it was a big disappointment for me, a disillusionment. I left the party in 1991. All this was a devastating blow to my spirit. You know, in the theory itself of communism there were in my opinion, grains of hope like those in the bright beginning of Christianity. But unfortunately, the theory and practice of communism were different. In general, it is no longer of any interest to talk about this subject.

Perhaps the only lasting benefit of her membership in the Comsomol was that in it she met the man she would marry. In an interview in 1980, she described how they met.

> In 1972 I was a member of the Comsomol Central Committee. There was another sportsman there, named Valeri Borzov, also an Olympic champion, having in the previous Olympics in Munich won the 100m and 200m. What a strange coincidence—she says and not only smiles but her eyes start sparkling, too—we got to like each other. First him, then me.
>
> **When did you get married?**
>
> In December 1977. On October 30, 1978, our daughter Tanya was born.
>
> **Do you want her to be a gymnast or perhaps a runner?**
>
> We want her only not to miss sports in her life. We shall not choose for her. Neither force her. She will do what she likes.[10]

More recently, she was interviewed in October 1993 by Lilya Kovalyova of Novosti Press. We conclude this biography with Kovalyova's article, *Ludmilla Turischeva: believing in herself.*

She has won every possible sporting title and was a member of the national team almost ten years—a period that for other gymnasts of her time seemed beyond one's strength. God did not deprive her either of beauty, character or charm.

Now Turischeva works in Kiev as senior coach of artistic gymnastics, acrobatics and rhythmic gymnastics of the Ukrainian Sports Club "Dynamo" and bears the responsibility of president of the Ukrainian gymnastics federation. As she did formerly in her sporting career, she carries out her work wholeheartedly and with improbable patience. Ludmilla says she inherited her purposefulness and sense of obligation from her father.

Do you consider your present work your second career after your gymnastics career? I asked Turischeva.

It is my responsibility, not a career. You know, I am only called the senior coach; in reality, I am an administrator. But I think that in this work I can be of use for I know all the fine points and nuances of big-time sports, in particular gymnastics. Besides I need something to do and these responsibilities are not a burden on me, although we experience certain difficulties, as does everyone in our country now. There's a lot of work to be done: to obtain apparatus for the gym and clothes for the gymnasts, to organize competitions, to bring about trips for the athletes around the country and abroad. In addition, I have been a member of the F.I.G. Women's Technical Committee for twelve years. That also demands a lot of effort and attention.

Where are you living now?

For more than sixteen years, in fact ever since I got married, I have been living in Kiev, in the center of town. We have a small but cozy apartment. We do not have a villa outside of town, but if we want to relax, we get into the car and drive out into the country.

Tell me about your marriage.

I consider my marriage with Valery Borzov to be successful. He is now Ukrainian minister for youth activities and sports and president of the country's national Olympic committee. Valery and I met after the 1976 Montreal Olympics and I am happy that fate sent me such a companion for my life.

Has your career affected your family life?

Valery and I were born into and grew up in sport. Therefore, we are able to understand each other and our enthusiasm for the work. We often discuss things but we don't argue. Now, if we were just to sit at home, perhaps there would arise some prickly moments, for we both have strong personalities. I say that without false modesty. We often go on business trips and are up to our neck in work. Besides, it is probably significant also that we married as adults and clearly understood family responsibilities, family life. We do not reproach each other if we are held up at work or on a trip. Most importantly, we strive for the same thing—to justify the responsibilities which people placed upon us.

I know you have a daughter. Please tell us about her.

Tanyusha was born a year after our marriage. She is now 15. She is studying at a mathematics lycée. She tried both artistic and rhythmic gymnastics, but when she was nine, she chose athletics. She loves to run short distances. She is the champion of Kiev both last year and this year in her age group for the hundred meter dash. We try not to protect our daughter unnecessarily. We give her the opportunity to make mistakes and then look into and correct her mistakes. We discuss family questions with her, especially questions of our way of life. She has a good taste for design. We have full mutual understanding with her and I consider myself a happy mother.

What was the most unhappy moment in your life?

Previously, I had thought it was the closing day of my last Olympics. Now I realize that the biggest grief in life is the loss of those people you are closest to. The death of my mother, who died young in 1981, is for me an irreplaceable loss. Twelve years have passed since that sad day, but she is still before my eyes. All my life I felt the ardent support of my mother. I am grateful to her in that whether in difficult moments in gymnastics or in life, she was my chief spiritual support. She had an unusually sensitive character. She never said a superfluous word, but she did everything that was necessary. She was able to protect me from all complications and anxieties before all crucial competitions. She made every effort that everything should go well. I consider it was because of her that I achieved so much. Several years ago Valery's father died. For me it was also a great blow because ever since we first met we hard a warm relationship together.

And the happiest moment of your life?

In sport, it was when I became all around gymnastics champion in the 1972 Munich Olympic Games. Generally speaking, it is very pleasant to stand on the top step of the victory pedestal. In life, my moments of happiness were my marriage and the birth of my daughter.

What do you imagine will be the future of gymnastics?

Everything in the world moves in spirals. Gymnastics is no exception. You cannot arrest its complexity. It will become more and more perfected and interesting for the spectators. Gymnastics of the future will consist of complexity, grace and maturity.

Do you participate in any sport now? Since your floor exercises were so full of dance, do you dance?

Right now, most of my dancing is around the stove. But periodically, though not systematically, I do a morning workout.[11]

References

[1]Valentin Lyashenko, "Leader," *Nedelya* (weekly), 1975, 46 : 14.

[2]Natalya Kolesnikova and Mikhail Esterlis, "Olympic Stars," *Soviet Woman,* 1973: 1: 16.

[3]Natalya Kolesnikova, "I Want to Repeat Everything," *Soviet Woman,* 1974: 8: 36–37.

[4]*Sport in the USSR,* 1971: No. 3.

[5]Larissa Latynina, "The Authority of a Champion," *Soviet Union,* 1974: 1: 54–55.

[6]Stanislav Tokarev, "Lessons of an Enviable Destiny," *Sovietsky Sport,* 25 Sept.1976.

[7]Lilya Kovalyova, "Ludmilla Turischeva: Leader of Soviet Gymnastics," Novosti Press Agency, APN 402K619/K.

[8]*Sport in the USSR,* 1975: No. 2.

[9]Ludmilla Turischeva, "We the Members of the Comsomol," *Sovietsky Sport,* 27 Nov. 1976.

[10]Istvan Gyulai, "Turischeva Today," *World Gymnastics,* Vol. 2, No. 4, 1980: 37-38.

[11]Lilya Kovalyova, "Ludmilla Turischeva: Believing in Herself," article written for this book, Nov. 1993.

Shown are the domes of St. Basil's Cathedral located in Red Square, Moscow. The Cathedral was erected in the mid-16th century to commemorate the victories that the troops of Ivan IV (the Terrible—Ivan Groznyy) won in the field against the khanates of Kazan and Astrakhan.

Olga Valentinovna Korbut

The Mystery and the Mastery

1955 Born, May 16, in Grodno, Belarus.
1964 Enrolled in children's gymnastics school, age 9.
1966 Joined gymnastics school of Renald Knysh who became her coach.
1967 Participated in Junior Championships of the then Byelo Russian Republic, later Belarus.
1968 Participated in Spartakiade for school children. 1st, vault, bars, beam.
1969 USSR National Championships, Rostov, October, age 14: 5th, all-around; selected for national team.
1970 USSR National Championships, Minsk, May: 1st, vault.
1971 Spartakiade, Moscow, July (USSR National Championships): 4th, all-around (tie–Turischeva).
1972 USSR National Championships, Kiev, April: 3rd, all-around.
1972 Riga Cup, Riga, Latvia, April: 1st, all-around.
1972 June, graduated from secondary school in Grodno; after Munich Olympics, entered Teacher Training College.
1972 USSR Cup, Minsk, July (Olympic selection trials): 1st, all-around.
1972 Olympics, Munich, August 27 to 31: 7th, all-around; 1st, beam, floor; 2nd, bars (tie–Zuchold); 5th, vault.
1972 Voted Associated Press Female Athlete of the Year.
1973 University Games, Moscow, August: 1st, all-around; 1st, bars, beam, floor.
1973 European Championship, London, October: 2nd, all-around.
1974 World Championships, Varna, Bulgaria, October: 2nd, all-around; 1st, vault; 2nd, bars, beam, floor.
1975 Spartakiade, Moscow, July (USSR National Championships): 1st , all-around (tie–Kim); 1st, beam (tie–Kim).
1975 World Cup, London, October: 2nd, all-around.
1976 Olympics, Montreal, July 18 to 22: 5th, all-around; 5th, bars; 2nd, beam.

Olga Korbut was the most romantic, the most famous and the best-loved person in the history of gymnastics. She stirred emotions as no one had before or has since. The desire to see her in person when she was performing became frantic; her appearance alone guaranteed a sell-out crowd.

Her story is a romance. When she became famous at Munich, journalists searched for words to describe her. They called her "pixie," "woodsprite," "elf," "the girl next door" (as opposed to a mysterious Russian); her gymnastic elements were said to "defy gravity." On television, they went so far as to say that her appearance at Munich was almost an accident, that she was only put in at the last minute. In so doing, they added to the unexpectedness of what people were witnessing.

The initial effect she created was that of stunning the spectators with moves never seen before: on the uneven bars, her back flip to recatch the high bar, and on beam, her back somersault. Then she conquered everyone's hearts and emotions with the appeal of her smile, the magic, the sauciness of her personality and yet also the complicated gymnastics of her floor exercise. After she first performed her optional exercises in team competitions, she became the toast of Munich. In fact, she almost *was* Munich. No event was more eagerly awaited that her return two days later for the all-around competition. Then, since she had the whole world in her little hand, and since perhaps millions of people were watching her second appearance and were wanting desperately for her to do well, disaster, when it stuck, struck everyone. We were all there when her foot rubbed the ground and upset the rhythm of her uneven bars routine; we agonized with her as she struggled through the rest of it; and we almost cried with her as she wept her bitter tears.

If any other Soviet gymnast had fallen from the apparatus, nobody would have cared. "That's life," we would have said. But with Olga, it was almost, "That's *our* life!" and we did care.

Consequently, when she came back in the apparatus finals and won her gold medals on beam and floor, we cheered all the more. It was as though we had won them ourselves, we wanted them so much for her.

Thus, with her we experienced the depths of her grief and then the heights of her joy. Our joy was all the greater because of her grief. With Olga, there was not only mastery of her gymnastics; there was also the mystery of how that little person could make everyone fall in love with her.

Part 1: The Mastery

In writing about Olga Korbut, it is necessary to dispel the notion that she was not a great gymnast. It has often been said that she owed her success to her charisma and not to her gymnastic ability. One highly placed American coach even went so far as to say in an important press conference that "Olga was not that great a gymnast." He based his assertion on the famous error just described on the uneven bars at Munich which cost her a high all-around standing. Both the statement by the coach and the concept of her charisma's being her primary asset ignore her long record of achievement.

This record began in the Soviet National Championships of October 1969 in Rostov. Fourteen-year-old Olga was too young, according to the rules governing Soviet gymnasts at the time, to participate in senior-level competition. The minimum age was sixteen. The national coach of the women's team, Larissa Latynina, decided, however, that Olga was capable of handling herself in adult competition and made an exception. Little Olga was, therefore, allowed to compete against the top gymnasts of her day for the title of Soviet national champion.

Her performance then had the same effect upon the Soviet people as it did in Munich three and a half years later. The reputation of her coach, Renald Knysh, as a bold innovator had preceded her and people were asking, "What does Renald Ivanovich have up his sleeve this time?" No amount of guesswork prepared the public, however, for what they saw when this little slip of a girl performed her back flip off the high bar to recatch it and her back somersault on the beam. They gasped when they saw the back flip but groaned when they saw the back somersault, wondering where all this would lead. What would happen to their lovely, artistic sport if what some people were referring to as "circus acts" were allowed to be performed?[1] Then, within the Soviet Union, as later after Munich in the gymnastic community at large, there were demands that such moves be banned. Renald Knysh stuck to his guns, however, and to his belief that, "gymnastics is acrobatics on the apparatus."[2] His tenacity, of course, was rewarded.

For Olga, the championships were significant not only because, through the daring innovations of her coach, she became immediately and widely known but also because in this her first appearance on what the Soviets called "the big podium," she placed fifth all-around.

"I might even have taken a prize," she said, meaning she could have placed first, second or third, "but what a pity—I fell from the bars."

"Were you scared performing such risky moves?" she was asked.

"At the beginning I was afraid," she replied. "I could not get the back salto on the beam. Now I'm not afraid. I'm not afraid at all."[1]

In those pre–Nadia days, girls of such a young age did not appear before the public in international competition. Olga, therefore, continued to make progress but at home, not out in the world.

Six months after the October 1969 national championships in Rostov, she competed in the 1970 national championships in Minsk in May. Although she did not place in the top six all-around, she won the gold medal in vault.

In November 1970, she was taken to Ljubljana, Yugoslavia, as a reserve on the Soviet team that was to participate in the World Championships. She helped set up the apparatus for the other gymnasts and she demonstrated her routines outside the competition before the judges. Her appearance was successful and she was highly praised. This praise went to her head, especially since she thought she should have been brought along as part of the team. For a time she became difficult and her teammates lost their affection for her.

1971 started off badly for Olga. She fell ill and missed her training for a long time. Nevertheless, in the 1971 Spartakiade—the Soviet summer games, held every four years in the year before the Olympics—Olga placed fourth, tying the gymnast who was to become her arch rival, Ludmilla Turischeva. Thus, she was moving up and at sixteen was consistently placed among the top gymnasts of her county.

Tamara Lazakovich, winner of the Spartakiade, and Ludmilla Turischeva, winner of the previous year's World Championships in Ljubljana, were the Soviet Union's two entries in the 1971 European Championship held in November in Minsk. There, as in Ljubljana, Olga was allowed to demonstrate her own gymnastics, outside the competition. This time, she performed not just before the judges, but before the public. Her time was coming.

Indeed it was: 1972 was to be her big year. After a series of smaller competitions with teams mostly from European countries, Olga participated in what was a crucial test for her: the 1972 USSR Cup, held June 29 to July 4 in Minsk. The USSR Cup is a principal competition in any year, but in 1972 it was to be the selection trials for the Munich Olympics. For gymnasts of this generation or age group, it was the make-or-break contest. No charisma counted here. The judges and Soviet officials wanted to determine whose gymnastics would stand up best under the extremely high-pressure conditions that would exist in the Munich Sport Hall. The competition was run according to procedures for the Olympic Games.

Ludmilla Turischeva won the first stage of the competition—the compulsory and optional programs. In the individual all-around competition, however, the order was suddenly reversed. In the all-around, the first two days' scores were averaged and counted as half the score, the other half being that obtained during the all-around. Ludmilla lost her balance on the beam and had to jump off. Olga then finished her own beam routine with her famous back somersault and took the lead, with 0.35 points advantage. Ludmilla made a desperate attempt to recover the lead and scored 9.8 in floor exercise, the highest mark awarded during the competition. It was not enough, however. She placed second; Olga Korbut placed first. In so doing, she won the USSR Cup, entered the Munich Olympic Olympics with the prestige of being number one on the Soviet team and proved herself to be the best gymnast in the Soviet Union.

Is this the sort of accomplishment that can be attributed only to charisma? Is this what a girl who "was not all that great a gymnast" can do? Hardly. Olga was technically as well as artistically one of the great gymnasts of her day.

One final note needs to be added to this discussion of Olga's gymnastic ability: it is her record in the 1974 World Championships in Varna, Bulgaria. This was an unhappy, frustrating time for Olga. No matter what she did, she was almost always scored a point lower than Ludmilla. Those of us who were there felt she was consistently underscored and that Ludmilla was receiving the benefit of any doubts simply because she was the Olympic champion. Nevertheless, Olga held her own. She placed second all-around, second on bars, beam, and floor exercise but won the gold medal on vault. Thus, her record in competition against the best in the world in 1974 was one gold and three silver medals for her, personally, and a gold medal for her contribution to the Soviet team victory. Olga proved once again her technical superiority as a gymnast in competition where serious-minded judges were not being swayed by emotions. In the remote Bulgarian town of Varna, there was not the same volume of enthusiasm for Olga as there had been in Munich.

Incidentally, in that championship, Olga dispelled another myth that had dogged her. It was that she could not twist. It was said that the extreme flexibility of her back that enabled her to perform certain of her elements prevented her from executing twists in floor exercise somersaults or in her vaults. In fact, the vault that won her the gold medal in Varna consisted of a full twist onto the horse and a handspring with full twist off.

It is important in recalling Olga's gymnastics to keep in mind the gymnastics of her day. In 1972, nobody was doing double-back somersaults in floor exercise or double-back somersault dismounts from bars or beam. The standard vault was the Yamashita, nowadays considered almost an elementary vault. It was a handspring onto the horse followed by a piking of the body in after-flight. Some gymnasts were performing handsprings onto the horse followed by half or full twists of the body off the horse; some gymnasts were performing half twists onto the horse with a half twist off. There were no back somersaults off the horse, however. These were introduced by Nelli Kim and Nadia Comaneci in the 1976 Montreal Olympics.

Olga was, perhaps, fortunate that she lived when she did. At 4 feet, 11 inches, and weighing only 82 pounds, she was of about the same height as the top gymnasts of ten and twenty years later. Could she have performed the gymnastics they were performing? It is quite possible, because she understood so well the learning requirements leading up to the performance of a difficult gymnastic element. In gymnastics, these are known as progressions, or progressive steps. That she did understand this science of gymnastic development is illustrated by an article she wrote about the 1981 Soviet National Championships where she was judging vault. Her article appeared in the October 1, 1981 issue of the newspaper, *Sovietsky Sport*,[3] and I quote it in full:

> There were many flagrant failures in the national championships. Coaches justified them by saying that a new Olympic cycle had just begun and that they are just smoothing out their modernized programs. They say they have all the time they need to perfect these programs. I do not accept such an explanation.
>
> I would like to look into the nature of these falls. At times they try to explain them using psychological reasons. In my opinion, this is only an attempt to cover up errors in work by means of the wisdom of science. That's not the reason. When Olga Bicherova completed her "Cuervo-360" vault, I was prepared to start clapping and only refrained because I was judging the competition on that apparatus. Really, Olga performed a record vault that none of the other women had mastered. The main thing is that she was ready for it.
>
> However, when Ira Bregina, who is just as young, brilliantly performed on the beam her stretched salto with a twist and then fell from her quite simple side aerial, that is difficult to excuse.
>
> Once I was the first to perform a back salto, tuck position on the beam. This innovative element even frightened some people. It was named after me. But they should have called it the "Knysh salto" and not the "Korbut salto" because coach Renald Ivanovich thought up the unbelievable number of exercises which brought us to that element which was unheard of in those times. That salto was only the result, the logical conclusion of a huge creative work, in which the birth of a new element became the last point.

> Sometimes people confuse the concept of a trick with that of stunting. In the word "trick" I do not hear a deprecating nuance. They often call a trick that which is the result of a long search by coach and athlete for new paths in sport. But stunting—that is an attempt to outshine, to dumbfound. As a rule, it results in failure. It is very bad when competitions of athletes are changed into a race between coaches to see who is the most daring. We don't need that kind of a race. As for the trick—long live the trick![3]

We will never know whether Olga would have been able to perform all the tricks that gymnasts who came along twenty years later could perform. The important point is that Olga's gymnastics was as advanced as that of any gymnast of her day and her execution was equally good.

Part II: The Mystery

For 99 per cent of the gymnasts who compete in Olympic competition, there is no mystery. They are very good, or they're brash, or they're shy and inhibited in interviews, or they're just average girls. In 1976, we watched Nadia Comaneci. We admired the perfection of her movements but wondered at the apparent absence of any emotional involvement. In 1984, we watched Mary Lou Retton. Again we admired her virtuosity and had no trouble appreciating that she was just a bouncy kid, laughing and enjoying herself enormously. Most gymnasts fall somewhere in between.

Not Olga Korbut. She is the one exception, the one girl who was both a gymnast of the highest caliber and a woman who defied comprehension. She was highly trained and muscular but also intensely feminine, almost aggressively feminine. She took advantage of her femininity. She behaved often with abandon because she knew she was Olga Korbut, that she could get away with things that the others could not and because she knew her country needed her as she was.

She was feminine because she had a woman's nature. She could cry and she did so openly. Perhaps, most importantly, she had a woman's intuition.

Olga Korbut was the consummate gymnastic artist. She intuitively understood what it takes to establish a personal rapport with the audience. "I can feel the mood of the people always," she explained once. "I know just when to smile. And when my eyes make contact with people in the audience, I try to make them feel as if I am going to present them with my soul."[4]

She was deeply affected by the public. "When I'm loosening up before going out to perform, I already sense the audience's attitude to me. If there's a real rapport, my success is assured; but if the spectators' faces look grim and indifferent, my spirits are immediately dampened. I love to perform to fans who aren't afraid of hurting their hands."[5]

Her rapport with the public not only came naturally to her but was encouraged by her coach, Renald Knysh, who said, "What I am interested in is how the spectators react to Olga and I try to get her to think in the same way."[6]

Not only did she understand how to establish a personal rapport with her audience, but she had an inner need to do so. In an interview in the Soviet newspaper *Komsomolskaya Pravda,* she said,

> I'm not interested at the thought of medals and titles. I don't particularly want them."
>
> **What do you want, then?**
>
> The affection of the public! That's what I fight for.[5]

To stay close to her public, to win their hearts, sometimes required a special sacrifice on her part. At one stop along the line during her first American tour, she reportedly was advised by her coach not to perform her back salto on beam because of an injured foot, but she did it anyway.

> They wait for me to do it and I do it no matter how much it hurts me.[7]

There was magic in Olga. One writer wrote:

> What the world needs every so often is something new, something spontaneous, even transcendent.
>
> She shed energy on anyone who saw her. Her wide-mouth smile was out of control most of the time, and it drew the kind of reaction that only a 6-month-old baby can usually manage. When Olga laughed, everyone laughed with her; when she wept, it turned out, she had plenty of company, too.
>
> She seemed to have wings, but at one point in one event (Munich), executing a simple glide kip she had done countless times before, she tripped badly. She was clearly out of the running and she went back to the bench and wept. The camera, already transfixed by her, caught every tear. From an earthly sprite, a durable human heroine emerged.[6]

The earthly heroine was human in another way: she could be very difficult. Knysh and Korbut are complete opposites. The coach is a modest, quiet man; Olga has a temper, is easily hurt and wants to do everything her own way. According to Knysh, relations with his pupil were not easy. Olga has a stubborn streak, and he has to keep convincing her that success only comes with a tremendous amount of hard work. Talent is not enough. When he talks about her obstinacy, however, Knysh is not complaining. He believes it is just such stubborn characters who become outstanding sports personalities.[8]

How difficult she could be and what a trial she was to her coach is revealed in the following excerpt from the Soviet magazine, Youth:

> "God, how she wore me out!" said Knysh. "If you only knew what she was like! I tell you she was difficult! And all in such a small person. It's hard to believe we didn't break up forever. There were a lot of such moments. She is hard as a rock. Convincing her took up three fourths of practice time. At times I would say, to hell with it, would leave the gym and think: 'This is it, I've had it. I'm pooped.' But the next day she would perform everything with such willingness and confidence that I would forget about the day before. . . . Then it would begin all over again."

On her part, Olga said:

> It's this way with me. If I think that something should be done a certain way and not differently, I'm going to do it the way I want to. There's nothing I can do about it. It's as if I had fallen into a cloud. If I don't do it my way, it's not going to work. I'll curse myself if it doesn't turn out the way I wanted, but the way Renald Ivanovich told me. . . . At such times I hate myself and promise myself that I'll have nothing more to do with the coach. Knysh proves a point, I scream against it, he proves it again, I run from the gym, and he's right again.[9]

Part of her make-up, of course, was a tremendous sense of humor. A reporter wrote:

> "It was comical to watch her at Earls Court (London) in 1973 on the occasion of the first Soviet visit, in the warm-up area out of sight of the public, having fun on the floor with the acrobats in the Soviet party. The two Vladimirs, as the two are known, were trying to teach her a trick and for some time they were not aware that she was having fun at their expense. When the 'penny dropped,' one of the Vladimirs picked Olga up and held her high above her head for all of two minutes, until she apologised. Her laughter could be heard ringing around that great barn of the warm-up area."[10]
>
> In the beginning of a workout there is some horseplay—always with 85 pound Olga in the middle. Two teammates swing her like a jump rope. She does a stag leap into another's arms, mocking the bravura of a classical ballet pas de deux. Then all the girls lose themselves in dodge ball.[6]

Olga's tears at Munich and her comeback the next day cannot account for the depth and intensity of her appeal. The answer lies with Olga herself, who has never ceased to be a lovable little urchin wiggling and tumbling her way into the hearts of others.[4]

Olga with President Nixon.

"To tell the truth, I really don't know why they love me so," Korbut tells an interviewer. "But I see myself in the public, my own character . . . . There's a simplicity there. We're very much the same. We are very close. You see it in their eyes when they look at you, a simplicity of honesty and good feelings."[11]

"Sometimes I look at a picture of myself in a magazine and I can't believe that girl who won all the medals and did no much to make gymnastics popular is really me. Sometimes I really envy the girl in the picture. Even now I can't understand how it all came about."[4]

How it all came about is simply that she was the prima donna of gymnastics. She made no effort to conceal her thoughts or her emotions. She had an independence of spirit that was at once her glory and the cause of her problems.

Criticism seemed to dog her frequently and often it seemed unfair. At the 1973 European Championship in London, Olga injured her left ankle again—it had been a recurring injury—and she had to withdraw. Although she took a silver medal in the all-around competition, during which she was in great pain, she could not complete even the first event—the vault—on the second day's apparatus finals because her ankle would not allow her to gain sufficient speed on her run-in. One reporter wrote:

> Olga was third to vault and one instinctively sensed she wasn't going to make it. She shied away and collapsed against the wall in a floor of tears. 'Poor little mite,' I heard said as she limped out of the arena and out of the competition—three words that show exactly where Olga's appeal lies. Suddenly we were right back to that night on the bars at Munich where the Korbut fairytale began. For a hopeless romantic like me, it was just too much.[10]

It was not too much, however, for the senior coach of the Soviet women's team, Larissa Latynina, who publicly criticized her in an article in Komsomolskaya Pravda. Larissa rebuked Olga for her lack of proper attitude, saying that Olga had been blaming accidents and illness for her mediocre performances.

"A true leader," said Latynina, "should win in any situation. And for that one must be a complete person in every respect—in relations to sport, to yourself, to your own triumphs and to the triumphs of others.

"And Olga Korbut," she continued, "does not yet have enough of these qualities."[5]

Olga was expected to perform in spite of physical setbacks; furthermore, she was expected to be a star but not to behave like one. There was no easy solution.

One thing she would not do is give up, retire, and rest on her laurels. One of Olga's relatives tried suggesting this to Olga: "What do you need all this for? You've already got to the top. Now you can be like everyone else. Don't torment yourself with training, slimming and diets. Go to sleep when you feel like it, be cheerful, enjoy yourself!" To Olga that meant surrender. It meant everything must remain as before, and she could not imagine that.[2]

She had become accustomed to the rule of gymnastics. "My teachers impressed on me from the very beginning, before I had learned to somersault or do handstands, that gymnastics recognizes only one love and demands everything of you. I suppose that's why the process of training and everyday work attracts me as much as competitions do. Only not competing with rivals but with myself. It's easier to win over a rival than it is to surpass oneself."[12]

Olga is, of course, a person of contradictions. She would express her devotion to the sport one day, as she did above, and at another time say, "Yes, I'm tired. Sometimes I feel like just throwing it all up, to be like other girls. Sometimes I get fed up with gymnastics—feel I just can't go on."[5]

In this she was not alone. Nelli Kim felt the same way before her great successes at the Montreal Olympics. They both, however, had the incentive of competition. In competition, all doubts were erased. In competition, the volatility of Olga's personality was leveled and unified into one thing: a flaming desire.

This was evident even in compulsory exercises. In her compulsory floor routine in the 1974 World Championships, she was on fire. Even though she was doing the same exercise as everyone else, she added a passion, a fervor that surpassed that of her teammates.

A similar instance was that of the selection trials to determine who would win a place on the 1976 Montreal Olympic team. Note this paragraph from the reporting of the first day's trials from the newspaper *Sovietsky Sport:*

> We interrupted yesterday's afternoon report at that moment when the gymnasts of the strongest Olympic group were warming up in their training room. We have never seen a warming up like that one—the room was filled with such a tense, strained silence, like the calm before a storm. The coaches were quiet, the girls were quiet, only asking each other who was next on the beam. Thus on the three training beams went Korbut, Kim and Saadi and their faces, when turned to us, were so different and yet were equally strained and reserved.[3]

When a place on the team was on the line, Korbut submerged her prima donna character, made the team, won a silver medal on beam but did not live up to the expectations of all those who were looking forward to the Nadia-Olga confrontation.

"It did not turn out," she said. "There were traumas; my freshness was missing. Contemporary gymnastics demands exceptional heartfelt enthusiasm and sharpness of perception. Of course, I have thought also of the Moscow Olympics, but I think that priority will be given to the young girls, I would say to the dashing gymnasts. To be fifth or sixth place on the team, that is not for me."

"And you decided to leave the podium."

"Yes. At first I was sad and was planning to start training again. Then other concerns took my attention. Thus, in January I had my wedding."[1]

Part III

It is significant that Olga Korbut was selected by *Sports Illustrated* in its 40th anniversary issue (September 19, 1994) as the gymnast who had made the greatest impact on her sport. It is a fitting reminder that it was she who changed gymnastics into what it is today from what it was before her appearance at Munich.

The public side of Olga's life is well-known. Much of it has been narrated elsewhere in this book. The inside story, however, primarily one of human relationships, did not become known until the publication of *My Story: The Autobiography of Olga Korbut*. It is a translation and adaptation of the autobiography she published in the Soviet Union, *There Lived a Girl*.

Olga Korbut's early life was a triumph over many difficulties, the first of which was that her family was very poor. They lived in Grodno, a small town in what is now Belarus. There were six of them: her father, Valentin, who was an army veteran of the second world war and who worked as a construction engineer; her mother, Valentina, who was a cook; older sisters Irina and Zemfira, nine and seven years older than Olga, who looked after her and her sister Ludmilla, who was two years older. They all lived in a one-room apartment of only 180 square feet. These conditions of poverty, from which she was desperate to escape, presented her with a challenge. She loved her gymnastics from the moment she was introduced to it and saw it as her means of escape. The more difficult and demanding it became, the harder she worked.

Later on, the story of her life became one of the interaction of her character and that of her coach, Renald Knysh. Under other circumstances or in other walks of life, they could not have tolerated each other. In their chosen life of gymnastics, however, they were able to work together for many years because coach and pupil needed each other. Olga needed Knysh because only he could teach her the gymnastics she wanted to learn; Knysh needed Olga because only she could perform the tricks he devised for her and only she had the desire and the perseverance to learn them.

Besides the gymnastics and acrobatics he taught her (there is a difference between gymnastics and acrobatics; see glossary) Knysh taught her to smile. He was aware of the effect the spectators had on judges in determining scores; he taught her to play to people in the stands.

> Ren always reminded me to smile, even when I was lying on the floor after a bad fall and wanted to do nothing but burst into tears.
>
> "Smile all the time," he would say. "When approaching the apparatus, when performing the loop, during your dismount. Smile! Otherwise, the spectators will see how hard you're working and the illusion will be lost."
>
> It disturbed me to remember that Ren trained me to execute that smile, exactly as he would train me to do a difficult element. That smile took years of zealous work-outs. So, I guess that smile is really Ren's creation. But if it is, why does it look so sincere? I really hope that the smile is one thing that is completely mine.[14]

Each achieved the desired goal at Munich, but from then on their relationship deteriorated. Undesirable traits in Knysh's character appeared and he became abusive, often hitting her. As if her relationship with Knysh was not difficult enough, the problems in her life were compounded by a never-ending succession of exhibition tours all over the world which exhausted her. (The American tours, on the contrary, refreshed her. She thrived on the adoration of the American crowds and appreciated the schedules which were less strenuous than those in Europe.) She struggled against the corruption of the Soviet sports committee which had no interest in her personally but only in the money her exhibition tours could earn.

Between Munich and Montreal, she was on a downward spiral caused by problems with her coach—from whom she parted in 1974—and by her physical exhaustion. Thus the much-touted confrontation with Nadia Comaneci was a non-event. As far as Olga was concerned, however, "getting to Montreal at all was itself a victory. I got there alone, without him (Ren), fighting injuries and depression every step of the way. Maybe I hadn't dazzled or amazed anyone this time, but I had won. Over whom? Maybe just myself."[15]

Her story, so far, has a happier ending. Flying to the United States on one of her exhibition tours, she met her future husband, Leonid Bortkevich, a singer, who was himself about to go on tour in the United States with a popular group. "I don't know what would have happened to me if I hadn't met Lenya. Thanks to him, I became a much nicer person. I'm sure he had a hard time with my explosive temperament, but I loved him very much and we were very happy."[16] They soon had a son, Richard. Since 1988, Olga and her family have been living in the United States, their home now being near Atlanta. It has long been Olga's desire to set up her own gymnastics club. Perhaps she will do it.

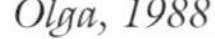

Olga, 1988

References

[1]Vladimir Golubev, "Sport Gave Me Happiness," *Sovietsky Sport,* 30 Mar. 1978.

[2]Michael Suponev, *Olga Korbut. A Biographical Portrait,* (New York: Doubleday, 1978.)

[3]Olga Korbut, "Long Live the Trick!" *Sovietsky Sport,* 1 Oct. 1981.

[4]Jim Gallagher, *Chicago Tribune,* 8 Dec. 1976.

[5]Nikolai Dolgopolov, *Komsomolskaya Pravda,* 5 Dec. 1975.

[6]Martha Duffy, "Hello to a Russian Pixie," *Sports Illustrated,* 19 Mar. 1973: 24–27.

[7]William Gildes, *Washington Post,* 22 Mar. 1973.

[8]Vladimir Golubev, "Olga Korbut," *Soviet Life,* Feb. 1973: 56–59.

[9]Mikhail Katyushenko, "Is Knysh Strict?" *Youth,* 1973, Sport section: 101–102

[10]Tony Murdock, OLGA poster booklet, British Amateur Gymnastics Association.

[11]Kenneth A Weiss, *Times-Picayune,* New Orleans, 5 Dec. 1976.

[12]Boris Semyonov, "About Olga Korbut," *Soviet Woman,* 1973: No. 3.

[13]Vladimir Golubev and Stanislav Tokarev, "There was Such a Silence," *Sovietsky Sport,* 20 May 1976.

[14]Olga Korbut. *My Story: The Autobiography of Olga Korbut,* (London: Century, 1992), 37

[15]Ibid: 132

[16]Ibid: 140

Angelika Reilig-Hellmann

1970 World Championships, Ljubljana, Slovenia, October: 10th, all-around; 6th, vault; 5th, bars.

1971 European Championship, Minsk, Belarus: 6th all-around; 3rd, bars.

1972 Olympics, Munich, August: 6th, all-around; 6th, bars, floor.

1973 Champions All, London, April: 2nd, all-around.

1973 Chunichi Cup, Nagoya, Japan, November: 2nd, all-around; Tokyo: 4th, all-around.

1973 European Championship, London, October: 6th, all-around; 1st, vault; 2nd, bars

1974 World Championships, Varna, Bulgaria, October: 3rd, all-around; 5th, vault; 4th, bars; 6th, beam, floor.

1976 Olympics, Montreal, July: 5th, beam.

Miss Hellmann's life has been devoted to gymnastics. She was six years old when she first started. Her gymnastics life from the beginning has been centered around the Berlin Sports Club, in which her coach throughout her active career was Jurgen Heritz. In 1975, while still a member of the GDR national team, she began to attend a sport high school in Leipzig. She stayed for four years and studied the methodology of coaching. She studied the coaching of artistic gymnastics during her first year but went on to other sports, including rhythmic gymnastics, swimming, athletics, and football. In 1979 she returned to the Berlin Sports Club and worked as a coach of 9-year-old girls. In 1984 she came to the national team as coach of beam and floor exercise, her principal student being the famous Maxi Gnauck. In addition, she spent two years studying at the ballet school in Berlin. During this time, she coached many other top German gymnasts, including 1985 World Championship medalists Gabrielle Fahnrich and Dagmar Kersten. She did not, however, travel with the team as national coach. This duty devolved upon the long-time senior coach, Hannelore Sauer.

In 1991 she became national coach of the new women's team. About the only good thing that can be said about her position is that she has the use of the large, well-equipped gymnasium at the Berlin Sports Club. The situation today is entirely different from what it used to be. Angelika says that in the glory days of the old GDR, it was as though women's gymnastics was one big family from the youngest, beginning girl right up through the members of the national team, the coaches and managers. Now there is no such team feeling. The managers are indifferent and there is very little money. In this unencouraging situation, Angelika has her work cut out for her. She is a cheerful, optimistic person, however. We should not count the Germans out yet.

She lives with her family in an apartment not far from the Sports Club.

Reference

Personal interview, Sept. 1994.

Elvira Fuadovna Saadi

Fans holding out their 1974 Moscow News *programs for Saadi to autograph.*

1952	Born, January 2 in Tashkent, Uzbekistan.
1961	Began gymnastics.
1967	Took first place in Spartakiade for school girls in Leningrad. Became a member of Soviet youth team. In her first international tournament, one between socialist countries, she won the gold medal on floor.
1969	Became a member of Soviet National Team.
1970	USSR National Championships, Minsk, May: 4th, all-around.
1971	Spartakiade, Moscow, July (USSR National Championships): 7th, all-around.
1972	Olympics, Munich, August: 8th, all-around.
1972	Entered Uzbekistan State University, majoring in biology.
1973	USSR National Championships: 1st, all-around; 1st, beam, floor.
1973	Champions All, London, April: 1st, all-around.
1973	University Games, Moscow, August: 3rd, all-around; 1st, vault (tie–Bogdanova).

1974 Married; moved from Tashkent to Moscow. Joined Dynamo Club, Moscow. Her coach: Vladimir Aksyonov.

1974 *Moscow News* competition, March: 3rd, all-around; 1st, beam, floor

1974 World Championships, Varna, Bulgaria, October: 4th, all-around; 3rd floor (tie-Sikharulidze).

1975 Spartakiade, Moscow, July (USSR National Championships): 5th, all-around; 2nd, floor; 3rd, bars, beam.

1975 World Cup, London, October: 3rd, all-around. 2nd, vault; 3rd, beam.

1976 Olympics, Montreal, July: 7th, all-around.

1976 Became childrens' coach at Dynamo Club in Moscow.

1979 Daughter Diana born.

1980 Daughter Leana born.

Elvira Saadi was one of those gymnasts a team cannot be without. She did not win a medal in finals on the apparatus at either the Munich or Montreal Olympics. Yet she was on both Olympic teams, a middle member of each team, and made significant contributions to her teams' gold medal performances by placing eighth and seventh all-around. She did, however, win individual gold medals in other tournaments.

She was valuable to her team in other ways. Debbie Hill, a U.S. team member in the early 1970s who had known the Soviet team of that day, said that Saadi was the most popular of team members. "Whenever one of the Soviet gymnasts had a problem, they went to her," Debbie said. One Soviet writer said she was "the most sociable of all our team members . . . . She was the most talkative, the most sensitive, the most enthusiastic."[2]

Saadi is a Tatar: that is, she comes from the Turkic people who live in a region of east central European Russia, the Crimea and parts of Asia.[2,3] She was born in Tashkent, Uzbekistan, an only child. Her father worked in a scientific research institute; her mother worked in a sewing machine factory. One of the ways in which her parents contributed to her development was that they took her frequently to the theater. This practice may have been an influence in developing her artistic qualities. These qualities and her natural physical abilities caused her physical education teacher at school to take a lively interest in her.[1]

"I do not want gymnastics to lose a future champion," he said. "She can achieve much, especially in floor exercise." [2]

Indeed, Saadi possessed remarkable gifts. Supple, with surprisingly expressive arms, she seemed in workouts to fly about lightly in her floor exercise.[2]

The gymnastic community took notice of her at the 1967 Spartakiade for schoolgirls in Leningrad where she took first place. Her floor exercise in which she combined parts of a Tatar dance with difficult gymnastics elements made a special impression.[2]

After this success, she was included in the Soviet youth team and her career took off, as can be seen from the chronology. Her greatest individual achievements came in the two years after the 1972 Munich Olympics. Then she won the 1973 National Championships and 1973 Champions All in London. She took 3rd place in the 1973 Moscow University Games and won a bronze medal in floor exercise at the 1974 World Championships in Varna, Bulgaria. During these years, Saadi was a fixture along with Korbut and Turischeva in the Soviet exhibition performances around the world.

One would have thought that after these two high-achieving years she might have been willing to retire. Though she did not, perhaps, expect to win an individual medal in the 1976 Olympics, she was not ready to give up her status as one of the Soviet "triumvirate"—Korbut, Turischeva and Saadi—that endured from Munich to Montreal.

One writer related, "as 1976 approached, the young steel-like girls captivated the podium and the style of Saadi seemed like a beautiful anachronism. Nobody believed she would really in be in Montreal.

"The word 'nobody' is not quite true. She says that at the time, exactly three people believed in her: she herself, her coach Vladimir Aksyonov and her husband. She says that their quiet, firm faith in her enabled her to live through those difficult times."

Her making the team for Montreal resulted in part from her training philosophy. "She said it was unbearable for her to train without a goal in mind. She always trained with an eye on victory, either over somebody or over herself. In sport, self-affirmation is for her the highest form of self-expression and if she cannot strive above all to win, then what is the point of sport."[4]

So she made the Montreal team and after the Olympics, like Olga and Ludmilla, she retired. She was already prepared for what she would do.

> Somewhere about the tenth grade, I understood that I would not be able to live without gymnastics. Then I decided to become a coach and, when the opportunity presented itself, I entered the biological department of Moscow State University. (She had moved to Moscow in 1974.) I did so because I thought that a teacher ought to understand the vital functions of the body. I studied hard but the pre-Olympic training load grew so much that I simply did not have time to prepare for my exams. So I entered the

> Institute of Physical Culture. It was not easier, but at least they gave me a little breathing space in the sessions.
>
> Even then, in the gym I could not just work for myself, but I needed to coach. I helped my coach Vladimir Aksyonov, in whose group of young gymnasts was the bright young girl, Olga Mostepanova. I knew that the Olympics in Montreal would be my last tournament. Therefore, over and over I thought about Aksyonov's method of work. Yet it became evident to me that I needed to be on my own, not under somebody's patronage or guardianship.[4]

She got her own group of very young, beginning girls together. Just as had been Lyubov Burda's initial experience in coaching young girls, Saadi found the experience difficult.

> How unbelievably difficult it is to be a coach! Everything turned out to be much more difficult than I expected. It was necessary, however, for me to go ahead in spite of cruel disappointments and to understand that the most important quality necessary in our work is patience, patience and still more patience.[4]
>
> In her gym, dozens of little boys and girls are busy on the apparatus. At first, it looks like an anthill; but when you look more carefully, you see that all the activity is in order: nobody is interfering with anybody else. We recognize Elvira Saadi immediately. She has not changed in any way, still as impetuous as ever, with her very black short haircut. She doesn't notice anything around her: her whole attention is on her students. Saadi does not sit down for a minute; she is fascinated by her work. She might become angry and could shout at a naughty girl; but then she sees a well-performed element and there is joy on her face.[4]

After beginning her coaching career in 1976, by 1981 her work was paying off. In the youth national championships for girls 11 to 14 in Moscow of that year, her twelve-year-old Natasha Timakova tied for first place in compulsories. In that same championship was Oksana Omelyanchick and Elena Shushunova, who four years later would become co-world champions.[5]

The girls were all boarded at the training center. Saadi had this story to tell: she went to her student's room, opened the door and threw up her arms at what she saw.

"Natasha what is the meaning of this?"

"What's the matter, Elvira Fuadovna?" asked Natasha in her tender, descant voice, as she raised her innocent eyes. "See how well my favorite doll performs the splits. Now we're doing a pirouette."

"Timakova," said Saadi in a severe voice. "We soon have the championships, you are late for workout and you are playing with dolls. Now quickly get ready!"

Later in the championships, as Timakova slipped, Saadi lamented, "In general, I am very upset. Two weeks ago, Natasha was well prepared for the championship. Now she's in a slump, is listless and is making mistakes. My heart aches. Such is a coach's portion."[6]

In a later interview she was asked, "Elvira, your ten- to twelve-year-old students have already mastered the most contemporary routines and elements. Are you not forcing the training of your young athletes?"

To this she replied,

> . . . in the specialized sport schools, we begin to train the girls at the age of six. Natural gifts for this or that sport show up within two years. Some of them cannot stand it, are not strong, do not have the needed coordination and courage. Those who drop behind move to a weaker group, others choose a sport more suited to themselves. My girls went exactly according to the gymnastic progressions. They are themselves interested in not repeating what they already know but in mastering something new or unusual. I myself cannot mark time. Probably I schooled my girls in this way, too. For me, the biggest joy is when we think up something new together. That means we have learned to think, to create!
>
> I admit I am myself sometimes frightened by this incredible difficulty. What tricks! What saturated routines! But at the competitions, if you look around, you will see that everyone is searching for something, everyone is looking ahead. Here all fears vanish into thin air. And I tell the girls: 'Are we worse than the others? Not worse! Yes, you can win over everyone!'
>
> I try to cultivate ambition and a thirst for victory in them. Without these in sport, and by the way in life, you cannot achieve anything. Before, I did not understand the words of my coach, 'I give all of myself to my students,' but now I do understand. Perhaps I devote less time to my children, Diana and Leana, than I do to my girls. You have to keep your eyes on the girls constantly. At this age, they have a sweet tooth, are capricious, touchy and mischievous. It is so difficult with them, but without them my world would lose its luster.[4]

In another five years, Saadi's leading student was Tanya Groshkova, with whom she gave clinics in the U.S.A. in 1987. Groshkova achieved more than Timakova. She won floor exercise in the 1989 Tokyo Cup that followed the Chunichi Cup. In 1990, Groshkova placed tenth in the European Championship in Athens and second in floor exercise. She came to Seattle as a reserve for the Goodwill Games, competed in the following U.S.A./U.S.S.R. meet in

San Jose and then won a tournament between the USSR and the rest of the world. In spite of the burgeoning success of her leading student, the worsening economic and political situation in Russia and the deterioration of the long-established order of things in gymnastics caused Saadi to leave her position at Moscow's Dynamo club and accept an offer to move to Canada. As of 1994, she is head coach of the Cambridge Kips Gymnastics Club in Cambridge, Ontario. She and her husband, Valery Chernyshev, plan to stay in Canada for the rest of their lives.

References

[1]Stansilav Tokarev, "A Clue to Saadi," *Sovietsky Sport,* 21 Nov. 1976.

[2]Boris Kaimakov, "The Most Lyrical Gymnast of the Soviet Team," (article) Novosti Press, 1973.

[3]Webster's *New World* Dictionary.

[4]Vladimir Golubev and Natalya Smyrnova, "Without Them My World Would Lose Its Luster," *Sovietsky Sport,* 18 Mar. 1987.

[5]Vladimir Golubev, "Dreams of Dolls and Double Saltos," *Sovietsky Sport,* 4 Nov. 1981.

[6]Vladimir Golubev, "One Step Up the Ladder," *Sovietsky Sport,* 6 Nov. 1981.

Nina Dronova

1967 Spartakiade for schoolgirls: 1st, all-around, age 13.
1971 East Bloc Tournament of Friendship: 1st, all-around.
1971 Chunichi Cup, Japan, November: 1st, all-around.
1974 Champions All, London, April: 1st all-around.
1974 World Championships, Varna, Bulgaria, October: 7th, all-around; 4th, beam; 5th, floor.
1975 World Cup, London, October: 7th, all-around.

Nina Dronova, who comes from Tbilisi in Georgia (as does her Varna teammate Rusiko Sikharulidze), had a short career. She was an expressive dancer and earned the title, "The Mozart of Gymnastics," from the London press for her performance in Champions All.

As related in the narrative of the 1974 championships, Nina had some elegant elements in her beam routine; similarly she had some original, artistic steps in her floor exercise. After Varna, she could not keep up, however, with the newcomers who were making their way toward the 1976 Olympics: Svetlana Grozdova, Lydia Gorbick, and Maria Filatova.

She is a choreographer in the gymnastics school run by an aircraft factory in Tbilisi and helps coach floor exercise with the Georgian team; but these jobs have been hampered by the civil war in Georgia. Her main occupations are as wife to her businessman husband and mother to their daughter Natasha. Natasha took up gymnastics but switched to swimming as she grew. Her godmother is Rusudan Sikharulidze. (Notes by Lera Mironova of the Russian magazine *Family*.)

The Soviet team outside their hotel in Varna. Left to right: Olga Korbut, Ludmilla Turischeva, Elvira Saadi, Nelli Kim, Rusiko Sikharulidze, Nina Dronova.

Rusudan Sikharulidze

1953 Born and raised in Batumi, a Georgian city on the coast of the Black Sea.
1969 Candidate for membership on the 1970 World Championships team.
1970 USSR National Championships, Minsk, May: 6th, all-around.
1971 Spartakiade, Moscow, July (USSR National Championships): 6th, all-around.
1974 World Championships, Varna, Bulgaria, October: 5th, all-around.
3rd (tie–Saadi) floor.

Like Saadi, Sikharulidze was a strong supporting member of the Soviet team, as evidenced by her 5th place all-around standing in the 1974 World Championships. In floor exercise, which they tied for the bronze medal, the outstanding characteristic of both of them was the eye contact with spectators that they maintained. Sikharulidze's floor exercise to "Malaguena" was Larissa Latynina's favorite of all the floor exercises she had seen.

She continued her association with gymnastics after she retired from competition. She coaches the Georgian team in Tbilisi, where she now lives, and is President of the Georgian Gymnastics Federation. She is an international judge who judged the 1990 Goodwill Games in Seattle. She is a strikingly beautiful woman about whom one correspondent in Seattle said, "She carries herself well."

She and her businessman husband Nodar Gulisashvili, a former gymnast, have one son, Irakli. A former player for the "Adzharia" football team in Batumi, he is a student at the Physical Culture Institute in Batumi. (Notes by Lera Mironova of the Russian magazine *Family*.)

Joan Moore Rice

1954 Born, August 14.

1960 Began gymnastics, age 6, at Mannettes Gym Club, Philadelphia. Her coaches throughout her career were Bill and Ginny Coco.

1968–1972
Attended Philadelphia High School for Girls.

1970 World Championships, Ljubljana, Slovenia, October: 33rd, all-around, as Joan Moore.

1971, 1972, 1973, 1974
U.S. National Champion (USGF) (1971 tie–Metheny).

1972 Japan vs. U.S.A., January: 2nd, all-around. (1st, Cathy Rigby).

1972 South African Cup: 1st, all-around.

1972 Olympics, Munich, August: 21st, all-around.

1972 Married Bob Rice.

1972 Chunichi Cup, Japan, November: 1st, all-around.

1973 French Invitational, Antibes: 1st, all-around.

1974 World Championships, Varna, Slovenia; October: 18th, all-around. (See competition narrative for story of her experience in floor exercise.)

1974 Honored by USGF as élite gymnast of the year.

1974 Retired. Moved to Edina, Minnesota, and purchased a gym club. Coached all levels through élite.

Joan Moore was one of the stars of U.S. gymnastics during its growing years. She was especially noted for her dance in floor exercise. Her interest in dance encouraged her to major in dance for two years at Temple University.

Gymnastics is in her bones, she says; so she will continue in the sport as her life's work. She has three children: two sons, Stephen, born 1976, and Sean, born 1977, and a daughter, Jeana, born 1981. Jeana is a gymnast. In 1984, the family moved to Hilton Head, South Carolina, to be closer to her family and to Bob's. They opened a brand new gym, Rice's Gymnastics Center in which they coached all levels for six years. In 1990, she and Bob divorced. Joan subsequently moved to Orlando, Florida, to work for Brown's gymnastics, where she choreographs and coaches beam and floor. In 1992, she married Ray Gnat and was expecting a baby in November 1994.

She began judging in 1984, when she moved to South Carolina and received her brevet (international) rating in 1989. Since then, among other competitions, she has judged three Championships of the USA, the trials for the 1991 World Championships, an American Cup and Mixed Pairs.

In 1990, she was elected to the USGF Board of Directors as representative for women; in 1994, she was elected to the Executive Committee for USA Gymnastics, where she currently serves. In 1994, she was elected to the U.S.A. Gymnastics Hall of Fame.

Other Events 1974 Internationally

March – November

In 1974, the international schedule of events expanded with one important addition: the competition sponsored by the newspaper *Moscow News.* The inaugural competition was won by Svetlana Grozdova, an attractive gymnast who became immensely popular, especially with the British, who called her "Grozzy." Second place was won by one of those unfortunate gymnasts who shows great promise, who would be a leader in any other country, but who could not make it past the barrier of the Soviet front line. Her name was Elena Primak. Like a comet, she made a brief appearance and then disappeared.

The 1974 *Moscow News* competition was important to the United States because of the performances by the American gymnasts Debbie Fike, who placed sixth, and Kyle Gaynor, who placed eighth. Their standings were impressive because they came behind four Soviet gymnasts and the leader of the Hungarian team. They beat entrants from all the other countries.

The 1974 *Moscow News* competition was also noteworthy in that 14-year-old Maria Abramova performed the double salto backward tucked in floor exercise. An official of the Hungarian team, Mr. Sandor Urvari, reported this in a letter published in the June 1974 issue of *Olympische Turnkunst* and stated that Abramova was the first girl to perform the double tuck in competition.

After the meet, the American girls immediately traveled by train to Riga, Latvia, for the "Riga Cup." There they encountered a new contingent of Soviet gymnasts. "Moscow News" and "Riga" came to be part of the Soviet selection process for the 1976 Olympics in Montreal, along with the Spartakiade and the national championships. Results of these two competitions were as follows:

"Moscow News," 1974

March 22nd to 24th

1.	Svetlana Grozdova	37.90
2.	Elena Primak	37.50
3.	Elvira Saadi	36.85
4.	Maria Abramova	36.65
5.	Marta Egervari, HUN	36.35
6.	Debbie Fike	36.30
	M. Blagoeva, BUL	36.30
8.	Kyle Gaynor	36.25

"Riga Cup," 1974

March 27th to 29th

1.	Lydia Gorbick, URS	37.80
2.	Nelli Kim	37.75
3.	Ludmilla Savina, URS	37.55
4.	Kyle Gaynor	36.80
5.	Stodulkova, TCH	36.40
6.	Rodika Sabau, ROM	36.35
7.	Debbie Fike	36.30

In April, in London, the British Amateur Gymnastics Association conducted its 1974 Champions All, the leaders of which were as follows:

1.	Nina Dronova	37.45
2.	Sylvia Schäfer, GDR	36.90
3.	Zsuzsa Nagy, HUN	36.70

In July, Olga Korbut, Lydia Gorbick and Ludmilla Savina performed in exhibition for five days at the Expo '74 in Spokane, Washington. Performing with them were Debbie Fike, Kyle Gaynor, and other members of the United States team.

The last major event of the year was Japan's Chunichi cup in November, the results of which were as follows:

1.	Nina Dronova	38.25
2.	Rusudan Siharulidze	38.05
3.	Gitta Escher, GDR	37.95
	Richarda Schmeisser	37.95
5.	Miyuki Matsuhisa, JPN	37.35
6.	F. Hayashida, JPN	37.25
7.	Zdena Dornakova, TCH	36.95
	Debbie Fike	36.95

Besides the World Championships in Varna, two other events took place between Champions All in April and the Chunichi Cup in November that had significance for the future. In June, Rod Hill took his team from the Denver School of Gymnastics—it included his wife Debbie—to a competition with the Junior Team at the National Training Center for Romanian Gymnasts in Onesti. Nadia won the meet and Rod Hill wrote a glowing report about the 13-year-old superstar in the August/September 1974 issue of *Gymnast*. The occasion was the United States' first introduction to Nadia Comaneci and her soon-to-be-famous teammates. Nadia was already well known in the east because of her 1971 and 1973 victories in the so-called Friendship meets between the Soviet Union and East Bloc countries, but the west was no more aware of her than they had been of Olga Korbut before Munich in 1972.

In October, the Romanian Gymnastics Federation received an urgent request for two gymnasts to appear in Paris for a gymnastics demonstration. The French Federation needed "a couple of bodies to make up the numbers. It was obviously an important occasion because the top Soviet gymnast, Ludmilla Turischeva, was going to be present."[1] To their surprise, the Romanian Federation decided to send Nadia and Teodora Ungureanu and their coach Bela Karolyi instead of Alina Goreac, the national champion. The decision created unprecedented excitement for the chosen three, who had to pack immediately, take the train to Bucharest the next day, and fly to Paris the day after.

When they arrived at the arena where the exhibition would take place that same day, Bela told the organizers whom he had brought along. They scoffed at the idea of two 13-year-olds performing alongside the World and Olympic Champion and sent him and his gymnasts to a secondary meet in another part of the city. They quickly won this meet and then returned to the scene of the major exhibition. They arrived five minutes after it had begun.

With his gymnasts in tow, Bela barged past the guards, hid his gymnasts behind a pile of crash pads and watched as Ludmilla Turischeva completed her vault. Seeing his opening, Bela said, "Right, Nadia, forget everything else, go and throw your Tsukahara. There's no time to measure your run, but you ought to be able to gauge it by now. Stun them."[1]

So, as Nadia said, "I tore off my coat and track suit, launched myself down the run and performed my Tsukahara."[1]

She did, in fact, stun them. The same thing happened on beam. As Ludmilla finished her routine, Nadia jumped up and performed hers.

By then, the organizers relented and allowed Nadia and Teodora to do an improvised floor display. The large Paris audience was entranced by the young Romanians and wanted to know all about them. Bela was proved right by his decision to have them jump in and perform without permission or warm-up. They returned to Romania confident in their ability to win medals in the European Championship the next year in Skien, Norway.

Volume II will open with Nadia's great victory at Champions All and Nelli Kim's emergence as the Soviet Union's strongest gymnast as the Soviets try to contend with Nadia at Skien and Montreal.

Reference

[1]Nadia Comaneci, *Nadia. The Autobiography of Nadia Comaneci,* (London/New York: Proteus Books, 1981.)

Scenes from Skien

A pictorial story from the
1975 European Championship,
the first competition in Volume II.

00

Albrecht Gaebele:
The Fascination of the Crucial Moment

In split second passes, the ball oscillates across the enemy goal from player to player. Suddenly there is an opening, and—beyond the reach of the goal-keeper—it lands in the net. In the succeeding moments when the stadium is ringing with the cheers of countless football fans, the technician in the television studio is running back the video tape a few metres, ready to replay the scene at the goal mouth—this time, however, in slow motion. Carefully watching the monitor screen, the director stops the tape at the crucial moment so as to give viewers a still of the whole situation in front of the goal and enable them to study in detail the rapid action of the defence.

This service provided by the television studio is not just a technical gimmick: it is simply and solely a concession to human vision. Our visual equipment is not capable of absorbing every detail of a rapid process of movement. Were it otherwise, the "illusion" upon which the moving picture is based would technically never have been possible. Whatever discoveries may in the future be made in the field of visual communications, and however the information media may one day be operated, one thing is certain: we shall never be able to dispense with the still picture.

If any proof were needed for such a contention, it will be found in the photographs taken by Albrecht Gaebele, many examples which have been published in this book. One thing is common to them all: they are photographic records of instantaneous phases from sports events caught by the fast reaction of a photographer at the crucial moment, the high spot, no matter whether its value lies in the gymnastics or in the pictorial aspect. High spots so perfectly frozen that the viewer can subsequently, at his leisure, fully experience the aesthetic satisfaction of an incident whose fascination details—because of the rapidity with which they occurred—inevitably eluded him at the time.

Every one of Gaebele's photographs provides that possible additional experience to which . . . we have our "third eye," photography, solely to thank. To take, as an example, the colour cover picture on the jacket of this book: it shows the Russian gymnast Elvira Saadi in the execution of an aerial walkover forward—legs astraddle, arms spread as though in flight, head down as though weightless in space. Newton's law of gravitation seems no longer to exist. The relaxed expression on the face of the gymnast completely obscures the difficulty of the exercise, demanding as it does split-second precision replacement of the feet upon the narrow beam. Whether it be

Richarda Schmeisser . . . seen apparently suspended off the upper bar (see page 317) or the Bulgarian Maria Gigova performing her famous and for a long time unique jump one arm handstand in stag position—the fascination in these and all other pictures is that the performance, the perfect body control, is part and parcel of an aesthetic experience of the highest level. Such photographs are just simply beautiful.

Gaebele has an inborn talent, and, like many other professional photographers, was self-taught. Beginning with his father's locksmith's shop in Öhringen and a

The photographer made many unsuccessful attempts to catch Kasamatsu of Japan in this phase of his inverted giant (with the emblem in the background) before he succeeded in achieving this perfect picture.

vocational training to begin with in his father's business, after passing his journeyman's examination in art metalwork, his future career seemed to be mapped out. But the security of citizenship means nothing to a young man. His mother encouraged him to "have a look around the world before you settle down." In Zurich, where he worked as a locksmith, he did not remain long. With a rucksack and a Kodak box camera, he tramped all the way through Europe. Later, he visited North Africa, traversed the Near East, Scandinavia, and—as a steerage passenger—traveled

Albrecht Gaebele is justly proud of this picture, which has caught the most difficult element in the exercise with the ball of rhythmic gymnast Maria Gigova of Bulgaria.

to India, Pakistan and Nepal. He never had much in his purse, and in consequence took such temporary jobs as welding operator, potato peeler, dish washer, and scrubber. More and more he recorded his travel experiences with the camera. The box camera was replaced by a Kodak Retina 1a, succeeded by a Contaflex and an Exakta Verax with a number of interchangeable lenses. The expenses of travel were eked out by slide lectures and the publication of photographs. On a journey across the South American continent (an expedition which included the Amazon region) Gaebele took with him highly professional equipment: three cameras with a range of lenses and a 16mm movie camera. (Today Gaebele uses a Leica and a Leica Contaflex SL, and Hasselblad.) At long last he was in a position to fulfill a long cherished wish: an extended world trip. When after seven months absence, he returned to his home town of Öhringen, Gaebele received from his sports club—apart from hectic games of handball—a commission to decorate the club room with good sports photographs. This provided a new twist to his globetrotting activities: his sports photographs, which had been acclaimed with loud praise by his club associates, also aroused the enthusiasm of the German Olympic Committee, and he was invited to contribute photographs for the calendar planned by the organization.

In 1967, Gaebele ventured on the crucial step: he leased his paternal workshop and devoted himself wholly to photography. At the 1968 Olympic Games in Grenoble and Mexico, he formed part of the team of three exclusive photographers who were commissioned to provide the photographic material for the official record of the German National Olympic Committee. Since then, Gaebele has been at . . . the 1972 Olympic Games in Sapporo and Munich, the Universiade in Moscow in 1973, the World Football Championships in 1974 in West Germany, to mention only a few. The nostalgia-motivated globetrotter has become a globetrotting sports photographer, a professional who made a record climb to the top in his career: in their annual photographic competition, the German sports press voted Gaebele in 1972 the most successful sports photographer and won the prize of "Sports Photo of the Year."

Only when light conditions are very bad, and the situation demands the combination of coincidence rangefinder and a giant aperture lens from the Leitz lens program, does Albrecht Gaebele resort to the M5. In the great majority of cases, however, he uses the Leicaflex: "I have to see what I'm taking: for sports photography the large, brilliant view-finder is indispensable." He has long since provided his Leicaflex with a motor attachment: "Not just so that I can rattle off some three pictures a second. Anyone who thinks that such a series automatically records the high spots of a sports incident would quickly discover his mistake if he tried it out in practice: in point of fact, the said high spot frequently lies between two exposures. No, I am concerned only with the rapid film wind, the increased readiness for action, which the motor affords." His favourite lenses: the Elmar-R f/2, 90 mm, the Elmarit-R f/2.8, 35 mm, and also the Elmarit-R f/2.8 180 mm, and lastly the 400 mm Telyt-R. On account of the usually unfavourable light conditions, not only are wide aperture lenses vitally necessary, but also fast films. For black-and-white work, he uses Kodak Tri-X film out of which he frequently squeezes an effective speed of 1600 ASA; colour photographs he takes on Kodak High Speed Ektachrome film exposed as for 650 ASA with forced development. If then with a sophisticated technical equipment there are combined an eye for a good picture, a fast reaction, imagination, and, occasionally, a skillful pair of elbows, it becomes possible to handle what would seem to be quite hopeless situations.

Albrecht Gaebele, who developed his hobby into a profession, began in quite a small way: in the sports club of his home town. Which only goes to show that it does not require attendance at international sporting events to become a good sports photographer. Gaebele's advice to young amateurs who want to experiment in the rewarding field of sports photography: "Begin with gymnastics—with the horizontal bar, parallel bars, vaulting horse, and rings. If you watch carefully the details of the exercise, you will quickly get to know the high spots of greatest pictorial interest. On these you must concentrate. And don't give up if you don't succeed in getting a good picture first time. Like the gymnast, you have to practice pressing the release at the right moment." And one more tip in conclusion: Make friends with the trainer of a gymnastic club. He will introduce you to the best gymnasts in the club, and will also tell you what phases of the exercise are of special interest. And to help to make your first attempts easier, ask the trainer to tip you off shortly before the photographic high spot is due to occur.

—By Horst W. Staubach in the journal "LEICA Fotographie," Number 2/1975.

Other photographs in this book which are notable for having been taken at the crucial moment are as follows: